Elvis Album

PUBLICATIONS INTERNATIONAL, LTD.

TABLE OF CONTENTS

4

Tupelo & Memphis
1935-1954

"Elvis would hear us worrying about our debts, being out of work and sickness and so on. He would say, 'Don't you worry none, when I grow up, I'm going to buy you a fine house and pay everything you owe at the grocery store and get two Cadillacs — one for you and Daddy and one for me! Little as he was, the way he'd look up at me, holding onto my skirt — you know, I'd believe him."

— Gladys Presley

Elvis at about age 3

The Presleys' first home in Tupelo — a two-room shotgun shack where Elvis was born

TUPELO

Elvis's twin brother, Jesse Garon, died at birth and is buried in Priceville Cemetery.

Gladys bought a guitar for Elvis at Tupelo Hardware.

As a child, Elvis greatly resembled Gladys.

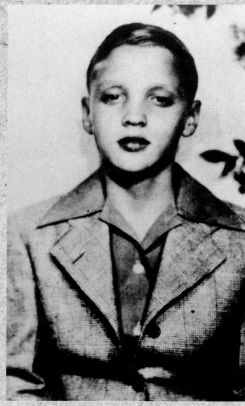

The store sold just about everything.

At age 11, Elvis won second prize in a talent contest at the local fair.

Buckaroo Elvis

In grade school, Elvis often wore blue jeans, which he would later despise.

MEMPHIS

The Presleys rented a tiny apartment at 462 Alabama St. in 1953.

Lauderdale Courts was home for the Presleys for 3½ years.

Just hangin' out — Elvis is second from the left.

Welcome to
Lauderdale Courts

A teenage "KING"
and his court

Could she have been his first love?

9

Some neighbors complained 'cause Elvis played his guitar at night, but others liked his music.

MEMPHIS

Elvis was fired from Loew's State for punching a fellow usher.

Looking cool on a hot Memphis day

Young and Handsome

MEMPHIS

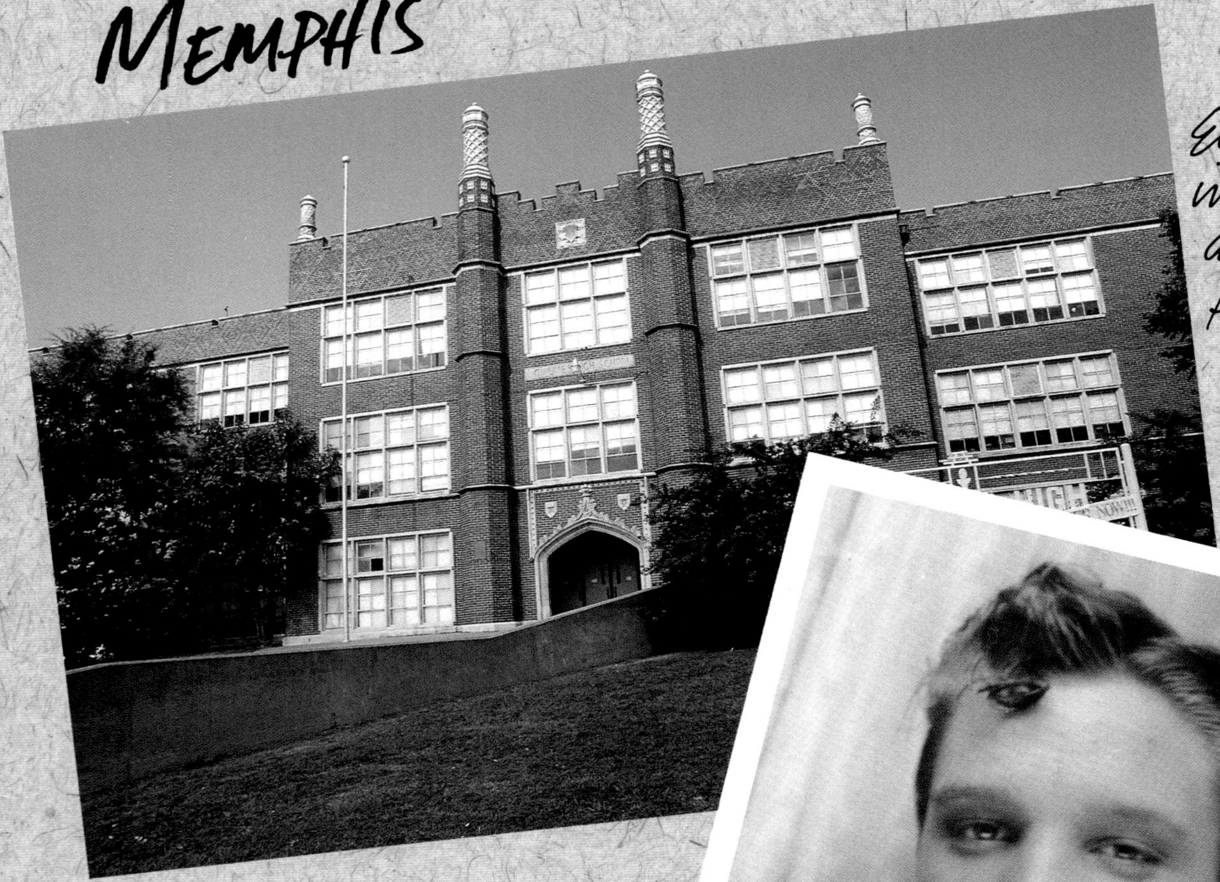

Elvis majored in industrial arts at Humes High.

An early high-school yearbook photo

HOME OF THE COTTON CARNIVAL

MEMPHIS

HUMES HIGH BAND

presents its

ANNUAL MINSTREL

Thursday, April 9, 1953--8 P.M.

HUMES AUDITORIUM

...PROGRAM...

Directed by
R. ROY COATS

Interlocutor
JIMMY CUNNINGHAM

Student Director
CHRIS KOLIVAS

MAURY SPIRO
L. D. LEDBETTER

End Men
GLENN YARBROUGH
BOB HALEY
ROBERT BARNES

VERNON YARBROUGH
JAMES YARBROUGH

1—Grand Opening	ENTIRE COMPANY
2—Twirler	HELEN PITTMAN, 5 years old
3—Carolina in the Morning	MAURICE BIGGS AND BAND
4—Darktown Strutters Ball	GLENN YARBROUGH AND BAND
5—Merry Makers	Featuring: VERNON YARBROUGH
6—Kentucky Babe	BAND
7—Male Quartet	SIDNEY McKINNEY, DWIGHT MALONE, GEORGE GRIMES and BILLY WOOLEY.
8—Louisiana Hayride	BAND
9—Electric Guitar	W. H. YARBROUGH
10—Xylophone Trio	SUSIE GARRETT, NANCY TURNER, and LALA WILLIAMS.
11—Accordion Solo	JOANN MASSERANO
12—Old Man River	GLENN YARBROUGH
13—Twirlers	ARWOOD TWINS
14—Trombonium	Featuring: TROMBONES
15—Beautiful Ohio	BAND
16—Guitarist	ELVIS PRESTLY
17—Tap Dancing	JERRY BLANTON
18—Acrobatic	SIDNEY EMBREY
19—Joshua	BAND
20—Dance Artist	GLORIA TROUT
21—Commercial Appeal March	BAND
F.E.—ENTIRE COMPANY	

13

PHILLIPS, JAMES ARNETT
Major: Science, Special Studies, Drafting, English.
Activities: Thespian, National Forensic, Debate Team, Spanish Club, Hi-Y, Biology Club, History Club, Speech Club, Student Council Representative, Non-Com Officer in R.O.T.C., Vice-President Speech Club, Vice-President History Club.
Awards: Winner District Debate Tournament, Winner "I Speak For Democracy" Contest.

ROBINSON, KATIE MAE
Major: Commercial, Home Ec., English.
Activities: F.H.A., History Club, English Club, Vice-President History Club.

RULEMAN, SHIRLEY
Major: Home Ec., Commercial, English.
Activities: National Honor Society, F.H.A., Y-Teens, Latin Club, Jr. Cheerleader, Sabre Club, History Club, English Club, Honorary Captain in R.O.T.C., President Home Ec. Class.

PRESLEY, ELVIS ARON
Major: Shop, History, English.
Activities: R.O.T.C., Biology Club, English Club, History Club, Speech Club.

Elvis in high school—A yearbook photo and a cryptic entry into the senior class's "Last will and Testament."

LAST WILL AND TESTAMENT

Section 74, Ruby Hankins and Katie Robinson leave asking, "May I borrow a pencil."

Section 75, Barbara Logan, Mattie Rainey and Billie Hill follow behind the above girls asking, "May I have a piece of paper?"☐

Section 76, Kenneth Doyle leaves to follow his brother —U.S.A.F.

Section 77, William Baxter Tatum, Jr. and Kenneth Don Wrey leave to take the place of "Mutt and Jeff."☐

Section 78, James Durham leaves his position on the bench. (Who wants it?)☐

Section 79, Perry Donnelley and Carl Hayes leave singing, "O Happy Day." (I ask you, "Is that any way to be?")

Section 80, Shirley Lee Bizzell and Juanita Morrow leave hoping there will always be some Gladiator wrappers so that the teachers can continue to buy a new pencil sharpener every two years.

Section 81, Fannie Mae Crowder and Lydia May Tucker leave their middle names to anyone who enjoys having them spelled "right" at the "wrong" times.

Section 82, William Barrett, Albert Teague and Edwin Leak leave—(What can they leave, they're using all that was pushed off and graciously given to them.)

Section 83, Donald Williams, Raymond McCraig and Elvis Presley leave hoping there will be some one to take their places as "teachers' pets" ??????

Section 84, Verna Faverly and Ada Lee Thompson leave their ability to "fix" some ones hair to anyone who isn't discouraged easily.

Section 85, Carol Kimbrell, Barbara Henderson and Bessie Gkikas leave as sweet as ever, which goes to prove that the senior year did not change everyone.

Section 86, Harry Karris, Billy Eggers and Charles Wells leave just as they came — empty-handed.

Section 87, Ann Norton leaves her naturally blond hair to all who acquire their's from a bottle.

Section 88, Ray Lofton and James Thomas leave the 12th grade to next year's seniors.

Section 89, Juanita Richardson leaves with the Woodards. (Martha and Carolyn.)

Section 90, Bob Smith, Scott Nolen and Edward Robinson leave their "love" of R.O.T.C. to President Eisenhower.

Section 91, June Forshee and Edna Ruth Griffith leave their stools in the lunch room to the lucky Jrs., who are now moving in.

Section 92, Shirley Slate and Mona Raburn leave their empty coke bottles on the table in order to give the Student Council Monitors something to do.

Section 93, Robert Rice and Carlton McFadin leave their studiousness to anyone else who can keep people fooled.

Section 94, Barbara Rafferty leaves her ability to write letters and English essays the same night.

The typewriter has burned out; the authors pooped, the words are few, the hands of time are pushing (the authors to sleep); the pencil point worn, the witnesses tired and so we close this, our "Last Will and Testament."

Duely Witnessed by
POGO
WIMPY

Elvis hired on as a truck driver with Crown Electric just after High school.

In high school, Elvis aquired a taste for flashy clothes.

Rock'n'Roller

1953-1958

"People say I'm vulgar. They say I use my hips disgustingly. But that's my way of putting over a song. I have to move. When I have a lot of energy, I move more. I lose three to four pounds a performance. I've always done it this way."

— Elvis Presley

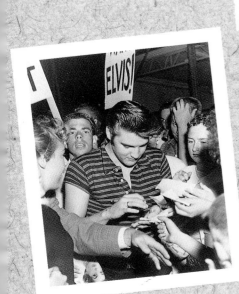

17

Elvis Presley — the living end!

New singing sensation
Elvis Presley in 1954

Memphis Press-Scimitar, July 28, 1954

IN A SPIN—Elvis Presley can be forgiven for going round and round in more ways than one these days. A 19-year-old Humes High graduate, he has just signed a recording contract with Sun Record Co. of Memphis, and already has a disk out that promises to be the biggest hit that Sun has ever pressed.

It all started when Elvis dropped into Sun's studios one day to cut a personal record at his own expense. Sam Phillips, president of the company, monitored the session and was so impressed with the unusual quality in the young man's voice that he jotted down his name and address. Some time later, Phillips came across a ballad which he thought might be right for Presley's voice. They recorded it; it didn't click. But they tried again; this time with "Blue Moon of Kentucky," a folk standard, backed by "That's All Right Mama."

Just now reaching dealers' shelves, the record is getting an amazing number of plays on all Memphis radio stations. "The odd thing about it," says Marion Keisker of the Sun office, "is that both sides seem to be equally popular on popular, folk and race record programs. This boy has something that seems to appeal to everybody."

"We've just gotten the sample records out to the disk jockeys and distributors in other cities," she said, "but we got big orders yesterday from Dallas and Atlanta." Sun, started by Sam Phillips, former WREC engineer, several years ago, has 40 distributors from coast to coast, so there's a good chance of a big national sale.

Elvis, son of Mr. and Mrs. Vernon Presley, 462 Alabama, is a truck driver for Crown Electric Co. He has been singing and playing the guitar since he was about 13—just picked it up himself. The home folks who have been hearing him on records so often during the past few weeks can see Elvis in person when he's presented by Disk Jockey Bob Neal in a hillbilly show at Overton Park Shell Friday night along with veteran entertainers from the *Louisiana Hayride.*

Marion Keisker, the secretary at Sun, was the first to hear Elvis sing. She knew he had talent.

SUN RECORD COMPANY
INCORPORATED

RECORDS THAT SELL!

TO:

639 MADISON   MEMPHIS, TENN.

POSTMASTER: CONTENTS: MERCHANDISE, MAY BE OPENED FOR INSPECTION

The Legendary SUN RECORDING STUDIO 706 UNION

Elvis recorded his first hit "That's All Right" at Sun Studio in July 1954.

Wabash BMI

Vocal U-128

"THAT'S ALL RIGHT"
(Arthur Crudup)
ELVIS PRESLEY
SCOTTY and BILL
209

MEMPHIS, TENNESSEE

Elvis performed at Slim Whitman's "hillbilly hoedown". The ad misspelled his first name.

in person
THE SENSATIONAL
RADIO · RECORDING
STAR

Slim WHITMAN

with Billy Walker, Ellis Presley and many others
Tonight One Big Show—8:00 P.M.
Adv. reserved seats today at Walgreen's, Main and Union,
$1.00. Tonight at Shell, $1.25 reserved; kids, 75c; general admission $1.00.

OVERTON PARK SHELL

The Commercial Appeal, Memphis,
July 25, 1954

SHELL SHOW FRIDAY

Hillbilly Hoedown Features Popular Music Favorites

Favorite folk ballads in a sylvan setting are on the entertainment bill this week as Slim Whitman, one of the top-ranking rural rhythm experts, brings his troupe here for a show at 8 p.m. Friday at the Overton Park Shell.

Whitman is based with the *Louisiana Hayride* group at Shreveport, La., and is currently hitting the top with a variety of rustic records. His left-handed style with the guitar is as unusual as his style of singing.

Also featured will be Billy Walker, a tall Texan, "Sugar-Foot" Collins, "Sonny" Harvelle, Tinker Fry, and "Curly" Harris along for the laughs.

Advance tickets go on sale tomorrow at Walgreen's Main and Union, Bob Neal, WMPS disc jockey and impresario of the Friday show, said yesterday.

19

Taylor's restaurant is next door to Sun studio.

Sam Phillips and Elvis share a tasty treat at Taylor's.

Elvis with his combo: Bill Black on doghouse bass and Scotty Moore on Electric Guitar

Dewey Phillips at WHBQ played "That's All Right" 14 times the night it premiered on his "Red Hot and Blue" Radio program.

Sam Phillips — the owner, chief engineer, and producer at Sun

Dewey Phillips and Elvis stir up the crowd at a local club.

Elvis poses in the parking lot of the Eagle's Nest, where he frequently performed.

SLEEPY-EYED JOHN
Presents

ELVIS PRESLEY
At the Air-Cooled

EAGLE'S NEST

At CLEARPOOL on LAMAR

TONIGHT

See and Hear Elvis Singing
"That's All Right" and
"Blue Moon of Kentucky"
—PLUS—

TINY DIXON BAND

Doors Open 8:30—Dancing 9-1
Admission $1.20 (Including Tax)

Elvis's second record, "Good Rockin' Tonight," backed by "I Don't Care if the Sun Don't Shine," was issued on September 25, 1954.

SUN

Vocal 2:10

U-131
210

GOOD ROCKIN' TONIGHT
(Ray Brown)
ELVIS PRESLEY
SCOTTY and BILL

MEMPHIS, TENNESSEE

Elvis rocks at the Eagle's Nest. The club's motto was, "Don't wear a tie unless your wife makes you."

Elvis's backup musicians were known as the Blue Moon Boys.

Memphis Press-Scimitar   October 13, 1954

Hayride Show Signs Elvis Presley

Elvis Presley, Memphis boy who made so good singing and playing the guitar that he has recorded for Sun Record Co. ("Blue Moon of Kentucky" and "That's All Right, Mama"), was a guest on *Louisiana Hayride.* And now he has made even better, Sun announced. He has been signed up for a year's contract with Louisiana Hayride and will be heard in Memphis every third Saturday when CBS picks up the show.

THE COMMERCIAL APPEAL   OCTOBER 14, 1954

PRESLEY TO SING ON RADIO SHOW SATURDAY NIGHT

Elvis Presley, our homegrown hillbilly singer, is continuing his swift, steady stride toward national prominence in the rural rhythm field. Latest honor to come his way is as guest performer with the *Louisiana Hayride,* to be broadcast Saturday night over KWKH, Shreveport.

Louisiana Hayride is about the second or third most popular hillbilly program on the air. The tops is Nashville's *Grand Ole Opry,* which never takes anyone but long-established stars in the country music field.

But Presley has already appeared on *Grand Ole Opry* — on Oct. 2 and neither customer nor fellow performers wanted him to quit. It is unprecedented for *Grand Ole Opry* to take a performer on the basis of a single record, which is what Presley had until two weeks ago.

Presley, 19, is the son of Mr. and Mrs. Vernon Presley, 462 Alabama, and was graduated from Humes High School in June, 1953.

His first record release, for Sun Record Co. of Memphis, backed "Blue Moon of Kentucky" with "That's All Right," and sold a sturdy 6,300 discs in Memphis in less than three weeks.

His second record, released two weeks ago Monday in the Memphis market alone, has already logged an astonishing 4,000 copies of "I Don't Care If the Sun Don't Shine" and "Good Rockin' Tonight." National distribution is expected to get the Presley name and fame really booming.

KWKH's *Louisiana Hayride* roster at the moment comprises Slim Whitman and band, Red Sovine and band, Johnny Hordot, Elvis Presley, Jim Reeves and band, Jimmy Newman, Tibby Edwards, Jimmy and Johnny, Hoot and Curley, J.E. and Maxine Brown, Jerry and Dido Rowley, Jeanette Hicks, Betty Amos, the Circle 6 Ranch Boys, Ginny Wright, Carolyn Bradshaw, Jack Ford, Buddy Attaway and the Lump Lump Boys, with Bill Walker slated to join on the 20th.

The _Hayride_ troupe performed in Meridian, Miss. They included Elvis (far right), Jim Reeves (center in black hat), Luke McDaniel (third from right), and Joe Clay (second from right).

Elvis waits backstage to rock the _Hayride_.

Elvis performs on the *Louisiana Hayride* which was broadcast Saturday nights on radio station KWKH from Shreveport.

Lucky Strike cigarets sponsored the segment of the Hayride that featured Elvis.

Memphis Press-Scimitar, October 20, 1954

ELVIS PRESLEY 'CLICKS'

Young Memphis Singer Now In Louisiana Show

Elvis Presley, Memphis' swiftly rising young hillbilly singing star is now a regular member of the *Louisiana Hayride*, broadcast each Saturday night over KWKH, Shreveport, La., and in part each third week over CBS, heard locally over WREC at 8pm.

The *Hayride* specializes in picking promising young rural rhythm talent—and it took just one guest appearance last Saturday for the young Memphian to become a regular. He had been heard about two weeks earlier on *Grand Ole Opry* from Nashville.

Presley was assured by A.M. "Pappy" Covington of the *Hayride* staff that he will be heard over the network portion of the show after he wowed 'em with the songs from his two jukebox hit records made for the Sun Record Co. of Memphis.

Elvis backstage

Elvis with Horace Logan, manager of the Hayride

October 23, 1954

Elvis Presley, who bowed into the pro ranks just two months ago, and who since has enjoyed much success with his initial release, "Blue Moon of Kentucky" and "That's All Right," appeared recently on the *Grand Ole Opry* in Nashville on the same segment of the program with Hank Snow, the Davis Sisters and Eddie Hill.

Presley, with his guitar and bass men, Scotty and Bill, made an appearance recently at Texas Bill Strength's nitery in Atlanta, and last Saturday (16) were guests on *Louisiana Hayride* in Shreveport.

AROUND THE HORN

Bob Neal, veteran c.&w. deejay of WMPS, Memphis, has taken over the personal management of Elvis Presley, 19-year-old country singer who in a few short months has catapulted to a top spot on *Louisiana Hayride*, Shreveport. Presley and his supporting team, Scotty Moore and Bill Black, plus J.E. and Maxine Brown and a *Hayride* show will appear in Clarksdale, Miss., January 12; Helena, Ark., January 13; and Booneville, Miss., Sheffield, Ala., Leachville, Ark., and Sikeston, Mo., the week of January 16. The following week the Presley unit will work a series of East Texas dates with Tom Perryman, of Gladewater, Tex. For the time being, Neal will continue his deejay chores at WMPS.

Bob Neal and Elvis check the charts in Cash Box.

Elvis signs a management contract with Bob Neal. Sam Phillips looks on.

Bob Neal was a local D.J. for country station WMPS.

27

Memphis Press-Scimitar   February 5, 1955

Thru the Patience of Sam Phillips—

SUDDENLY SINGING ELVIS PRESLEY ZOOMS INTO RECORDING STARDOM

That 'Something' Has Captivated Fans Over the U.S.

By Robert Johnson
Press-Scimitar Staff Writer

One sultry night late last July, Dewey Phillips flicked a turntable switch with one of his cotton-pickin' hands and sent a strange rhythmic chant spinning out from WHBQ.

"Well that's all right Baby . . . that's all right, Baby. . . ."

The record ended. Radio like Nature, abhors a void and Mr. Phillips hastens to fill the breach.

"That'll flat git it," he said authoritatively.

That same night, Sleepy Eye John over WHHM tossed the other side of the record on his admirers—and the same voice which had been reassuring Baby now sang plaintive praise of "Blue Moon of Kentucky."

Someth'ng Happened

Time didn't exactly stand still, but something happened. Bob Neal of WMPS played the record, too. The pop jockeys, entranced by something new, began slipping "That's All Right" and "Blue Moon" in among the more sophisticated glucose and bedlam of Teresa Brewer, Nat Cole and Tony Bennett.

In less than a week, a momentous change began for a young teen-ager, working on an assembly line, who liked to sing and play the guitar.

His name: Elvis Presley.

Elvis' first record was on the Sun label of Sam Phillips' small but ambitious Memphis Recording Service, 706 Union. It wasn't the first time that Sam's Sun has created a good-sized ripple in the frenzied circles of record business. Sam is largely responsible for a new trend in the field which the trade publications call R&B (for rhythm and blues) and country (or hillbilly) music, and for making Memphis the R&B capital, as Nashville is for rustic rhythm.

Within a Week

Within less than a week, Sam was frantically and painfully trying to press enough copies of Elvis' debut platter to catch up with a 6000 back-order which hit him before the record had even gone on sale, before it had been released in any market outside Memphis.

And overnight, a restricted but indubitable mantle of fame settled about Elvis, as the record went spinning out across the country—100,000 . . . 200,000 . . . 300,000 . . . still going.

Within a month, Elvis was invited to appear on hillbilly heaven: Nashville's *Grand Ole Opry*. Veteran entertainers kept him singing backstage, after the show.

On Juke Box Jury

The record was played on *Juke Box Jury*. "Blue Moon" had been written and first recorded some years earlier by a famous, *Grand Ole Opry* entertainer, Bill Monroe of Kentucky. Tennessee Ernie Ford, on *Juke Box Jury* that night, drawled: "If ole Bill Monroe hears this, he'll just take his li'l ole country band and head back for the hills." Monroe himself, far from being offended, sent Elvis a note of thanks, After Elvis brought it out, six other companies made it with their stars.

Billboard gave Elvis' first record an 85 score, very high, on both sides. Over a 15-week period, only one other record in the same category had an equal rating, and that was by the established star, Webb Pierce.

Sam Phillips still hasn't figured out which was the big side. "That's All Right" was in the R&B idiom of negro field jazz, "Blue Moon" more in the country field, but there was a curious blending of the two different musics in both.

Two More

Sun brought out two more Elvis records—"I Don't Care" and "Good Rockin' Tonight"; "Milk Cow, Blues Boogie" and "You're a Heartbreaker." Billboard's annual poll of disk jockeys of 1954 landed Elvis in the list of Ten Most Promising artists on the strength of them. . . .

In A Class Alone

Sam doesn't know how to catalog Elvis exactly. He has a white voice, sings with a negro rhythm which borrows in mood and emphasis from country style.

Marion Keisker, who is WREC's Kitty Kelly and Sam's office staff, calls Elvis "a hillbilly cat."

While he appears with so-called hillbilly shows, Elvis' clothes are strictly sharp. His eyes are darkly slumbrous, his hair sleekly long, his sideburns low, and there is a lazy, sexy, tough, good-looking manner which bobby soxers like. Not all records stars go over as well on stage as they do on records. Elvis sells.

If the merry-go-round doesn't start spinning too fast for a 20-year-old, he'll end-up with enough cheeseburgers to last a Blue Moon.

Spin 'em again boys.

October 22, 1955
Bob Neal, Manager of Elvis Presley Enterprises, Memphis, advises that deejay copies of Presley's latest Sun recording, "Mystery Train" b.w. "I Forgot to Remember," are available to those who write to Neal at 160 Union Avenue, Memphis.

Elvis Presley a new kind of country singer

Reviews of New C&W Records

THE BILLBOARD

Elvis Presley
Milkcow Blues Boogie **80**
Sun 215— Presley continues to impress with each release as one of the slickest talents to come up in the country field in a long, long time. Item here is based on some of the best folk blues. The guy sells all the way. Ops will particularly like it. (Leeds, ASCAP)

You're a Heartbreaker **76**
Here Presley tackles the rhythmic material for a slick country-style reading. What with the good backing this one should get action, too. (Hi Lo, BMI)

MUSIC-RADIO

Elvis Presley (Sun) and unit plus **Bud Deckleman** headed up a show in New Orleans last Friday night (4), with **Red Smith**, WBOK deejay, handling the promotion. **Bob Neal**, Presley's personal manager, announces that a new office is being opened at 160 Union Avenue Memphis, to handle Presley's affairs. Neal invites deejays to write in for samples. Presley is also set for a show and dance appearance with **Lee Hamric** in Carlsbad, N.M., February 14, with the deal set by Neal and **Col. Tom Parker** of Jamboree Attractions, Madison, Tenn.

Wilson writes that he emceed a recent **Ferlin Huskey** show in Gainesville, Fla . . . From KSIJ, Gladewater, Tex., **Tom Perryman** infos that he celebrated his sixth anniversary with the station recently by taking a week's tour with **Elvis Presley, Scotty and Bill** and **J.E. and Maxine Brown.** Perryman wound up the celebration with **Hank Thompson.** He adds that **Dowell Bushnell** is now doing two hours of c.w. spinning on *Dal's Corral*, from 1-3 p.m. each day. This gives KSIJ six hours a day across the board of country music, says Perryman.

Cal Shrum, country and western spinner at WMAY, Springfield, Il., infos that credit for the lyrics on his new tune, "Lonesome Lover," should go to **Gordon Forster,** not **Tim Spencer,** as he previously reported. Spencer is publishing the tune . . . **Col. Tom Parker** and Victor artist **Charley Stewart** guested recently with **Cottonseed Jones** on KXLR, North Little Rock, Ark. . . . **Shorty Long**, WPAZ, Pottstown, Pa., currently doing two folk shows a day, Monday thru Saturday, 11-12a.m., and 1-2pm., besides spinning a hit parade every Sunday.

In addition to her one-hour *Cousin Carroll Calling*, heard five days a week over KXAR, Hope, Ark., **Carroll A. Wynn** is doing a 10-minute sponsored show, *Country Music Time.* Carroll types that she helped promote a jamboree, held in Hope, February 22, which included the **Duke of Padukah, Mother Maybelle, the Carter Sisters, Elvis Presley, Bill and Scotty, Jimmy Rodgers Snow, Charley Stewart,** and **Uncle Dudley.** Also appearing in Hope recently were **Jimmy and Johnny, T. Tommy Cutre** and **Merel (More and More) Kilgore.**

MILKCOW BLUES BOOGIE
ELVIS PRESLEY
(Arnold)
SCOTTY and BILL
215
MEMPHIS, TENNESSEE

Leeds Ascap

Vocal U-140

FOLK TALENT AND TUNES

Hank Snow's All-Star Jamboree, underwritten by Hank Snow and Col. Tom Parker, kicked off a three-week tour of Louisiana, Alabama, Florida, Georgia, Virginia, North Carolina and Tennessee at New Orleans May 1. Trek winds up in Chattanooga May 20. Headlined by Snow, the unit includes Faron Young, the Wilburn Brothers, Slim Whitman, Martha Carson, Elvis Presley, the Davis Sisters, Mother Maybelle Carter and Troupe is playing auditoriums in the various spots. Colonel Parker, assisted by Tom Diskin, is using radio, TV, newspapers and circus billing to herald the mammoth show. Deejays along the route are also co-operating on the venture.

Elvis and Hank Snow

May 14, 1955

Bob Neal, currently working with Col. Tom Parker on promotion for the *Hank Snow Show* in the South reports that he has Elvis Presley, Martha Carson, the Carlisles, Ferlin Huskey, J.E. and Maxine Brown and Onie Wheeler set for a week's trek beginning May 29. Neal, who is Presley's personal manager, says the latter has a new release on Sun, "Baby, Let's Play House" b/w "You're Right, I'm Left, She's Gone." Deejays may receive a copy by writing him at 160 Union Street, Memphis, Neal says.

Unknown store owner, Elvis, Col. Tom Parker, and singer Faron Young

Faron Young and Elvis

30

JUNE 1955

"Elvis Presley continues to gather speed over the South," writes **Cecil Holifield,** operator of the Record Shops in Midland and Odessa, Tex. "West Texas is his hottest territory to date," continues Holifield, "and he is the teen-agers' favorite wherever he appears. His original appearance in the area was in January, with **Billy Walker** at Midland, Tex., to more than 1,600 paid admissions. In February, with **Hank Snow** at Odessa, 20 miles from Midland, paid attendance hit over 4,000. On April 1, we booked only Elvis and his boys, **Bill and Scotty,** plus **Floyd Cramer** on piano and a local boy on drums for a rockin' and rollin' dance for teen-agers, and pulled 850 paid admissions. We are booking Elvis for May 31, heading his own show with **Ferlin Huskey, the Carlisles, Martha Carson, J.E. and Maxine Brown** and **Onie Wheeler** on a round robin starting at 7:30 p.m. in Midland and 8:30 p.m. in Odessa. Incidentally, our sales of Presley's four records have beat any individual artist in our eight years in the record business."

First Annual Country and Western Popularity Poll, a three-week contest run recently by Bobby Ritter over WTUP, Tupelo, Miss., drew 1,016 cards and letters from 16 States. In the contest's three categories, **Kitty Wells** placed first among the top 10 female singers; **Elvis Presley,** was first among the top 10 male vocalists, and the **Simmons Brothers,** WTUP artists, wound up in the no. 1 spot among c.&w. bands . . .

The *Hank Snow Show,* with **Faron Young, the Wilburn Brothers** and **Elvis Presley,** played before an overflow crowd of 2,700 in Ocala, Fla., May 10, reports **Nervous Ned Needham,** c.& w. deejay at WMOP, Ocala . . . .

Elvis and Scotty Moore tune up before the show.

July 23, 1955

Deejay Lee Alexander is now spinning the *Lee Alexander Show* six days a week over KECK, Odessa, Tex. In addition, he's also working *Pioneer Jamboree,* which features guest artists every Friday night in Odessa. Guesting with Alexander recently were Ferlin Huskey, J.E. and Maxine Brown, Simon Crumm, Elvis Presley, Bill and Scotty, Tibby Edwards and Sonny James.

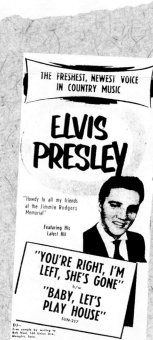

THE FRESHEST, NEWEST VOICE
IN COUNTRY MUSIC

ELVIS PRESLEY

"Howdy to all my friends at the Jimmie Rodgers Memorial"

Featuring His
Latest Hit

"YOU'RE RIGHT, I'M LEFT, SHE'S GONE"
b/w
"BABY, LET'S PLAY HOUSE"
SUN-217

DJ—
Free sample by writing to
Bob Neal, 160 Union Ave.,
Memphis, Tenn.

Featured Star,
KWKH Louisiana Hayride

For available dates

WRITE
WIRE
PHONE

BOB NEAL Exclusive Personal Management
160 Union Ave., Memphis, Tennessee
Phone: Office 8-3667 ● Home 4-4029

July 1955

ELVIS PRESLEY FOR JAMBOREE

The Big D Jamboree country music show at the Sportatorium Saturday night will feature one of the brightest new stars in the field when Elvis Presley returns for a special guest booking.

Presley will have Scotty and Bill as sidemen to back him up on his latest tunes, three of which are listed in the top 10 on the country music charts.

Presley hit first with "That's All Right" and followed with "Baby, Let's Play House." His latest which had got off to a good start saleswise, is called "Mystery Train." Presley, now 21 years old, has his largest following in the bobby-sox field.

A special feature of the Jamboree starting this Saturday will be the show's new policy of paying bus fare home for patrons.

Scotty and Bill often wore western attire; Elvis preferred outrageous suits.

Austin, Texas   The American Statesman

Chance Record Gives Presley Start to Top

Elvis Presley, a young man whose boppish approach to hill-billy music has made him one of the hottest performers of the day, will be headlining a troupe of *Louisiana Hayride* stars when they stage a Western music jam-boree Thursday at 8 p.m. in the Sportcenter.

Appearing with Presley will be guitarist Scotty Moore and bassist Bill Black, his recording partners, plus a dozen or so headliners from the nationally famed *Louisiana Hayride* show in Shreveport.

Included on the bill will be such folk music specialists as Johnny Horton, Betty Amos, David Houston, Dalton and Lulu Jo, Sonny Tremmell, Ray Gomer, Tillman Franks and Willie Bird-brain, the hillbilly comic.

During his comparatively short career in the music world, young Presley, the star of the show, has made a spectacular climb to nationwide popularity.

About a year ago, Presley, Moore and Black were teaming up to make a personal record when they were accidentally heard by a recording manager. Impressed by the rocking style of Presley and his friends, the mana-ger contracted the group to make a pressing whose immediate suc-cess started the 20-year-old Presley on the way to his present position of prominence.

Since that first disc—"That's All Right, Mama"—Presley has applied his half-bop, half-Western style to such tunes as "I Don't Care if the Sun Don't Shine," "Good Rockin' Tonight," "You're a Heart-breaker," and "Milk Cow Blues Boogie," each of which has en-joyed wide popularity throughout the country.

While on the road, Elvis poses with a youthful singing trio.

Brenda Lee and Elvis

THE BILLBOARD

The Billboard Music Popularity Charts

JULY 16, 1955

WESTERN RECORDS COUNTRY &

• Best Sellers in Stores

1. I DON'T CARE (BMI)—W. Pierce 3   5
   YOUR GOOD FOR NOTHING HEART (BMI)—Dec 29480
2. IN THE JAILHOUSE NOW (BMI)—W. Pierce 1   24
   I'm Gonna Fall Out of Love With You (BMI)—Dec 29391
2. MAKING BELIEVE (BMI)—K. Wells 2   19
   WHOSE SHOULDER WILL YOU CRY ON? (BMI) Dec 29419
4. YELLOW ROSES (BMI)—H. Snow 4   15
   WOULD YOU MIND? (ASCAP)—Vic 20-6057
5. SATISFIED MIND (BMI)—P. Wagoner 5   8
   Itchin' for My Baby (BMI)—Vic 20-6105
6. CATTLE CALL (ASCAP)—
   E. Arnold & H. Winterhalter 6   4
   Kentuckian Song (ASCAP)—Vic 20-6139
7. THERE SHE GOES (BMI)—C. Smith 9   10
   Old Lonesome Times (BMI)—Col 21382
8. SATISFIED MIND (BMI)—R. & B. Foley 8   4
   How About Me? (BMI)—Dec 29526
9. LIVE FAST, LOVE HARD, DIE YOUNG
   (BMI)—F. Young 7   16
   Forgive Me, Dear (BMI)—Cap 3056
10. SATISFIED MIND (BMI)—J. Shepard 11   4
    You Can Take Possession (ASCAP)—Cap 3118
11. IN THE JAILHOUSE NOW, NO. 2
    (BMI)—J. Rodgers 13   8
    Peach Pickin' Time Down in Georgia (BMI)—Vic 20-6092
12. I'VE BEEN THINKING (BMI)—E. Arnold 13   24
    Don't Forget (BMI)—Vic 20-6000
13. HIS HANDS (BMI)—Tennessee Ernie 15   1
    I'm a Pilgrim (BMI)—Cap 3135
14. BLUE DARLIN' (BMI)—J. Newman 12   7
    Let Me Stay in Your Arms (BMI)—Dot 1260
15. WILDWOOD FLOWER (ASCAP)—H. Thompson . . .
    BREAKIN' IN ANOTHER HEART (ASCAP)—Cap 3106
15. BABY, LETS PLAY HOUSE (BMI)—E. Presley . . . . —   1
    I'm Left, You're Right, She's Gone (BMI)—Sun 217

Elvis toured the entire South in the spring and summer of 1955.

Memphis Press-Scimitar   AUGUST 6, 1955

AUDIENCE PULLERS . . . . Overton Park Shell was jammed with an overflow audience last night for the wind-up of the eighth annual Bob Neal country music jamboree series.

Several hundred who wanted to hear in person Johnny Cash and Elvis Presley and Webb Pierce and some 22 other country music and comedy performers had to be turned away, while 4000 more lucky people enjoyed the show. The company also toured Little Rock, Ark., 3000 listeners; Camden, Ark., 2000; Sheffield, Ala, 2800; and Tupelo, Miss., 300, this week.

Both Cash and Presley record for Memphis' own Sun Record label.

Johnny Cash, Sun's latest singer, performed with Elvis at Bob Neal's Jamboree in August 1955.

FOLK MUSIC FIREBALL

ELVIS PRESLEY

Every so often a newcomer to the Country music scene stirs up a fuss with a different kind of record, an unusual singing style or a "gimmick" of one sort or another. The latest sensation these days is a 19-year-old Elvis Presley, a handsome, strapping Mississippi boy who's a ball of fire when it comes to putting over a tune. Recording on the Sun label and a regular member of the KWKH *Louisiana Hayride,* in Shreveport, young Presley is enjoying the reality of his life's dream: to sing for people and hear the spontaneous applause that means he's a hit.

When Elvis was a youngster down in Tupelo, Mississippi, folks used to stop him on the street and say, "Sing for us, Elvis." And he would . . . standing on the street corners, in the hot Mississippi sun . . . or in church . . . or at school . . . anywhere someone wanted to hear him, he'd sing. Now the same thing is happening all over again. When he's recognized on the street or at any public place, people call out: "Sing for us, Elvis."

"That's All Right" and "Blue Moon Of Kentucky," Elvis' first Sun waxings, were also his first professional work of any kind. He's a self-taught musician and worked out his unique style while listening to records and picking out the tunes on a cheap ($2.98) guitar. One day he drifted into a Memphis recording studio to make a personal record—just to get an idea about how he sounded—and was heard by Sam Phillips, prexy of Sun Record Company, who thought that with a little work and polish the boy might make the grade as a commercial artist. Several months of hard work did the trick, and "That's All Right" and "Blue Moon Of Kentucky" had an astounding reception all over the nation. The disc also represented something new in records: the unusual pairing of an R&B number with a Country standard.

Just 19, Elvis has been out of high school but one year—and the big (6-footer) blonde guy likes nothing better than to spend an afternoon practicing football with some of the youngsters in his neighborhood. Other hobbies of Elvis' include movies, listening to records—and eating! Stories of the singer's appetite are many. His girl friend, Dixie, declares that recently, at one sitting, he ate 8 Deluxe Cheeseburgers, 2 Bacon-Lettuce-Tomato sandwiches—and topped it off with three chocolate milk shakes.

Since the release of his two-sided hit, Elvis has been making personal appearances and bringing the house down every time. As the featured entertainer at the grand opening of a new business arcade, he played to a wildly enthusiastic audience of more that 3,000 who couldn't restrain themselves and started dancing and jitterbugging when Elvis sang "That's All Right." At the recent Jimmie Rodgers Day celebration in Meridian, Mississippi, Elvis was called back for encore after encore, singing such tunes as "Milk Cow Blues Boogie," "You're A Heartbreaker" and his latest pairing: "I'm Left, You're Right, She's Gone" and "Baby, Let's Play House."

There's no doubt about it—this youngster is a real "Folk Music Fireball."

Rock n' roller Bill Haley toured with Elvis in the fall of 1955.

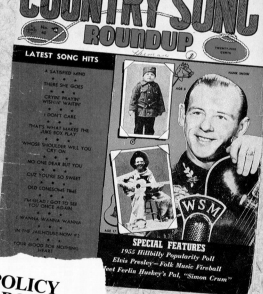

The first national magazine to feature Elvis

NEW POLICY COMBINES POPS-C&W

New York— Col. Tom Parker of Jamboree Attractions, one of the nation's major bookers and promoters of country & western talent, instituted a new policy when he presented a combination of popular and country & western music on a recent one-nighter tour.

Parker teamed Bill Haley and His Comets with Hank Snow for an extended tour, which opened in Omaha, Oct. 10. Jimmie Rodgers Snow replaced his father on the show in Lubbock and Amarillo while Hank hopped to Nashville for an appearance on the *Grand Ole Opry* TV show. Elvis Presley joined the Snow-Haley tour in Oklahoma City.

35

Memphis Press-Scimitar   November 22, 1955

Memphis Singer Presley Signed By RCA-Victor for Recording Work

By ROBERT JOHNSON *Press-Scimitar Staff*

Elvis Presley, 20, Memphis recording star and entertainer who zoomed into bigtime and the big money almost overnight, has been released from his contract with Sun Record Co. of Memphis and will record exclusively for RCA-Victor, it was announced by Sam C. Phillips, Sun President.

Phillips and RCA officials did not reveal terms, but said the money involved is probably the highest ever paid for a contract release for a country-western recording artist.

"I feel Elvis is one of the most talented youngsters today," Phillips said, "and by releasing his contract to RCA-Victor we will give him the opportunity of entering the largest organization of its kind in the world, so his talents can be given the fullest opportunity."

Handled by Parker

Negotiations were handled by Col. Tom Parker of Hank Snow-Jamboree Attractions, Madison, Tenn., Bob Neal, Presley's personal manager, and Coleman Tiley III of RCA-Victor.

Elvis Presley Music, a publishing firm, has been set up to handle much of Presley's music, in conjunction with Hill and Range Music, Inc., New York City.

Bob Neal, WMPS personality, continues as Presley's personal manager and will handle his personal appearances and other activities, but Hank Snow-Jamboree Attractions will handle Presley enterprises in radio, TV, movies and theaters.

Also taking part in negotiations were Hank Snow himself, RCA-Victor's longest-term western star; Sam Eagre, RCA-Victor regional sales manager; Ben Starr of Hill and Range music, and Jim Crudington, local RCA-Victor representative.

Presley, who lived in Tupelo, Miss., until he was 14 and is a graduate of Humes High.

Phillips signed him for Sun Records after Presley wandered in one day and wanted to have a recording made at his own expense.

Best-Seller Fast

His first record, "That's All Right, Mama" and "Blue Moon of Kentucky" hit the best-seller lists immediately after its release in July last year, and both *Billboard* and *Cashbox,* trade journals, named him the most promising western star. He became a regular on *Louisiana Hayride* on CBS. His newest record, "Mystery Train" and "I Forgot to Remember," is his best-seller so far. Both songs were written by Stan Kesler and Charlie Feathers, a Memphis team. Tony Arden has just recorded "I Forgot to Remember" for Victor, and Peewee King's latest is also a Kesler-Feathers composition. All five Presley records have made the best-seller list.

Presley's "Mystery Train" is now being played by pop disk jockeys as well as c&w in the east.

Sun has 10 country-western artists remaining on its label, including Johnny Cash and a newcomer, Carl Perkins of Bermis, Tenn., who writes his own music and is causing a stir. This week Sun brings out a new feminine vocalist, Maggie Sun Wimberly of Florence, Ala., with songs by another Memphis composing team, Bill Cantrell and Quentin Church, who wrote a previous substantial country-western hit, "Day Dreaming."

Steve Sholes of RCA welcomes Elvis.

From left: Bob Neal, Sam Phillips, an RCA executive, Elvis, and Col. Tom Parker

Memphis Press-Scimitar   January 11, 1956

Memphis Boy, Elvis Presley, Signs Contract With Gleason

By ROBERT JOHNSON, Press-Scimitar Staff Writer

One more giant step toward the biggest time by Elvis Presley, the 20-year-old former Humes High boy whose career has zoomed in little more than a year.

Elvis, whose recording contract with Sun Records was recently acquired by RCA-Victor, has been contracted for four appearances by Jackie Gleason on the half-hour *Stage Show* which Gleason produces along with his own show on Saturday nights.

The first appearance on the CBS show, which we get through WREC-TV, will be Jan. 28, with others on Feb. 4, 11, and 18.

NBC also was reported as having been bidding for Elvis. They wanted him for *The Perry Como Show,* opposite Gleason.

Events are spinning faster than his records for the Memphis youngster whose songs have appealed to fans of three musical categories—country and western, rock 'n' roll and straight pop. Don't let your head spin with them Elvis!

Elvis performs on national TV on Stage Show.

In March 1956, the Colonel officially became Elvis's manager.

Elvis's first national hit

ELVIS PRESLEY

Heartbreak Hotel (Tree, BMI)
I Was the One (Jungnickel, ASCAP)—Victor 6420—Presley's first Victor disk might easily break in both markets. "Heartbreak Hotel" is a strong blues item wrapped up in his usual powerful style and a great beat. "I Was the One" is about as close to r&b as you can get without horns, and has more pop appeal. Presley is riding high right now with network TV appearances, and the disc should benefit from all the special plugging.

April 14, 1956

When Carl Perkins' "Blue Suede Shoes" made the r&b charts five weeks ago, it was the first time within memory that a disc by a country artist had made it in this field. This week, Perkins is joined by another country cat, namely Elvis Presley. Presley, like Perkins, is powerfully inspired by authentic r&b, and he's top seller in every field. The disk to break thru is "Heartbreak Hotel," which already has hit a total sales mark of [over 750,000] and is traveling at the rate of between 25,000 and 30,000 disks per day. It's certain to hit a million soon, and a good portion of this will be the r&b market.

Elvis's first album

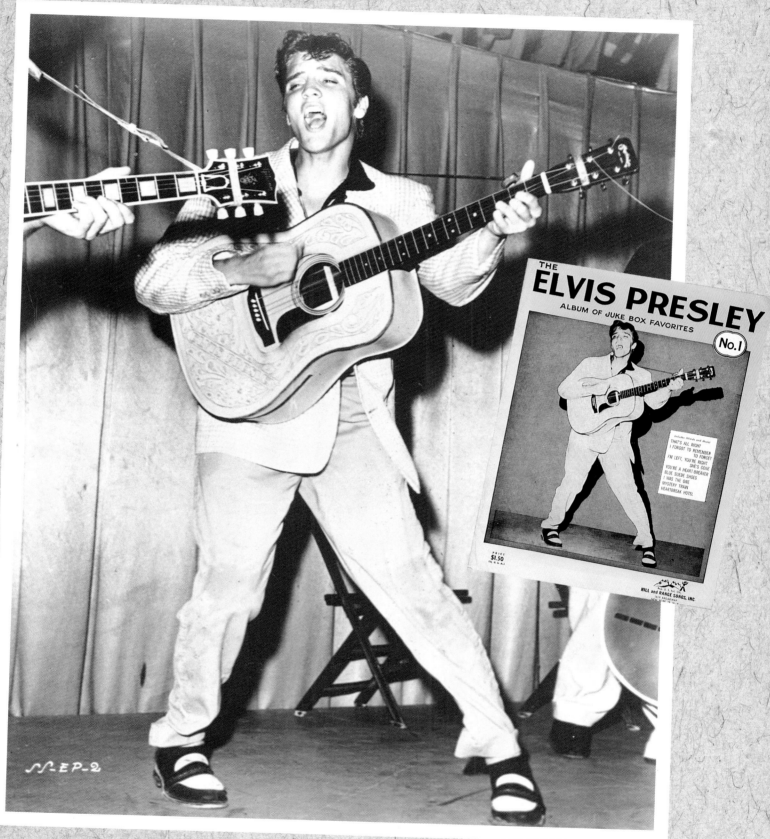

This photo became famous. It was used throughout 1956 to promote Elvis.

The Boundless Future
MOVIES SIGN ELVIS

Hal Wallis, motion-picture producer in Hollywood, heard the screams of the teen-agers as clearly as if he'd been accompanying Elvis Presley on his sensational cross-country tour. They sounded louder in his ear as he sat in a crowded night-club room in Las Vegas—sounded louder than the sophisticated sneers of the well-groomed audience who came to stare at Elvis. Quietly, Hal Wallis made his way backstage after the show and without fanfare, held out the promise of a screen test for Elvis, the screen test that this boy has longed for ever since he dreamed the big dreams of long ago. Skeptics in Hollywood laughed. But Wallis sensed an ability in Elvis far and above that exhibited by his singing and his guitar playing.

To quote the Western Editor of PHOTOPLAY magazine: "I went to look at the screen test that Presley made, with considerable doubt in my mind about this boy's acting ability," Norman Siegal wrote. "But, when he went into his scene with veteran Frank Faylen, I got excited. This boy is an actor." Norman Siegal was seeing in this test what Hal Wallis instinctively knew was there. Hal is having a screenplay written especially for Elvis and his name will soon be on every movie marquee in the country. Watch for it and see for yourself whether PHOTOPLAY and Hal Wallis are any judges of talent.

Hal Wallis (right) was convinced Elvis would be a star.

Elvis in the recording studio

Life   April 30, 1956

A HOWLING HILLBILLY SUCCESS

YOUNG ELVIS PRESLEY'S COMPLAINT BECOMES NATION'S TOP POP TUNE

A lover's lament called "Heartbreak Hotel" sung by Elvis Presley is the best-selling record in the country this week, and the 21-year-old hillbilly who howls, mumbles, coos and cries his way through it has overnight become the biggest singing attraction for teen-agers in the U.S. A $35-a-week Memphis truck driver two years ago, Presley appeared on a few TV shows last fall with a guitar in his hands and a sob around every note. Shortly girls were quivering and fainting wherever he turned up to sing "Long Tall Sally," "I Got a Woman" and "Blue Suede Shoes." On a tour of Texas last week they kicked through a plate-glass door in Amarillo to get him to autograph their arms and underclothes. In San Diego, the Shore Patrol was called out to save him from an over-enthusiastic audience.

This week Elvis headed into Las Vegas to pick up about $12,500 for a week's wailing. Asked what it is about him that makes all the ladies go limp, Elvis answers, "I don't know, but I sure hope it doesn't stop. . . ."

The press swarmed around Elvis wherever he performed.

April 19, 1956

KNOW WHAT I MEAN?

Elvis Gives Out With Crazy Cool Interview

Shortly before he was to go on stage at the Heart O' Texas Coliseum, Elvis Presley, the new 21-year-old king of the nation's rock n' roll set, sat in a darkened Cadillac limousine for an interview—well hidden from the sight of nearly 4,000 screaming squealing teen-agers who were on hand to welcome him Tuesday night.

All the hep cats were there and not enough fuzz (cops).

Out in the stands and on the floor, his audience of idolizing teen-agers did all but hiss and boo to rid the stage of a group of other hillbilly entertainers and bring Presley out behind the microphone that he handles more like a limp blond than a mechanical gadget.

Still Elvis made them wait . . . and he stared out at them, half scared and half unbelieving.

Then with some sort of spasmodic movement, he turned to talk about himself.

"What do you want to know about me, honey?"

"Elvis, have you any idea at all about just what it was that started the girls going crazy over you?"

"No, I don't. I guess it's just something God gave me. I believe that, you know. Know what I mean, honey? And I am grateful. Only I'm afraid. I'm afraid I'll go out like a light, just like I came on. Know what I mean, honey?"

Presley has a way with that "honey" business. When he talks, he looks straight ahead, or sort of dreamy like in no direction at all. Then he turns with that "know what I mean, honey?" His face is close, real close. Right in your face—almost.

"When do you start making your first movie, Elvis?" (Everybody calls him Elvis.)

"Oh, early in June, I think, because . . ."

At this point he stopped talking and stared ahead into the crowd. He squinted his eyes, jerked up a pencil (which had no lead) and began scribbling on the dash of the car. Then he turned and said:

"Huh, did you say something."

"Elvis, when you start acting, will you keep the sideburns?" (The sideburns come down below his ears).

"Oh, I don't know, it depends on what type part they put me in. You know, I'm supposed to do 'Billy the Kid' pretty soon."

"But Elvis, 'Billy the Kid' has been done to the ground."

"Yeah, I know, but this time it will be different." The way he says "different" it really will be.

"Elvis, will you sing in your first movie?"

"No honey, sure won't. Going to be in it with Katharine Hepburn and Burt Lancaster, and I won't sing. I don't want to, I want to be an actor."

Then he turns and stares into the crowd again, listens to one of the other entertainers singing and grins slowly.

"But Elvis, have you thought how unhappy all these girls are going to be if you stop singing?"

"Huh, what was that? Oh, I'll never stop singing, honey, never."

He was beginning to make me wonder if I knew what I was talking about, so I changed the subject:

"Elvis, I hear you walk in your sleep."

"Well, I have nightmares."

"What kind?"

"I dream I'm about to fight somebody or about to be in a car wreck or that I'm breaking things. Know what I mean, honey?" (I don't have any idea what he means).

"Where are you from?"

"From Memphis, Tennessee."

"Oh, yes, that's where all the hillbilly singers come from, isn't it?"

"Maybe so, but I'm no hill-billy singer."

"Well, have you typed yourself . . . . I mean your type of singing?"

"No, I don't dare."

"Why?"

"Cause I'm scared, know what I mean, honey? Real scared."

"What of?"

"I don't know . . . I don't know. Know what I mean, honey?"

At this point I thanked him for his time and started to make a beeline for the door. He grabbed my hand, sat there looking sleepy-eyed into my face and fanned his long lashes while he said:

"Write me up good, will you, honey?"

And he drove out to meet the hysterical adoration of young girls and boys whose emotions he has found are easy to stir up with a song.

San Diego, April 6, 1956

SCREAMS, CHEERS

Teens Yell For Songs By Elvis

Elvis Presley, a 21-year-old singer from Tennessee, rocked and rolled for 5,000 teen-agers last night as he ended his two-night stand in the Arena on Harbor Drive.

Both nights were sellouts.

Presley pumped his guitar, slapped it, and made it play accompaniment to his octave-sliding voice.

The Presley part of the show was brief. He followed a woman vocalist, an acrobatic dance team, a comedian, and a xylophone player.

The audience stomped their feet. 'We want Elvis.'

And then he appeared. The boys cheered and whistled. The girls screamed, jumped, and clapped.

Presley played and sang six tunes. The crowd was too noisy for most of the numbers to be heard.

But it made no difference. The teen-agers knew them by heart.

Elvis signs autographs at a San Diego record store.

41

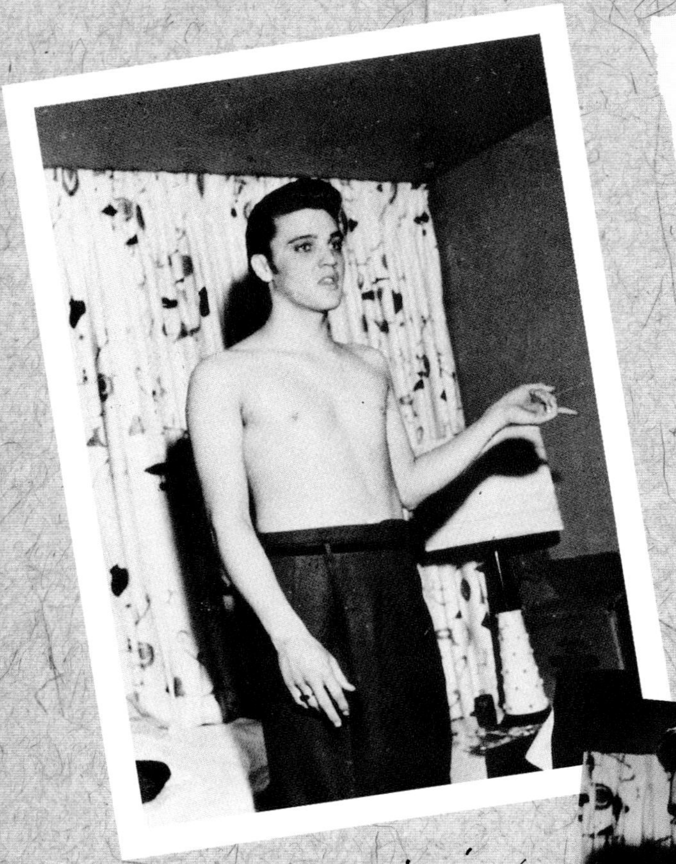

Variety   May 2, 1956

New Frontier, Las Vegas

Las Vegas, April 25
Freddy Martin Orch (17) with Martin Men (5), Johnny Cochrane, Dave Leonard, Bob Hunter, Shecky Green, Elvis Presley & Combo (3), Venus Starlets (14), Jack Teigen, Marge Baker; $2 minimum. . .

. . . Elvis Presley, coming in on a wing of advance hoopla, doesn't hit the mark here in a spot surfeited with rock and rollers playing in shifts in every cocktail lounge all over the Strip. The loud braying of the tunes which rocketed him to the bigtime is wearing, and the applause comes back edged with a polite sound . . . .

Elvis in Las Vegas

Newsweek   May 14, 1956

Music:
Hillbilly on a Pedestal

The high-pitched squeals of females in fanatic teen-age packs are being heard again. Elvis Presley, a hillbilly singer capable of impressive bodily contortions has moved onto the pedestal lately occupied by Johnnie Ray and, before him, by Frank Sinatra . . . .

Last week Presley wound up his first night-club date, a two-week stand at the New Frontier Hotel in Las Vegas. Wedged into a show built around Freddy Martin's silken arrangements of Tchaikovsky and show tunes, Elvis was somewhat like a jug of corn liquor at a champagne party. He hollered songs like "Blue Suede Shoes" and "Heartbreak Hotel," and his bodily motions were embarrassingly specific . . . .

Drummer D.J. Fontana, Scotty, Bill, and Elvis lounge around the pool in Vegas.

Minneapolis, May 13, 1956

AFTER LAST NIGHT   By Will Jones

Squeals Drown Presley's Songs

Elvis Presley, young bump and grind artist, turned a rainy Sunday afternoon into an orgy of squealing in St. Paul auditorium.

He vibrated his hips so much, and the 3,000 customers squealed so insistently at the vibrations, it was impossible to hear him sing. None of the smitten seemed to care . . . .

. . . A radio interviewer asked him about his record successes.

'I switched to Victor because that's the biggest company there is,' drawled Presley.

'You 19 or 21?' asked another. 'I've heard both.'

'Twenty-one,' answered Presley. 'Wish ah was 19.'

Presley came here from Memphis, Tennessee, his home. He's been so busy he hasn't had a chance to get home for awhile. He got a few free days by surprise after he flopped at a Las Vegas, Nevada, night club. They replaced him with a girl singer. The older customers in Las Vegas just didn't dig him . . . .

Elvis flopped in Vegas...

...The older crowd just didn't dig him.

Elvis's scintillating performing style made the girls swoon, the boys jealous, and their parents cringe.

Time   May 14, 1956

Teeners' Hero

. . . He is Elvis Aaron Presley, a drape-suited, tight-trousered young man of 21 and the sight and sound of him drive teenage girls wild . . .

Item: In Fort Worth 16-year-olds have carved his name into their forearms with clasp knives (one did it four times), and an older woman was heard to plead with him, "I've got my husband's Cadillac outside, come with me?"

Item: In Oklahoma City he was safely whisked away in a police car after his show, but a reporter who had interviewed him was mobbed by the stage-door Jennies. "Touch him," yelled one, "Maybe he's touched Elvis!"

Item: In Amarillo, when asked if he intended to marry, Elvis answered, "Why buy a cow when you get milk through the fence?" . . .

Time   June 18, 1956

Yeh-Heh-Heh-Hes, Baby

In Boston, Roman Catholic leaders urged that the offensive music be boycotted. In Hartford city officials considered revoking the State Theater's license after several audiences got too rowdy during a musical stage show. In Washington the police chief recommended banning such shows from the National Guard Armory after brawls in which several people were injured . . .

. . . The object of all this attention is a musical style known as "rock 'n' roll," which has captivated U.S. adolescents as swing captivated prewar teen-agers and ragtime vibrated those of the '20s . . .

. . . There is no denying that rock 'n' roll evokes a physical response from even its most reluctant listeners, for that giant pulse matches the rhythmical operations of the human body, and the performers are all too willing to specify it. Said an Oakland, California policeman, after watching Elvis ("The Pelvis") Presley . . . last week: "If he did that in the street, we'd arrest him . . . ."

A reflective moment

Elvis was considered dangerous by adults.

Presley Gets Blamed

Ottawa, July 14. Even up in Ottawa, Elvis Presley gets blamed for [teenagers' bad actions.] The latest incident was a court appearance of five teenagers held after police raided a beer party where the president of the Ottawa Elvis Presley Fan Club pleaded guilty to participating . . . .

. . . Peter Mercer, club secretary, denied the club had any connection with the beer party. "We have," he said, "no intentions of being connected with these so-called rock 'n' roll violence worshippers" . . . .

45

Elvis clowns it up with Milton Berle on Berle's TV variety show.

America   June 23, 1956

Beware Elvis Presley

Does the name Elvis Presley mean anything to you? If it doesn't the chances are that it does to your children. He is a "singer" of rock 'n' roll songs and his records are top favorites with the juke-box audience. If his "entertainment" could be confined to records, it might not be too bad an influence on the young, but unfortunately Presley makes personal appearances . . .

. . . Yet the National Broadcasting Company wasn't loathe to bring Presley into the living-rooms of the nation on the evening of June 5. Appearing on *The Milton Berle Show*, Presley fortunately, didn't go so far as he did in LaCrosse, but his routine was "in appalling taste" (said the San Francisco *Chronicle*) . . . .

That Scream You Heard Was Presley's Audience

An atomic explosion of juvenile emotion hit the Fox Theater last night. It was triggered by Elvis Presley, the singer with the profile of a Greek god and the motions of a Gilda Gray who is the current sensation of the rock 'n' roll business.

Sporting a green jacket, tight pants and a guitar, Elvis loped onto the stage for three performances. The guitar seldom got twanged, because Elvis was too busy flexing his knees and swinging his thighs like a soubrette in the palmy days of burlesque.

NEW HIGH REACHED

With each manipulation, local adherents of the Presley cult cut loose with screams that put to shame the pandemonium raised by Frankie Sinatra, Tony Martin and Martin and Lewis, prime favorites of the old swooning days at the Fox. Elvis was singing to a wicked beat, but only the cool heads knew he was doing 'Heartbreak Hotel,' 'Blue Suede Shoes,' 'Long Tall Sally,' and 'I Got a Woman' and 'My Baby Left Me,' all milestones in his meteoric career as a recording artist.

OTHER ACTS

There were other acts, including the Jordanaires, who did an excellent job of setting up Presley's stint with some bouncy quartet singing, but they served merely to mark time until the Marlon Brando of the mountain music set arrived.

A stout cordon of city and private police kept in hand the 12,500 teen-agers and others who attended the three shows. It is estimated that Presley got close to $10,000 for his chore of about an hour and a half.

Not bad for a 21-year-old who was driving a truck in Memphis, Tennessee, only a year and a half ago.

This provocative version of "Hound Dog" on Berle's show caused an uproar.

Elvis sings "I Want You, I Need You, I Love You," with the Jordanaires.

Allen Gives No. 2 Spot to Sullivan via "New" Presley

Time   July 23, 1956

Sunday at 8

When NBC's Steve Allen decisively beat CBS's Ed Sullivan a fortnight ago in the battle for TV's Sunday-at-8 audience . . . , the burning question among television's hucksters was: Who had done it, Allen or his guest star Elvis ("The Pelvis") Presley? Sullivan, in the unaccustomed position of runner-up, affected disdain for the Pelvis, snorted that he would not have the gyrating groaner at any price on his family-type program. "He is not my cup of tea," Sullivan said loftily . . . .

Elvis appears in a tux on The Steve Allen Show.

Rehearsing for Steve Allen's show

A Tux for TV

A bubblegum card commemorating the occasion

48

Newsweek   July 16, 1956

Lardner's Week

Devitalizing Elvis

by John Lardner

. . . Live and let live—that is how most of us boys in the upper crust of sociology look at it. Nonetheless, we all watched with interest last week when one of our number, Steve Allen (who has his own show, as we say in the scientific game), made a public attempt to neutralize, calm, or de-twitch Elvis Presley, the lively singer . . . .

. . . Allen's ethics were questionable from the start. He fouled Presley, a fair-minded judge would say, by dressing him like a corpse, in white tie and tails. This is a costume often seen on star performers at funerals, but only when the deceased has specifically requested it in his will. Elvis had made no such request—or, for that matter, no will. He was framed . . . .

HOUND DOG

HOUND DOG
WORDS AND MUSIC BY JERRY LEIBER AND MIKE STOLLER

As Recorded by
ELVIS PRESLEY
on RCA Victor

50¢

REG. U.S. PAT. OFF.
ELVIS PRESLEY MUSIC, INC.
and LION PUBLISHING COMPANY, INC.
Sole Selling Agent,
HILL AND RANGE SONGS, INC.
1650 Broadway, New York 19, N. Y.

"Hound Dog" was Elvis's trademark song in 1956.

DON'T BE CRUEL
(To a Heart that's True)
Words and Music by OTIS BLACKWELL and ELVIS PRESLEY
As Recorded by ELVIS PRESLEY on RCA Victor

PRINTED IN U.S.A.

SHALIMAR MUSIC CORP.—ELVIS PRESLEY MUSIC, INC.
Sole Selling Agents:
SHELDON MUSIC, INC.
48 West 48th Street
New York 36, N. Y.

PRICE 50¢ IN U.S.A.

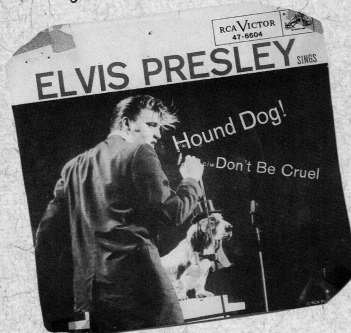

RCA VICTOR
47-6604

ELVIS PRESLEY SINGS

Hound Dog!
b/w Don't Be Cruel

"Hound Dog" backed with "Don't Be Cruel" was released in July 1956. The record sold 6 million copies that year alone.

Elvis on Vacation!

Elvis with June Juanico

Elvis and Red West vacationed at Ocean Springs, Miss., in July.

June Juanico, who lived in Biloxi, Miss., visited Elvis in Ocean Springs.

Elvis and Red try out a new rifle.

While on holiday, Elvis took waterskiing lessons.

By the end of his vacation, Elvis could ski quite well.

51

ELVIS PRESLEY: MUSIC TO SIN BY!

The fans go wild...

... as Elvis moves to his music.

Ocean of Screams Breaks Over Elvis

Elvis Presley, a big shouldered kid in a pink coat and long black pants, staggered onto the stage of the Olympia Theater Friday like a drunken Brando.

And the mob, which stretched way up into the darkness of the theater, stood up and shrieked.

Even when Marciano was belting the sense out of Moore in the ball park of New York there was no such shriek. It vibrated the air, piercing everything like a trillion tiny knives in the dimness.

"Oh, go man, go!" one kid girl in shorts screamed, her frantic hands at her black hair, eyes stunned and face contorted. And how they screamed.

Presley jogged around the mike, and opened his mouth, and the mob drowned the sound away. He loosened his white tie and licked his lips and tried again, but the jam of teenage girls wouldn't let his voice go.

They had started lining up outside the theater at midnight Thursday.

Before noon Friday, the crowd had grown into a line around the block, and then packed the theater to standing room, waiting just to see this mumbling, swaying kid in the pink coat.

The bedlam trembled. "I want you," sang Presley, "I need you . . ."

The mob of girls surged to the stage, where they knelt, arms upraised.

A band of policemen, who were standing around shaking their heads in disbelief, rushed in and pried the kids from the stage.

Presley smiled, his shaggy brown hair began to fall like a horse's mane, and even that brought a thundering of delighted squeals.

"Nothin' like it since Sinatra started," one cop said. "I don't see how these kids can get so excited."

Excitement was the word. Among the hundreds of teenage girls, some clutched photographs of Presley fondly, others wore straw cowboy hats, others had magazines with his picture printed brightly on the front.

And on the stage, the kid in the pink coat closed his eyes and strummed his guitar and swayed passionately, "I need you-oo, I want you-oo." And a 1956 hysteria swelled and smashed away the sound of his music.

52

Ticket 'Rocks' Elvis Presley

HATTIESBURG, Miss., July 31—Constable Charlie Ward figured he had caught just another speeder when he picked up a Tennessee motorist.

But it took his teen-age son just a split second to realize his dad had arrested rock-n-roll sensation Elvis Presley.

. . . Presley is mostly nightmare. On-stage, his gyrations, his nose wiping, his leers are vulgar. When asked about the sex element in his act, he answers without blinking his big brown eyes: "Ah don't see anything wrong with it. Ah just act the way Ah feel." But Elvis will also grin and say, "Without mah left leg, Ah'd be dead." Old friends, like the Memphis Press-Scimitar's Bob Johnson, advise him to clean up his "dances."

Presley has taken the rock 'n' roll craze to new sales heights. He has also dragged "big beat" music to new lows in taste.

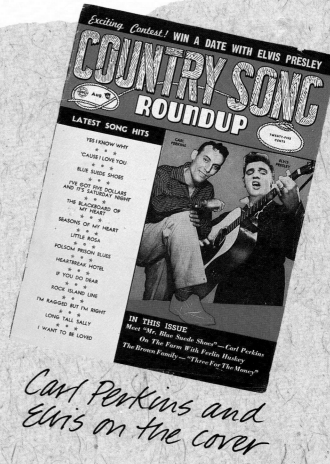

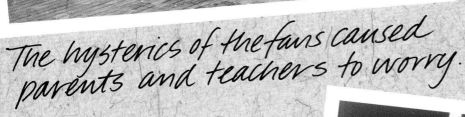

The hysterics of the fans caused parents and teachers to worry.

Carl Perkins and Elvis on the cover

Q

Do Elvis' parents mind his shaking?
—Nancy Johnson, Nyack, N.Y.

A

Mr. and Mrs. Presley appreciate their son's singing style as an outgrowth of southern-style jazz and blues and rhythm singing. They don't object; in fact, Elvis' grandfather is now singing on discs, too.

Trying to make contact

Elvis' Performance Satisfies Gooding

Elvis Presley, minus his bump and grind dance, continued his two-day show in Jacksonville today after a hectic time yesterday—a warning from a judge and trouble with the Variety Artist Guild.

The teen-age rock 'n' roll idol, who was advised before his first show here yesterday to 'keep it clean' or face court charges, met with local Juvenile Court Judge Marion Gooding after the opening performance and was warned sternly to remove the objectionable hip movements from the act.

Judge Gooding, who watched the first performance along with 2,200 screaming youngsters, said today apparently Presley has complied with the order, judging from reports of the later shows last night.

Before talking to Gooding yesterday, Presley appeared bewildered at the request. 'I can't figure out what I'm doing wrong,' he told reporters backstage.

'I know my mother approves of what I'm doing . . . If I had a teen-age sister, I certainly would not object to her coming to watch a show like this,' he said.

Meanwhile, a representative of the American Guild of Variety Artists told Presley yesterday that unless he joined AGVA and his manager, Tom Parker, posted bond and insurance for other acts in the Presley show, AGVA would prevent other acts from appearing.

The matter was cleared up shortly before show time when Presley accepted membership in the organization and his manager accepted bond and insurance obligations to AGVA.

Presley, who kept a nonchalant attitude throughout the day, spent his spare time between performances posing for magazine, television and newspaper photographers and answering reporters' questions.

Elvis kisses Helen Putnam, Founder of Fat Girls Anonymous.

THE ELVIS PRESLEY SHOW
STARRING
IN PERSON

ELVIS PRESLEY

WITH AN ALL STAR CAST
THE JORDONAIRES
PHIL MARAQUIN
FRANKIE CONNORS
BLUE MOON BOYS & Others

RCA Victor Recording Star
HEAR HIS SONG
"HEARTBREAK HOTEL"
"HOUND DOG"
AND HIS OTHER GREAT
RECORDING HITS

FLORIDA THEATRE
JACKSONVILLE - FLORIDA
FRI · SAT AUG 10 - 11
MATINEE AND NIGHT SHOWS

NEWSWEEK   August 27, 1956

Inextinguishable

Despite repeated efforts by critics to cool his sex-hot flame, Elvis Presley has remained the most incendiary figure in the world of rock 'n' roll. Last week, his latest hit, a tuneless ditty called "Hound Dog," was lurching inexorably toward the top of the best-seller lists. If this were not enough, there was other proof that interest in the singer was still burning.* . . .

*Many Democrats who heard of it felt that Presley's endorsement of Stevenson was a below-the-belt blow—the first, possibly, of the '56 campaign.

In Jacksonville, a judge made Elvis tone down his act.

Dewey Phillips, Wink Martindale, and Elvis on Martindale's Memphis TV show.

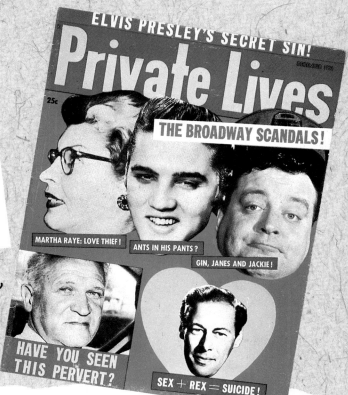

ELVIS PRESLEY'S SECRET SIN!

Private Lives

25c

THE BROADWAY SCANDALS!

MARTHA RAYE: LOVE THIEF!   ANTS IN HIS PANTS?

GIN, JANES AND JACKIE!

HAVE YOU SEEN THIS PERVERT?

SEX + REX = SUICIDE!

IS ROCK 'N ROLL MAKING SAVAGE SEX SINNERS OF SIMPLE TEEN-AGERS? IS YOUNG ELVIS PRESLEY THE BIG ANSWER?

Since the advent of rock 'n roll rhythms, music has been blamed for making savage sex sinners of simple teen-agers. And the symbol of rock 'n roll music—"music to sin by," as one observer put it—is hip-swinging Elvis Presley.

Detractors can cite an almost endless list of examples to show why rock 'n roll is more madness than music, why Elvis ("Hi-luh-huh-huh-huv-yew-hew") Presley is more seducer than singer. Here are a few authenticated cases:

Police Arrest 14

After a rock 'n roll "concert" in New Haven, Connecticut, police arrested 14 teen-agers and charged them with fighting and drunkenness. New Haven Police Chief Francis V. McManus said thousands of the teen-aged fans at the session "wound up in a state of drunken abandon." He said "we don't stand for that sort of thing . . . ."

"The musicians," added the police chief, "rolled around the floor like a bunch of dervishes. One musician would lie on the floor and the other would crouch over him, playing his instrument. It was very suggestive . . ."

Elvis, Elvis!

Elvis Presley is a young man of 21. He wears a drape suit and tight trousers. He also sings and plays a guitar. Yet this youth is capable of driving women wild with desire for him.

In Fort Worth, Texas, girls have proudly showed off their forearms that they have disfigured with knives by scratching out

in blood his name. One girl cut his name into her forearm flesh no less than four times!

In Fort Worth, too, it was reported that one woman waited for Elvis to beg him to come away with her. Said she: "I've got my husband's Cadillac outside. Come with me! . . ."

What Elvis Has

Why has Elvis been called more a seducer than a singer? Why is rock 'n roll, Elvis Presley's specialty, blamed for making young innocents into savage sex sinners?

The answers lie in the way Elvis delivers a song, the kind of songs rock 'n' roll favors, the manner in which musicians play rock rhythms.

Let us take a look at Presley putting a song over. On a stage, his hips swing from side to side, his entire body quivering rapidly, his full lips knowingly shaping lyrics of love and desire and longing.

It's almost dangerous to criticize Presley for his showmanship, so violent do his fans get. For example, Ben Gross in his New York Daily News TV-radio column "What's On?" criticized him, and these are but a few of the letters he got back:

(1) "You're a dirty, lousy _ _ _ _ _ and ought to be put in jail."

(2) "Elvis is the world's greatest singer and people who say bad things about him should be cut to pieces alive and thrown in the river."

(3) "You're a dirty filthy slob—Some night while you are walking home from

work you might accidentally get run over by a car. This is some friendly advice."

(4) "You're going to get into lots of trouble, you _ _ _ _ _."

(5) "The day The News hired you they lowered themselves lower than a rattlesnake . . . Is it true that you get paid off in morphine? Drop dead!"

(6) "You _ _ _ _ _ jerk. You need a dose of poison and I'll come up and give it to you myself."

(7) "Older people don't like Elvis. I hope they all croak."

(8) "The next time you write anything about Elvis Presley I hope and pray that you will break your ten little fingers on the typewriter . . . . Yes, Elvis does rotate his pelvis, but he sure knows how to do it."

And on the letters go, much in the same tone, 99 per cent of them from teen-agers, according to columnist Gross.

The Music Itself

Rock 'n' roll music is simple music, very repetitious music, with a strong beat. When teen-agers hear songs like "Rock Around the Clock," "Heartbreak Hotel," "Rock Me All Night Long," "Annie Had A Baby," "Tweedle Dee," and "Long Tall Sally," they wail, scream unearthly moans, and even dance excitedly in public, losing all inhibitions. Sometimes the thousands gathered in a theatre to listen to a rock 'n' roll show act more like a convention of hop-heads rather than an audience merely being entertained by music.

Listening to it, no one can ever deny that rock 'n roll is full of sensuousness . . . .

LETTERS To The Editors

ELVIS

Sirs:
I'm an Elvis Presley fan writing you to thank you for the nine-page article on him ("Elvis—a Different Kind of Idol," Life, August 27). Some time ago you had a short article on him. That was good but I really flipped when I saw this story.
JUDY McCLELLAND

White Plains, N.Y.

Sirs:
We want to thank you for that picture spread you had about our "dream baby"—Elvis. It was the "badest," and when I say the "badest," that means the "greatest." The "cats" here in Philly are wild about Elvis. He's the "king," the supreme ruler.
STELLA VERBIT

Philadelphia, Pa.

Sirs:
Please don't give people the wrong impressions of Elvis Presley. We think he's the absolute end.
JANIS OLSEN

Grand Junction, Colo.

Sirs:
No one complains about the female strip-teasers but when it comes to Elvis, it's a different story. When he was on the Milton Berle show the criticisms started flying. But when a girl danced the way an uncivilized native would, no one said a thing. That really scorched me.
CAROL PARKER

Rochester, N.Y.

Sirs:
Few stories featuring Elvis Presley seem to include much about his family or his parents. Could you tell me if he has any brothers or sisters?
BOBBIE JEAN POLEET

Hanover, Ind.

No sisters; a twin brother died at birth.—ED.

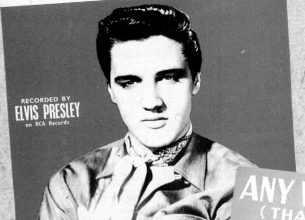

BLUE SUEDE SHOES
Words and Music by CARL LEE PERKINS

RECORDED BY
ELVIS PRESLEY
on RCA Records

ABERBACH (LONDON) LTD.
Sole Selling Agents
BELINDA (London) LTD
142, Charing Cross Road, LONDON, W.C.2

Sheet music

Sirs:
I honestly believe the kids just enjoy his performances because they are full of vivacity. I'd hate to think the years the church and I have spent on training my teen-age daughters could be obliterated by watching a performance or two by Elvis.
VERNA B. GORDON

Atlanta, Ga.

Sirs:
I hate Elvis Presley!
DANNY ROSE

Rye, N.Y.

Sirs:
I wasn't sure whether my aversion to him was due to ignorance of facts or just plain disgust. However, your story certainly clinched it. I just don't "dig" Brother Elvis.
BARBARA CZWOJDAK

Buffalo, N.Y.

Sirs:
The actions of those teen-age girls made me realize how silly and simple I was when I almost went haywire over Johnny Ray. I guess it is just a phase we all go through.
JERRY SMITH

Ambler, Pa

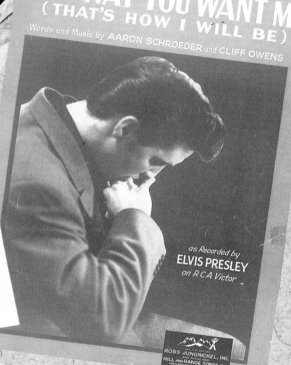

ANY WAY YOU WANT ME
(THAT'S HOW I WILL BE)
Words and Music by AARON SCHROEDER and CLIFF OWENS

as Recorded by
ELVIS PRESLEY
on RCA Victor

ROSS JUNGNICKEL, INC.
Sole Selling
HILL and RANGE SONGS, INC.
1650 BROADWAY, NEW YORK, N.Y.

Elvis liked to tease the girls by moving close to them on-stage.

Elvis Presley

Part I: The People Who Know Say He Does Have Talent

. . . Elvis Presley, who was driving a truck in Memphis two years ago, made his debut with Tommy and Jimmy Dorsey on *Stage Show* last spring. The Dorsey rating, which had been drooping like a noodle, came to life. "The Pelvis" was invited to return. Appearing on Milton Berle's show, Elvis brought screams of joy from his followers, howls of rage from older viewers, and achieved for Berle his first top audience in months.

Despite the protest, Steve Allen invited Presley to sing—without wiggles—on his new Sunday night show. Dressed in top hat and tails, Elvis sang. That night *The Steve Allen Show* drew a bigger audience than *The Ed Sullivan Show*, no mean feat.

Sullivan's response was immediate. "I wouldn't have him (Presley) on my show at any price," said Ed sanctimoniously. "He's not my cup of tea."

But the following week, Ed, like the great broken-field runner he is, reversed his field, quietly signed Presley for three appearances at eight-week intervals at a total of $50,000 . . .

. . . Ed Sullivan's explanation of why he signed Presley seems to indicate that he carries his own estimate of the Sideburn Kid's talent.

"I've never met Presley. I've never seen him on TV, except for those kinescopes of the Dorsey Brothers' show and the Berle show I watched. I thought he was perfectly okay with the Dorseys. As for the Berle show, I don't see why everybody picked on Presley. I thought the whole show was dirty and vulgar.

"In signing Presley, I'm stringing along with the kids. I think he has some kind of tone in his voice that scores with them, the same as Frank Sinatra had.

"I can tell you now that he'll sing no suggestive lyrics for us. As for his gyrations, the whole thing can be controlled by camera shots."

When apprised of this news, Allen made the following statement: "I hereby offer Ed Sullivan $60,000 to make three appearances on my show. He will not, however, be permitted to bump, grind, wiggle, waggle or smile . . . ."

The Plain Truth About Elvis Presley

TV GUIDE

LOCAL PROGRAM LISTINGS
WEEK OF SEPTEMBER 8-14

15¢

Elvis Presley

Part 3:
He Tells How The Little Wiggle Grew

. . . Presley had arrived in Lakeland, Fla., a few hours before. In 10 minutes, the first of his two scheduled performances in Lakeland's armory would begin. Now he was talking about himself to a visiting reporter.

"Naw, sir," he said, "I don't like them to call me Elvis the Pelvis. It's the most childish expression I ever heard from an adult. Elvis the Pelvis . . . ."

Elvis Presley

Part 2: The Folks He Left Behind Him

. . . Robert Johnson, TV columnist for the Memphis Press-Scimitar, believes that Presley has now reached the point where he can sing more with his voice and less with his pelvis. "His records sell in England, where no one has even seen Presley," he says.

Perhaps the picture of Elvis Presley, as composed by the folks back home, can best be completed with two final quotations, one from Presley's father, the other from one of the band.

From Vernon Presley:

"Anyone like Elvis, it's easy for them to criticize him. I think some of it's jealousy. Whenever someone writes that he should change, the kids write letters saying they like him the way he is. I don't want him to change . . . ."

And from the musician:

"Only one trouble with Elvis: he thinks he's not going over unless the audience is tearing the place up and screaming . . . ."

TV RADIO MIRROR

RADIO MIRROR
DEC.

NEW!

BETTY OAKES
of Valiant Lady

TEAL AMES
The Edge of Night

Ed Sullivan
and Elvis Presley

EXCLUSIVE!
THE GIRL
WHO GOT
TO PRESLEY

Presley's 82.6% Share

Ed Sullivan show hit an all-time peak in share of audience Sunday night (9), swamping NBC-TV's feature film showing of "The Magic Box" with an 82.6% share, compared with NBC's 8.3% . . . .

Elvis rehearses for The Ed Sullivan Show.

Tupelo, Miss., Fair, With Elvis, Sets Gate, Grandstand Records

Tupelo, Miss.—Elvis Presley and the Mississippi-Alabama Fair & Dairy Show rocked and rolled to smashing success.

The six-day fair, which closed Saturday (29), piled up an all-time record attendance of 180,000. Grandstand receipts were 40 percent higher than last year, and the midway gross (by the Olson Shows) topped that for 1955 by 12 per cent.

Presley, in for his home-coming (he was born in East Tupelo), wowed 'em on his day, Wednesday (26). No fewer than 100 special police, including 50 State highway patrolman, were called in to control the crowd that stormed the grandstand to see the Tupelo boy made good.

His End $11,000

Mississippi's Gov. J. P. Coleman was on hand to present a scroll to Presley and say the State was proud of Tupelo's native son. Mayor James Vallard joined in like expressions.

Presley received $11,800 for his appearance, with his end based on 60 per cent of grandstand receipts. He was in on a guarantee of $5,000 against the percentage. For his appearance the usual grandstand price was upped from 75 cents to $1.50. The capacity, moreover, had been increased by the addition of 3,000 seats in front of the stage.

Bill Changed Daily

The rock and roll headliner provided the highlight of the fair, but actually was part of the sweeping changes effected by the fair's manager, J. M. Savery. Each day, for the first time, the fair offered name or semi-name talent in front of the grandstand at 75 cents admission.

Ernest Tubb and His Texas Troubadours, the Wilburn Brothers, Hank Locklin and Bobb Helms were in opening day, The Blackwood Brothers and the Statesmen were offered Thursday (27). Wally Fowler and His Chuck Wagon Gang, the Bond Sisters, Oak Ridge Quartet and Sister Kate Freeman were in Friday (28), and Carl Perkins, Johnny Mack Brown, Smiley Burnette, Warren (rock and roll Ruby) Smith and Eddy Bond and the Stompers the final day, all on a two-a-day basis.

In prior years the fair offered the same show for the duration of its run.

Savery, commenting on the success this year, said that the fair will continue to offer different attractions each day next year.

22G for Attractions

The grandstand attraction outlay was $22,000, an all-time high here but more than warranted, Savery said. The fair's attendance surpassed the old mark by 24,000, but receipts from all sources were proportionately higher than the jump in attendance.

Besides the shift in attractions, the fair made many other changes. A new stage was built, new cattle and swine barns were erected, premiums were hiked to $20,000 and there were more industrial exhibits because space was freed by reducing the independent midway. An automobile was given away nightly. All available exhibit space was sold out, and livestock entries hit a new high.

Elvis performed two shows at the Miss.-Ala. Fair and Dairy Show in his hometown of Tupelo on Sept. 26, 1956.

Two of Elvis's cars, a Chevy Bel Air convertible and a Lincoln Premiere, sit behind his house on Audubon Dr.

MEMPHIS: Elvis Presley relaxes by playing the organ at his home here as girl friend Barbara Hearn looks on. The singer shows no battle scars after a three-blow fracas with two service station attendants. Witnesses say the fight began when Elvis didn't move his car fast enough for one of the attendants, who shoved Presley. All three were released on $52 bond on [pending] charges of assault and battery and disorderly conduct.

Barbara Hearn was Elvis's girl in 1956.

Memphis Commercial Appeal   October 20, 1956

Assignment: Memphis—

Was The Judge Injudicious? New Presley Puzzle Is Born

By LYDEL SIMS

Winding up the week's work:
On historic occasions, reporters are expected to weigh and analyze every word uttered, however casually, in search of secret significance.

Thus it becomes necessary to study a word spoken by acting Judge Sam Friedman yesterday during the Presley Trial.

"You," he told Elvis, "because of your avocation wherever you go, you have a large following . . ."

Now the question is, what is the significance of the judge's choice of "avocation"? And did he choose it consciously, or did some judicially-repressed opinion cause his tongue to trip?

Called Away?

I have consulted Webster on this, and there are several possibilities.

He could have meant that Elvis' singing is a "subordinate occupation, esp. one pursued with enjoyment." He could have been identifying it as a "hobby."

Perhaps he meant the Presley voice is "that which calls one away from one's regular employment." If so, for better or for worse?

Was he suggesting a new teen-age idiom, in that when Elvis lights into "Hound Dog" he is in the "state of being called away"?

Finally, could he have been using "avocation" in its outmoded meaning, "vocation," and if so, why?

Social historians will long ponder this puzzle.

Elvis was acquitted of all charges related to a fight with two gas station attendants.

HEARTBREAK: HOUND DOGS PUT SALES ZIP INTO PRESLEY PRODUCTS

Firms turn out Elvis-labeled shoes, jeans, lipstick but fear fate of Davy Crockett.

Hank Saperstein and Elvis look over the Elvis merchandise.

European postcard

Foto: Camera Press/Ufa   Elvis Presley   Reproduktion verboten.

Ufa/Film-Foto

Flasher buttons

Elvis Presley

[OFFICIAL]

3 Inch PHOTO BUTTONS

in Beautiful Color

$2.00 Per Doz.

3" round celluloid buttons.

25% deposit with order, balance C.O.D.

Kim & Cioffi is the Official Elvis Presley Licensee for Photo Buttons.

KIM & CIOFFI   926 Filbert St., Philadelphia 7, Pa.
Market 7-2283   Market 7-1225

NEWSWEEK

ENTERPRISE:

Presley Spells Profit

. . . "It's nothing new," [Hank] Saperstein explains. "It happened with Valentino, Theda Bara, and Clara Bow. We are each of us insecure in our way. We like to identify ourselves with people who are somebody." Identifying himself with Presley seemed the thing for Saperstein to do; already handling products with the imprimaturs of Wyatt Earp, the Lone Ranger, and Lassie, Saperstein signed up Elvis for an exclusive merchandising deal, pledging to do for Presley at the retail counter what Col. Tom Parker did for him on stage, screen, TV, and records.

Presley Products: Teen-agers have since mobbed the retail counters in search of Presley products. Dollar lipsticks (in exotic shades of Hound Dog Orange and Tutti Frutti Red) have passed the 450,000 mark in sales. A Providence, R.I., costume-jewelry firm has turned out 350,000 charm bracelets ($1 plus tax), jangling with such Presley symbols as a hound dog, guitar, or a cracked heart. Another $150,000 has gone for the same number of statuettes of Elvis, complete with guitar. A New York clothing manufacturer has moved 80,000 pairs of $2.98 jeans bearing Presley's photo and has expanded the line to include Presley "Ivy League" girls' shirts. ("Ivy League" pants are next . . . .)

Bubblegum cards

Hound Dog

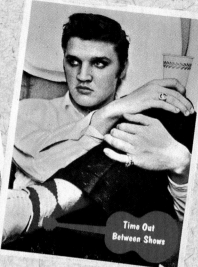

Time Out Between Shows

The Fan's Friend

ELVIS PRESLEY HEAD SCARF
Four-color print on pastel silk rayon blends. Colors: white, pink and copen. Retails at $1.49

Now Elvis can keep your head warm!

61

LOOK   November 13, 1956

The Great Elvis Presley Industry

Teen-agers pay nearly $20,000,000 a year to worship the young rock-'n'-roller

... It's hard to believe that the teen-age girls of the land could carry that much dough in the pockets of their green-stitched black-denim Elvis Presley jeans, but they are the ones who make the Presley Industry pay off. There must be a couple of million awkward, unjelled American females who, in the next five years or so, will be reasonably intelligent American women. But today, an appalling number of them insist on knowing nearly all the details of Elvis Presley's life and times and make a great nuisance of themselves playing Presley records at home and squealing at his concerts.

If you are troubled by all this, you needn't be; they will get over it. Some day, they will all yawn at once when Elvis comes bleating out of the loud speaker. They will lay away the green-stitched jeans, the sneakers, bobby sox, T-shirts and funny hats with the Presley imprimatur. They'll lose the Presley charm bracelets for which they paid a dollar, and the two-dollar plaster-of-Paris Presley bust will be covered with dust. They'll outgrow the Elvis Presley lipstick in Hound Dog Orange, and they'll stop anointing themselves with Elvis Presley perfume. They may even stop spending Pop's money on long-distance telephone calls to Elvis, whom they seldom get to speak to, anyway.

When that happens, Colonel Parker and Hank Saperstein will be sorry, but by then, they will be laboring in other vineyards and the world will not be deprived of their good works. Perhaps it is to lighten our burdens that the Lord sends us from time to time gay and imaginative men like Colonel Parker, who realize that life is a great big hilarious fruitcake loaded with potential profits. It was Parker who founded and nourished the Great Elvis Presley Industry. Saperstein joined the firm only four months ago to expand operations . . . .

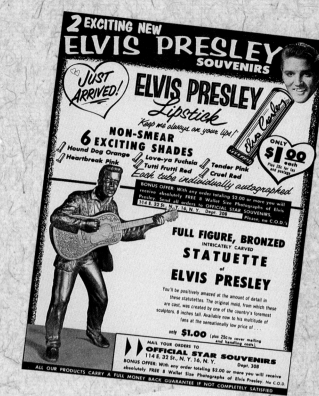

If your heart belongs to Elvis . . . and you don't care who knows it . . .

Here's a bracelet that shows it!

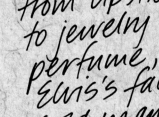

From lipstick to jewelry to perfume, Elvis's face sold many products.

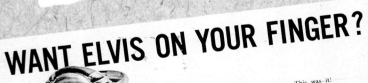

WANT ELVIS ON YOUR FINGER?

This was it!

Here was something that you could have with you always, wear on your finger and look at whenever you got the urge. But it was more than having Elvis with you morning, noon and night. It was a darned attractive piece of jewelry! Adjustable to fit any finger, 18-carat gold plate that's guaranteed never to tarnish, an unusual groove design, and—best of all: a life-like, four-color picture of Elvis sealed in clear lucite and magnified, and it makes his face just seem to jump out at you.

Right now MODERN SCREEN is handling the ring exclusively, through the mails. It will be available some time in the future at some stores, but right now, $1 and the filled-in coupon gets you Elvis—on your finger, twenty-four hours a day! Live a little.

David Myers
EDITOR

Tear on dotted line

Tinted postcard

A fan shows off her "Love Me Tender" necklace.

An Elvis charm

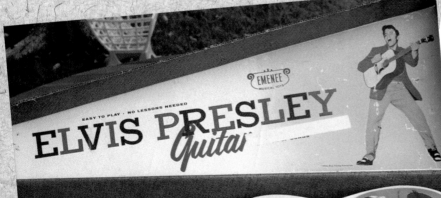

Toy guitar

Elvis distributes some special souvenirs to fan club members.

Memphis Commercial Appeal   November 24, 1956

Foe of Presley Punches Himself Into Workhouse

TOLEDO, Ohio, Nov. 23— (AP) Jealous of his wife's admiration for Elvis Presley, Louis John Balint, 19, tried to throw a punch at the singer in a hotel bar early Friday. The punch didn't land, but the effort landed Balint in the county workhouse for disorderly conduct. Presley, who said he didn't want to press any charges as a result of the fight, was driving through snow flurries to Cleveland when Balint's case came up in municipal court. The unemployed sheet metal worker was unable to pay a fine of $10 and $9.60 in costs and was taken to the workhouse to serve seven days.

No one was hurt, and Balint admitted afterward that none of his punches connected with the rock and roll idol of teenagers. The Memphis singer said Balint had lunged at him while he sat at a table with his manager and a group of musicians with whom he is making a personal appearance tour.

Before pleading guilty to the disorderly conduct charge, Balint told police he resented having his wife, from whom he is separated, carry Presley's picture instead of his.

November 1956 – trouble in Toledo

Elvis reads about himself.

"ELVIS" DANCE

The Elvis Presley craze has even spread to the college campus. The Alpha Epsilon Pi fraternity at Bradley University in Peoria, Ill., held one of the wildest parties of the entire social season entitled "Elvis goes collegiate."

Some one hundred and fifty couples danced clad in jeans, sharp shirts and the paraphernalia that is so typical of Elvis. All the males in attendance at the party were required to grow sideburns to be admitted.

In front of the AEPi house speakers blared out tape recorded music by Elvis to add to the deafening roar of the combo which was playing in the basement. Couples were greeted at the door by the fraternity's social chairman, Dave Horowitz, who gave out favors which consisted of a folder and a picture of Elvis reading DIG Magazine.

Across the porch of the house was a twenty foot sign announcing the party and a ten foot high drawing of Elvis playing his guitar.

Highlight of the evening was the crowning of Bradley's answer to Elvis. Chuck Arnold of WIRL in Peoria made the presentation to the winner along with an album of Elvis' recordings.

Entertainment was supplied by members of Bradley University's championship NIT basketball team. Some of the members of the team went into some of Elvis' convulsive movements and added shrill voices for realism.

On the road

Is he a new JAMES DEAN?

When Elvis got into close-up love scenes ... with Debra Paget "the camera boys hung their eyes out a foot." "What technique!" one of them said later.

And Debra said: "That Elvis Presley! He doesn't need any stand-ins!"—a crack at some of the matinee idols who reach Hollywood via a boast about their ability to slay the lady stars.

"Oh brother!" said movie director Robert Webb when they told him he had to handle the rock 'n' roll phenomenon.

"Oh Elvis? He's a nice, co-operative guy," Webb was soon saying.

Studio chief Hal Wallis has let it leak that he considers Presley the natural successor to his discovery of four years ago, the late James Dean.

Critics who have seen the film rushes say Presley sometimes looks as if he could emulate Dean in the intensity of his screen work. But they wonder if he's not the "singing Marlon Brando."

The three songs in the film, in addition to the title tune, are "Poor Boy," "You're Gonna Move," and "Let Me." The discs will be out shortly in advance of the film due here in December.

Presley has been good enough actor for the studios to bring forward the date of his second picture, *Lonesome Cowboy,* in which he stars with bare-all Jayne Mansfield . . . .

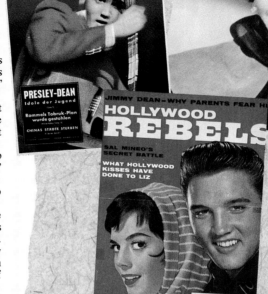

Elvis dated Natalie Wood, James Dean's one-time costar.

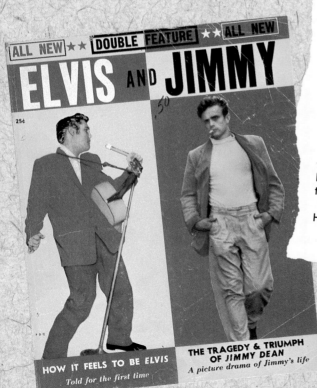

Can Elvis fill James Dean's shoes?

THE TRAGEDY and TRIUMPH of JIMMY DEAN

Here, in pictures, is the story of Jimmy Dean that has never been told—

Here are the dramatic scenes of Jimmy's life that have never been shown before—

No photographer was there to film these intimate moments of Jimmy's life. But here you will see them, in all their drama.

HERE IS JIMMY AS HE REALLY WAS

HOW IT FEELS TO BE ELVIS

WHEN you start reading this magazine on page 6, YOU are going to be Elvis Presley . . . .

YOU are going to find out just how it feels to sing as Elvis sings . . . .

YOU are going to feel the emotions that pass through Elvis' mind as he is singing . . . .

YOU are going to go out with Elvis on a date with a girl friend . . . .

. . . and hear just what Elvis says to her . . . and see how he behaves . . .

IN THE NEXT HOUR, YOU ARE GOING TO BE ELVIS—AND FEEL HIS MOST INTIMATE EMOTIONS.

—And also you are going to know how it feels to be so idolized that your very appearance anywhere draws throngs of people around you —anxious to hear you, to touch you if they can—but if not, only to be near you.

Elvis Draws 'Em; So Does 'Giant'; Theaters Happy

The Elvis Presley film at Loew's State, *Love Me Tender,* may have started off slowly Wednesday, but it revved up into high yesterday and Thanksgiving.

"We had a good crowd Wednesday night," Manager Arthur Groom said yesterday, "and Thanksgiving Day we broke all cash receipt records, including that of *Gone With the Wind.*

"And *Love Me Tender* is at regular prices, while *Gone With the Wind* was at advanced prices."

Yesterday at 11 a.m., there was a line waiting for the box office to open which stretched up Main and down Gayoso, Mgr. Groom said, and when he arrived at the theater at 9:50 a.m., there were about 30 waiting.

"We're going to open at 9:30 Saturday morning so as to get in an extra show," Mr. Groom added.

Meantime, up at Warner, *Giant* has been packing them in to what Manager Eli H. 'Slim' Arkins calls "all-time record business."

The Warner, a slightly smaller theater than Loew's State, has been bulging since its opening Wednesday a week ago. The night of the Christmas parade, Mr. Akin had to shut down his box office to keep people from getting hurt in the crush.

The Thanksgiving crowds at the Warner box office stretched around the corner of Main and Monroe down to the alley, and at one point, nearly to the Monroe-Second corner of the Bank of Commerce.

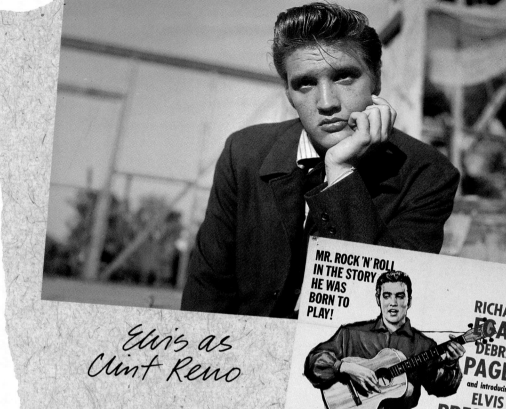

Elvis as Clint Reno

MR. ROCK 'N' ROLL IN THE STORY HE WAS BORN TO PLAY!

RICHARD EGAN
DEBRA PAGET
and introducing
ELVIS PRESLEY
in
LOVE ME TENDER
from 20th CENTURY-FOX

CINEMASCOPE PICTURE

CO-STARRING ROBERT MIDDLETON · WILLIAM CAMPBELL · NEVILLE BRAND
WITH MILDRED DUNNOCK · BRUCE BENNETT
PRODUCED BY DAVID WEISBART · DIRECTED BY ROBERT D. WEBB · SCREENPLAY BY ROBERT BUCKNER · BASED ON A STORY BY MAURICE GERAGHTY

Movie poster

Robert Wagner (center) was considered for the role of Clint Reno.

YOU-NEVER-KNOW-YOUR-LUCK.

When Hal Wallis couldn't find a story for his torso-tossin' film debut, **Elvis Presley** was growing impatient. The singing-geetar player would have received $20,000 from Hal. So, while Hal's still looking, 20th Century Fox comes up with *The Reno Brothers* co-starring Elvis and Dick Egan—and for his little stint Presley gets a hot $100,000.

No sir, he doesn't have to give a nickel of it to Hal. The contract Elvis has with him is "non-exclusive" and allows Presley outside pictures.

In French, the title was Twilight Cowboy.

NINOVE

CINEMASCOPE

RICHARD EGAN
DEBRA PAGET

et le Roi du ROCK and ROLL
4 chansons nouvelles

ELVIS PRESLEY

LE CAVALIER
DU CRÉPUSCULE

"LOVE ME TENDER"

ROBERT MIDDLETON — WILLIAM CAMPBELL — NEVILLE BRAND

EEN RUITER IN DE AVONDSTOND

PRODUCTION DAVID WEISBART — MISE EN SCÈNE ROBERT D. WEBB
SCÉNARIO ROBERT BUCKNER d'après un récit de MAURICE GERAGHTY

PAGE AFTER PAGE OF ALL-PICTURE ROMANCES

Mirabelle

4½d

The
GIRLS in
"LOVE ME TENDER"
PRESLEY's
LIFE

Richard Egan, Debra Paget and Elvis

Elvis poses with a couple of costars!

HOLLYWOOD IN PERSON:

Egan Provided Elvis With Helping Hand

By SHEILAH GRAHAM

Hollywood, Calif. (NANA)—
It's always a pleasure to interview Richard Egan. Some people attain fame overnight, but Richard did it the hard way, little theatres, taking bit roles, and always waiting, in a five-year struggle to stardom. And being a good sport, as he was again in making no fuss when 20th Century-Fox signed Elvis Presley at a salary of $100,000 to take over the other main role in *Love Me Tender*.

Elvis even took over the title. This picture was originally called *The Reno Brothers*, but with Presley singing the song of which

2,000,000 copies have already been sold, and with 20th wanting to cash in on the boy with the sideburns, Dick, who is now a big star in his own right, moved over a bit and helped Elvis with the new career.

"I even grew sideburns, because I'm playing his older brother," Dick laughed.

"Elvis is a surprising type of actor," said Egan. "He's the male Monroe. He's completely without guile. You give him lines and he says them the way he would in real life, and that's the best kind of acting, when you're not."

are they taming elvis?

And when *Love Me Tender* was released last month Elvis proved himself to the critics—his one-time detractors—as well as to the actors.

At the same time Elvis studied acting he studied improving his English. He toned down his gaudy style of dress—even wore a black tie to a premiere. He shortened his side-burns.

Though always polite to his elders—sir-ing, mister-ing and ma'am-ing—Elvis' background had not included refinement of manners. He used to lounge in a chair on the approach of a lady—scratched himself when he felt an itch. The new Elvis tried hard to change these old habits. And little by little Elvis is leaving behind the crude country boy.

Still enough of the free soul remains to suggest the role he's reportedly headed for after he completes *The Lonesome Cowboy* for Hal Wallis. The part Elvis really wants to play is the biography of the late Jimmy Dean. "I never met Jimmy Dean," said Elvis, "but how I wish I had."

Just the night before Elvis Presley had stood in an arena singing to a crowd of 3,000. Getting with the beat he commanded attention with all the confidence and assurance of a king of rock-'n'-roll well on the way to his first million.

Eight hours later Elvis was just a nervous youngster reporting for work on a new job.

The quick change marked Elvis' debut in movies—the first day he answered the call for his role in *Love Me Tender.*

Even by way of Memphis it's a long haul from Tupelo, Mississippi, to Hollywood. The stretch from soloist to novice actor in a group of professional players is even greater.

That August day Elvis felt his head bursting, hearing the refrain inside him, repeat: "You gotta prove yourself, prove yourself, prove yourself!"

A first movie is a test for anyone, but Elvis' strain was added to by fame acquired as a singer and the fact that many actors resented his selection for the coveted dramatic role of the youngest Reno brother.

Ambition and desire pressed Elvis, too. "I don't ever want to stop singing, but more than anything I want to be an actor."

There on the studio lot Elvis faced his most critical audience. Most of them expected him to walk through the part—to lend his name to the cast. They got a surprise.

For two months, except for time off to appear on Ed Sullivan's TV show (Elvis' next video date, Sunday, January 6, CBS-TV) Elvis worked 12 hours a day at acting. He won the respect of the entire troupe.

Elvis recorded the songs for Love Me Tender in Hollywood.

Love Me Tender

20TH, CINEMASCOPE

Elvis Presley's first picture shapes up as an agreeable Southern-type Western, sturdy in content but apparently slapped together in too much haste. As his older brothers, Richard Egan, William Campbell and James Drury have fought the losing battle of the Confederacy. The trio made off with a Union Army payroll, and they have the loot with them when they return to mother Mildred Dunnock. For Egan, who was believed dead, the homecoming is marred by the discovery that his ex-fiancee, Debra Paget, is now Elvis' wife. The emotional conflict between the brothers is brought to a climax when Union officials seek the missing payroll. Presley's song numbers fit into the proceedings pretty smoothly, and he's commendably relaxed in quiet scenes, but the dramatics at the end throw him.

FAMILY

Richard Egan, Debra Paget, and Elvis fool around behind the scenes.

LOVE ME TENDER

Elvis Presley's first

Elvis is here, and to say anything else is probably superfluous. But he's here, and of course he sings—four songs. And his guitar is here. Elvis has been home on the farm these several years while his big brothers (Richard Egan, William Campbell, James Drury) have been fighting for the South. On their last fight they divested some Union soldiers of 12,000 dollars cash. Unknown to them, the war was over. The brothers and their buddies—Neville Brand among them—sit down and decide to split the loot since the General they were going to deliver it to doesn't have an army to spend it on. Richard Egan can use the money because also home on the farm are his mother (Mildred Dunnock) and his intended (Debra Paget). Unknown to Egan they think he has been killed in the war and Debra has married Elvis. "Love Me Tender," Elvis sings on the front porch the first night the family is all together, and Richard can hardly stand it. He decides he must go away or his love for Debra will eat at him. But there's the money which the Union has come to claim. Hand it over, the U.S. Marshal (Russ Conway) tells Egan, and we'll drop all charges. He's willing to hand it over, so are his brothers, but their buddies—mainly Neville Brand—refuse. It's while Debra is helping Richard collect the money that Neville turns Elvis against them. Elvis becomes insanely jealous. He nearly shakes Debra to death and shoots, but does not kill, the brother he always loved. Then he comes to see that he was wrong. His acting—in this, his first picture—is as good as anyone else's. CinemaScope—20th-Fox.

Elvis signs an autograph for one of the extras.

ELVIS PRESLEY Becomes a Movie Star

sheet music

They were all set to jeer. They remained to cheer him instead...

As far as the people of Hollywood knew, Elvis Presley was merely the most sensational, controversial, personality to hit the town in a coon's age. Now they know different—at least the lucky few who really got close to Elvis. Listen to his co-players in *Love Me Tender*. Bill Campbell: "When you see a guy this sweet, who wants to work as hard, you have to like him. He's a smart boy and a good boy." Richard Egan: "He broke me up when we got in a scene together. He'd look me right in the eye and throw me. The right thing just seems to come naturally to him. I think he has an unlimited future, and I think he can do anything he attempts." Debra Paget: "He's amazing. He's so unspoiled and fresh, everybody is crazy about him. In fact, he's more fun than a barrel of monkeys! And he is a gentleman."

Elvis sings "We're Gonna Move".

ELVIS PRESLEY in Love Me Tender

One of the greatest assets of the Western as a form is its extreme flexibility; it can be and is, adjusted to accommodate just about any kind of story and any kind of artist. In the case of this week's Western, *Love Me Tender*, a traditional tale of outlawry at the end of the Civil War has been tailored to fit the talents of the king of the rock 'n' rollers, Elvis Presley.

This was Presley's first film, and tonight's screening is also his first appearance in a feature programme on British television—his managers have been careful to ensure that he is seen only rarely on the home screen, and never until now in full song. As Clint Reno, a youngster whose elder brothers are Confederate cavalrymen who capture a Union payroll and are accused of theft when the war ends, Presley not only sings several numbers (including of course the title song), but acquits himself very creditably in the many action sequences.

Love Me Tender was released by Twentieth Century-Fox in 1956 and produced by David Weisbart, who then went on to make most of the subsequent Presley films. Presley's co-stars in tonight's production are Richard Egan as his elder brother, and Debra Paget, who supplies the necessary romantic interest as Cathy, the girl loved by both Clint and his brother. The strong supporting cast includes Neville Brand, Bruce Bennett, and James Drury.

A young fan signs a *Love Me Tender* poster outside a theater.

Lobby Cards

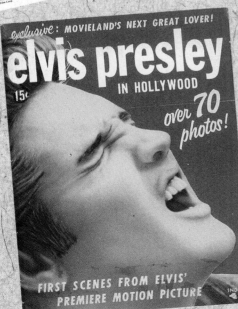

the joint rocked . . . . .

Two idols, two storm centers of controversy, exchange send-offs

Till Lee Liberace proved different, it was supposed that Liberace fans would walk out on Elvis Presley, and vice-versa. Lee's fans and Elvis' fans seemed poles apart except in the violent response each gave its idol. Matrons reacted to the appeal of smiling, pianist Lee. And oft-sullen Elvis thumped the heartstrings of teen-agers. Or so it was before the two stars collided with dazzling display in Vegas and triggered an explosion that may join still more conflicting forces—youth and age. The occasion was Lee's nightclub date on his return to the States. Elvis was at ringside to give him a rousing opening night. Spotting Elvis, Lee tore his act apart to insert tribute to the rock-'n'-roll king. He did take-offs on Elvis and kidded around with an exchange of jackets and trademarks. Then Lee turned serious and acclaimed Elvis "one fine American boy with a lot of talent—a boy who is good to his parents, too." The result was thunderous applause from Lee's fans for him—and Elvis.

ELVIS PRESLEY-LIBERACE

Elvis asked the famous entertainer for an autograph for his mother.

Elvis visits Liberace backstage after catching his act in Las Vegas.

From left: Jerry Lee Lewis, Carl Perkins, Johnny Cash and Elvis — the million dollar quartet

Memphis Press-Scimitar   December 3, 1956

TV News and Views

By ROBERT JOHNSON   Press-Scimitar Staff Writer

I never had a better time than yesterday afternoon when I dropped in at Sam Phillips' Sun Record bedlam on Union at Marshall. It was what you might call a barrel-house of fun. Carl Perkins was in a recording session . . . and he has one that's going to hit as hard as "Blue Suede Shoes." We're trying to arrange an advance audition for you Memphis fans before the song is released in January. Johnny Cash dropped in. Jerry Lee Lewis was there, too, and then Elvis stopped by.

Elvis headed for the piano and started to Fats Domino it on "Blueberry Hill." The joint was really rocking before they got thru.

Elvis is high on Jerry Lee Lewis. "That boy can go," he said. "I think he has a great future ahead of him. He has a different style, and the way he plays a piano just gets inside me."

Elvis debunked the newest rumor: "No, I haven't bought 200 acres at Collierville," he said. "How do those stories get started?"

He talked earnestly about the Toledo incident. "I talked to that fellow for at least 15 minutes, trying to be nice to him and keep him from starting anything, but finally it just got out of hand."

I never saw the boy more likeable than [when] he was just fooling around with these other fellows who have the same interest he does.

If Sam Phillips had been on his toes, he'd have turned the recorder on when that very unrehearsed but talented bunch got to cutting up on "Blueberry Hill" and a lot of other songs. That quartet could sell a million.

Elvis '56

Elvis poses with rhythm-and-blues singers Junior Parker (left) and Bobby Bland (right).

MASS HYSTERIA

Frenzied Elvis Fans Rock Youth Center

By BOB MASTERS   Member of Times Staff

Elvis (The Pelvis) Presley came to town yesterday, and last night 9,000 rock 'n' rollers 'flipped.'

His appearance on the stage of the Louisiana Hayride at the Fair Grounds Youth Center set off what was undoubtedly one of the finest displays of mass hysteria in Shreveport history.

Presumably he sang: you couldn't hear him over the screams of the frenzied 9,000. But at least his lips were moving, and his pelvis certainly was. He wasn't halfway through "Heartbreak Hotel" before it became apparent nobody ever had a more appropriate nickname.

It was a hectic evening for Elvis all around. A scheduled press conference more nearly resembled a mob scene, with representatives of the press and radio lost among the throngs of fans, autograph-seekers and the curious, who infiltrated the meeting.

A brief talk with the Pelvis—who finally managed to escape the mob with about two minutes remaining in his 60-minute "press conference,"—disclosed that he was glad to be back in Shreveport, has four Cadillacs and a Lincoln Continental and apparently enjoys all the fuss made over him.

GUARDED DURING DAY

But there wasn't any such commotion during most of Elvis' stay in town. Probably Khrushchev and Bulganin wouldn't have been better guarded than was the young singer during most of the day.

To get him in his room at the Captain Shreve you had to pass guards, policemen, business associates of one kind or another, and numerous members of his entourage whose immediate function was not apparent.

For his appearance on the Hayride, Elvis wore white shoes with blue soles, a green coat, blue pants, and white shirt, tie and silk scarf. At the hotel, he settled for slacks, the scarf and a kind of smoking jacket.

Despite adulation enough to turn the head of an oriental potentate, Elvis is friendly enough. He also appears to find plenty of humor in the spectacles he stimulates.

A talk with Jeanelle Alexander, president of the Shreveport-Bossier Presley fan club, and Kay Wheeler from Dallas, president of the first and biggest Presley club, amply illustrates the fervor The Pelvis stirs in the hearts of his admirers.

Says Kay, who has encountered the singer several times previously: "I flip every time I meet him."

"FLIPPING"

Jeanelle defines "flipping" as experiencing in an extreme form and simultaneously the emotions of love, hate, anger, hero worship, anxiety and a few others whose names she didn't have on the tip of her tongue. She said other teenagers react similarly.

She didn't speculate on the effect of all of this on the autonomic nervous system.

Kay says a little more conservatively: "He's the most fascinating human I've ever known." She adds, rather frighteningly, that "Elvis is a living denial of the notion teenagers should be seen and not heard."

Well, they could certainly be heard last night. If you haven't heard 9,000 persons shrieking for half an hour at the top of their lungs in a closed building there's no point trying to describe it. They couldn't hear Elvis—presumably why they were there—but they didn't seem to mind. Just looking at him must have been enough.

The motions, gyrations, bumps and grinds, or whatever you want to call them, Elvis goes through wouldn't be tolerated in most burlesque houses. They do, however, undoubtedly call for considerable acrobatic talent.

Probably never before have so many been stirred so much by an acrobat.

TO AID YMCA

Elvis has reportedly made a million dollars or more in the last couple of years—he commands top pay for his performances —but last night he did his gymnastics for nothing. Both the singer and the members of the KWKH Hayride contributed receipts to the Shreveport YMCA's expansion program.

Elvis seemed to be glad to perform for nothing—and certainly he didn't spare the gyrations. For 35 minutes or thereabouts he gave what can certainly be described as an "unforgettable" performance.

It was a big night for the Shreveport police force, too. With teenagers giving every indication of tearing the Pelvis limb from limb out of sheer admiration and animal spirits, the police threw up more or less effective barricades throughout the building.

They were effective enough to keep Presley from being mobbed, but just barely. It required considerable agility to keep up with him as he fled from one room to another—always a step or two ahead of his admirers.

All in all, it was a big event in several respects and a good time was had by all, maybe Elvis more than anybody else. Whether Shreveport will ever be the same again remains to be seen.

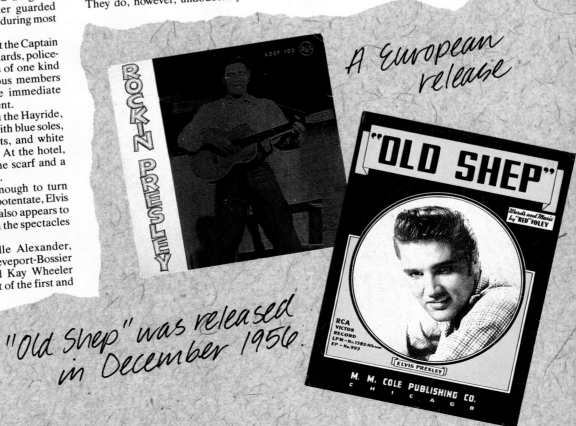

A European release

"Old Shep" was released in December 1956.

Shreveport Times 12-16-56

Everybody and His Dog Turns Out For Elvis

By PERICLES ALEXANDER
Times Amusement Editor

Everybody and his hound dog was out to see Elvis Presley wriggle and writhe on KWKH's *Louisiana Hayride* last night in the cavernous Youth Building at the Louisiana State Fair Grounds, the only structure large enough to hold his teeming, screaming following.

Coupling a double whammy with a pulsating body hold on every song he sang, the rock 'n' roll king whipped through most of his repertoire ("Love Me Tender," "Don't Be Cruel," "Heartbreak Hotel," etc.) assisted by the Jordanaires.

It was beside the point that the gyrating rotary troubadour was seldom if ever heard by an audience screaming like Zulus every time he moved a muscle. The Pelvis applies more "Body English" to a song than many a baseball pitcher and he has more movements than a well-oiled Swiss watch.

No entertainer in history has worked under greater audience handicaps, not even Sinatra at the Palace. Elvis' mere appearance on the *Hayride* stage last night set off a veritable atomic explosion of photographic flash bulbs and squeals from teenagers which crescendoed into pandemonium.

Next to Ethel Merman, who never had a singing lesson in her life, Presley stands or gyrates alone in belting across a song. If the tumult and shouting of an audience ever subsides, it may be even more surprising to discover that the kinetic singer has real vocal artistry. Until then, it will take an Elvis disc and not an in-person appearance to bear out this theory.

All the screams, squeals and audience commotion last night was not reserved for Presley alone. The Roman Circus Maximus atmosphere of the evening began early and the audience would erupt in screams for any *Louisiana Hayride* artist applying physical as well as vocal exertion to a song. Today's folk singers must work out daily in gyms.

Presiding over the *Hayride* program, Horace Logan made a real attempt to introduce Elvis but no introduction was necessary for the 21-year-old lad.

It was a blockbuster of an evening of entertainment and everybody came away satisfied, unless he went specifically to hear the rock 'n' roller sing.

December 16, 1956 — Elvis's last Hayride performance

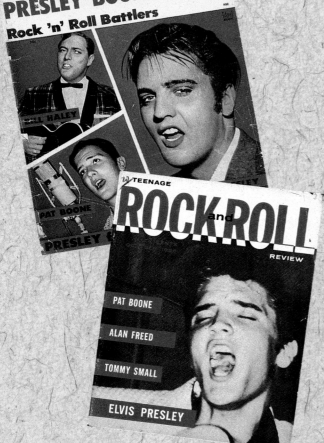

In performance, rivals Bill Haley and Pat Boone could not match Elvis's raw power.

PLAYING FOR KEEPS
and TOO MUCH

Sold over 1 million copies

Unlike other entertainers, Elvis was never too busy to pose with fans.

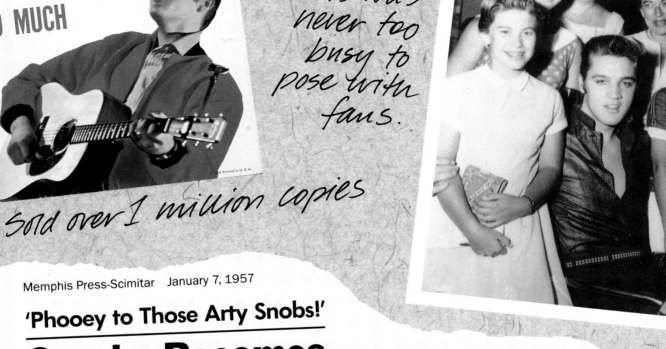

Memphis Press-Scimitar   January 7, 1957

'Phooey to Those Arty Snobs!'

Sparks Becomes an Elvis Admirer: 'He's Terrific!'

By FRED SPARKS   *Scripps-Howard Staff Writer*

I like Elvis Presley. I think his performance last night on *The Ed Sullivan Show* was terrific.

I gave it four stars, four bells, four hams for genuine, American-style, folk-type, grass-roots fun-singing.

I am bored to illness by the egg-heads, long-hairs, tea-cup tipplers, self-appointed moralists and arty snobs who are running around this country like Peeping Toms wired for sound saying: "Elvis Presley must go . . . He's a bad example for our young people."

Well, my dear, tut-tut and bosh-bosh. Judging by the anti-Elvis bellows in the parlors, press and pubs of those who would brain-wash anybody who doesn't meet with their approval, Elvis is a bigger menace to the U.S.A. than Bulganin, Khrushchev and opium smoking in high school lunch rooms.

Their hatred is rising to new hysterical heights as Elvis prepares to change his guitar for a rifle. He's to be silenced—but by the draft board, not the windy bores—and I'm sure, despite inevitable ribbings, he'll be a good soldier. For he is of the soil itself, like Will Rogers and Carl Sandburg.

The Millions

Yes, nobody likes Elvis—except maybe 40 million citizens from blue jeans to wheel chairs who keep feeding nickels into juke boxes and loving him on their tv screens.

One columnist—famous for changing her hats and opinions every day—says the main thing she wants less of is Elvis. Then, in the same breathless typewriter, she says wants more of Bing Crosby. Nothing wrong with Bing; but she probably also wants more of the Spanish-American War.

Circle a newsstand and you'll see magazine after magazine featuring articles like: "A Mother Demands They Gag Presley" and "Elvis Presley Is Indecent."

Indecent? Bah!

If he's indecent so are half the best seller books, three quarters of the paintings in the nation's galleries, Helen Hayes and one-piece bathing suits.

Me thinks most of those labeling Elvis "indecent" are the same frustrated frantics who during prohibition went around sniffing coffee cups for whisky and did their own private boozing behind locked washroom doors.

I wish Elvis—who is very competent in such matters—would punch a few of his more vicious critics in the nose before he becomes Pvt. Presley. He might also sue several for eight or ten million dollars.

I have traveled no small bit around the country, and while I am no music expert, the type of shouting, jumping, jiving Elvis does is as much a part of our basic fondness for noisy expression as the fife-and-drum-corps, which is also taboo around water holes frequented by our intellectual snoot set.

The Presley Motion

And as for his leg-wiggles and mouth-twistings, have you ever seen a man who calls the tune at a square dance stand quiet and erect as a totem pole? Anybody, who's happy—and Elvis couldn't do his jeeamberings if he wasn't having a good time—shifts and shuffles. If that is evil so is the classic ballet in which raw sex—tightly attired—is the backbone.

Most of the songs he has single-handedly rocketed to the hit parade stratosphere are also happy hollerings of Americana. I'm positive the words of "You're Nothing But a Hound Dog" and "Heartbreak Hotel" will be picked over by historians as mad, jolly mutterings of our golden era just like long hairs today treat as holy these medleys of our depression: "Brother, Can You Spare a Dime?" and "Let's Have Another Cup of Coffee."

And Clothes?

The carping critics also screech: "The clothes that Elvis wears set a bad example . . ."

Which proves again the America they know revolves around the Stock Club and the Brown Derby, with the vast spaces in between Manhattan and Hollywood a grim, ugly, darklands.

Statisticians tell us about one third the men in the U.S. don't bother to own a suit—they prefer the Elvis-type casual, open neck shirt and slacks and odd jackets. Maybe the critics think we all should dress like Anthony Eden and check our sombrero hats which entering Joe's Diner.

Memphis Press-Scimitar   January 8, 1957

It Won't Be Long Now
Elvis Scores Hit With Army—He's 1-A

By PAUL VANDERWOOD   Press-Scimitar Staff Writer

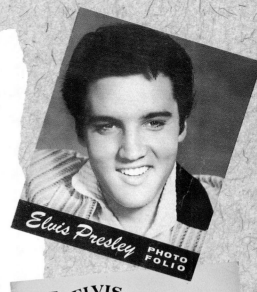

Elvis Presley PHOTO FOLIO

GIRLS DON'T LOOK NOW! Elvis doesn't even know yet. But he's 1-A.

"1-A" is a draft board lingo. It means, "You've had it," "Time to enlist" or "Prime draft bait"—depending how you look at it.

Capt. Elwyn P. (Rip) Rowan, Army recruiting Main Station Commander, today looked at Elvis' mental and physical test scores and decided, "He's in the 1-A class."

Presley says it doesn't much matter. He expected these results and said, "I'll go when they call me."

That can't be for at least 21 days, according to law. And recent practice has been to give draft notification six to eight months after the physical has been passed.

How did Elvis fare?

"Physically he's an A-profile, and that's as high as you can go," Capt. Rowan said.

Mentally? "Can't give you the exact score, but Presley's score was about average," the Captain said.

Draft Board 86 hasn't received notification of Elvis' test scores yet, but they're in the mail, Capt. Rowan said. The board officially designates classification, but Presley's scores place him in the 1-A group, he said.

The date Elvis is drafted depends upon the quota Board 86 must fill. Once "in" he'll head for Camp Chaffee in Fort Smith, Ark.

Basic training takes eight weeks. Then comes specialization, and as Elvis is something pretty special already, it probably means Special Service duty—entertaining the troops, etc.

He'll make $83.30 a month as a Private E-1, after four weeks basic training. However, Elvis said he'll probably record some records on passes and leaves.

"A-ten-chun," Elvis. "Take yer post."

THE ELVIS
PRESLEY
ALBUM No 2

Contents

ALL SHOOK UP
ANY WAY YOU WANT ME
(LET ME BE YOUR) TEDDY BEAR
LONESOME COWBOY
LOVE ME
FIRST IN LINE

SONGS and PHOTOGRAPHS

2'6

BELINDA (London) LTD.
142, Charing Cross Road
LONDON, W.C.2.

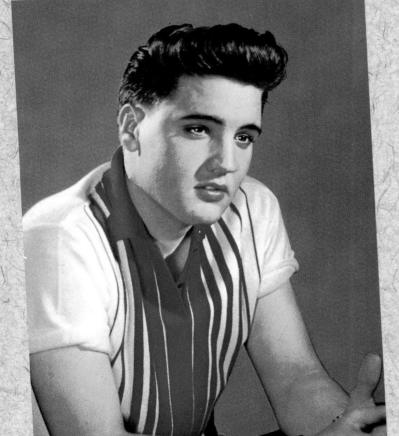

This retouched photo eliminated Elvis's sideburns, which many found offensive.

Elvis loved children.

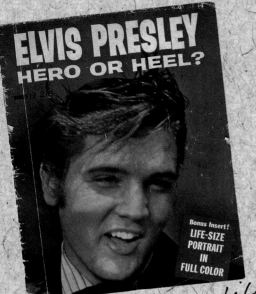

ELVIS PRESLEY
HERO OR HEEL?

Bonus Insert!
LIFE-SIZE
PORTRAIT
IN
FULL COLOR

The generous, polite Elvis vs. the sneering rebel

Elvis Fans Shape Up as 'Rebels' Who Can't Face Adult World

By EUGENE GILBERT

What sort of teen-ager really likes Elvis Presley—idolizes him from the top of his bushy brown hair to the soles of his blue suede shoes?

Is he (or she) a good student? A joiner? A churchgoer? A hero worshipper? Does he differ in any way from the average Perry Como or Frank Sinatra fan?

To get the answers to these questions we had to depart somewhat from our usual approach of public opinion research and delve into a scientific area known as motivational research.

THIS IS HOW we went about it. We selected about 100 teen-agers at random and questioned them extensively about their extra-curricular activities, their scholastic achievements and their plans for the future.

Individual answers varied, of course, but the aggregate produced a definite pattern, and from this pattern an outline sketch of a typical Presley fan emerged.

Presley fans, to begin with, are no joiners. Only 33% of his most enthusiastic admirers professed membership in a club, society or other group operated by their school, church or community.

Remarked one, "Who's got time for school clubs? I'd rather sit around with my pals."

FANS OF FRANK Sinatra, Perry Como and Pat Boone scored higher—about 50%—when it came to joining.

They also seemed to do better in school, receiving grades at least one and one-half times higher than the Presley followers. The average school grade for an Elvis man (or woman) was C, compared with B or better for the Sinatra-Como-Boone faction.

Of the latter, one out of every three said they strove to obtain the best possible grade. Only one out of every ten Presley fans could say the same. Two out of ten said emphatically they didn't care one way or the other where grades were concerned.

SIMILARLY PRESLEY fans were shockingly unconcerned about the future. A large number had no answer when asked what he or she aspired to become in life. At least 30% had never given it a thought and didn't want to be reminded of it.

Sinatra, Como and Boone addicts had a somewhat better score, but not much.

After tabulating these answers about club activities, school work

and future plans, our researchers next went to work analyzing them in the light of modern sociological findings.

We started with the fact that the teenager not only is experiencing physical change during these formative years, but also is undergoing changes in attitude toward social responsibilities and community activities.

MORE AND MORE demands are being imposed upon him by the adult world, yet he still clings to his dependent, infantile existence of former years.

The organized conventional clubs provide, for the well adjusted boy, a necessary outlet where he can express his independence and at the same time fulfill his adolescent yearning to belong.

But to the not so well adjusted teen-ager the problem is not quite so simple. He, too, needs a sense of belonging but cannot seem to satisfy it in acceptable outlets.

HE SHUNS THE conventions of the adult world, because he regards the world as a threatening place. It demands that he meet the obligations of school work. It asks him to plan for the future and his own economic security. It invites him to take his

place as a responsible citizen in an organized community.

In this nether world between childhood and manhood, Elvis Presley emerges as a symbol of destruction. Presley is unacceptable to the adult world, and, to the unadjusted teen-ager, he seems to mock its cultural taboos.

THROUGH AN ALLIANCE of the spirit with Presley, the teen-ager is able to act out his infantile desires of striving for power through the destruction of adult standards and symbols. He can satisfy his need to belong by uniting with other youngsters of similar aim.

This, then, is the picture that has emerged of the rabid Elvis Presley fan from our motivational research department.

It seems to be borne out in a letter we received recently from an irate teen-ager after one of our surveys showed a steady decline in Presley's popularity.

"You are out to destroy all the things we teen-agers sincerely like," wrote Barry, from Corona, New York. "You don't care about us at all. But Presley will live forever."

Like Peter Pan, you have to believe in him.

Exposed:
The Strange Cult of Rock-and-Roll

By Blake Martin

The drums pound incessantly, in a fierce, monotonous, emotional rhythm. A voice wails frantically, now and again reaching a falsetto shriek as it increases in frenzy. The dancers—young teenage boys and girls—leap and twist, now doing violent solo steps and now clutching each other in passionate dance duets. The sight and the sound merge into a mad maelstrom—furious, pagan, erotic.

Where do you think you are? Deep in the Belgian Congo? In the Australian bush? On some south sea island?

Nonsense—this is America, 1957.

It could be New York. Or Peoria, Ill. Or Waycross, Ga. Or Montpelier, Vt. Or any town in America where the rock-and-roll cult is operating.

For the similarity between rock-and-roll and primitive cults is now being explored by sociologists and anthropologists. Even theologians have noted it—Chicago's Catholic archbishop, Samuel Cardinal Stritch, in a pastoral letter denouncing rock-and-roll, referred to it as "tribal rhythms."

There is a good reason why the good Cardinal reached that conclusion. Rock-and-roll is a direct and linear descendant of African tribal music. And rock-and-roll dances bear a distinct resemblance to the ancient and unchanging dance steps of the most primitive African tribes . . .

. . . And it even has its own set of gods— Elvis Presley, Pat Boone, Little Richard, Bill Haley, Fats Domino.

And it has high priests—like Alan Freed, an Ohio-born disc jockey who claims to have invented the phrase "rock-and-roll." Like most high priests of most cults, Freed and his fellow rock-and-roll panjandrums make a good living out of it.

Recently, Freed promoted a rock-and-roll show at New York's Paramount Theater. The crowds of teenagers surged forward to see their gods and join in the cult songs and do the cult dances in the theater's aisles. The first day, they wrecked plate glass windows that lined their path and they knocked over the theater's box office. Almost 200 policemen were needed, inside and outside the place, to keep order. The line outside the theater stretched for blocks, and it took 18½ hours for all the teenagers to get in. That day, [the theater took in more money] than it had taken in in one day for any attraction, including the all-time greats of show business.

Freed's deal called for the first $50,000 taken in to go to the theater. Of the balance of the seven-day gross, he would keep 90 per cent. The week-long engagement grossed $125,000, meaning that he took 90 per cent of $75,000—or $67,500. Out of that, he had to pay the acts and the band, a figure he estimated at $32,000. This meant that, for the week-long rock-and-roll orgy, high priest Freed netted $35,500. It's a well-paying cult.

And the other parts of the cult are profitable, too. Records of the gods singing are fabulous money-makers. In '56, RCA-Victor sold 13,500,000 single records and 2,750,000 albums of Elvis Presley's performances. Other items that feature the god's side-burned picture and/or endorsement racked up a total sales estimated at well over $25,000,000.

Because of the millions upon millions of teenagers in America—and the more millions overseas, where the cult is fast-spreading— [this] would seem to be far and away the largest cult the world has ever known. And it is also the noisiest.

Rock-and-roll roars on—and it will probably crash with a bang like every other cult that has ever existed.

EXPOSED - THE STRANGE CULT OF ROCK AND ROLL

Attacked in the press

If Children Get No Understanding They Become Rebels
Elvis Worship, Hardened Criminal Laid to Same Cause—'Need to Be Needed'

CHICAGO, May (UP)—A noted psychologist said the "need to be needed" accounts for two controversial phenomena among humans —an Elvis Presley worshipper and a hardened criminal.

Dr. James G. Bond of the Toledo (Ohio) State and Receiving Hospital said "all people as youngsters reach out for understanding from their fellows.

"If rebuffed, they become rebels," said Bond, here to attend the annual convention of the Midwestern Psychological Assn.

"The lonely adolescent may become a lone wolf and turn into a hardened criminal at an early age," Bond said.

The so-called hardened criminal type has stumped psychologists, Bond said.

There is no way of reaching this man because he feels no guilt or pain about his behavior.

"He is termed 'socially psychotic,'" Bond said, "simply a misfit in our culture and one who has been rebuffed at an early age."

The adolescent rebel may turn, he said, to a rock 'n' roll type idol in an effort to find himself.

To this youthful rebel, Bond said, Elvis Presley "symbolizes nonconformity, power and rebellion against parents."

"The adolescent identified himself with these idols because he lacks strength of his own. He just needs to 'be one of the group.'"

Bond said idol worship may start a "confused teen-ager on the path to juvenile delinquency" because his "leaders become the people who most express their hostility against society, parent or whatever stands in his way to pleasure."

Bond said each adolescent should be made to realize his parents are walking several feet behind him.

"The youngster only wants to know that when he falls, someone will be there to pick up the pieces.

"Maybe it would help a little," he said, "if all parents grew sideburns and learned to play the guitar."

Memphis Press-Scimitar

Welcome Wagon Ladies Take Elvis a Gift—His 623rd Teddy Bear

Two Welcome Wagon ladies paid a visit to a rather well known family of newcomers to Whitehaven recently and learned that Elvis Presley now has a grand total of 623 teddy bears.

Mrs. Norma Provost and Mrs. Carol Godwin were the ladies who went bearing Welcome Wagon gifts, and they describe the experience as quite exciting.

There was one hitch.

"We had set up an appointment thru the gate man, explaining that we wanted to welcome the Presleys to the community," said Mrs. Provost.

"When we got there, we learned that Mrs. Presley had gone somewhere.

"It was a hot day, and as we stood there with all our presents in the heat with all the other people, we were very disappointed.

"But then we got a call setting up another appointment."

Enthusiasm Wilts

"Some of our enthusiasm had evaporated in the heat, but we got the gifts together again and went out.

"My little girl had lined up about 10 of her friends whom she thought would be able to ride right in with us, and they were disappointed when they found out of course that was impossible.

"We drove right in thru the gate while the people looked at us. We felt quite important.

"What we saw of the Presley home was perfectly gorgeous—not gaudy as we had thought it would be from reading about the colors.

"The living room has a red rug, blue walls and white draperies, and there's gold trim on practically everything.

"Elvis' music room is right off the living room, and it's mostly white.

"Elvis came in to see us while we were talking to his mother.

"It was 3 in the afternoon and he was wearing black satin pajamas.

"He explained that he has to do most of his living at night—not wild life, just plain living—because he can't go out much in the daytime because of the crowds.

'Real Wild' Shirt

"He was very nice and sincere. We gave him a shirt—a real wild one of the sort he likes.

"We also gave him a teddy bear for his collection."

It was at this point that Mrs. Presley told them that their teddy bear was No. 623.

Mrs. Provost said there were a number of teddy bears in their living room.

Most of the gifts which Mrs. Provost and Mrs. Godwin took with them from merchants they represented were for Mrs. Presley.

"We had two big baskets full," Mrs. Provost said.

"There were a lovely gold planter from a florist, some tea aprons, a sheet and pillow case set, a set of tea towels with favorite recipes, a massive ash tray and an unusual novelty tray."

Did the Presleys receive an unusually impressive welcome from the Welcome Wagoners?

"They certainly did," said Mrs. Provost.

"We carried gifts from 15 merchants. Fourteen of them wanted to give something special. The other one said no, they should be treated like any other newcomers."

Elvis and starlet Yvonne Lime tour his new mansion, Graceland.

Elvis greets fans at Graceland.

Elvis introduces Yvonne to his mom.

Cool outfit, Yvonne!

Elvis purchased Graceland in March of 1957.

Memphis Press-Scimitar

This Man Gets to Go to Elvis' Back Door Every Morning

by JIM WHITE *Press-Scimitar Staff Writer*

Jimmie Burns is a much envied man.

For Burns, 63, of 5162 Airways, is a postman—but not just an ordinary postman. He's Elvis Presley's postman. And as such, he is one of the few outsiders entitled to admittance behind the closely guarded walls at Graceland, Elvis' Whitehaven mansion.

Each morning at about 10:30 when Burns' red, white and blue truck pulls up to the gate, teenagers—they're always there—clamor up to his truck, chattering, "Oh, you lucky man...Tell Elvis hello for us . . . Can we ride with you?"

I always kid them, "Give me a quarter and I'll let you ride," Burns chuckled, "but of course I couldn't let anyone ride in the truck."

Was He Home?

A few minutes later, after dropping the rock an' roller's mail, Burns is met at the gate once more with eager faces exclaiming, "Did you see him? . . . Was he swimming? . . . He is home, isn't he?"

Elvis has a mailbox outside the gate—covered with scrawlings from admirers—but he gets so much mail that Burns gives him backdoor service.

"His father usually meets me in the rear to get the mail," said Burns "and often he invites me in for a minute—Mr. and Mrs. Presley are wonderful people."

How much mail does Elvis get?

"At least 500 or 600 letters a day," said Burns, "and usually two or three packages from all over the world. This would be a good place for a stamp collector to get some samples."

Lipstick Smears

What kind of mail does he receive?

"Most of it is from teen-age girls, judging from the lipstick smears and affectionate notes scribbled on the envelopes," laughed Burns, "but his father told me that Elvis gets many songs from amateur composers who want Elvis to record their masterpieces."

Burns said "in all my 35 years carrying mail, I have never had a customer who gets more mail."

What does he think of Elvis?

"I've never seen him—he's always still in bed or upstairs when I get there," he said, "but I can tell you this: He's got as nice parents as you'll find anywhere."

Burns is a rock 'n roll fan himself: "I like the tune and the melody."

Elvis has a dog, "but he doesn't bite," says Burns.

81

Marine Wants Elvis' Apology On Gun Threat

Memphis Commercial Appeal   March 25, 1957

A lanky young Marine said yesterday he feels Elvis Presley "owes me an apology" for pulling a toy pistol on him.

But Pfc. Hershel Nixon said he doesn't intend to make a formal complaint to police about an incident Friday night when the singer held a Hollywood prop gun in his hand and told the Marine: "You don't want to start trouble with me, do you?"

Elvis said he took the gun, used in making films, from his coat to scare Private Nixon away. He thought the Marine had been drinking and wanted to start a fight, he said.

"I didn't try to pick a fight with him and I wasn't drinking," Private Nixon said yesterday. "I had no way of knowing the pistol was a toy. He didn't tell me the gun wasn't real or let me inspect it."

The pair exchanged words on Third near Poplar where Elvis, sporting a fuzzy new moustache, had parked his white Continental Mark II and was signing autographs for several girls.

The Marine said he was walking to the Salvation Army USO at 174 North Third, where dances are often held, when he saw Elvis and went over to talk to him.

The Marine, stationed at the Naval Air Station at Millington, quoted the 22-year-old teenage idol as saying: "I'll blow your damn brains out, you punk."

Presley denied he used those words.

The Marine said: "I won't file a complaint because he didn't hurt me in any way except the name he called me—punk. Where I come from, St. Louis, punk is the lowest thing you can call a person. I'm a Marine and the Marines build men, not punks.

"I think he owes me an apology because nobody—not even Presley—has a right to pull a pistol on someone, even if it is just a toy."

Police said they would take no action in the matter unless Private Nixon files a complaint and swears out a warrant for the singer's arrest.

March 1957— In trouble again!

Elvis poses with some radio personalities.

Elvis Presley Drew A Pistol on Him, Marine Charges

Memphis, Tenn., March 25 (AP) —A lanky young Marine says he doesn't plan to file a complaint with police because Elvis Presley pulled a "pistol" on him.

But Pvt. Hershel Nixon, 18, says he feels the rock 'n' roll singer owes him an apology.

Police said they won't take any action in the Friday night incident unless Pvt. Nixon tried to pick a fight while the singer was signing autographs for admirers on a midtown street.

Pvt. Nixon said, "I didn't try to pick a fight and I wasn't drinking. I had no way of knowing the pistol was a toy . . ."

The Marine, stationed at the Memphis Naval Air Station, said he left after Presley pulled the prop gun and said, "I'll blow your brains out, you punk."

Presley, 22, said the Marine accused him of bumping into his wife as she walked out of a restaurant about two months ago.

"She told me all about it," he quoted the Marine as saying, "I want to get it straightened out right now."

Presley, who returned recently from Hollywood, said he edged away but the Marine followed.

"I told him I didn't know what he was talking about because I had been in Hollywood," Presley said. "Then I thought about that toy gun and I pulled it out. I said, "You don't want to start trouble with me, do you?

"I was smiling when I took it out of my coat. Everybody else standing around there knew it wasn't real."

Presley said he and a friend had been "playing" with the prop gun.

The singer was twice involved in fist fights last year. Both times he claimed the other party was the aggressor and the judge agreed.

Gov. Frank Clement (Tenn.), Elvis, and the Colonel

Elvis parties with a friend.

Elvis and d.j. Dewey Phillips (center) visit a local record store.

St. Louis Post-Dispatch March 30, 1957

Elvis Sings Here, but Squeals Of 11,000 Often Drown Him Out

A highlight of the 1957 tour was Elvis's gold tuxedo.

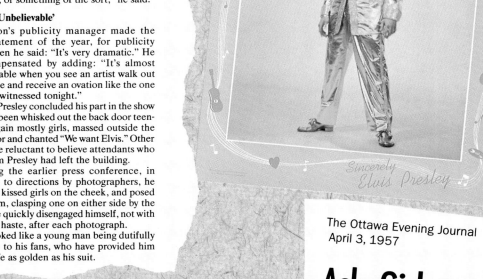

Sincerely
Elvis Presley

Elvis Presley shimmering in sequins and metallic gold cloth, writhed and sang last night in Kiel Auditorium convention hall before a capacity crowd of about 11,000 spectators most of them teen-age girls. Many times the appreciative din from the audience drowned out Presley.

The performer, who has secluded himself in a Hotel Chase room all day under an assumed name, had been spirited by police into the auditorium by an obscure alley entrance to avoid admirers standing guard at the stage door.

He had been escorted to the hall in time to avoid the Market Street traffic snarl caused by his scheduled appearance. Shortly before the 8 p.m. curtain time eastbound machines were inching along from the point west of Union Station.

The "rock and roll" singer did not go on stage until after the show's midpoint intermission. Entertainers accompanying him on a nine-performance tour did their turns while Presley talked to reporters and radio disc jockeys in assembly Hall 2. What was scheduled as a press conference turned out to be dominated by autograph-seeking teen-agers who had infiltrated the police lines.

After the intermission, during which spectators had another chance to buy Elvis Presley souvenirs, the 22-year-old performer bounded onto the stage and the uproar began. He glittered and grimaced. Rhinestones embedded even in the laces of his gold-colored, raised-heel shoes added to the dazzling sight.

Girls screamed and hundreds of flash bulbs were discharged, making the hall look as if it were under an artillery barrage. Presley clung to the microphone stand and staggered about in a distinctive, distraught manner, waiting for the noise to subside a bit.

Outnumbered and Outshrieked

When he mouthed the opening words of his first song, the uproar began again. Girls shrieked. Elvis shrieked, but he was outnumbered. His contortions were ecstatically received. His most appreciated medium of expression seemed to be burlesque's traditional hip movements.

Musicians from a jazz concert playing to a small audience in the auditorium's adjoining opera house sneaked into the wings to watch Presley perform.

"Man, how much do you suppose those yard goods cost him?" one of them speculated.

Elvis staggered and sang more songs evoking the same audience reaction, each presentation becoming a repetition of the first.

Australian promoter Lee Gordon said the gold suit had cost $2500.

"It's real gold, with impregnated unborn calf skin, or something of the sort," he said.

'Almost Unbelievable'

Gordon's publicity manager made the understatement of the year, for publicity men, when he said: "It's very dramatic." He overcompensated by adding: "It's almost unbelievable when you see an artist walk out on a stage and receive an ovation like the one we have witnessed tonight."

After Presley concluded his part in the show and had been whisked out the back door teen-agers, again mostly girls, massed outside the stage door and chanted "We want Elvis." Other girls were reluctant to believe attendants who told them Presley had left the building.

During the earlier press conference, in response to directions by photographers, he dutifully kissed girls on the cheek, and posed with them, clasping one on either side by the waist. He quickly disengaged himself, not with impolite haste, after each photograph.

He looked like a young man being dutifully attentive to his fans, who have provided him with a life as golden as his suit.

Nudie Cohen of Hollywood designed the gold lamé suit.

The Ottawa Evening Journal
April 3, 1957

Ask Girls Stay Away From Elvis

Students of Notre Dame Convent have been asked to promise they will take no part in either the reception for Elvis Presley today or his show at the Auditorium tonight.

The request, circulated throughout high school classes at the Convent, followed a speech over the public address system at another Ottawa school yesterday.

But, while the other simply warned students not to misbehave at the rock 'n' roll rally and to do nothing to bring dishonor on their school's name, the Notre Dame circular requested students not attend.

It was written on blackboards at the convent during routine class hours, students said, and they were asked to copy it, then sign it at the bottom.

It read:

'I promise that I shall not take part in the reception accorded Elvis Presley and I shall not be present at the program presented by him at the Auditorium on Wednesday, April 3, 1957. Signed . . . .'

Buffalo Courier-Express   April 1, 1957

Singer Real Showman
Elvis' Grin Enthralls Girl Fans

By Dick Hirsch

At 9:52 last night an earsplitting soprano ovation set the very foundations of Memorial Auditorium a-quaking.

Elvis Presley sauntered onto the floodlit stage and grinned a sheepish grin. The roar increased. And Elvis grinned.

For three solid minutes, like the high-pitched whines of a squadron of jet-planes, they screamed.

Elvis held up his hand for silence. He muttered something that was lost in the frenzy. Then he twitched his well-publicized pelvis, and the screams were louder than ever.

His gargantuan mop of hair spilled over his forehead. He cuddled the mike. He snickered at the gallery behind the bunting-draped stage. Young girls squeezed their temples with their hands as if in sublime agony. Elvis himself appeared as though afflicted by a serious case of stomach cramps.

Audience in Palm

But through it all, Elvis, Tennessee's gift to teen-agers, played his part to the hilt. He is an amazing phenomenon and he had the giant audience in the palm of his hand.

The giant crowd, mostly teen-agers and predominantly girls, began filtering into the Auditorium about 6:30 p.m. Some remained there for about an hour after Presley had sprinted from the stage.

Police Galore

"Are you sure there isn't a policeman's ball here tonight?" one early arrival asked. About 180 uniformed police and plainclothesmen, including auxiliary police, were in the audience. Capt. John F. Mahoney of the Franklin Station was in command. The large force of police helped keep the huge crowd well under control.

The only violence took place outside Memorial Auditorium about 10 when police arrested a youth who, they said, was throwing stones at auditorium windows. The youth, who identified himself as John Jerry, 16, of 228 Pratt St., was arrested on a charge of malicious mischief.

Lew Horschel, veteran Auditorium concessionaire, said the house was the largest and most enthusiastic he'd ever seen. And that goes back 40 years.

Spring 1957 — Elvis tours the midwest and Canada.

Elvis arrives in Vancouver. Pal George Klein is the man with the gym bag.

Elvis '57

The Ottawa Journal   April 4, 1957

Elvis Fans Give Helen a Headache

By HELEN PARMELER
of The Journal

Some wept, some moaned, some clutched their heads in ecstasy; everybody screamed, stamped, clapped hands, flailed arms; one person got down on all fours and pounded on the floor.

Elvis 'sent' them.

Elvis 'sent' me too—home with a busting headache!

This is supposed to be a 'woman's eye view' of Elvis Aron Presley. His fans will consider it a 'worm's eye view'.

I'm still bewildered. Last night's contortionist exhibition at the Auditorium was the closest to the jungle I'll ever get. But it isn't the Memphis wiggler who's the 'missing link'. It's his audiences—in Ottawa and elsewhere.

Let Off Steam

I don't know if his gyrations excite them, or if he merely gives off steam. But, let off steam they did, and I have a headache to vouch for it. Perhaps he hypnotized them.

For more than a hour and a half the seething mob sounded like 50 jet planes taking off at once.

The crowd was a mixture of teenagers, a fair sprinkling of adults and policemen, and the odd diplomat and socialite. One foreign embassy official (who begged to remain anonymous) claimed he was merely studying 'Canadian culture'.

The lad with the permanent sneer certainly gave them their money's worth. In spangled gold lamé he slithered and reeled until the sweat poured from his brow and his lank hair covered his eyes.

Couldn't Hear Him

By the time 'Houn' Dog' arrived for the third time around he had his audience in his hand, but not in his lap—the entourage of policemen saw to that.

Then in a last pop of flashlight bulbs he was gone. The lights switched on and that was all there was to it. They hadn't heard his voice, but they were happy. As they had shrieked their adulation, they drowned out his every word. But his hips had kept the beat for them.

Perhaps the words of one 15-year-old Hull High School student sum up the intensity of the girls' emotions. 'I love him', she sobbed, long after he had departed.

In the words of a cynical cop: 'Every time he took a dive, they hollered. They're crazy.'

As for me, I'm still bewildered.

I'd just like to own as much as that boy pays in taxes.

Anybody know how to get rid of a headache?

Life on the road: another city, another concert, another fan

Elvis greets a 4-legged fan.

Toronto Daily Star   April 8, 1957

400 AT SCHOOL WERE ASKED TO AVOID PRESLEY

Special to The Star

Ottawa, April 8—Eight girls have been expelled from Ottawa's Notre Dame convent because they attended a rock 'n roll show last week featuring Elvis Presley.

'It was not a show for young ladies to attend,' one official said today. 'The girls deliberately defied the regulations of the school so we asked their parents to withdraw them.'

Convent authorities said the action 'will not be reconsidered.'

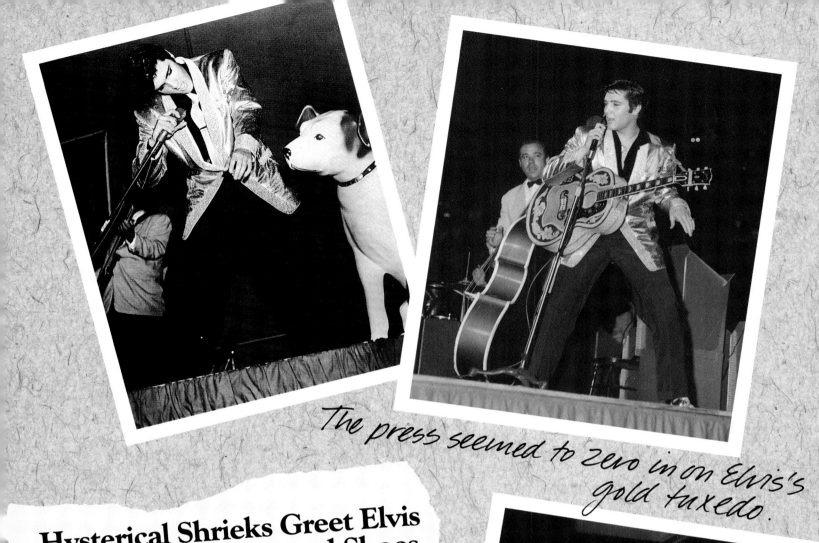

The press seemed to zero in on Elvis's gold tuxedo.

Hysterical Shrieks Greet Elvis In His Gold Jacket and Shoes

The trouble with going to see Elvis Presley is that you're liable to get killed. The experience is the closest thing to getting bashed on the head with an atomic bomb.

Elvis gave two performances Sunday in the Olympia—each to shrieking audiences of around 14,000. Presley, the singing troubadour with the long sideburns, gives off more electricity than the Detroit Edison Co.'s combined transmitters.

When he made his grand entrance, pandemonium broke loose and carnage waited in the wings. Most of the afternoon throng were little girls, nice little girls who just adore Elvis. They wore Elvis buttons, Elvis hats and carried Elvis pictures.

Before the show, Elvis sat still long enough for a brief press conference. He didn't seem a bit self-conscious in his red suede jacket, flashy blue shirt and blue pants. Elvis is very polite. "Yes, ma'am" and "yes sir" he was careful to say.

He was asked whether he worried about his popularity waning. "If they forgot me, I'll just have to do something worth remembering," he said. **And what about the Army, Elvis?**

"When I took my physical, they told me it might be three months, six months or a year."

Eight cars are a lot, aren't they, Elvis? Ever thought of selling any of them?

"If I wanted to sell them I wouldn't have bought them in the first place. I just built a new four-car garage. Guess I'll have to build another one for the other four cars."

Elvis came here in a Cadillac limousine from Ft. Wayne, Ind. His young fans were up early trying, to no avail, to track him down.

The young'uns started to congregate at the Olympia as early as 9 p.m. for the 2 o'clock show. Some tried the hotels with no luck.

Inside the Olympia, the youngsters surged against police lines in hope of getting an early look at their idol. "Insane, isn't it?" said one of the 175 policemen assigned to the "Sideburn Detail."

Except for climbing up each other's backs, the crowd was fairly orderly.

The 22-year-old Presley, who had changed into a gold jacket, gold shoes and a gold string tie, dashed on stage to the hysterical shrieks of unleashed bedlam.

Hundred of flashbulbs popped and swoons reached a crescendo, "Elvis, Elvis, Elvis, Elvis."

Before the show, Tom Parker, general manager of the Hillbilly singer, talked about Elvis' popularity.

"We get 25,000 to 30,000 fan letters a week," Parker said. "Why, he even got more than 270,000 Christmas cards, a lot of them from right here in Detroit."

Elvis is a nice boy, said Parker. "None of this has gone to his head."

There is a fanatical loyalty among Presley fans.

A teen-aged girl, sporting a "I Hate Elvis" button, was forced to remove it by a group of fans before they would allow her to reach her seat.

From here Presley will go to Buffalo, thence to Toronto, Ottawa and Philadelphia. Then Elvis will hike out to Hollywood, where eight movies await him. Apparently, Elvis is still the most.

Is Elvis in this magazine?

Memphis Press-Scimitar   July 10, 1957

Elvis Film Sets Record In Crowds at Strand

And First Day of 'Loving You' Also Breaks All Cash Records Except One

The first day of *Loving You* broke every existing attendance record in the history of the Strand. It also broke every money record except one. The first Saturday run of *The 10 Commandments* brought in $200 more. Its tickets were priced at $2 top, however, against 90 cent top for *Loving You.*

The Presley picture yesterday also almost broke the one-day gross record for Paramount Pictures releases playing at any Memphis theater. Only *The Greatest Show on Earth,* playing at the Malco, with higher prices and twice as many seats, and one other Paramount picture ever took in more money in Memphis in a single day.

Hal Wallis, producer of the picture, telephoned Manager Alex Thompson three times yesterday from Hollywood. The first time to inquire about attendance, the second time to see if the phenomenal business was holding up (it was increasing), and the third time to ask that clippings of reviews and news stories on the picture be airmailed to him.

Lloyd Bailey, theater manager said, "We've had some good movies here, but I've never seen anything like this."

Today, Presley followers were still flocking to see their idol in "unexpected numbers," according to Bailey. And there has been no letup of lung exercise. Bailey said today's customers were "as loud as yesterday's." He added: "They finally finished ripping off all my billboard displays," including, he said a cardboard cutout of Elvis "which gave them a little trouble at first."

Yesterday, most of the theater's 1100 seats emptied after each performance and were refilled in 15 minutes. Some dyed-in-the-wool Presley fans stayed for as many as five performances, however.

Lobby cards

Elvis's parents made a cameo appearance in Loving You near the end of the film.

10212-2/1

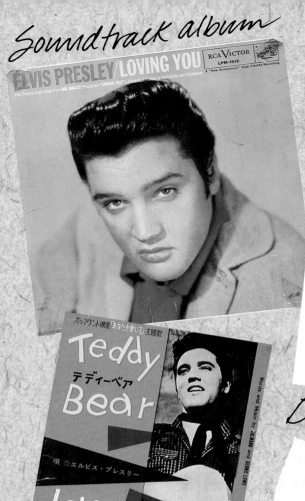

Dolores Hart made her film debut in <u>Loving You</u>.

She's Elvis' 'Hart' Interest

HER HART is in her work, you might say. Dolores Hart, Elvis Presley's new leading lady, who makes her film debut in Paramount's *Loving You,* and Elvis himself are said to have blushed repeatedly during the filming of this kissing sequence. According to their studio neither the star nor his leading lady had ever played a romantic scene in front of a 40-man movie crew. That should be enough to disconcert any pair of young lovers. You might say, in other words, they'd get all shook up.

Loving You

WALLIS, PARAMOUNT; VISTAVISION, TECHNICOLOR

Fashioned carefully to show off Elvis Presley in the best light, this drama-with-music casts him as a lonely young drifter, boomed into fame as a singing idol. It's press agent Lizabeth Scott who discovers him, hires him as vocalist with Wendell Corey's obscure band and promotes him with publicity stunts. Though Elvis gets entangled with the personal affairs of Liz and Wendell, he also shares a gentle romance with winsome Dolores Hart. Music is ladled out in generous portions—ballads, blues, but mostly rock 'n' roll.

MODERN TEEN

Loving You

Elvis' first motion picture, *Love Me Tender,* was admittedly not the greatest—but most everyone agreed that Elvis did very well for his first acting job.

However, we hear that Elvis' current flicker, *Loving You,* is a real goodie.

It's the story of a small town guy named Deke Rivers. Deke (Elvis) is discovered by a female press agent who hires him to sing with a hillbilly-type band which is conducted by her ex-husband (Wendell Corey). Lizabeth Scott plays the pretty press agent. She decided Deke's rock and roll brand of singing is just the thing to put the band into the big time. They all go out on tour and Deke becomes an overnight sensation.

Teenagers flip over Deke—including (now the plot thickens) a pretty teenager who is a vocalist with the band. A new discovery, Dolores Hart (a teenager herself) plays the band vocalist who adores Deke. But Deke is all shook up about glamorous Lizabeth Scott.

Then Lizabeth goes a little too far with a press agent stunt involving a fabulous car, supposedly the gift of an older woman. The people in the town where the band is currently appearing are furious about the stunt. They insist that the Sheriff stop the show.

Deke concludes his gorgeous press agent and her ex-husband are both false friends. He leaves town.

We won't tell you exactly how everything works out but you can be sure that Dolores and Elvis are together in a clinch at the end of the picture.

Elvis kisses a girl for the first time in this film. We mean he kisses a girl for the first time in a motion picture—we strongly suspect he has already kissed a girl off screen.

Elvis' romance in the movie, Dolores Hart, was a freshman at Marymount College in West Los Angles when she was discovered and cast in the role which easily qualifies her as Most Envied Teenage Girl of the Year.

89

behind the scenes with / LOVING YOU

Elvis Presley hadn't been kissed on screen until he made *Loving You*, but here he makes up for lost time. He gets smooched by three fetching females. Lizabeth Scott is strictly business; Jana Lund is definitely daring—but Dolores Hart makes her is positively for real! . . . Dolores is the eighteen-year-old newcomer who makes her film debut as Presley's teen-age romance in the picture. She's a freshman at Marymount College, in Westwood. . . . Elvis drives a $10,000 gorgeous white convertible in the picture, and one sequence called for the car to be covered with loving messages written in bright red lipstick by ardent teen-age fans. This posed a problem for the studio, for it was impossible to remove the lipstick without ruining the paint. A property man finally found a solution: a mixture of red show-card coloring, cornstarch and water looked exactly like lipstick, but rubbed off leaving the paint sparkling white. . . . During the shooting of the film at Paramount, the studio was deluged with an average of five hundred telephone calls a day for Elvis. Some came from as far away as London. While the callers were predominantly female, there was a surprising number of boys phoning. . . . One day the officer of duty at the main studio gate was approached by a couple, and the man said, with a Southern accent, "Howdy, officer. Can you tell me how to get into this place? We've got a boy working here." The officer politely inquired whom the lad might be. Before the man could finish Elvis Presley, the gates were opened, and Mr. and Mrs. Vernon Presley of Memphis, Tennessee, were ushered in. . . . Later, the parents played a bit part in one scene with Elvis. . . . Hundreds of teen-age fans lined up at the gate to watch their idol drive out in his white Eldorado Cadillac at the end of the day. They wanted to take photos, be photographed with him and have him sign autographs. This sometimes took as long as two hours, and while Elvis was cooperative, he came to work around eight each morning and didn't leave until almost seven p.m. So the police chief of the studio hired six extra security officers to clear the way for Elvis to drive out at night. . . . While Elvis was making the film, the mail department received conservatively two thousand pieces of mail each day for him; one teen-ager was sending him her 128th letter. The mail was turned over to Colonel Parker's secretary and it was her duty to see that it was sorted and answered correctly. . . . A great deal of the mail was shown to Elvis, and he spent a couple of hours each day signing letters and autographing specially requested photos. . . . Each day in the studio commissary at lunch time, Elvis would sit in the alcove dining room off the main room with three of his friends and associates. Two of them were buddies from Memphis; one cousin, was his private bodyguard and security officer. . . . Elvis' lunch was invariably the same each day: mashed potatoes with gravy, sauerkraut and crisp bacon. . . . On the set Elvis became nervous if interrupted by members of the press, so the set was closed during the shooting so that he could concentrate on his acting.

—Dick Williams

Elvis checks out a crane shot through the VistaVision camera.

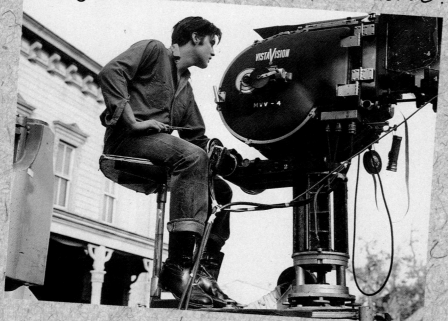

Elvis cuts loose on the final production number.

'Loving You' Draws Happy Shrieks From Elvis Presley's Fans

Audience shrieks to Elvis Presley's wriggles are available (for them as likes 'em) again in the Paramount Theater where Mr. Presley wriggles in Vistavision and Technicolor and the tale of an orphan boy's zoom to fame entitled *Loving You*.

Although Mr. Presley's art has improved to the extent that he can generate more shrieks out of much less wriggly wriggles the total shrieks are fewer than during his recent film, *Love Me Tender*, due to the increased amount of plot and high emotions in *Loving You*.

In *Loving You*, a truck-driver, Presley, is discovered by Lizabeth Scott, the very tricky press agent for a lame band, conducted by her divorced husband, Wendell Corey.

The Presley voice, charm and wriggle buoy up the band magnificently but complicated questions arise: Does Mr. Presley love Lizabeth and maybe she him or does he love Dolores Hart, more his age.

* * *

ANYWAY Mr. Corey loves Lizabeth though doubting her motives, and he is fond of Mr. Presley whom he describes as just the type of upstanding and shriek-inducing youth he would love to have for a son. As for Dolores her eyes brim with tears when Presley sings, an odd effect.

Despite all the adulation he inspires, Mr. P. feels friendless and is inclined to question that his rosy road to fame is wholly honorable or the perfect answer to his dreams.

He is saddened by evidence of self-interest on the part of Liz and the tendency of some of the most foolish adults ever seen on any screen to consider him a menace to youth and culture.

When these doddering middle-agers are persuaded by the director to respond to the Presley art with joyous semi-wriggles, you really have something.

All this, one senses, is rather a bore to the shriekers who are happier just shrieking to Presley songs, Hot Dog, Lonesome Cowboy, Let Me Be Your Teddy Bear and Mean Woman Blues.

* * *

IN ADDITION to these and other treats, the Paramount presents *Rock, Rock, Rock* which is more or less more of the same—though shriekless.—A.S.

LOVING YOU (*Paramount*)—This film, following the immense success of Elvis Presley in *Love Me Tender*, serves principally to allow him to sing between romantic scenes with Dolores Hart and dramatic ones with Lizabeth Scott.

Dolores Hart, as Susan, the singer's girl friend, is making her film debut in this picture, and Lizabeth Scott is a Press agent who discovers Deke's (Elvis Presley) singing talent and persuades her ex-husband (Wendell Corey), a band leader, to help her make a success of his career as a singer.

Among the many new songs which crowd the film are "Dancing on a Dare," "Got a Lotta Livin' to Do," "Candy Kisses," "Let Me Be Your Teddy Bear," "Hot Dog" and the title song, "Loving You."

Inside the album cover

Sal Mineo visits Elvis on the set.

Elvis obliges with some auto-graphs.

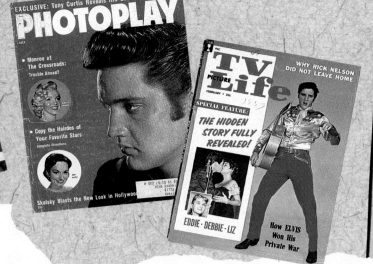

HELD OVER!

EVERYTHING YOU COULD WISH FOR IN A MUSICAL ENTERTAINMENT!

YOU'LL ROCK 'N' ROLL WITH ELVIS SINGING
"LOVING YOU"
"HOT DOG"
"LONESOME COWBOY"
"LET ME BE YOUR TEDDY BEAR"
"GOT A LOT OF LIVIN' TO DO"
"MEAN WOMAN BLUES"
"LET'S HAVE A PARTY"

YOU'LL LOVE ELVIS IN HIS FIRST BIG MUSICAL IN TECHNICOLOR

ELVIS PRESLEY
ELIZABETH SCOTT · WENDELL COREY

You'll love
LOVING YOU

FIRST PITTSBURGH SHOWING!

★ NOW PLAYING AT THE FOLLOWING ★
DRIVE-IN AND NABORHOOD THEATRES

BELLEVUE .... Bellevue	LEONA .... Homestead
ARCADE .... South Side	MANOS .... Tarentum, Pa.
CAMP HORNE DR. IN. North Hills	MT. OLIVER .... Brownsville Rd.
COLONIAL DR. IN. ..... Route 51	RIVOLI .... East Pittsburgh
DEPENDABLE DR. IN. Near Airport	SEWICKLEY ...... Sewickley, Pa.
FAMILY DR. IN.. New Kensington	SHADYSIDE .... Walnut St.
GARDEN .... North Side	SILVER LAKE DR. IN. Wash. Blvd.
GREATER PGH. DR. IN. Route 30	TWIN HI-WAY DR. IN. Rts. 22-30

July 27, 1957   MELODY MAKER

AT LAST!
—the truth about Elvis Presley

People have tried to write Elvis Presley off—and there are many more who would if they could. To many, he's an unpleasing sign of the times, something they dislike without really understanding.

Last week, the MELODY MAKER met a man who believes he does understand.

Charles O'Curran—Patti Page's husband—is a dance director, who has been working with Elvis on the paramount film, *Loving You*.

"Actually, I selected his songs," says O'Curran. "Hal Wallis is a great producer, but he doesn't know much about pop songs. One of the numbers I picked was 'Teddy Bear,' which is doing very well.

"How is Elvis? You're going to love him. I hear he is coming over here. Let's put it this way: you're going to like him a lot more than some of the people around him.

"When I say that he's a simple lad, don't get me wrong. He's sharp enough mentally. But, in a way, he's still unspoiled and unaffected. Childlike, perhaps.

"And he's so willing to learn. If you told him to go over in the corner and stand on his head, I think he'd do it. . . .

PATIENT

. . . Don't take my word for it. Everyone who has worked with him says the same. Naturally, he's made some enemies. In his position, that's unavoidable. He has to be smuggled in and out of hotels and theatres, and in general keep to a plan of campaign mapped out by others. That's bound to offend some.

"But I've seen him signing autographs and he's much more patient than most of us would be. If two hundred people are there, he'll just go on writing his signature until he's satisfied everybody.

"Presley has become an industry. He's so big that ordinary standards don't apply. For example: one magazine wanted him for a special

Charles O'Curran,

Hollywood dance director and husband of singer Patti Page, worked with Elvis Presley on his film, *Loving You*. Here, in an exclusive interview with TONY BROWN, he gives the facts about the teenagers' idol.

---

photographic session. That kind of co-operation is normally given free in the name of publicity. But Presley's handlers demanded a fee—a huge one. And I believe they got it.

"How can his teenage appeal be explained? I think it's simple.

"How free is a teenager?

"They're told not to do this, not to do that all day in school. And it's No, No, No, all the rest of the time at home —a constant process of repression.

"So then they go to an Elvis Presley concert and watch the uninhibited performance of someone who seems just about in their own age group. They get his smoldering, rebellious appearance. And they catch on that this is one time when they can let themselves go, let their hair down, squeal and scream and clap. It's actually allowed.

"Once they've enjoyed that sort of freedom, no adult can ever tell them to stay away from Elvis. Oh, they've tried it.

"Religious organizations put the ban on him, sent the word out to parents to forbid their daughters and all that. Did it make a scrap of difference? What do you think? You've heard about forbidden fruit. . . .

"And so what happens? He's banned and people write about him. The kids refuse to stay away—and they write some more. If it seems at any time that he's unco-operative, newspapers put in a beef. Does it

touch Elvis? Of course not. It's all publicity.

"And, incidentally, although I've heard that Presley has come in for some criticism over here, I notice that you claim to have your own Elvis Presley, Tommy Steele.

"I caught his act on television the other night.

"Cute.

"How does it compare with a real Presley performance?

"I'm afraid it doesn't."

Sheet music

PARTY
Words and Music by JESSIE MAE ROBINSON

SUNG BY ELVIS

PRESLEY

IN THE
HAL WALLIS PRODUCTION

LOVING YOU

A PARAMOUNT PICTURE

TECHNICOLOR
VISTAVISION

PRICE 60c

as Recorded by ELVIS PRESLEY on RCA Victor

GLADYS MUSIC, INC.
HILL AND RANGE SONGS, INC.

Loving You

WALLIS, PARAMOUNT; VISTAVISION, TECHNICOLOR

✓✓✓ In a part neatly tailored to fit his own personality, Elvis Presley comes off much better than in his first picture. Off-and-on lovers, press agent Lizabeth Scott and has-been bandleader Wendell Corey are touring small towns in the South when they meet Elvis. Liz realizes that the shy youngster could be a singing smash, so she hires him as vocalist with Corey's band—and secretly puts him under personal contract to herself. Gaudy publicity fast gets Elvis into the limelight and onto a spot that he finds uncomfortable. But even Liz's overpowering influence can't keep him from falling for sweet young singer Dolores Hart. Though the story line is strong enough, there's never too long an interlude between musical numbers, all done in lively style. FAMILY

Wendell Corey, Elvis, Dolores Hart, and Lizabeth Scott

Elvis's musicians Scotty Moore (far right) and D.J. Fontana (striped jacket) were in Loving You.

LOVING YOU

Elvis Presley's second movie (from Paramount) allows him to play a swivel-hipped singer whose style brings him the adulation of teen-agers and the condemnation of parents. Around this made-to-order character has been built a fairly complicated story of backstage double-dealing with Lizabeth Scott as a press agent, Wendell Corey as the bandleader who loves her and cute newcomer Dolores Hart as a singer who loves Elvis. As the plot twists and turns so does Elvis; his fans will be delighted with his songs and those not his fans may be surprised by his acting competence. Hal Wallis produced.

Jana Lund gave Elvis his first screen kiss.

THESE REPORTS TRUE— ELVIS AND DEWEY HAD A FALLING OUT

By ROBERT JOHNSON *Press-Scimitar Staff Writer*

A nationally famous friendship has recently been real cool, and a tragedy of personal relations based on trifles has developed.

Elvis and Dewey haven't been on speaking terms for some weeks.

There has been a lot of gossip and some of it has got pretty far afield.

It was Dewey Phillips who helped make Elvis a sensation by playing his first record, "That's All Right, Mama," on his *Red, Hot & Blue* radio show. He called up Elvis, got him out of the Suzore Theater, asked him to come down and be on the program because he wanted to help plug the record.

Dewey was one of Elvis' most enthusiastic fans. He still is. Elvis appreciated it, frequently turned up to be on Dewey's show free—even after he became the highest-paid entertainer in broadcasting.

But since Dewey went out to Hollywood to visit Elvis—as Elvis' guest—things haven't been the same.

Here's the way the story has been told:

Elvis paid Dewey's way to Hollywood. He didn't put him in with the other fellows, but put Dewey up in a room in his own personal suite.

He had planned a lot of things he wanted Dewey to do. Most of all, he wanted Dewey to spend a lot of time with him, and to watch him at work at MGM.

Dewey showed up the first day, stayed about 15 minutes, got nervous and bored, left.

Elvis took Dewey to his dentist and spent about $400 getting Dewey some of those fancy porcelain caps just like Elvis' for his teeth. He took him around to the various studios and stars' homes, proud of his strange friend from Memphis.

Dewey tried to take pictures at MGM, and they wouldn't let him.

At the Moulin Rouge, the management asked Elvis if he would acknowledge an introduction. Elvis said he would. They threw the spotlight on him, and Dewey got up, stood in front of him and started taking bows. Elvis was embarrassed.

Elvis introduced Dewey to Yul Brynner. Dewey is supposed to have said something like, "You sure are a shortie, Mother." Elvis is reported to have gone back and apologized to Brynner later.

A source which gave some of this information said: "Part of the trouble was that those people in Hollywood just didn't understand Phillips."

The biggest breach of all, it is stated, was that Elvis let Dewey hear his recording of "Teddy Bear" but warned him not to take one, as he only had a few samples and the Victor people would be furious if anyone jumped the release. Dewey, it is stated, put one in his suitcase, put it jubilantly on the air a considerable time before it was released generally, causing great unhappiness among local distributors, who couldn't supply demand, and they complained.

This last is said to have been the most serious fracture of all.

"Elvis was furious," it was said. When Dewey got back to Memphis, word of some of these matters got to a friend of his who took him aside and did a little woodshedding, the general tenor of which was: "You behaved badly. You owe Elvis an apology."

So Dewey said maybe he did, and he would apologize.

He did apologize, and they spent a happy night of reunion together, and their newly-cemented friendship lasted at least two or three days.

Still, however, Elvis didn't go down to visit Dewey's show as he had of yore, and Dewey began to think that Elvis didn't really like him any more.

So, according to this much-gossiped version of the story, Dewey went out at 3 o'clock one morning, was turned down at the gate, climbed the fence and went in and roused the household shouting: "I'm thru with you, Elvis." Elvis is said to have doubled him in spades.

One person close to Elvis said: "What made it especially bad is that Mrs. Presley is so nervous, especially since Liberace's mother got hurt."

Friends of Phillips have known for some time that he has been very upset and brooded about his differences with Elvis.

Dewey said today:

"I still love that boy like a brother. Or maybe it would be better to say like a son.

"It's not true that I quit playing his records. I played five of them last night.

"I like what he did. You know what I mean—he really got in there and did something.

"There was nothing wrong when I left Hollywood.

THEY EVEN WEPT

"When we said goodbye, we even shed a few tears, I told him I'd never be able to repay him for all the nice things he had done for me.

"His last words to me were, 'Phillips, be sure and say a prayer before you get on that plane.' (Elvis has been plane-wary ever since a near crack-up in a chartered plane, does all his traveling by train.)

"I went out to Hollywood on vacation, and I wanted to have some fun.

"I've got a lot of friends out there—some of them I just know by talking to them, on the phone—and I wanted to see them. You know, record people . . .

"About this Yul Brynner thing, I didn't realize I was embarrassing anyone. Elvis introduced us, and I said 'How you getting along, old buddy,' just like I would to anyone.

"Then I said, 'My gosh, you look shorter than you do in pictures.' It was just that he wasn't near as big as I thought of him. He said, 'That's how they put the cameras, Phillips,' and that's all there was to it."

FEELING GOOD

"At the Moulin Rouge, I was just feeling good, playing around. They put the spotlight on Elvis, and I jumped up and waved my hand. Just feeling good. I was on vacation.

"I didn't want to stay at the studio all day. I wanted to see a little of the town.

"That thing out at Elvis' house . . . I didn't go over the fence, I walked right thru the cotton-pickin' gate. The guard left it open.

"It was only about 1 a.m. I'd just finished my work, and Barbara Pittman (singer) and a couple of other girls who wanted to see Elvis were with me. I'd had two or three beers, but I wasn't drunk.

"What I really went out there for was for my Polaroid camera that Sam Phillips gave me for Christmas. I let Elvis have it, and I wanted it because I was going to take the rest of my vacation at Pickwick and I would need the camera.

"It wasn't really late for Elvis. He stays up late almost every night. You know, we just live that way.

"They wouldn't let me in and I still haven't got my camera.

"I said some things I shouldn't have said."

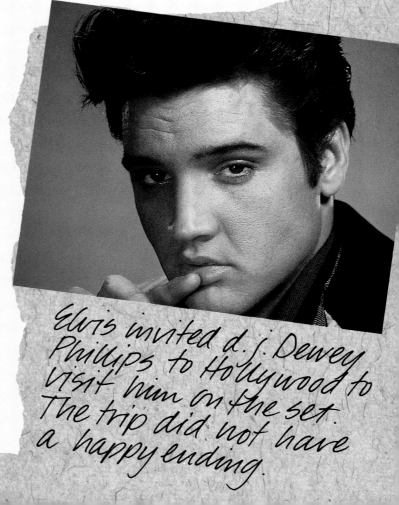

Elvis invited d.j. Dewey Phillips to Hollywood to visit him on the set. The trip did not have a happy ending.

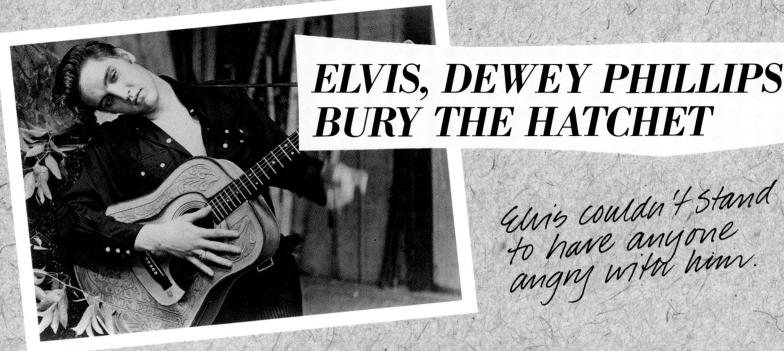

ELVIS, DEWEY PHILLIPS BURY THE HATCHET

Elvis couldn't stand to have anyone angry with him.

By Robert Johnson *Press-Scimitar Staff Writer*

Elvis Presley and Dewey Phillips are friends again.

Elvis himself took the initiative in renewing their friendship and dropped in to see Dewey during Dewey's radio broadcast on WHBQ last night. However, Dewey had previously stated at the time when the story about the break in their friendship first appeared that he still felt deep affection for Elvis and hoped their friendship could continue. Dewey had continued to play Elvis' records on his radio and live shows even when they were not seeing one another.

The break-up had come as the result of some incidents when Dewey visited Elvis as Elvis' guest in Hollywood.

After the broadcast last night, Elvis and Dewey and a number of friends went to Sam Phillips' place and played records and discussed them.

But if one wound was healed, Elvis was still troubled about another, it was indicated.

He has been deluged with stacks of telegrams from musicians all over the country asking for the jobs left vacant by the resignations of Scotty Moore, guitarist, and Bill Black, bass fiddle player, who had been with Elvis since the beginning of his career.

Elvis could have his pick of musicians, but he isn't happy about it.

He wants Scotty and Bill back, if it can be graciously arranged.

You don't wipe out with a few days of unpleasantness the memories of four years together, including times when they pinched pennies for hamburgers, rode rutty roads to tanktowns, talked long hours in cheap hotel rooms, snatched sleep in speeding cars, watched the crowds begin to grow and grow, first began to know that something big was happening.

Word has come to this writer that Elvis would like to try to get together with Scotty and Bill on a mutually satisfactory basis if he could be sure of just one thing— that they did not go to The Press-Scimitar with their story.

For the benefit of Elvis and whoever else might be interested —Scotty and Bill did not come to me with the story, altho many persons who feel aggrieved quite properly do so. I went to them. The story of their resignation was known in its general outline to me before I even knew Scotty and Bill had returned to Memphis. Because I know many people in music and because I have written about Elvis so much, it was natural that word of the matter would reach me.

Elvis can learn from Sam Phillips that I called Phillips at Sun Records and asked him where I could reach Scotty. I told Phillips: "I suppose you know what I want to talk to him about." Sam said: "Yes, I guess so. It's a shame."

Later I called Bill Black and put it to him point-blank. Bill said: "I haven't been making any secret of it. I've got to make a living somehow. No, we're not with Elvis any more."

I called Scotty. I told him I had this information, that it was just a questions of time until it became rather general knowledge, and that if I didn't write it some other reporter would.

Scotty and Bill did not bring their troubles to the paper.

Elvis graciously mended fences with Phillips, and Dewey continued to play Elvis's records on the air.

Teen-Agers Scream—Presley Bends

Backstage in Seattle

The Spokane Review   August 30, 1957

Elvis poses with a local fan club before the concert.

Well-Guarded Elvis Arrives 'Safe'

Elvis Presley and six of his "buddies" breezed into Spokane last night, "ready teddy" for a big show at Memorial stadium tonight.

They whisked through the Great Northern depot in a tight football-like formation much more suited to a crowd of hundreds than the 15 or 20 fans who turned out to get a close look at him.

At least two of the fans, Marge Street, 13, and her brother, Rick, 15, W2325 Dean, said they were disappointed.

"He doesn't look anything like he does on television," Marge said. "Only his hair. Guess they make him up to look different."

They couldn't break through the rock 'n' roll idol's convoy to get an autograph or to touch him but they seemed satisfied with just a look up close.

Presley said the train ride from

Memphis, Tenn. was "very enjoyable" and that he ate in the diner "just like regular folks."

"We had some nice crowds along the way," he volunteered, wearing the characteristic smirk that never left his face from the time he stepped off the Empire Builder until he slipped into the limousine that took him to the Ridpath Hotel.

Asked on the run if he was ready for the big show at the stadium, he replied, "Yeah, ready. Ready teddy."

That was about all the conversation a reporter could get out of him. Presley was too busy slipping quickly but gently past a few female fans who approached him like a lost brother.

Just the same though three of them nailed him for autographs before he got into the car. When cornered, Presley signed gracefully but quickly.

His tour manager was on hand when Presley got off the train at the east end of the station. Two or three of his "buddies" got off first though to check the crowd and possibly plan strategy for the exodus from the station.

The singer with six "buddies" (the name he gave to friends and guards with him) crowded behind and beside him shoulder to shoulder, walked west for a block through the station and got into the car at Washington Street.

They said Presley travels by train because he has a fear of planes, brought on by a near crash when he was in a chartered plane and by the collision of two air liners over the Grand Canyon last year.

The show at the stadium starts at 8 tonight.

The Spokane Review   August 31, 1957

Presley Whips 12,000 Into Near-Hysteria

Any description of what happened last night at Memorial Stadium could be but a pale picture of an event that had to be seen to be believed.

Elvis Presley, his long hair flopping and his sequined gold jacket glittering in the pink footlights, sang 13 songs in the midst of a huge, solid bubble of sound.

It was an unreal atmosphere. On one side of the infield were about as many police officers as appear in New York's St. Patrick's Day parade. Behind them in the stands was a near-hysterical sounding crowd of more than 12,000. Mostly girls, a big percentage 14 and younger.

Ushers Helpless

On your other side, spotlighted and vibrating, was a young man who embodies more sheer animal magnetism than many of the "captive" audience—police, reporters, photographers, ushers, first-aid men—were able to believe had existed.

The crowd jammed the west stands, sitting in the aisles with a complete disregard for order—many of the standees ruefully displayed stubs for $3.50 seats to the helpless ushers. The seats had long since been filled and the crowd was so jammed in it was impossible to sort out individual rights.

During the first hour of the show, while Presley confronted a room filled with hostile reporters and radio men and with doe-eyed young women representing high school papers and the like, the crowd was average in its approbation.

Attitude Changes

But their attitude changed dramatically after Presley came on, trailing a group of dazed reporters and radio men who were immeasurably impressed with the way he handled himself under their sharp fire.

Presley, who talked with assurance despite giving the impression he was—in the vernacular of his follower—a Rube from Rubeville ("if you wanta see somebody make a idiot outta theirself, you should see me tryin' to stand still . . ."), took the crowd in the palm of his hand.

From the time he rode through a double line of police in a Cadillac until he left after a startling rendition of "Houn' Dog," flash bulbs bloomed like sunflowers in Kansas. White-sweatered arms swept in imitative circles and once, when he gave his famous thumb-twirling gesture, the stadium was a waving field of twirling thumbs.

Seemed To Have Fun

And all through it, twisting, bouncing, vibrating and at times sliding back and forth behind a guitar, was Presley. Often his face wore the sneer that his critics find so abhorrent. But mostly he looked like a 10-year-old who was having the time of his life—but a 10-year-old with the showmanship of a P. T. Barnum.

Presley's last song, "Houn' Dog," added enough sounds to the bubble to force grinning police-officers to throw their hands over their ears.

The sideburned singer climbed off the stage, dragging the microphone he had cuddled for more than 40 minutes, and crawled toward the crowd on his knees. It was impossible to hear him.

Nothing Out Of Line

City juvenile probation officer Robert Brumblay, who was sitting in the infield, had worried a little before Presley came on the stage. He wasn't sure what avenue the exuberance would take.

When it was all over, nothing out of line had happened. There has been an indication that a rush for the stage might be coming as Presley left, but master of ceremonies Harwood Hardin adroitly parried that.

About all the city could complain of was a few youngsters who were stealing soil from the stadium infield. Presley's feet had touched it.—G.H.

Onstage in Seattle

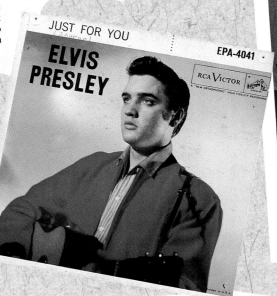

This EP album was released during Elvis's fall tour.

JUST FOR YOU
ELVIS PRESLEY
RCA VICTOR
EPA-4041
A "NEW ORTHOPHONIC" HIGH FIDELITY RECORDING

Elvis with the Jordanaires

—and the Stadium Shakes

Portland Teenagers Frenzied Over Elvis

A gold suit, an oft-plucked guitar and a sideburned bundle of the most enchanting, gyrating and just plain droolin' rock 'n' roll charmer ever to hit this world plopped right into the laps Monday of thousands of hysterical Portland teenagers.

How they loved it!

They jammed the Union station, the Multnomah hotel, the Multnomah stadium gateways. They thrilled to every word, every breath of the famed entertainer. Here was a haven in otherwise conservative life of studies, dishes and mowing the lawn.

Here was a miracle wrapped handsomely in a single package—a miracle wearing the exciting name of Elvis Presley.

THERE WERE many who at the end of the day were slightly frustrated, in some cases even disillusioned. Some of these were among the 500 first jubilant and later disappointed Presley fans who crowded Union station at 4:30 p.m. Monday for a glimpse—oh, please, just a glimpse—of the man. Others were included in the hundreds who blocked the front entrance of the Multnomah hotel where the man of the hour was to while away several of his Portland hours only to later discover that clever agents had smuggled him through the side door, unobserved by teenage eyes.

At the station he escaped the crowd by edging quickly from the last car on the train to a waiting convertible. Scarcely more than 15 fans not among the official party were able to reach the scene before the auto made its fast exit. Meanwhile, those 500

Presleyites at the station slowly grew aware of the disappearing act.

IN THE eighth-floor governor's suite at the hotel he stayed with 12 troupe headliners, eating and making merry over the sounds of Presley records. No unauthorized persons were allowed near the floor, and the few diehards who did slip by advance guards were halted and quickly ushered from the area by an efficient squad of policemen. Presley's three security officers and cleaning women.

Then at 8 p.m., on to the stadium, where again he bypassed scores of you-know-who expecting their idol to travel down the ramp into the stadium. No sir. Instead, he jumped from a cab at the head of the Multnomah Athletic club, adjacent to the stadium, where he met with newsmen and photographers in a half-hour press conference.

Numerous winners of local disc jockey shows posed with him following the conference. Everywhere, photographers' shutters clicked.

BUT BY NOW the stadium show was in progress, mellowing an estimated 14,000 persons. Band instrumentals, tapdancing, comedy routines, vocals and numbers by the four Jordanaires all brought polite applause from a crowd still thirsting for Mr. Elvis.

And he didn't disappoint. Not this time. It was 10 p.m. on the nose. The second act started with a rambunctious vibraphone player setting the pace. It was zero hour. . . .

Crooning a more mellow tune

A crowd of 14,000 people came to see Elvis rock Portland, Oregon.

In Vancouver, Elvis worked the crowd into such a frenzy...

...that a mob rushed the stage, girls' dresses were torn from their bodies, and fights broke out between teens and police.

Elvis Fans Fight Police In Wild Vancouver Show

VANCOUVER. Sept. 3, (CP)— The Province, in three articles spread across two inside pages, today bitterly criticized a Saturday night concert here by Elvis Presley.

Feature writer Ben Metcalfe said: "A gang moved into our town to exploit 22,000 pre-conditioned adolescents, hired OUR policemen to stop anybody who wanted to get too close, then left with the loot and let the police and the kids fight it out for what was left—nothing."

Entertainment editor Les Wedman wrote: "It was planned artificiality at its best, and gullible and truly worshipful Elvis Presley fans bit."

Policemen, ushers at Empire Stadium and air cadets could not hold the first mob which rushed the stage.

"The kids moved back. A girl, her dress torn, was carried screaming in very real hysteria off the field," Metcalfe said. "Presley came forward, winking gleefully at his cronies, and started it again.

"This time the kids met the full force of the law and the ushers while Presley urged them on from the stage.

"Girls were punched. Lifted bodily back into the heaving mass. Their escorts, teenagers like themselves, threatened the police and cadets. One bulky youth, his nose spurting blood, was hurt til he screamed.

"On stage, Presley winked again for his cronies to move into another wiggling song. It was obvious that he was enjoying himself."

Wedman estimated the night's take at between $30,000 and $40,000 and Presley, who appeared for an hour, received close to $20,000.

Memphis Press-Scimitar   September 21, 1957

Elvis Is 'Shocked' At Musicians Quitting

But He Goes Ahead Auditioning To Get Replacements on Team

A Message to the Musicians

An open message from Elvis Presley to Bill Black and Scotty Moore, the musicians who quit him last week after being with him since before stardom:

"Scotty, I hope you fellows have good luck. I will give you fellows good recommendations. If you had come to me, we would have worked things out. I would have always taken care of you.

"But you went to the papers and tried to make me look bad, instead of coming to me so we could work things out. All I can say to you is 'good luck.'"

By Bill E. Burk,
Press-Scimitar Staff Writer

Even tho he had been warned that some of his group might quit, Elvis Presley said in Memphis last night that he was "shocked" when the two registered letters came to him in Hollywood announcing the resignations of Bill Black and Scotty Moore, musicians who had been with him since before his sudden rise to the top began.

"The news of their quitting me came as a shock," Elvis told this reporter in an interview at his home at Graceland. "It is a mystery to me why they didn't come to me and ask for more money," he said. "They never did, believe me they didn't."

"We've had our problems before—even some arguments—but we always settled them," he continued. "Every time they ever came to me and asked for something, they got it, no matter what. Had they come to me, we would have worked it out and they would have got more money."

Elvis said he had an idea that some outsiders (he didn't know who) had made offers to the boys. He said he talked with Scotty after receiving the letter of resignation and Scotty admitted to him that he had other offers.

"They expressed to the paper their respect and admiration for me," Elvis said. "If they had that much, why didn't they come to me instead of going to the paper?" Again he repeated that neither of them had ever come to him asking for more money.

In his conversation with Scotty, Elvis said he offered to give him $150 a week while working (representing a $50 a week increase), but that Scotty told him it would take that, plus a sizable sum to get him out of debt.

Elvis said, "Scotty said that I said the more money I made the more he and Black would make. I have a good memory and I don't remember ever telling them that."

Elvis told of the many times he had gone to bat for the boys: ". . . I've been paying them $100 each and every week. People thought I was crazy for doing this. There are a lot of good musicians around. I could have picked a new group every week, but no, I wanted Scotty and Bill."

Elvis said their resignations came at a crucial time. He plays the Tupelo Fair (which he called "my homecoming"), Sept. 27. He said he just received the date of his next tour, which will be in October at a spot not yet named. And then it's back to Hollywood for work on two more films.

Elvis said he would immediately begin auditioning for a new guitar and bass player during the two weeks before the Tupelo Fair. "It might take a while," he said, "but it's not impossible to find replacements."

In Sept. 1957, Bill and Scotty quit Elvis's band.

That's Scotty under the RCA dog in the background.

Musician Denies Elvis' Statement

By ELTON WHISENHUNT
Press-Scimitar Staff Writer

Scotty Moore, Elvis Presley's guitar player, said today no one had hired him and bass player Bill Black "out from under Elvis." Moore also denied the rock 'n' roll king's statement that "they never asked me for a raise—if they had they would have got it."

Moore said numerous times in the last 18 months he and Black had asked Presley for more money. They were not requests for salary increases as such, Moore said, but money from the gate receipts on shows they played.

October 29, 1957

Elvis Wriggles, Fans Scream at Pan-Pacific

The screams were fairly audible two blocks away from the Pan-Pacific Auditorium last night.

They were anticipating Elvis Presley, who hadn't left his hotel room at that moment. However, even a mental suggestion of his name seemed to wring a sustained, almost frightening screech from the 9000 teenagers who had jammed the hall to hear their idol . . .

Press Conference

One hour before he was to go before this pulsing mob of an audience, Elvis was whisked into a hot back room of the auditorium for a press conference.

'What's your emotional power over women?' demanded one obviously influenced female reporter.

'Gosh . . .' replied Elvis, whispering something inaudible into a mike provided for the occasion.

'Read this!' snapped another reporter, shoving a magazine article into Elvis' hands. It was an article supposedly by Frank Sinatra attacking the institution of rock 'n' roll music.

'I admire the man, he has a right to his own opinions,' carefully replied the black-shirted Elvis.

'That's all you have to say?'

'You can't knock success,' said Elvis. How much money is he making?

Over a million a year, he's not sure of the exact figures.

All in all, he was a pleasant, mild-mannered person who might have been any other 22-year-old young man, were it not for the high gleaming pompadour, the rhinestone belt, the gold evening jacket. He was quiet, polite, somewhat shy and made sure to sprinkle in plenty of 'sirs' when he answered newsmen. Perhaps it was rehearsed that way, who can say for sure . . .

. . . He sang for 50 minutes, offering 18 of his biggest hits, from 'Heartbreak Hotel' to 'Jailhouse Rock' and no one could have possibly understood a word. Partly it was the constant shriek, partly the frightfully poor audio system.

Musically speaking, it was not the music that sold them. It was his hips. They wiggled, they bumped, they twisted. 'I don't sing,' he had said earlier, 'I yell.' Last night, he yelled and his army of faithful yelled back. With the flashbulbs and spotlights it was exactly like a battlefield.

'It's doggone crazy,' said Elvis, 'but it's worth it. After all, you can't knock success.'

The L.A. police called Elvis's opening-night show lewd . . .

First Presley L.A. Gigs, Oct. 28-29 At Pan Pacific

Elvis Presley will play his first L.A. dates Oct. 28-29 in a two-night performance at Pan Pacific Auditorium. Concerts are being promoted by Lee Gordon, who previously had booked Presley through a series of mid-western stands after an agreement for Presley to trek to Australia had fallen through because of other commitments.

Presley will solo for the second half of the show. His manager, Col. Tom Parker, now is setting acts for the first half of the bill. House will be scaled from $2.75 to $3.75, with all seats reserved.

Meanwhile, Metro will world-preem its Elvis Presley starrer, *Jailhouse Rock,* in rock 'n' roller's hometown, Memphis, next Thursday.

. . . So he had to tone it down.

L.A. Police Order Presley 'Clean Up' His Pan-Pac Show

"Clean it up and tone it down."

That was the crisp order issued by L.A. police last night prior to the second and last Elvis Presley performance at the Pan-Pacific Auditorium. [This] came on the heels of the opening night performance which provided a chilling picture of Presley's impact on adolescent minds. Many sources flatly labeled the show "lewd," police reported. Others described it as the "most disgusting and most frightening" show they had seen.

However, city officials said that while the show probably was in "questionable taste," it did not violate any obscenity laws and no action was planned. But Deputy Chief Richard Simmons ordered his vice squad to give Presley strict orders that the alleged sexy stuff be cut.

Following last night's performance, Presley left immediately for his home in Memphis, for a two-month vacation before reporting back to Hollywood in January for another film assignment. He has just completed *Jailhouse Rock* for Metro and the film goes into release next month.

KING ELVIS
ON THE "JAILHOUSE ROCK" MOVIE SET

This single was #1 for 7 weeks.

King Elvis stars in M-G-M's dramatic new story with music, an Avon Production directed by Richard Thorpe and produced by Pandro S. Berman. Co-starring is the late Judy Tyler, with Mickey Shaughnessy, Dean Jones and Jennifer Holden. Guy Trosper wrote the terrific screen play . . . and it turns out to be Elvis Presley's greatest picture. King Elvis sings six hit songs that will meet with your approval.

During the filming of this great M-G-M production . . . the candid photographs on this and the next two following pages were taken for your Hep Cats magazine.

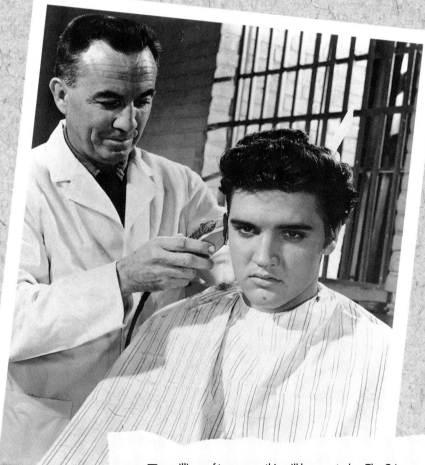

Fans flipped when Elvis's character got his hair cut.

For millions of teenagers this will be counted as The Crime Of The Century. Wars may come and peace may go . . . but his fans believed that Elvis Presley's sideburns and mane were here to stay. But how wrong were the fans! As these pictures prove conclusively. For the sake of his rock 'n' rolling art (and a substantial salary), Presley's locks have been shorn for M-G-M's *Jailhouse Rock.*

The film? A dramatic story set to music. And there's plenty of drama in the expressions on Presley's face as the hair falls from his head. At first: laughing-devil-may-care. Then: realization sinks in. Last: MISERY. Scene of the crime was M-G-M Studios. And the name of the demon barber, the villain of the piece: actor Jack Lorenz. **BURT RAINER**

An EP album

JAILHOUSE ROCK ELVIS PRESLEY

Jailhouse Rock
Young and Beautiful
I Want To Be Free
Don't Leave Me Now
Baby I Don't Care

Elvis with Judy Tyler

This photograph was taken before the tragic death of Judy Tyler in a car accident. She is seen with Elvis Presley and blonde Jennifer Holden, between scenes of M-G-M's Jailhouse Rock. Judy starred in a Broadway show, Pipe Dream, before getting her role with Elvis Presley. Jennifer hails from Chicago and makes her screen debut in the film.

Memphis Commercial Appeal

Presley Weeps Upon Learning Starlet In New Movie Killed

By TED SMITH

Pretty Hollywood starlet Judy Tyler, co-star of Elvis Presley in *Jailhouse Rock,* was killed late Wednesday in a Wyoming traffic crash that took two other lives.

Her identity was established yesterday.

When Elvis heard the news at his home in Whitehaven he turned to Vernon Presley and said, "Daddy, I have to go to the funeral."

Then tears came.

"She was at the peak of success," Elvis said. "Nothing has hurt me as bad in my life."

Miss Tyler and her husband of 10 months, Gregory Lafayette, were on their way to New York when the two-car crash occurred near Billy the Kid, Wyoming.

Starlet Killed Outright

The starlet was killed outright in the grinding crash. Her body was severed by the impact. Her husband died early yesterday of chest injuries. The other victim was Donald D. Jones, 23, of Hanna, Wyo. A companion in his car was injured.

Officers said the Lafayette car apparently swung into the lane of oncoming traffic to avoid hitting a car pulling onto the highway from a tourist shop.

Shooting on *Jailhouse Rock* ended only last week in Hollywood. Metro-Goldwyn-Mayer studios said both Miss Tyler and her husband were 24.

"I remember the last night I saw them," Elvis said. "They were leaving on a trip. Even remember what she was wearing."

'Can't See Movie'

Elvis said Miss Tyler and her husband were saving money from the movie so they could take a trip around the world.

"All of us boys really loved that girl," the famous singer said. "She meant a lot to all of us. I don't believe I can stand to see the movie we made together now, just don't believe I can."

The starlet's body will be sent to New York tomorrow for funeral services. No time has been announced.

Elvis said he will attend the services even if it means missing the premiere of *Loving You,* which is scheduled to open at the Strand Tuesday.

'Jailhouse Rock' Opens With Presley Starred

Rock 'n' roll was given a back-handed slap last night when *Jailhouse Rock*, starring Elvis Presley, opened.

Why a popular teen-age idol like Presley and the contemporary musical rage of rock 'n' roll must be associated and identified with crime, greed, profanity, vulgarity and brutality is beyond imagination.

If Screenwriter Guy Trosper, Producer Pandro S. Berman and MGM want to capitalize on the tremendous popularity of Presley, more power to them; if they want to wax rich on teen-age dollars, none can object. However, it would seem to be wise to do something FOR the rock 'n' rollers and not something TO them.

Vicious Character

The kids flock to see and hear Presley sing. Yet in this picture the leading character plays a vicious, rude and unpleasant individual.

Presley portrays a kid with a temper who goes to prison on a manslaughter charge for beating a man to death with his hands. His cellmate teaches Presley what he knows about singing and when the boy quits prison, wiser yet more bitter, he determines to become famous as soon as possible.

Not Realistic

However, it is hard to accept this story of a repentant soul told in words of realism. It is hardly realistic for one to make $1,000,000 being a heel and then be sorry for it.

Judy Tyler is costarred with Presley and the cast features Mickey Shaughnessy, Dean Jones and Jennifer Holden. Richard Thorpe directed. . . .

Lobby cards

Elvis plays Vince Everett, who accidentally kills a man in a fight.

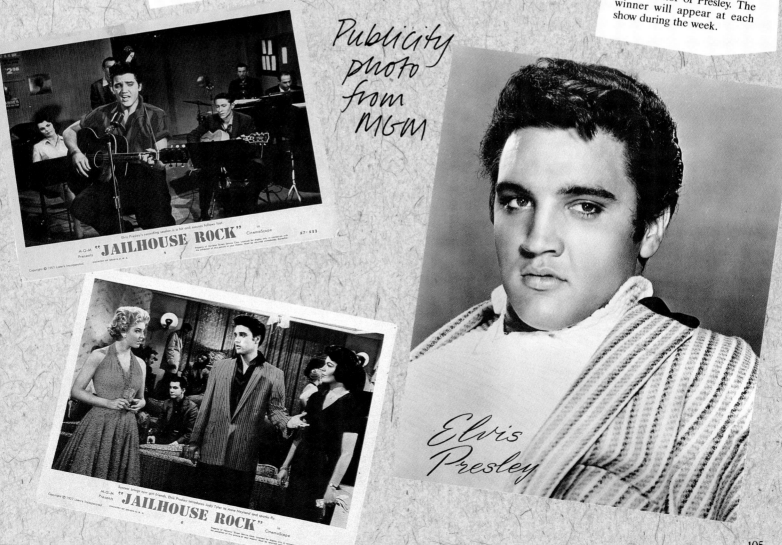

Presley 'Rocks' Cap Right Off His Tooth

Elvis Presley entered Cedars of Lebanon yesterday afternoon after swallowing a cap off one of his teeth. It became imbedded close to a lung.

Following surgery, the singer is in good condition and is expected to return to work shortly in *Jailhouse Rock* at Metro.

'Jailhouse Rock' Opens First Run

Elvis Presley portrays an ex-jailbird who becomes a recording star after he is released from prison in his new MGM picture, *Jailhouse Rock*, opening today at the State, New Fox, Capitol, UA Pasadena, Fox Beverly, Paradise, Cornell and 10 drive-ins.

Appearing on stage at the State only, starting today, will be the winner of the Betty Yeakel TV show contest to find Southern California's best impersonator of Presley. The winner will appear at each show during the week.

WHO is Jennifer? What is she? Jennifer Holden was an unknown. But now she's in the swim in Hollywood—because of this lucky break! It's her first film role and here she is, playing opposite Elvis Presley—NO LESS—in his newest picture, *Jailhouse Rock*. She's the envy of a million girls!

Publicity photo from MGM

M-G-M Presents "JAILHOUSE ROCK" in CinemaScope

M-G-M Presents "JAILHOUSE ROCK" in CinemaScope

Elvis Presley

Presley gets better and better

JAILHOUSE ROCK   ★★★

For Presley addicts there's only one thing you need to know. Here's Elvis: go to it! But for the rest of you there's a glimmer of hope, too—the boy actually improves on acquaintance. This is the third round in the Presley screen barrage. And certainly it's the liveliest so far.

As to his singing, it's still a case of either you do or you don't go for it—and, if you don't, this film won't make you change your mind. But as a personality Presley finds the right sort of niche here.

Instead of the darling of *Loving You*, it's a rough, tough, get-up-and-go type of Presley who even manages to have a sense of humor about that awesome subject—the Elvis hair-cut!

As a sharpie from the wrong side of the tracks with a lethal way with his fists, Presley is sent to jail for accidental manslaughter.

In prison, he meets a broken-down hillbilly singer (Mickey Shaughnessy) who gets him interested in the guitar and show business through a prison TV show.

Released from prison, Presley tries to break into show business, but at first manages only to break a couple of belligerent jaws, until a helpful publicity girl (Judy Tyler) takes him in hand. Then comes the big-time and with-it Presley grows a big head.

It's a slick, entertaining job of film-making that starts out better than it finishes. Judy Tyler—alas, recently killed in a car crash—is a charming heroine. And, as usual, Mickey Shaughnessy is a tower of strength.

While Presley may not be everyone's idea of a favorite star, at least now he looks like a performer with a screen future.

Vince Everett . . . . Elvis Presley
Peggy Van Alden . . . . Judy Tyler
Hunk Houghton . . . Mickey Shaughnessy
Mr. Shores . . . . Vaughan Taylor
Sherry Wilson . . . . Jennifer Holden
Teddie Talbot . . . . Dean Jones
Laurie Jackson . . . . Anne Neyland

Metro-Goldwyn-Mayer-Avon. American. CinemaScope. "A." 97 Minutes. Producer: Pandro S. Berman. Director: Richard Thorpe. Photographed by Robert Bronner. Music Supervision: Jess Alexander. Screenplay: Guy Trosper. Release: Feb. 17.

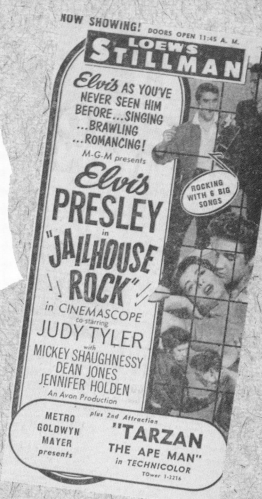

Elvis choreographed the "Jailhouse Rock" number himself.

106

Newspaper ads

— NOW —
ELVIS PRESLEY IS BACK!

7 PRESLEY HITS!

MGM
Jailhouse Rock

Judy Tyler In CinemaScope An Avon Production

PLUS — 2nd FEATURE

TODAY THROUGH NEXT WED.

ROXY

Eve. Shows 7 p.m. and 9 Continuous

Millions of New Fans for **Elvis Presley**

THIS PICTURE PACKS A PUNCH!

7 NEW SONGS
Jailhouse Rock
Treat Me Nice
Young and Beautiful
I Wanna Be Free
Don't Leave Me Now
Baby, I Don't Care
One More Day

in His First Big Dramatic Singing Role!

M-G-M — **Jailhouse Rock**

In CinemaScope An Avon Production

Sheilah Graham In Hollywood

'Jailhouse Rock' Is Gold Brick to Elvis

HOLLYWOOD, Nov. 21.—Elvis Presley stands to make $2,500,000 as his share of *Jailhouse Rock*, currently a smash hit throughout the country. Elvis was paid $250,000 plus 50 percent of everything taken in above the cost of the picture—which was $1,000,000. The box-office take is tabbed at $6,000,000—approximately a dollar for each Presley wiggle.

French poster

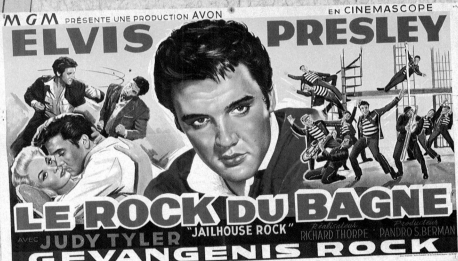

MGM PRÉSENTE UNE PRODUCTION AVON   EN CINEMASCOPE

ELVIS PRESLEY

LE ROCK DU BAGNE

AVEC **JUDY TYLER**   *"JAILHOUSE ROCK"*   Réalisateur **RICHARD THORPE**   Producteur **PANDRO S. BERMAN**

GEVANGENIS ROCK

"Jailhouse Rock"

(MGM)   CinemaScope   96 Min.

Cast: Elvis Presley, Judy Tyler, Mickey Shaughnessy, Vaughan Taylor, Jennifer Holden, Dean Jones, Anne Neyland.

Credits: An Avon Prod.; Produced by Pandro S. Berman; Directed by Richard Thorpe; Screenplay by Guy Trosper; Based on a story by Ned Young.

Elvis Presley fans should have a field day with this musical melodrama showcasing their boy. The CinemaScope camera seldom leaves his ever-movin' person as he romps through six songs, becomes involved with three girls, throws several punches, has his sideburns and long hair shorn, displays his bare chest, gets tangled up in a big dance production number and performs countless other acts that have endeared him to his followers in the past. The barely discernible story-line traces the fall and rise of Presley from his jailhouse days to Hollywood.

Serving a prison stretch for an accidental murder, Elvis takes up singing and shortly after his release is on his way to stardom, on records, radio, TV, in clubs and finally in the movies. Embittered, heartless, mercenary, short-tempered, yet somehow sympathetic, Presley is reformed at the end and wins his loyal lady. To be sure, there are a few others in the cast, notably the late Judy Tyler, as his business partner who loses her head over the heel, and Mickey Shaughnessy as a cynical convict. Given some particularly colloquial dialogue, Presley seems to be right at home in the part. Teenagers who like their Elvis all shook up will find much to cheer about here, and the picture should gross accordingly.

lookin' lean and mean

To Play Or Not To Play Is '?'

HOLLYWOOD—To play or not to play Elvis Presley's Christmas package—that seemed to be the puzzler for disk jockeys last week.

Portland, Ore., disk jockey Al Priddy, KEX, chose to air Presley's "White Christmas" and promptly got fired for it. Station management had banned the playing of the wax, averring that the "treatment of the song was in extremely poor taste."

Conversely, Dick Whittinghill, KMPC, Los Angeles, answered a request to play the Presley album, with "No, I won't play it. That's like having Tempest Storm (stripper) give Christmas gifts to my kids."

Elvis cuts a few more tunes for RCA.

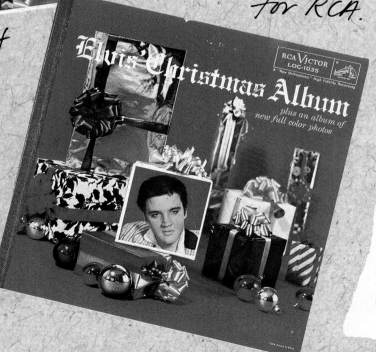

Many thought it was sacrilegious for Elvis to record Christmas carols.

ANTI-PRESLEY JOCKS ATTENTION: Young Mary Ellen Cantor of Pennsylvania in an "open letter to any disk jockey who ever criticized an Elvis Presley record" writes: "I think it's a shame, that Pat Boone can make a rock and roll record out of a spiritual ('Wonderful Time Up There') and hardly anyone, including disk jockeys, think anything of it. I bet if Presley made that same record half of the deejays wouldn't play it, or else it would be banned by their stations. If any deejay reading this has an answer to why Presley gets criticized and Boone doesn't, I think it would be only fair to Presley fans to know the reason."

'I Want to Go Where I Can Do the Best Job for the Army,' Says Elvis

Elvis in the army— oh no!

Memphis Press-Scimitar

Army, Navy Recruiters Make Offers to Elvis

Competition Spurred by Reports Singer's Draft Status is 'Hot'

By ROBERT JOHNSON AND THOMAS N. PAPPAS
Press-Scimitar Staff Writers

The Army and Navy were close on Elvis Presley's heels today.

Reason: The news that his draft status is "hot."

There were indications Elvis might be wearing one of Uncle Sam's uniforms by next month.

Nobody was flatly stating anything about Elvis' draft status—Army, Navy or draft board.

Elvis was classified 1-A a year ago, took his pre-induction exams and passed last Jan. 4.

He has been on the "wait and see" list since.

Elvis is 22. He will be 23 on January 8.

It is this age group that is most vulnerable in the draft: Both Army and Navy recruiters have made efforts to contact Elvis this week.

Both want him to enlist, not wait for the draft.

Army, Navy Make Offers

The Navy has this to offer:

An "Elvis Presley Company" to train together.

The Army offers this:

A two-year enlistment with a 120-day deferment which would give Elvis time to complete his new picture, *Sing You Sinners*, which starts shooting on location Jan. 20 in New Orleans.

Elvis' draft board No. 86, would give out no information today on his draft status.

The board said no information is given out on any registrant.

But this much is certain:

Elvis has been 1-A for a year.

He has asked for no deferment, has simply said he's ready to go "when they want me."

That time may be soon.

Memphis Press-Scimitar   December 12, 1957

'What's the Fuss About?' Elvis Asks as Fans Cry

Draft Notice Comes, Girl Moans: 'I Never Thought It'd Happen'

BY JAMES F. PAGE, JR.   *Press-Scimitar Staff Writer*

"Dream," sang Elvis, "dream when you're feelin' blue . . ."

"Does that draft notice make you blue?" someone cracked.

"Who—me?" grinned E. P.

And that's the way it is with Uncle Sam's new prospective soldier—"ready to go—glad it's now"—at 22.

It was early this morning at Graceland, and Elvis plus buddies were ready for bed after a night on the town—maybe one of his last for awhile.

"I don't know what all the fuss is about," he said, running a comb thru his hair. "I'm just a guy who makes music—no different from anybody else."

But to millions of teen-agers he is different—something special.

They proved it while Elvis was at the movie.

"I feel like crying," said one girl, and she wasn't alone.

Fans began to crowd their hero's front gate early—and they stayed late.

He Won't Sing Until Presley Wears Khaki

HOLLYWOOD—(AP)— Singer Johnny Desmond has become so busy as a straight dramatic actor that he seldom sings any more except for recordings.

"I'm waiting for Elvis Presley to be drafted," he said. "Presley's draft notice is the greatest thing that ever happened to the music business. Once he's in the army, then the rest of the rock 'n' roll fad will disappear."

December 27, 1957

Elvis Given 60-Day Draft Deferment

MEMPHIS, Tenn., Dec. 27 (INS) —Singer Elvis Presley received a 60-day draft deferment today because of movie-making commitments.

Milton Bowers, chairman of the 23-year-old Presley's draft board, said it had been unanimously decided to allow the delay so his Hollywood studio could complete a picture already arranged.

The studio had asked for an eight-week extension, claiming that it would lose approximately $300,000 if Elvis reported for induction on Jan. 20, as scheduled.

The draft board refused the Hollywood request but said the rock-and-roll singer would have to ask for the additional time himself. He thereupon wrote, "Not on my behalf, but so these folks will not lose so much money with everything they have done so far."

Presley claimed from the start that he wanted no special favors for himself. He had said, "I'll go where they want me, when they want me."

"Postman, Postman, don't be slow— be like Elvis, and...

GO MAN GO!"

Am I The Girl for Elvis?

I'M 18 YEARS OLD and I'd make a perfect wife for Elvis. I have good muscles so I could fight off girls that tried to take him. Please tell him my telephone number and he can call collect!

Tessie Cass, Timberton, Mich.

I DON'T KNOW if you would like to get stuck with me. I am 15 and well-developed. My measurements are 36-21-35. Have big blue eyes, pretty lips, like yours.

Patti Coplen, San Francisco, Cal.

I'D DO FINE FOR ELVIS as a wife because I can't talk very well, but I know how to listen. I also know how to kiss. I've tried it on other boys—just getting in practice for him. I am 15, but old for my age.

Martha Reo, Chicago, Ill.

I HEARD ABOUT your romances—Nat Wood, Barbara Hearn, Dixie Locke, Debra Paget, etc. I counted 24 of them, El. I thought about it for a long time, a very long time. Then, just like God was talking to me, I realized it was a lie. You can't get married. You said so yourself. You can't even take a girl to the movies without the entire United States knowing about it. Elvis, you said you want a girl who believes in God as much as you do. I would like a husband who is tall, dark and handsome, who is something—not just a bum, a man who will treat me like a woman. I believe in God. I was confirmed a while back. If you were confirmed, you know how scared you were. Well, I was not scared very much because I believed God was with me. El, have faith in God. I know its lonesome at the top, but if you have a talk with God once in a while, you'll be O.K. God put you on this earth for a purpose, El, remember that.

JoAnn Weddington, Rocksprings, Tex.

I AM 19 YEARS OLD, five-feet-five, weigh 107, have brown hair and grey eyes. I've been married once before, and I've got a baby six months old. I hope it wouldn't make any difference to you. Nothing has ever gone right for me.

Pat Whitely, Woburn, Mass.

I HAVE AN ELVIS SCARF, Elvis pins, Elvis shoes, an Elvis sweater, Elvis hat and all of his records. All I need now is Elvis himself. I even had my hair cut in a boyish bob and I have Elvis sideburns.

Bobbyjean Saxon, Seattle, Wash.

I HAVE A VERY SPECIAL REASON why I am interested in Elvis. And it is far different from the other millions of girls across the country. But I'll not try voodoo. I have read some girls have. I'll just keep my trust in God. And if it is His will, someday I'll meet him. If I were you, Elvis, I'd put her through a test and find out whether it's you yourself she loves. Something like this should do this trick. Tell her you invested your money and lost it.

Carol Kurt, Decatur, Alabama

ALL MY FRIENDS tell me I look just as much like Elvis as a girl possibly could. I think I do, too. I even wriggle like he does. Now if Elvis married me, we would be sure to have children that looked like him. That way, there would always be an Elvis Presley.

Jean Goshner, Charleston, S.C.

I BAKE GOOD SHOOFLY pie and cook spareribs and sauerkraut, too. I can play the organ and am learning to play the guitar which means I could play while Elvis sings so he wouldn't get so tired. I have saved my money and have $24.87 which I would give to Elvis if he married me. He could buy me a wedding ring with it and keep the rest for himself. I think he would like a girl so thrifty.

Mamie Diefendorfer, Quakertown, Pa.

JUST TELL ELVIS I dig that wedding bells rumble and he'll know I'm the one gal he's tuned to.

Elva Parsley (real name!)
Hopkins, Tenn.

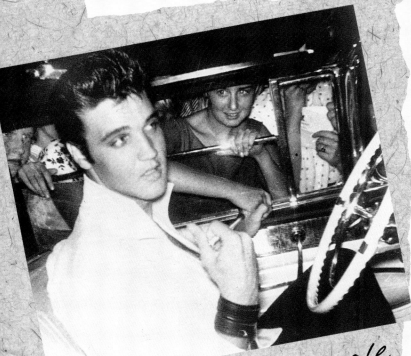

Elvis was always considerate of his fans, and they repaid him with intense loyalty.

The ELVIS THEY DIG Fan Club Publication

PLANET EL ★

discovered by A. Hand on the night of 15th August, 1959

THE COVER drawing was done by Geoffrey W. Gibson, of 29 Kerry Drive, Smalley, Derbyshire, and illustrates his impression of a typical scene on Planet El.

Actually, little is known about the Planet, so should any readers have any further information, it would be greatly appreciated if they would pass this on to me.

Certain facts that are definitely confirmed are that El first appeared in 1956, and has since proved to be the greatest body in the Universe. It is surrounded by golden disc-like rings, which tend to increase about every two months. Its atmosphere is electrifying, and every activity shoots out at least a million shocks, and in one instance six million has been recorded.

When El first appeared, it was thought by many experts to be just another comet that would quickly fade and die, but the reverse has been the case. It shot from nowhere, and has in fact increased in stature and brilliance since that date. Since its appearance, many other stars have passed over El, temporarily dimming its greatness, but it now seems a certainty that it will never be eclipsed.

The Planet itself was thought at first to be made almost entirely of rock, with just a trace of gold dust in it, but since then it has shown it has many lush fields of different qualities, and gold deposits are very heavy. Many issues of El are argued on, but one thing every expert is agreed upon: El certainly has atmosphere.

It has been established for some time that life exists on the Planet. The inhabitants have peculiar guitar-shaped faces, are very nimble, and pass a considerable amount of spare time digging this, and digging that . . . but mainly digging El. Their chief industry is manufacturing juke boxes, guitars, and smelling salts for reviving personnel who receive "a message" (a term often used there).

The Elvisians are also very fond of animals. Teddy Bears, Hound Dogs and Cats are in great profusion. This, also, according to the wise professors who have studied the subject at length, is due to El's most electrifying atmosphere.

A. HAND

Jan Shepard,
Dolores Hart, Elvis,
Carolyn Jones,
and Lilliane
Montevecchi

HOW'S ELVIS AS SCREEN ROMEO?

Co-Star Says He's . . . er . . . Well . . .

The girl who got Elvis Presley's first screen kiss (not yet seen in Chicago) is a Chicago girl with a round face, big blue eyes and a level head.

How about that kiss? She had to take it from him. "It wasn't a love scene, really," recalled Dolores Hart, front runner for the wriggling guitarist's new movie, *King Creole.* "The only time we kiss is when I take the initiative."

* * *

HOW DOES ELVIS rate as a screen lover?

Dolores, sitting in a suite at the Ambassador East, squirmed slightly and dabbed at her nose. She caught a cold on this tour to whip up interest in the movie, which opens July 25 at the Chicago Theater.

"I don't know," she said, at which it was the turn of a press agent seated nearby to squirm slightly.

Dolores hastened to explain: "I never played a love scene with anyone else. But he must have done well, judging by the letters from people who saw preview showings."

* * *

WELL, SHE MUST have firm opinions, as the press agent said she would, about how Elvis might topple from their thrones such kings of the screen as Clark Gable, Gary Cooper and Errol Flynn?

"Oh, a person like Elvis, no matter what anyone says, deserves credit as a person of talent. There is no reason he shouldn't soar to the heights the kings occupy now," she said.

"But it's difficult to compare one actor with another, because an actor brings so much of himself to a role."

* * *

BUT SHE AND ELVIS never dated, she said, and as for making another movie with him, well—.

"An audience," she said, "gets tired of seeing the same two people teamed together."

Dolores used to live at 5830 N. Hermitage, where her grandparents, Esther and Fred Kude, still live. She attended St. Gregory's parochial school until her family moved west.

'I THINK OF HIM AS BIG SEXY POT'

French actress Lilianne Montevecchi is most outspoken on the subject of Elvis as a screen Romeo.

"I don't want to get too close to him," said Lilianne, who also plays opposite the hip-swinging singer in *King Creole.*

Here's her statement to reporters in New York recently:

"When they tell me I am to do picture with that man, I am devastated. I think of him only as the belly dancer, the big sexy pot."

"Then he comes to my dressing room and says to me, 'Why you no like me.' He is like little boy, very sweet. So I am nice to him, only I do not want to get too close."

"He is too much complexes, young spoiled."

goes to the movies

King Creole

PARAMOUNT, VISTAVISION

Elvis Presley does his strongest acting job so far, as a New Orleans kid who thinks you have to be tough to get ahead. His singing success finally entangles him with a gangster —and the gangster's girl (Carolyn Jones). But sweet Dolores Hart stands by. There's plenty of music as well as plot, the tempo shifting from folk song to rock to tender ballad. Elvis has given his fans a movie to remember him by during the coming two years.

European Fanzine

French film magazine

KING CREOLE, completed just before singer-actor Elvis Presley left for two years in the Army, is Elvis' best movie to date. It's an exciting story of a New Orleans high school boy who takes up singing as a career. Filmed against a backdrop of violence and crime, it gives Presley his chance at a more substantial dramatic role than he has had before, and he rises to the occasion. (Hal Wallis—Paramount)

Billy Competes With Presley

MELBOURNE (AP)—Billy Graham's evangelistic crusade had strong competition Saturday night from Elvis Presley's new movie King Creole, playing at a Melbourne theater.

Graham's service was devoted to "Bodgies and Widgies"— Australia's young hoodlums, distinguished by their purple trousers, and their girls, who wear short skirts. Only three turned up, at least in costume.

Young people thronged the open air Music Bowl, however, and more than 2,000 made "decisions for Christ" after Graham made his appeal in "bop" talk.

As they filed in, Graham said: "Crazy man, crazy—dad, you really blasted me this morning—you were really cool, dad, cool, I mean cool."

Director Michael Curtiz, producer Hal Wallis, and Elvis work through a scene.

Elvis and the Jordanaires chat with Dolores Hart.

'KING CREOLE'
Offers Elvis—Little Else

"King Creole"

Produced by Hal B. Wallis, directed by Michael Curtiz, from a novel *A Stone for Danny Fisher,* by Harold Robbins, released by Paramount Pictures, and presented in the Chicago Theater.

THE CAST

Danny Fisher	Elvis Presley
Ronnie	Carolyn Jones
Nellie	Dolores Hart
Mr. Fisher	Dean Jagger
"Forty" Nina	Lilianne Montevecchi
Maxie Fields	Walter Matthau
Mimi	Jan Shepard
Charlie LeGrand	Paul Stewart
Shark	Vic Morrow

This shoddily produced film offers Elvis Presley and little else.

The script is aimed at generating sympathy for the hero who is forced to live in a slum because his pappy lost everything after his mama died. He works after school in a night club, and while he's protecting a woman from the unwanted attentions of a customer, he gets in all kinds of trouble. Bad company leads him from the straight and narrow and there is plenty of violence plus a number of murders before it's all over. The action is, of course, well laced with Presley singing in his usual unintelligible fashion.

Customers were rather scarce on opening day but a group of girls tried to stir up some excitement with their senseless squealing every time their hero opened his mouth. This in turn evoked a couple of good-natured boos from a trio of young sailors who watched the proceedings disdainfully. Personally I was on the side of the navy.

KING CREOLE
PARAMOUNT, VISTAVISION

✔✔✔This'll hold 'em! As a temporary-farewell gesture, Elvis Presley not only proves he's still top man in the r 'n' r field—he shows rapidly acquired extra poise as an actor. Full of rhythm and action, Elvis' best picture so far casts him as a boy with a grudge. Because his ineffectual father (Dean Jagger) can't hold a job, Elvis has to work part-time in a lowdown New Orleans night club. A teenage gang tempts him toward petty crime; but, after he's flunked his senior high-school year, a singing career comes his way by chance. Even this involves him with the underworld, in the persons of racketeer Walter Matthau and Carolyn Jones, Matthau's mistreated girl. On the sunny side is Elvis' romance with Dolores Hart, his *Loving You* leading lady. A fuzzy moral outlook and an excess of plot twists hamper the film, but the music's the thing. With the opening number, Elvis hints at a big future beyond rock 'n' roll. ADULT

Lobby cards

Carolyn Jones Femme Lead in 'King Creole'

Carolyn Jones, who won an Academy Award nomination for her performance in *The Bachelor Party,* has another demanding role in Hal Wallis' new Elvis Presley production, *King Creole.*

Carolyn, who is being described by critics as a "young Bette Davis," has the role of Ronnie, the racketeer's girl who befriends Presley, a New Orleans singer, in the musical dramatization of Harold Robbins' best-seller, *A Stone for Danny Fisher.*

Kissing Carolyn!

Movie poster

Rockin' onstage Dixieland-style

Newspaper ad

TV STAR ANNUAL

He's traded stardom for a soldier's stripes, leaves behind his golden records and one slam-bang movie.

KING CREOLE is Elvis's last Paramount release; he was given an extension on his draft notice to complete it. Elvis himself was too modest to request this; his bosses, who knew how many people's incomes depended on the picture, asked for the delay. With Dolores Hart, Carolyn Jones and a bevy of other beauties, he delivers the most telling love scenes of his career. He's just as hard-hitting in the rough-and-tumble action; to delight his fans, there are ten songs . . .

. . . How about marriage? Of course that's part of Elvis' long-range plan but he's in no hurry. Quick vacation trip to Hawaii just before his induction gave him a taste for travel. He'll tour Europe when he can get time off from German army base, will probably see a lot more of the world (and the world's girls) before he settles down. Just about the most eligible bachelor in the entertainment spotlight, he's 6' tall, weighs 175, turned 23 last January 8. Who's his best girl today? His mom.

A NEW, EXCITING ELVIS PRESLEY EMERGES IN DRAMA-WITH-MUSIC FILM, 'KING CREOLE'

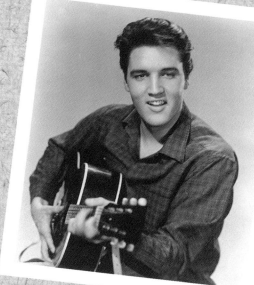

Since a certain entertainer took leave of his fans to serve his country, the lyrics of the Army song, at least in his outfit, have probably undergone a change to: "The caissons go rock-'n'-rolling along." On the civilian front the millions of fans soldier Elvis Presley left behind can take heart from the news that Paramount is now releasing the last picture the star made prior to his induction, Hal Wallis' exciting drama-with-music, *King Creole*.

King Creole represents a big first for Presley in that it marks the singing star's premier plunge into big-league acting, for in this film the nation's rock-'n'-roll idol assays a James Dean-Marlon Brando type of role. And what's more, he does it to the tune of a musical score of thirteen hits.

Co-starred in *King Creole*, most of which was filmed in the colorful and exciting French Quarter of New Orleans, are Carolyn Jones (who won an Academy Award nomination for *The Bachelor Party*), Walter Matthau, Dolores Hart, Dean Jagger and Vic Morrow, with top featured roles filled by shapely Lilianne Montevecchi and Paul Stewart. The film, based on *A Stone for Danny Fisher*, tells the tense and emotional story of hard-loving, hard-hitting Danny, who sang his way up from the gutters of lusty, brawling New Orleans against tremendous odds.

Elvis as Danny Fisher

KING CREOLE ★★★

Two years ago, Presley on the screen was a laughing stock. But nobody's laughing now. After that abysmal beginning—in *Love Me Tender*—the boy goes from length to strength. And this film hits the perfect formula for Elvis. That isn't to say it's a perfect film—far from it: just that it's perfect for Presley.

The setting is the steamy, sleazy tough quarter of New Orleans, in which the indolent intensity of Presley seems right at home.

And to match the atmosphere, the production is fast-paced, vicious, with a beat as insistent as the most vigorous rock 'n' roll.

The producer, Hal Wallis, has surrounded his star with players—notably Carolyn Jones, Dean Jagger, Paul Stewart—some of whose excellence and experience can't fail to rub off on Presley.

The grimy plot has him as a disgruntled teenager, who flunks his graduation and gets mixed up with thugs, racketeers and a good-hearted bad girl (Carolyn Jones). Inevitably, nightclub manager Paul Stewart discovers Presley has a voice: and naturally the customers go for it.

His down-at-heel father (Dean Jagger) disapproves and not even the love of a good woman (Dolores Hart) can prevent Presley from getting deep in trouble with a sadistic gang leader (Walter Matthau).

The story's hokum, but it's put over with a knowing air and acted with spirit; while a couple of the songs are better-than-average Presley. With this kind of backing there seems no reason why, after his army stint, he shouldn't become the big screen personality I thought he couldn't be.

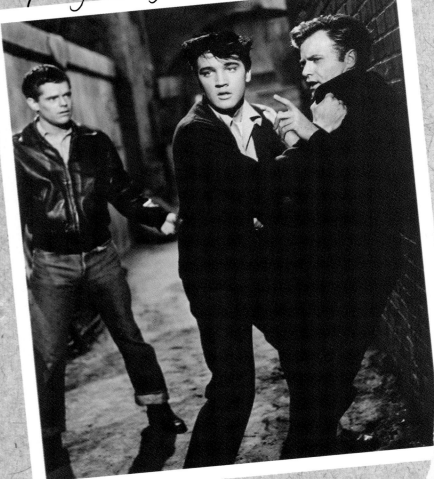

Danny roughs up "shark", played by Vic Morrow.

Danny Fisher	ELVIS PRESLEY
Ronnie	CAROLYN JONES
Nellie	DOLORES HART
Mr. Fisher	DEAN JAGGER
"Forty" Nina	LILIANNE MONTEVECCHI
Maxie Fields	WALTER MATTHAU
Mimi Fisher	JAN SHEPARD
Charlie	PAUL STEWART
Shark	VIC MORROW
Sal	BRIAN HUTTON

Paramount American. "A." 116 minutes. Producer: Hal Wallis. Director: Michael Curtiz. Photographed by Russell Harlan. Screenplay: Herbert B. Baker and Michael Vincente Gazzo. From a novel, *A Stone For Danny Fisher*, By Harold Robbins. Release: September 21.

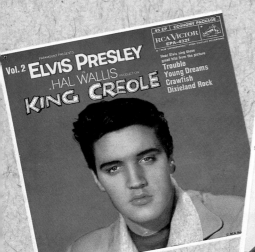

Soundtrack EP albums

Sheet music

Elvis records the soundtrack for King Creole. Of the 11 songs in the film "Hard Headed Woman" achieved the most recognition.

117

'Heartbreak Hotel' . . . 'Blue Suede Shoes' . . . 'Hound Dog' . . . 'Rip It Up' . . . 'All Shook Up' . . . and now 'Jailhouse Rock.' Hit follows hit . . .

But how long can Presley keep it up?

The unprecedented success of Elvis Presley's latest disc, "Jailhouse Rock," seems to have quieted the cynics once and for all. Or has it? Certainly no new-comer to the record field could have had a stormier passage from critics and disc jockeys when Presley first burst upon us during the early part of 1956.

Remember that record? Of course you do. It was "Heartbreak Hotel" and, though it seems so long ago now, it only appears that way through the fabulous succession of hit discs that Presley has since sent our way.

If America wishes to boast of "flying platters" they can claim a whole armada of them with Presley at the helm, long before their now much-publicized "Explorer!"

Through all of Presley's earlier successes the cry has continually been from the cynics, "He'll never last." But having taken stock of the Presley legend I am beginning to see that most of our original thoughts were made in haste.

The record buyer continued to prove us wrong, but even in the face of fantastic disc sales we didn't retreat from our original outbursts too quickly.

It's possible, of course, that we weren't quite prepared for this Elvis bombardment. After all, he can claim to be the forerunner of the current vogue. Since then we have had a host of imitators. Mostly very bad copies, as copies usually prove themselves to be.

It is mainly these also-rans that have demonstrated to us quite forcibly that Elvis has his own special brand of vocal excitement to transmit to us on wax.

This excitement is, of course, more easily understood by the younger generation, and there's no doubt that through his discs he provides a means of "letting off steam . . ."

• FILM FUTURE IS ASSURED

Now more recently, the film *Jailhouse Rock* has caught the imagination and Presley's future in the film field is assured.

All along the line he is proving that he has got the talent that few people were prepared to consider when his first discs came our way.

The big point is, however, that not only is Elvis proving his own lasting powers, but he is constantly dispelling all thoughts that rock is a dying musical style. Just when there seems to be an abatement—so Presley comes bursting back with a bigger and better example.

In the States, his popularity still commands high figures at the box office. He is still the biggest money-spinner that country has seen in show-business for many a long year.

Right now Elvis has a new issue in America with the simple title "Don't." Presumably everyone has ignored his statement, for they have flocked in their thousands to purchase this newest release. So much so, the disc has already jumped from nowhere to No. 40 in the American charts.

• HE HAS DONE IT AGAIN

Following the usual formula, it would seem that when "Don't" eventually arrives on the British music scene—Do, for it looks as if the lad has done it again.

Soon Elvis will be called upon to do his American service time. Have no fear, his record company RCA is stockpiling future discs, so that the supply will never run dry whilst he is doing his bit.

One thing is certain, Private Presley will be one of the wealthiest soldiers ever to serve in the American army.

His record royalties will continue to pour in whilst he is serving, and no doubt he will still find time to do the odd concert somewhere in his travels.

No one will deny him any of this. He has proved his point as an entertainer. He has shown that he can act, and most of all has amply proved that he can give the customer what he (and she) wants disc-wise.

Elvis '58

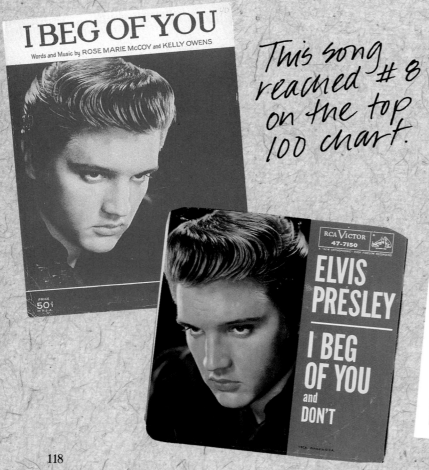

This song reached #8 on the top 100 chart.

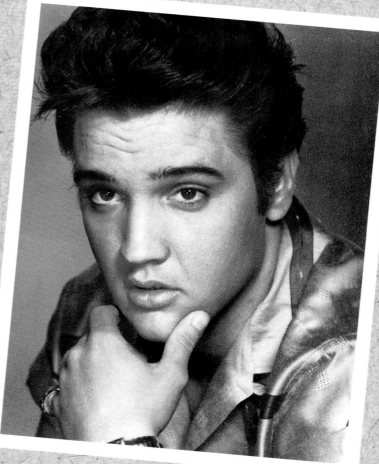

Elvis Presley received a Pops-Rite Popstar award, for being the star of the pictures selling the most popcorn in 1956-57, from Jim Blevins, Mayor of Popcorn Village, near Nashville, Tenn., recently. The award was for the star's contribution to the popcorn industry after a poll was made by movie theatres. The award was made in Memphis a few hours before Presley was inducted into the United States Army.

Before his army induction, Elvis spends time with his parents.

Dolores and Valerie Kiss Elvis good-bye.

ELVIS GETS THE STANDARD HOLLYWOOD FAREWELL

Houn' dog Presley left his blue suede shoes behind when he left for his Memphis home last night. He carried a prop blunderbuss to the commissary party at Paramount Studio, where he just finished his last movie before his Army draft call. Dolores Hart kisses him good-bye and Valerie Allen waits her turn.

DRAFT BOARD HAS HEADACHE, NAMED ELVIS

The draft board here used to be a rather quiet place. That, of course, was before Elvis Presley was drafted.

Since then—especially after the rock and roll idol was granted an eight week deferment to complete a movie—letters have poured in.

And Milton Bowers, Sr., board chairman, is "fed to the teeth" with the outcries of those who think Elvis is the greatest, and those who think he is the least.

Others More Important

"With all due respect to Elvis, who's a nice boy, we've drafted people who are far, far more important than he is," said Bowers. "After all, when you take him out of the entertainment business what have you got left? A truck driver.

"One woman in a letter yesterday called us a bunch of damn southern goons. Well, she's the one who's a goon.

"I talk Elvis Presley more than I sleep. A crackpot called me out of bed last night and complained that we didn't put Beethoven in the army.

Put Ike in Army, Too

"Considering that Beethoven was not an American and has been dead for some time, I suppose he felt we were discriminating against rock and roll music.

"I told him we put Mr. Eisenhower in the army and that ought to count for something. Then I asked him how old he was and he told me he was 52. I asked him how he got so stupid in 52 years."

Army Days

1958 - 1960

"You can treat Presley like any other soldier. He never asked for one special preference. He went along with the Boys. He is a fine lad".

— First Sgt. Daniel S. Brunetti

March 19, 1958

Army Sharpens Shears for Elvis
'Operation Haircut' Is On

FORT CHAFFEE, Ark., March 19 (UP)—The Army assured Elvis Presley fans today that their hero's debut as a soldier will be fully publicized from blood tests to haircut.

The change from blue suede shoes to combat boots will be as fully documented as any other historical event.

Realistically admitting Pvt. Presley won't be "just another GI," the public information office here is preparing for his arrival on March 24 or 25 with enthusiasm usually reserved for approaching command inspections.

But "Operation Haircut" won't be the production one would expect. It seems Elvis accepted the inevitable and had his luxuriant growth sheared last week at his home in Memphis. His sideburns are gone.

However, the usual Army haircut and other induction ritual will be covered by the press.

Capt. Arlie Metheny, public information office, said yesterday a press center for visiting newsmen, photographers and television crews is being established.

"We got loads of letters from girls," Metheny said, "who wanted us to save them a lock of Elvis' hair when he gets a GI haircut.

"I hated to disappoint them, but we couldn't do it," he said.

"I issued a statement saying the hair will go in the trash with all the rest."

Operation Haircut!

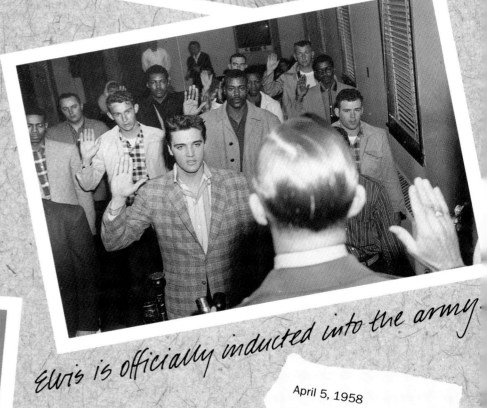

Elvis is officially inducted into the army.

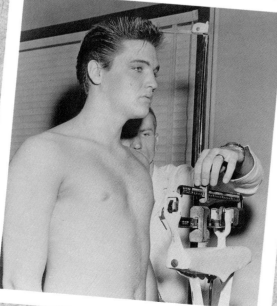

Every step of the process was photographed.

April 5, 1958

ELVIS' TRESSES FALL VICTIM TO ARMY BARBERS

Fort Hood, Tex., April 5 (AP)—Rock 'n' roller Elvis Presley is wearing the same crew cut as others in his company, an information officer said today.

Capt. R. L. Kingsbury said one trainee shaved his head completely on his own volition but the others, looking like "peas in a pod," wore the crew cuts they got before being sent here.

The captain said the army is "leaning over backward to accord Presley the same treatment as the others." In private life, Elvis wore curly locks and long sideburns.

Just another soldier

Serial number US 53310761

Memphis Commercial Appeal, March 25, 1958

Pvt. Elvis Begins Army Life In Sentry-Guarded Barracks

Rock and Roll King Attempts To Be Good Soldier Despite Hordes Of Photographers, Newsmen And Squealing Greeters At Fort Chaffee

by LOUIS SILVER staff writer

FORT CHAFFEE, Ark., March 25 (Tuesday) Pvt. Elvis Presley slept early Tuesday morning in an Army barricade guarded by a pair of gentries armed with automatic carbines.

From Elvis' military performance thus far, there was little likelihood they were there to keep him in—but rather to keep others out of his new home. Despite sleepiness and . . . a horde of newsmen which has dogged his first day in service, he is making every attempt to be a good soldier.

Elvis in Command

He and the 20 other inductees from Memphis—with Elvis in command—arrived here by bus at 11:25 p.m. Monday. As the bus rolled to a halt 10 screaming, squealing youngsters greeted the rock and roller as if he were already a military hero.

They were children of the military men on this post. Their actions were, to be mild, extreme. Guards finally shooed them away.

The new GI's were lined up in their first formation. An enduring corporal—ordered around ceaselessly by photographers, finally got them issued bedding and two towels.

They were marched—with Elvis performing in a military manner—to renovated World War II Wooden barracks. Each was assigned a built-in closet and cabinet—in place of the foot lockers known to millions of earlier draftees.

The patient corporal explained the Army method of making a bed. Presley repeated it, only to find it torn up by photographers who wanted him to do it all over.

Guards At Entrance

Then the guards were posted at the entrance, although the newsmen were not ordered out. The guards were less than enthusiastic over their unusual duty.

When the traditional First Call is blown at 5:30 Tuesday morning Elvis will have 15 minutes to make his first reveille formation.

Then it will be a fast round of classification tests, lectures, a $7 partial pay and haircuts for those who need them. Elvis does and knows it.

Uniforms come Wednesday—along with inoculations.

Monday, in Memphis, Elvis was placed in charge of the new inductees and volunteers by Maj. Elbert Turner, commander of the Armed Forces Examining Station at Kennedy Veterans Hospital.

Elvis, smiled, waved and saluted as he boarded the bus . . . leaving for the Arkansas camp near Fort Smith—where he will spend the next three days being processed.

Sorry, Gals, Elvis Gets No Leave

MEMPHIS, Tenn., July 29 (AP)— Sorry, girls, but it'll probably be a long time before you see Elvis Presley again.

The Army plans to send the rock 'n' roll idol directly to Germany—with no leave time en route.

The Memphis Press-Scimitar learned that today in a telephone chat with a public information officer at Fort Hood, Tex., where Elvis is stationed.

Lt. Col. Marjorie Schulten, a WAC officer, said:

"The program which Pvt. Presley is training under does not provide for leave time off upon completion. He'll be on orders for his next assignment the day he completes his training— probably the first week in September."

The Memphis singer is undergoing 14 weeks of advanced training at Fort Hood. He entered the Army last March.

Elvis at Ft. Hood

Boot camp

ELVIS BOARDS TROOPSHIP, HEADS FOR GERMANY

Carrying his duffel bag up gangplank, Pvt. Elvis Presley boards transport which yesterday sailed for Bremerhaven, Germany, where it is scheduled to arrive Oct. 1. Army says singer will be assigned as a tank crewman with unit at Friedberg. Presley said he hopes to meet Actress Brigitte Bardot.

D. 63   Elvis Presley

An Elvis bubblegum card commemorates his army service.

PVT. PRESLEY'S SCHEDULED FOR GERMAN DUTY

Fort Hood, Tex., May 27 (AP)— Pvt. Elvis Presley will leave here after Sept. 20 for military duty in Germany. That was the official word today from this central Texas fort which trains crewmen and teams.

Presley will finish basic training Saturday and will go into advanced training at Fort Hood after a two week leave. After eight weeks of advanced training as a tank crewman he will undergo six weeks of basic unit training. This creates the tank team. He will then be sent to New York to board ship for Germany.

Promotion? That can't come, a Fort Hood spokesman said, before July 28. At that time Elvis will become private 2. That's equal to buck private in the old army.

Memphis Commercial Appeal August 15, 1958

New Fame Failed To Change Elvis' Love For His Mother

By THOMAS MICHAEL

Many things changed for Elvis Presley after the millions started rolling in too fast to count and the adulation became such that thousands came from far off just to see from a distance the house he lived in.

Probably the thing that changed least of all was his relationship with his mother, who died yesterday.

In his almost incredible wealth and fame of recent years he was a dutiful and loving son to Mrs. Gladys Presley, just as he had been in the poor and obscure years of his early youth.

As the bright new star of the entertainment world, he gave her a mansion to live in and many gifts. But the instant and respectful attention he gave her when she spoke to him seemed more nearly the true mark of his affection.

Her Tasks Were Simple

It was plain that Elvis would have liked to have lavished upon his mother all the things he could so easily afford—diamonds, mink coats, fancy cars, clothes from Paris, travel. But her tastes never ran that way. He did send or bring her a gift whenever he left home.

Once he sent her a large collection of expensive hats. She kept a few and gave the rest away to friends.

One gift to her was a pink Cadillac. She delighted in it, but clearly because it was a gift from her son, and not because it was big and expensive. She used it little.

The best gift Elvis could give his mother was his time, of which he came to have less and less as he came to have more and more money and fame. In this he was as generous as his panting public would let him be. He nearly always rushed home at the end of an engagement.

Worried By Letters

Mrs. Presley didn't like her son to fly. It worried her. So he traveled by train or car—except once when he wanted to spend an extra night at home before returning to his Army base in Texas, and again when he flew home Monday after getting an emergency leave because of his mother's last illness.

Mrs. Presley worried too about the crank letters; her son got many threatening him with death for "taking my girl away from me". But these were [usually] kept from her, as were most of the printed accusations that Elvis' act was vulgar.

PRESLEY'S MOTHER DIES AT 42

MEMPHIS, TENN.—(UPI)—Mrs. Gladys Presley, 42, mother of singer Elvis Presley, died of an apparent heart attack Thursday only a short while after reporting she felt "so much better."

Presley, on a seven-day emergency furlough granted when his mother's liver ailment grew more serious earlier this week, was reported grief-stricken.

Mrs. Presley's husband, Vernon, was at her bedside in a local hospital when she died. Elvis who was asleep at his $100,000 suburban mansion "Graceland," arrived shortly after his mother's doctor had pronounced her dead.

* * *

THE SINGER, now as Army private stationed at Ft. Hood, Tex., was deeply attached to his mother. Friends said much of his devotion probably was a result of his twin brother's death at birth.

In achieving fame and wealth as a rock and roll entertainer, Elvis made good a promise made to his mother when the father was working as a Mississippi sharecropper and later when Elvis was driving a truck.

* * *

During her son's rise in the entertainment world, Mrs. Presley said very little in public, letting Elvis and her husband answer the questions of newsmen and the curious.

When the family moved from a $40,000 home in Memphis to the mansion, she commented. "I think I am going to like this new home. We will have a lot more privacy and a lot more room to put some of the things we have accumulated over the last few years."

Elvis's heart was broken when Gladys died on Aug 14, 1958.

What he is, she made him. He'll never forget her, and he'll never be quite the same as he was before. These were Elvis's hours of tenderness—and torment.

Pvt. Presley answers his private mail... from you

An English fanzine devoted entirely to Elvis

PHOTOPLAY
THE WORLD'S TOP FILM MAGAZINE

FANS' STAR LIBRARY 10D
No 13
EXCITING GLAMOUR PHOTOS
ELVIS in the army

Elvis reads about himself.

DEAR ELVIS:
DO YOU MIND IF GIRLS CALL YOU? DO YOU EXPECT TO DATE MUCH WHILE YOU'RE IN THE ARMY? WHERE DO YOU LIKE TO TAKE YOUR GIRLS AND DO YOU SEND THEM FLOWERS?

Dusty Towers
Washington, D.C.

I'm pleased when girls call me ... and flattered. Yes, I hope to meet lots of new girls while I'm in service. It will be a long, long time before I'm a civilian again—and naturally I love all pretty girls. When they come running at me, I want to run to them—not away from them. I'm a great movie fan. I like to go to the movies with my dates. The flower bit? No, I don't send flowers to a girl unless she dies. I'm kidding, I send flowers if they are sick or if it's their birthday.

ELVIS:
I'M HEARTBROKEN. I HEARD YOU'RE LOOKING FORWARD TO BEING SHIPPED OVERSEAS BECAUSE FOREIGN GIRLS TREAT THEIR MEN MUCH BETTER THAN AMERICAN GIRLS DO!

Jenny Lincoln
Lordsburg, New Mexico

Honey, you heard wrong. American girls suit me just fine.

DEAR ELVIS:
WHY DO YOU ALWAYS TAKE BEAUTIFUL GIRLS TO MEMPHIS TO MEET YOUR FOLKS WHEN YOU HAVE NO INTENTION OF MARRYING THESE GIRLS?

N.W.
San Francisco

My folks always like to know my friends and the girls I date ... and I like them to.

DEAR PRIVATE PRESLEY:
MY DADDY TELLS ME THE ARMY IS GOING TO MAKE IT REAL HARD FOR YOU BECAUSE YOU ARE FAMOUS. DADDY SERVED WITH GLENN FORD IN THE MARINES AND SAYS MR. FORD WAS KEPT ON LATRINE DUTY AND ASSIGNED OTHER DIFFICULT JOBS TO PROVE HE WAS NOT PRIVILEGED. ARE THEY TREATING YOU BAD? IF THEY ARE, I'LL FIX THEM GOOD.

Elinore Stevens
Los Angeles, California

In the Army, I'm just another trainee, just another guy. Sure I did KP, stood guard, went through combat training in the field, made the fifteen-mile hike with sixty-five pounds on my back—but so did all the other fellows. The officers are strict but fair. They have a job to do and won't stand for nonsense. And I'm flexible. I expected to conform. I've never been accustomed to things real easy. If I make it hard, the only one it's going to be hard on is me. I certainly don't mind hard work. I've done plenty of it before this. I worked as a laborer, up at three every morning, working in a defense plant. When I was in high school I'd get out at 3:30 and be on the job at 6:30 for $12.50 a week ushering. And I'd be up at dawn every morning to complete my homework. This is nothing to me. I can always make out.

DEAR ELVIS:
PLEASE TELL ME—ARE YOU HAPPY, REALLY HAPPY IN THE ARMY? ARE THE REST OF THE FELLOWS FRIENDLY? DO YOU GET HOMESICK MUCH?

Cynthia Goldstein
New York City

I like the Army and I like the fellows just fine. Nope—the guys haven't needled me about my career. Only time they seem conscious of it is in the evenings when they drop into the barracks to get autographs for their sisters or friends. About getting homesick—there's been so much to learn and to that few of us have had the time to get homesick after a day filled with climbing mountains, hopping fences, shooting at targets, etc. I had looked forward to going into the Army as a new experience. And it sure has been, I miss my buddies back home and my friends, but you can't go through life depending on friends. You have to depend on yourself. And you learn to do that in the Army.

Out of uniform—Elvis in Germany, 1959

The first book to be published about Elvis

A MUST FOR EVERY ELVIS FAN!

130
35¢

the ELVIS PRESLEY story

Edited by JAMES GREGORY
Editor of MOVIELAND and TV TIME
With an Introduction by DICK CLARK

32 PAGES OF PHOTOS PLUS A FULL-PAGE PINUP OF ELVIS IN COLOR
A NEVER-BEFORE-PUBLISHED
THE WHOLE STORY OF ELVIS

YEARLY "POP POLL" CHAMPS: Patti, Ricky, Everlys!

TEEN
JUNE 1958
25¢

D'JEVER EAT A HOAGIE?
Flick Stars Try New Food Fun Fads

TOMMY STEELE
England's Answer To U.S. Rock 'n Rollers

WILL THE ARMY CHANGE...

ELVIS?

'A Perfect Gentleman All The Time':
Dating Elvis Thrills Girl, 16

By Serge Fliegers

WEISBADEN, Germany, March 1 —"He's the greatest" is the way 16-year-old Priscilla Beaulieu expresses her feelings about her latest steady date—a sergeant named Presley.

Elvis admitted Tuesday he'd been "seeing quite a lot of" the bouncy, curved daughter of Air Force Capt. Joseph P. Beaulieu, from Austin, Tex. now stationed at headquarters of the United States Air Force, Europe.

"He's been a perfect gentleman all the time I've known him," Priscilla trilled. "He doesn't drink, doesn't smoke and doesn't even use bad words like some other boys do.

"I never dreamed this could happen to me. Of course, I've been a Presley fan for years. What teen-ager isn't? I saw all his films and bought all his records."

Presley, stationed with the Third Armored Division in this town 25 miles from Frankfurt, carried out the last of his Army duties today. He leaves by plane for the United States tomorrow for discharge and a return to his million-dollar stage career.

Elvis signs autographs for his German fans.

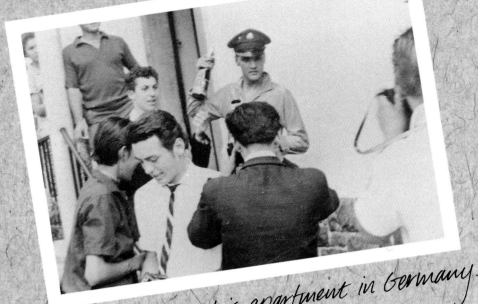

Elvis celebrates near his apartment in Germany.

A fan's photo of Elvis, 1959

Elvis Presley's Pocket Biography

VITAL STATISTICS
Real Name: Elvis Aron Presley
Birth Date: January 8, 1935
Birth Place: Tupelo, Mississippi
Height: 6' 1"
Weight: 180 pounds
Hair: Brown
Eyes: Blue
Chest: 40"
Waist: 32"
Hips: 41"

FAMILY
Mother: Gladys Love Presley, formerly a nurse's aide, now deceased
Father: Vernon Elvis Presley, formerly a tenant farmer, carpenter, truck driver, factory worker
Brothers: A twin, Jesse Garon, who died at birth
Sisters: None

RELIGIOUS BACKGROUND
As a child he attended services at the Fundamentalist Assembly of God with his parents. He now feels believing in God is more important than going to church.

SCHOOL DAYS
He graduated from L. C. Humes High School in Memphis. His teachers there report he was a good student, rather quiet, but did well in most of his studies and managed to get by in the others. His fellow students assessed him with this prediction in their year book: "Elvis Presley—Most Likely To Succeed. Haw! Haw!" (Were they ever wrong.)

JOBS BEFORE SINGING
He first earned about $8 a week mowing lawns. While in high school he made $14 a week as a movie house usher, also worked in a furniture factory. After high school he drove an electrical supply truck for $40 a week, later worked a full eight-hour shift at a tool company making artillery shells.

HIS FIRST RECORD
"That's All Right, Mama" backed by "Blue Moon of Kentucky" on the Sun label.

IDIOSYNCRASIES
He gains weight easily, prefers to eat one or two meals a day instead of three.
He dreads being alone.
He likes flashy clothes.
He likes teddy bears.

FAVORITE BRAND OF CIGARETTES
He doesn't smoke.

FAVORITE DRINK
He likes soft drinks, no liquor.

FAVORITE FOODS
Pork chops, brown gravy, apple pie, vegetable soup, beans, fried potatoes, ketchup, corn pone.

FAVORITE COLORS
Pink and black

GREATEST AMBITION
He wants to be a great actor.

HIS ONLY VICE
Nail-biting

STRONGEST VIRTUE
Loyalty—to friends and fans

SADDEST MOMENT
His mother's death on August 14, 1958

FAVORITE SINGER
Pat Boone

HIS CURRENT MAIL
About 80,000 letters a week

CURRENT ADDRESS
Private Elvis Presley
Third Armored Division
A.P.O. 39
c/o Postmaster
New York City

Elvis trades his guitar for an accordian.

Elvis on furlough in Paris, June 1959

Parisian shoeshine

A fan's-eye view of ELVIS PRESLEY at a famous Parisian night club

"**My** daughter and niece will be so disappointed that Elvis isn't coming tonight," said Zoe Gail to me as we sat at a stage-side table in the fabulous Lido Club, Paris, in July.

At the word "Elvis" I gave a start. "You mean Elvis Presley," I said. Miss Gail, the singer-actress who was famous in Britain for introducing the wartime song "I'm Gonna Get Lit Up When The Lights Go On In London," nodded quite casually.

"He was here last night and we thought he would be back tonight," she continued. She is of course, the wife of Bert Bernard, one of the miming Bernard Brothers, who are the stars of the Lido show.

She went on to explain that her young daughter and niece had been allowed to wait up late in the hope of seeing Elvis, and further explained that Elvis had flown for a weekend in Paris from Frankfurt and had been sitting at the very table we were at the night before.

This information threw me and my American cousin, Jerome Sirt, of Chicago. We didn't know whether to believe it or not, but I must admit that I got rather excited at the prospect of Mr. Rock 'n' Roll himself coming to the Lido.

There are two different shows each night at this famous night club. After the first one Bert Bernard came to the table and told his wife and the young girls that Elvis had phoned and said he would be in for the second show.

When we heard this news I must admit that we were as excited as the girls were.

And sure enough, just after the second show commenced, in came Elvis smartly dressed in his Army uniform and accompanied by a couple of his Servicemen pals. Very quietly and unobtrusively they sat down at the table next to ours—no more than a couple of feet away!

I found it really difficult to be calm and although the show was a superb spectacle, I was more interested in how Elvis was enjoying it.

In a little while a girl joined Presley's party and Elvis greeted her very politely, but extremely inconspicuously so that he would not take anyone's attention from the show.

During the performance he was only troubled to sign an autograph, which he did quickly and politely.

When the show finished and the lights went up, however, the news soon got around that Elvis was present. He was quickly surrounded by eager fans and autograph hunters, who, I am glad to say, were level-headed and well behaved, except for one girl who was slightly overcome by it all . . .

Soft drink

Elvis won further favour in my estimation by the fact that he must have been the only person in the vast packed room that night who didn't touch a drop of alcohol of any kind. He ordered and sipped quietly a glass of tomato juice.

He didn't smoke, and at all times he looked and acted like a real gentleman. He called everybody "Sir" or "Ma'am" and was most humble, and throughout the evening there was no sign of showing off in any way.

He chatted to us as if we had known him personally all our lives. My cousin asked Elvis if he had ever played in Chicago and he replied that he had just done a one-night there, but hoped to go back after his [discharge from the Army.]

The question I wanted to ask Elvis was the one every British fan wants to ask—when he is coming to make his debut in Great Britain.

He laughed and said: "That remains to be seen. I certainly want to appear there before all those wonderful and kind people who have so consistently bought my records. Any time my manager, who looks after all my dates, says I am playing Britain then I'll be a mighty happy fellow."

Elvis says everything in a soft, Southern drawl, which is most pleasant to the ear and when you ask a question he listens intently and gives you an answer directly and sincerely. We talked together for a full ten minutes, but I was so excited inwardly that I must honestly confess that I cannot remember much of our conversation.

He autographed our programmes and I asked him if he would mind having his photograph taken with us.

129

Anita Wood waited for Elvis while he was in the army.

ANITA WOOD REVEALS—
WHY ELVIS AND I COULDN'T MARRY

"Oh, we can't get married now," Anita was telling the Memphis newspaperman. "We both have too much to do. With Elvis going to Germany and me really just getting started with my career, we're neither one ready to get married."

The question that prompted this reply came up after Elvis had returned to Fort Hood following a two-week furlough. He had about 13 long weeks more of specialized training in the Armored Division, then was leaving with his group for Europe. It seemed to most observers that Elvis had spent a lot of time with his beautiful, blonde honey, Anita Wood—enough time to make the Memphis reporter wonder whether they were planning a fast wedding ceremony before he shipped overseas. It was no secret they'd been together the last few hours of his leave without his friends or parents around. If they weren't planning an immediate marriage, were they perhaps arranging for her to visit him in Germany after he got there the last week of September?

Anita didn't hedge. "I'd love to go visit him in Germany if his family goes over, and Elvis says he's going to have them go over when he can. But I don't know! What would people say about me going to Germany, after all the rumors that started just because I went down to Texas to see him?

"Really, I saw very little of Elvis in Texas. He hardly ever got off the post. Luckily, I met these real wonderful people, Sgt. Bill Norwood and his wife, and they invited me to stay at their house on the post. But I still didn't see Elvis much —sometimes just for five minutes at a time. And we couldn't go anywhere, even on the post, without him being mobbed. Really, those boys were just as bad as the girls ever

are about Elvis. If he went into the PX or to the movies, they would mob him every time. About the only place we could go without a whole lot of people crowding around was one of the Snow Queen ice places at the edge of the post. I'm so proud of the way Elvis has done in the Army, though. Being made an acting assistant squad leader and winning those marksmanship medals and everything!"

"You mentioned your career before," the reporter continued. "Would it really come between you and Elvis?"

"Naturally we both just felt awful when I had to go to New York for my recording session just when he got home on furlough," Anita answered, "but we both knew it just had to be. When something like that comes along, you just have to go on and do it, and nobody knows that better than Elvis. But missing a whole week at home with him was awful. Of course I talked to him on the phone—to tell him I was going to be on the Jack Paar Show, and how my picture had been in two New York papers and about the songs the Am-Par people had for me to record—but it wasn't like being back in Memphis with him. I wanted to know what he was doing and be in on the fun. I heard he bought a brand-new red Continental convertible right after I left for New York and I was dying to see it. He had told me he was going to the Lincoln place but I didn't know if he was really going to buy something, or what kind.

As for the most important question, "Would they ever marry?" even Anita didn't seem to know the answer. "Well," she said slowly, "It's like we've both always said. Our careers come first. I guess we'll just have to wait and see what happens. How things work out, I mean."

Presley Wins Army Promotion

FRIEDBERG, Germany (AP) — Elvis Presley had a new job and a new stripe in the U.S. Army Wednesday — but no pay raise.

The singer was promoted to acting sergeant and squad leader in the 3rd Armored Division's 32nd Armor Scout Platoon.

Presley had been a scout jeep driver. The promotion does not mean a pay hike because it is only temporary. It does mean that Presley can sew a third stripe to the sleeves of his uniform and he has more responsibility. As acting sergeant he commands a three-man reconnaissance team.

French music magazine

Dutch magazine of radio & TV stars

Communists Call Elvis Presley American Weapon In Cold War

BERLIN (UPI) — Communists are complaining about a new American weapon in the cold war named Elvis Presley.

The Communist youth newspaper "Young World" Saturday called Elvis a "Weapon in the American psychological war to infect a part of the population with the philosophical outlook of inhumanity . . . to destroy everything that is beautiful . . . to prepare for war."

He's public enemy no. 1, the Communists said, and western intelligence agencies are using him to recruit youths with "nuclear political views . . . for provocations."

The Red attacks on the gyrating singer followed a rock 'n' riot, at Chemnitz in East Germany. A group of rock 'n' roll fans who call themselves "The Presley Band" started the ruckus.

Seventeen youths have been arrested and police are seeking other ringleaders in the riot, Young World said.

The riot began in a square called the Scholssteich when teen-agers who gather there each night tuned their portable radios in on western stations which play the Presley records.

The people's police descended on the teen-agers and tried to confiscate the radios. The youths resisted and at first overpowered the police but reinforcements arrived and the youths were subdued.

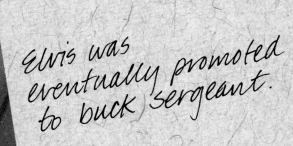

Elvis was eventually promoted to buck sergeant.

FAREWELL TO PRISCILLA. . .

Life, March 14, 1960

The Army's Sergeant Elvis comes back home to girls he left behind him

In a spectacular shift of power that critically exposed the flank of U.S. music lovers the Army returned US53310761 from Germany last week for mustering out at Fort Dix, N.J. Fans mobilized to fighting strength and tuned up their shrieks. Mimeographed directives sped from the Pentagon as the Army proudly staged a press conference. Elvis was back.

After his two-year hitch, twenty-five-year-old rock 'n' roll idol Elvis Presley wore a sergeant's chevrons but no sideburns. "If I say the Army made a man of me," he said, "it would give the impression I was an idiot before I was drafted. I wasn't exactly that."

Elvis was, in fact, a smart soldier. His agents back home had been pretty smart too, selling 20 million RCA Victor records to the jukebox set. These earned "The Pelvis" $1.3 million in addition to his $145.24 a month service pay. Elvis paid the U.S. 91% of the total in taxes, or enough to support about 150 of his fellow soldiers for a year.

Behind him at Ray Barracks near Friedberg, Elvis had left hordes of palpitating Frauleins and the pretty 16-year-old Priscilla Beaulieu, daughter of an Air Force captain stationed at Wiesbaden. Elvis kissed her before he flew to the aid of the girls back home, sorrowful at parting but anxious to get into his bright-colored pants and back to his hip-swinging singing.

Elvis waves goodbye to Priscilla Beaulieu.

Mister PRESLEY!

THE RETURN HOME recently of one of the county's most famous natives was almost a national event. Sgt. Elvis Presley flew home to the cheers of millions of fans, ready to resume his show business career after an enforced two-year hiatus in the Army.

After picking up his final paycheck of $109.54 at Fort Dix, N.J., Elvis hopped aboard a special railway car and headed for his sumptuous home in Memphis, Tenn. About 100 admirers were on hand to greet him, including teen-agers and gray-haired grandmas. Presley recommences his TV career May 12 when he will collect $125,000 for appearing on a Frank Sinatra special.

Elvis answers questions for the press before leaving Germany.

Final paycheck – $109.54

RCA's Waiting for Elvis to Call the Tune

By William A. Bruning

Memphis, Tenn., March 15— Elvis Presley apparently hasn't made up his mind about what his first record as a civilian will be.

But RCA Victor has made up its mind that the record will sell a million copies.

According to trade circles, the company has already assigned the record a number—7740—and set sales quotas for each of its major distributors.

Not only that, but RCA also has geared itself to ship 50 per cent of the million copies within 72 hours after the record is released.

In fact, the company is reported ready to press a fast second million after the first million is sold out.

Asked about these optimistic preparations, Presley indicated that he hasn't even caught his breath, much less figured out what to sing with it.

Since he got out of the Army last week, Elvis has been spending his time at Graceland, his suburban mansion, with various social trips to town. Sunday night he went to see "Holiday on Ice" in Memphis' Ellis Auditorium and spent most of his time backstage, mounting the elevated bandstand where he also wielded a lighted baton over the 17-piece band.

Later he signed autographs and photographs for members of the company. Still later, he invited everybody out to his house.

Before that, however, Elvis had left a mansion-full of company to go out and say hello to four specially selected youngsters who were among the hundreds waiting outside the Graceland gate.

One of them, Fletcher Davis, 16, said they drove out "just to look at Elvis's home."

Then one of Elvis' cousins, Wayne Presley, whom the four youngsters had met last summer, noticed them and told Elvis.

Travis Smith, Elvis' uncle and gate-keeper, called the four out of a line of 30 cars of sight-seers who had parked in front of Graceland.

"Elvis is a warm-hearted and thoughtful young man," Davis said. "He kissed the girls on the cheeks and they stood like rag dolls vowing they'd never wash their faces again. He shook hands and thanked us for coming to see him. We're all his fans."

Later, one of the Presleys explained that Elvis had done the favor because Davis and his companions were students at the Arkansas School for the Deaf.

133

Presley Home, Intends To Resume His Rockin' Role

FORT DIX, N.J. (UPI)—Sgt. Elvis Presley, setting foot on U.S. soil for the first time in 18 months Thursday, promptly vowed to stand by rock 'n' roll music as long as the public wants it.

"I will never abandon it as long as people keep appreciating it," Presley told a Hollywood-style news conference.

He arrived at this military base about 7:30 a.m. with 79 other GIs and their families after a flight from Frankfurt, Germany.

More than 200 persons, including several screaming teenagers, greeted Presley as he stepped off an Air Force transport in a snowstorm.

While newsmen and photographers delayed his run through the customs section, Presley said he had been "too nervous to sleep."

Later he held a news conference in a service club on the post.

It turned into a near-mob scene, with photographers pressing in for more and more pictures.

He posed with several female admirers and kissed them at the demand of the cameramen.

Hollywood added a touch of glamor to the scene. Nancy Sinatra, daughter of singer Frank Sinatra, and flame-haired actress Tina Louise were on hand.

Presley will appear on Sinatra's television show May 1.

Presley said his plans were to visit his home in Memphis and then to plunge into television and movie work.

Presley called his Army tour a "good experience," but said it left him little time for privacy.

He said he was glad it was over because he did not want military service "hanging over my head all my life."

Presley said he expected to do without the long sideburns of his pre-Army career.

He reiterated his desire to become an actor, but said that as long as people wanted it, he would never abandon rock 'n' roll singing, which brought him a million-dollar career.

"I will never take it on my own to change," he said. "It would be a foolish mistake. People tell you whether they like it or not."

Arriving at Ft. Dix, New Jersey to be discharged

Elvis prepares to return to Memphis.

Another press conference for the media

134

Elvis Is Back—SNAFU

By George McEvoy

Elvis Presley came home yesterday —Good Conduct Medal and all.

He hit McGuire Air Force base in a blinding snowstorm, and only historians will determine the greater impact. When his plane touched down at the New Jersey field at 7:30 a.m., a crowd of teen-age girls began caterwauling like so many demented banshees. There was a terrible moment of suspense as 79 other GIs and their families filed off the military transport. Then—HE appeared.

Elvis, with his sergeant's stripes, sharpshooter badge and the medal he won for being a very good boy, stood in the door of the plane for a moment and waved. The effect on the girls was electric. Then he strode quickly across the field until photographers and reporters surrounded him.

The first question they asked him was whether he was going to resume rock 'n' roll shouting or turn to music as a career.

"I will never abandon rock 'n' roll as long as people keep appreciating it," he drawled. **The bobby-soxers squealed that they appreciated it. Elvis smiled at them and they squealed again.**

Hollywood added glamour to the scene, if any was needed. Nancy Sinatra, whose father had a similar effect on young females some years ago, greeted Elvis and gave him two fancy shirts, gifts from Frankie.

Col. Tom Parker, Elvis' manager, was there with dollar signs in his eyes.

He said "l'il ole Elvis" will get $125,000 for a guest appearance on Frank Sinatra's TV show. Parker also said Elvis has seven motion pictures lined up and will earn nearly three-quarters of a million dollars in the next three years.

One fan on hand to greet Elvis was Mrs. Laura Driver, 19, who came from Brooklyn and waited in the storm for more than seven hours to greet her dream boy.

"He's just marvelous," she cooed. **"He's so dreamy. He's just a doll!"**

Then she added, "My husband, Morris, thinks I'm crazy."

Elvis finished his interview and left with the other soldiers for Ft. Dix, where he will be mustered out in about two days. In honor of his homecoming a radio station in Memphis, his hometown, will play nothing but Presley records for 24 hours.

Elvis was in Germany for most of his two-year Army hitch. It did seem quiet around here, didn't it?

ELVIS APPEARS IN UNDIES AT CAR WINDOW

Washington, March 6 (UPI)—Elvis Presley Sunday was rocking and rolling —by railroad this time— toward his Tennessee home for a rest.

The young teenage idol, discharged from the army Saturday after a two year hitch, spent Saturday night sleeping in a private railroad car parked in the Washington railroad station.

Col. Tom Parker, Presley's manager, refused requests by photographers for pictures of the singer. Just before the train pulled out Sunday morning, a curtain went up in the private car and there stood Presley—in his underwear.

Popular

Elvis To Rush 1st Disk

By Jack Karey

Without question, the major topic of discussion in the world of records is typified by the exclamation "Elvis is back!" Only time will tell what events will constitute the new chapters in the story of this showbiz phenomenon, but you can bank on the fact that practically his every turn will make news.

One of his very first moves, however, will be a rush recording session; very likely featuring civilian Presley performing a soft, sweet ballad on one side of the record, exhibiting a new mature mellowness—and on the other side, a red hot rock 'n' roll performance to prove that he hasn't lost any steam!

Elvis is set for plenty of activity in the year ahead. The exact tack his career will take is a matter of considerable conjecture. It's reasonably certain, however, that he'll make the most of any opportunity to turn serious actor.

But regardless of what the future holds, his army service certainly merited commendation. Sgt. Presley was no arrogant, free-loading, wild kid—he was a good soldier!

WHY DEBBIE MAY LOSE AT LOVE AGAIN

TV *and movie screen*
and Movie Screen

Elvis Presley's First Interview as a Civilian!

25¢

IS LIZ LIVING A LIE?

D HOLLYWOOD BREAK EDD BYRNES' HEART? Annette's Away f

PHOTOPLAY

why Liz had to leave the party so early

CONTEST win a "welcome home" DATE WITH ELVIS (see page 19)

MARCH 25¢

WHAT LIZ CAN TEACH YOU ABOUT MAKING LOVE

MOVIE STARS 25¢
TV CLOSE-UPS
APRIL

THE STRANGE MARRIAGE OF MICHAEL LANDON —can his wife compete with glamour?

BONUS ALBUM 50 STARS SIGN PIN-UPS FOR YOU plus handwriting analysis

WIN ELVIS' HOMECOMING GIFT

ELVIS PRESLEY

Movie Star
1960 - 1969

"I want to become a good actor, because you can't build a whole career on just singing. Look at Frank Sinatra. Until he added acting to singing he found himself slipping down hill."

— Elvis Presley

the KING of ROCK 'N' ROLL is DEAD

by MARY CULVER

IN SEPTEMBER, 1958, Elvis boarded the Navy transport ship—the U.S.S. Randall which was used in the U-I film, *Away All Boats*—to begin his Army stint in Germany. His departure was recorded by RCA Victor. The beginning of March, 1960, Elvis returned. His arrival was also recorded and will soon be available. But the Elvis who went away and the one who returned are very different people.

Elvis is older now. He celebrated his twenty-fifth birthday on January 8th. He has been under the rigorous discipline of the Army, and he is a serious man now.

When Elvis spoke to the press that September day in 1958, just before he walked up the gangplank, he was asked if he had a message for his fans. Elvis said, "Yes, I do. Tell them I hope to be able to pick up just where I left off. My fans have been very loyal. They've been mighty nice to me. But—if the singing situation changes and, if rock 'n' roll goes out while I'm gone—well, then I guess I'll be concentrating on movies more than ever. To be a good actor is my main ambition now."

The rock 'n' roll situation hasn't changed much. It's still going strong. But Elvis has changed. While he was still over in Germany, he was already fighting with Colonel Parker and everyone else who has an interest in his future about whether he'd pick up where he left off or not. Colonel Parker wants him to go on singing rock 'n' roll. Elvis wants to switch to ballads. He wants to sing straight, serious songs, and he wants to become a serious actor....

Elvis discusses his new image with the press as he enters a more conventional phase in his career.

The Rock n' Roll idol gives way...

Who said time doesn't fly? Remember the old side-burned, baggy-pants Elvis, who you wouldn't dare bring home to mother? Now he's a regular Beau Brummel, boasting a $9000 Sy Devore wardrobe. Not only is he sexier than ever, but we'd sure like to bring him home to mother.

A CONSERVATIVE ELVIS . . . !
Rocker Doffs the Cool Duds

Hollywood, Sept. 15 (AP)—Elvis Presley, who once wore long side-burns and gold lame jackets that even Liberace wouldn't be caught dead in, has become a fashion plate.

Movie stylist Sy Devore disclosed today that he has fashioned a new wardrobe for the onetime Beau Brummel of the black leather jacket and motorcycle boots set. (The sideburns went a couple years ago.)

END OF AN ERA

"It's the end of an era," said Mr. Devore. "The new Elvis now takes his place alongside such conservative and stylish dressers as Frank Sinatra, William Holden, Peter Lawford and even JFK himself.

"He could pass for a Wall Street banker."

Mr. Devore was commissioned by producer Ted Richmond to do a wardrobe for Elvis in his newest movie "Take Me to the Fair." The revolutionary attire—for Elvis—was all a surprise to him.

"We had a problem," Mr. Devore said. "Elvis gets $50,000 a week, which means that in order to call him in for pre-production fittings, it would have cost the picture $10,000 a day.

"So I got Elvis' measurements from his last movie and hired another actor his size for the fittings.

"I designed a $9,300 wardrobe and took a chance that Elvis would like it. We made everything before we let him take a look at it. Every piece was different from anything he had worn before.

"He flipped when he saw the clothes. He loved them. What's more he has a natural flair for wearing them."

He said there were 10 suits at $285 apiece, 30 custom-made dress shirts at $25 apiece; four sport coats at $200 apiece and two cashmere sport coats at $225 apiece, 15 pairs of slacks at $85 a pair, and 55 ties, some costing as much as $7 a piece.

There were all kinds of accessories except underwear.

"Elvis, I discovered, doesn't wear underwear," he revealed.

... to the handsome leading man.

Well, if Elvis Can Do It . . .

by Terry Turner

WHEN ELVIS Presley, a soldier, appears on a Frank Sinatra ABC-TV special in a few months, he'll receive a record payment for a guest appearance.

Elvis, tagged by some TV writers as "Our Leader," will receive $125,000.

Of course, you realize that Elvis will have expenses. He has to pay his manager and other people out of that salary. He won't be able to keep more than $100,000 or so. And then the government will step in to take a huge chunk.

* * *

NOBODY KNOWS, yet how long Elvis will be on camera when he appears with Sinatra. These are details that will be worked out later.

But assume he's on camera for half an hour.

He'll be making more than $4,000 a minute.

See, kiddies? Work hard, practice long hours, be blessed with talent. And you, too, may make $4,000 a minute one of these days.

(Who's bitter? I'm not bitter.)

Joey Bishop, Frank Sinatra, and Nancy Sinatra welcome Elvis to their TV special.

"The Voice" meets "the King"

ELVIS PRESLEY RETURNS

Unfortunately because one-half hour earlier begins a TV program so earth shaking that all the world will be tuned in to ABC. As everybody knows, Elvis Presley has been mustered out of the Army, and from 9:30 to 10:30 p.m. we'll all be able to see how he fared.

Elvis will sing two songs, "Fame and Fortune" and "Stuck on You," each of which has sold more than 1,000,000 records. If his position were not so unassailable, the thought would occur that Frank Sinatra was operating on the principle of "If you can't lick 'em, join 'em." It's Sinatra's show, and others in addition to the returning warrior to appear on it are Sammy Davis, Jr., Joey Bishop, Peter Lawford, and Nancy Sinatra.

Joey, Frank, Elvis, Nancy, and Sammy Davis, Jr. swing through a hip tune.

Elvis Comes Marching Home

By ALAN LEVY

Next Thursday (May 12), two generations of idolatry will be embodied on the television screen, when the 44-year-old son of a Hoboken boilermaker play host to a 25-year-old native of a "shotgun shanty" in Tupelo, Miss. Ex-bobby-soxers—who once risked truancy to venture within swooning distance of "The Voice"—will watch their idol nostalgically and view with parental alarm their daughters' raptures over "The Pelvis." The men of their houses will gaze at either millionaire and ponder the classic riddle: "What's he got that I haven't got? . . ."

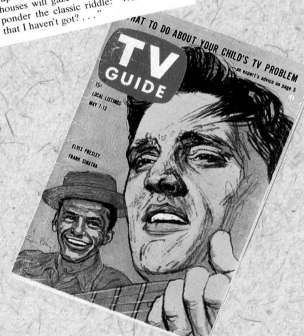

Elvis Restricted In TV Return
But It's Not Frank Sinatra's Fault That Presley Sings Only Two Songs

By ED SULLIVAN

Sure as shooting, when Frank Sinatra's TV show with Elvis Presley is shown on channel 7 Thursday night everyone will claim that Sinatra deliberately restricted Presley to two songs. Youthful TV fans will never forgive Sinatra for thus mistreating Elvis. The truth of the matter is that Presley's manager, astute Col. Tom Parker, flatly insisted Presley would sing only two songs!

Col. Tom, using the logic of a farmer, is a firm believer in not giving a hungry horse a bale of hay. The TV show was taped at the Fontainebleu hotel before an audience of thousands who jammed the big ballroom. They screamed so loud the plaster fell off the ceiling when Elvis appeared. In addition, guests in the hotel watched it on their TV sets via closed circuit.

Presley, minus his sideburns, has substituted what the ladies probably would call a "high hair-do." His hair is so high in front that it looks like a ski jump. He makes his first appearance in his army dress uniform and seems a bit ill at ease. Later in the show he does two songs, in one of them he does a bit of twitching. The cameras twice switch to head close-ups.

Throughout his last number the generation which developed in the two years of his army absence rocked the ballroom with the same shrill screams that have been the story of his singing life.

He then teams up with Sinatra, with Frank singing alternate bars of "Love Me Tender" while Elvis warbles phrases of "Witchcraft." And that's it! They also do a talking bit in which Nancy Sinatra chats briefly with her dad and Elvis.

Presley's share in the program is so limited that I made it a point to ask Col. Tom if he had insisted on this limited representation. "I certainly did," said he.

Presley's group now reports to Hal Wallis, in Hollywood, for his next flicker. He'll do the Wallis movie and then move over to Twentieth Century-Fox for two more pictures. In the meantime, orders for Presley's first record have mounted to 1,430,000 platters. He is about to start recording his first album. In other words, Elvis faces a future even more golden than it was two years ago when he became a GI.

ELVIS' German Stepmother

– can he learn to love her?

BY JANET McCUTCHEON

It was Friday night in the quiet town of Freiberg, Germany. In one of the trim frame houses on a pretty tree-lined block two men were getting dressed to go out. The younger one hummed as he peeled off his khaki-colored clothes, washed, shaved and donned a bulky blue sweater and tight white ducks. In contrast, his companion seemed unusually quiet, even troubled. Sometimes he would glance in the direction of the younger man, clear his throat as if to speak, then quickly turn his head and concentrate on the business of getting ready for his date. FOR HIS DATE! . . . He had to face up to reality now. And with that resolution Vernon Presley turned to Elvis and said:

"Son, there's something I must tell you." Elvis sensing the strain in his dad's voice, wheeled around.

"Son," Mr. Presley continued—and it was obvious he was struggling with inner emotion—"I have met a fine woman here I would like to marry. . . ."

No, this scene hasn't taken place—not yet. But, according to Elvis' pals abroad and his relatives in Memphis, this incident — and his father's marriage to a German woman—could happen any day. . . .

Presley Daddy-O Weds Divorcee

PANAMA CITY, Fla. July 17 (UPI)—Vernon E. Presley, 44, father of Elvis, beamingly presented his bride today.

He confirmed that he married silver blonde divorcee Davada 'Dee' Elliott, 34, in a quiet, secret ceremony at Huntsville, Ala., the night of July 3.

They have been honeymooning the past two weeks at a hideaway lodge at this Gulf Coast resort.

The new Mrs. Presley shyly held hands and stood close to her husband at the announcement.

NO OFFICIAL WORD

Despite reports of their marriage and discovery that the couple obtained a marriage license in Huntsville there had been no official word from the principals.

Sources in Huntsville said they were married by a judge in a civil ceremony and left immediately in a sports car packed with luggage.

Mr. Presley and his bride, mother of three sons, confirmed this today.

They indicated that Mr. Presley's famous son had not been told. Elvis, however, last week gave them his blessing and said he did not attend the wedding because his fans might have caused a public clamor and distraction.

The fanzines mistakenly thought Dee Stanley Presley was German.

Elvis did not attend Vernon's wedding because his ever-present fans might have caused a distraction.

Memphis Commercial Appeal

Presley Sales Spin To Tune Of 76 Million

Elvis Presley was paid tribute yesterday for reaching the 76-million mark in record sales.

A plaque revealing Elvis' astounding achievement was presented to the Memphis singer yesterday at the $100-a-plate luncheon in his honor at the Claridge.

Two minutes after the announcement by George R. Marek, vice president and general manager of RCA Victor records, it was revealed that since the plaque was inscribed the latest Presley record has passed the million mark in sales. Elvis' latest record is "Surrender."

RCA also presented the Memphis singer-actor with an assortment of awards for record-breaking record sales in foreign countries.

The awards were for record sales in Australia, Belgium, Brazil, Denmark, England, France, Germany, Japan, The Netherlands, Norway, Sweden, and the Union of South Africa.

"It's Now or Never" heads the list with an old number, "Jailhouse Rock." Brazilians also like "It's Now or Never" and the favorite Presley disk in Japan is the same. In fact, this song heads the list of bestsellers or is a close second in most of the foreign countries.

Other awards presented to Elvis yesterday included the American Bandstand TV program for the "best male vocalist" in 1960 and Billboard magazine's award for disk jockeys' selection of "It's Now Or Never."

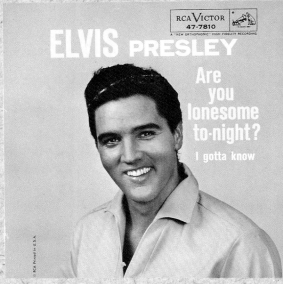

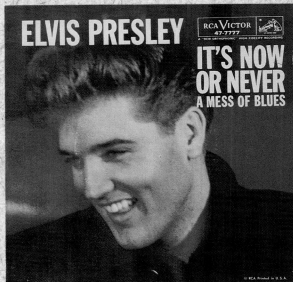

Two of Elvis's biggest hits after his return from the army

IT'S NOW OR NEVER

Words and Music by Aaron Schroeder and Wally Gold

As recorded by Elvis Presley on RCA Victor

Price 60¢ (In U.S.A.)

Gladys Music, Inc.
Sole Selling Agent:
Hill and Range Songs, Inc.
1619 Broadway, New York 19, N. Y.

Sheet Music

ELVIS PRESLEY already has sold 1,600,000 copies of "It's Now or Never," which makes the 26th gold record for the Memphis flash.

Right now he's in Hollywood shooting *Flaming Star* and in a recent interview contended rock and roll is here to stay.

His remarks on the subject: "Most of the records in the top 50 sellers are rock and roll. But in the two years I was in the army, I think the music got better. There wasn't so much of the wild stuff."

143

SCREEN IN REVIEW:
Presley Updated For His Comeback

Elvis was gone but not forgotten from 1958 to 1960. His astute manager, Col. Tom Parker, saw to that.

The comeback film, *G.I. Blues,* is designed to show what a model soldier he was around Frankfurt on the Main. It isn't all biographical. The plot idea is lifted from the 1933 Kenyon Nicholson play, *Sailor Beware!* which has not been purged of all impurities for Mr. Presley's teenage following. Recent surveys of the age group, however, disclose that only their elders are surprised at what their children are not surprised at.

With obscene hip-wiggle eliminated and hair trimmed to country club length, Elvis is an obedient draftee and a whizz at special services. He has an on-limits, off-hour combo for entertainment and sings at least uncredited 10 ditties of the type for which he is renowned. When not otherwise engaged he is the nicest guy on the post. He espouses the glacial Juliet Prowse (gratefully remembered from *Can-Can*) to save a bet for a pal. They fall in love, but she becomes indignant when she hears she is a game, then forgives when she looks in Elvis' bovine eyes.

He baby-sits for another buddy who has gone off to marry the infant's German mother. But as we said, teenagers are not even bewildered by such notions. Hal Wallis has given *G.I. Blues* a slightly self-conscious production, aware, doubtless, that Elvis Presley is social influence second only to hard drink. Norman Taurog's practiced hand was in the direction, making tolerable many digressions such as a scenic ride on the historic river.

AS FOR PERFORMANCES, for once we did not feel inclined to exterminate Elvis, found only three or four of his uniformed associates obnoxious, and continued to like Miss Prowse, the Bombay-Capetown-London dancer, who has an elfin charm to go with a brassy manner and sensational hoofing. Leticia Roman from Italy and Sigred Maier from Germany are two other comely adornments. The top sergeant, played by Arch Johnson, is dumb and what's new cinematically?

IN A WORD: Seasoned turkey dish for Thanksgiving.
—JOHN ROSENFIELD

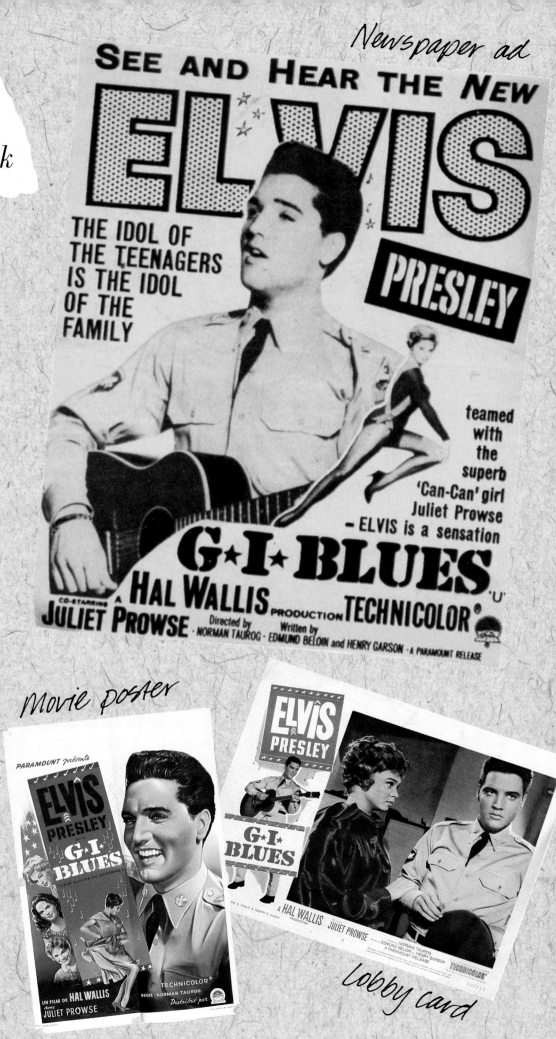

Newspaper ad

SEE AND HEAR THE NEW

ELVIS PRESLEY

THE IDOL OF THE TEENAGERS IS THE IDOL OF THE FAMILY

teamed with the superb 'Can-Can' girl Juliet Prowse — ELVIS is a sensation

G·I·BLUES 'U'

CO-STARRING A HAL WALLIS PRODUCTION TECHNICOLOR
JULIET PROWSE Directed by NORMAN TAUROG · Written by EDMUND BELOIN and HENRY GARSON · A PARAMOUNT RELEASE

Movie poster

Lobby card

Elvis as
Lady Killer
Tulsa MacLean

New Elvis Presley Stars in 'G.I. Blues'

BY JOHN L. SCOTT

Gone are the snake-hips gyrations, fish-eye look and sullen attitude. Elvis Presley, late of the U.S. Army and back on the screen, is the smiling All-American Boy in his first post-service picture, *G.I. Blues*.

The Hal Wallis production opened Tuesday night with premiere festivities at the Fox Wilshire Theater. This first-night event benefited the Hemophilia Foundation.

Elvis portrays an upstanding, trim G.I. on duty in Germany who carries around his guitar when not riding a tank and sings at the drop of a soldier's cap with his buddies who eventually hope to open a night club in Oklahoma.

Falls for Dancer

Elvis has some gambling pals, too, who fast-talk him into seeking an all-night date with a notoriously frigid night club dancer (Juliet Prowse) in order to win a $300 bet with some other GI's.

When Presley first watches Juliet dance he becomes one of the wow boys, then after winning

her attention by his respectable, non-wolfish tactics, he falls hard for her.

Yes, indeed, Elvis is a real nice Joe about the whole thing, taking the delectable Miss Prowse riding on a Rhine steamer, on a scenic tram car and eventually to a park where he sings a little tune while participating in a kiddies puppet show.

Oh, he spends the night in Miss Prowse's apartment all right, but as a baby sitter for a G.I. friend who is marrying hastily and tardily. Ulterior motive—nothing of the kind.

Elvis sings some 10 numbers in *G.I. Blues*, including a few tunes about the army and some items called "Wooden Heart," "Didja Ever?" He has reduced that old rock and roll wiggle to a rhythmical shaking of knees; he doesn't leer, and his formerly oily mop of hair is no more.

I wouldn't actually call Elvis sophisticated in the picture, but he has grown up, for which we give thanks. And he's learning how to act, too, particularly in the lighter sequences.

I'm certain most mature theatergoers will welcome the change in Presley. Now as to his squealing teen-age fans—it is hoped they also will go along with the metamorphosis.

Miss Prowse's portrayal of the torrid entertainer with a supposed cold heart reveals that she has more talents than just dancing. Elvis' G.I. pals—Robert Ivers, James Douglas and Arch Johnson —are interesting in conventional roles. Leticia Roman, beautiful young brunette from Italy, and Sigrid Maier, handsome blond from Germany, please in their screen debuts.

Norman Taurog's direction is satisfactory and commercial. It is interesting to note that Taurog— who almost always manages to get at least one infant into each of his pictures does it again. Edmund Beloin and Henry Garson wrote the script.

G.I. Blues begins regular runs today at Fox Wilshire, Hillstreet, Iris, Compton, Gage, Pickwick and various other theaters and drive-ins.

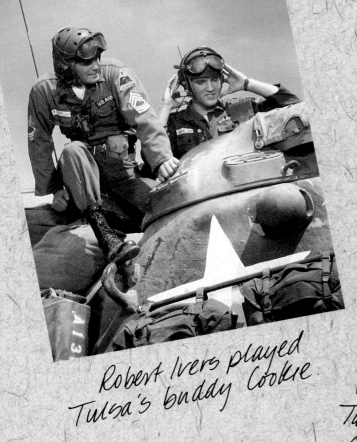

Robert Ivers played
Tulsa's buddy Cookie.

Tulsa was part of an army tank
crew just as Elvis had been.

145

Elvis—On Love And Marriage

Hollywood, June 4—Elvis Presley is 25 and still unmarried, girls, but he often thinks about getting hitched.

His thoughts mostly center on what it would do to his career—but he will marry when the right girl comes along.

Presley's comments on marriage were triggered by a wedding scene in *GI Blues*, wherein he marries Juliet Prowse, Frank Sinatra's girl friend in real life.

"Love and marriage," says Elvis, "are the most important things in life. Even more than one's career." He intends to remain choosy about his girl friends.

"By the time I've been out with a girl three times," he comments, "I can tell for sure if she is interested in me or what I can get for her."

ELVIS PRESLEY was supposed to do a 100 city personal appearance tour to ballyhoo his picture *G.I. Blues*, but Paramount reluctantly cancelled the tour because so many local police officers refused to guarantee Elvis' safety. There are just that many fans who want to tear him apart in sheer adoration.

UNSPEAKABLE

IN **G.I. Blues** (Plaza)—which in passing I would call the most witless, vulgar, and boring musical of the year—Elvis Presley achieves a notable fusion of the unspeakable and the unsingable.

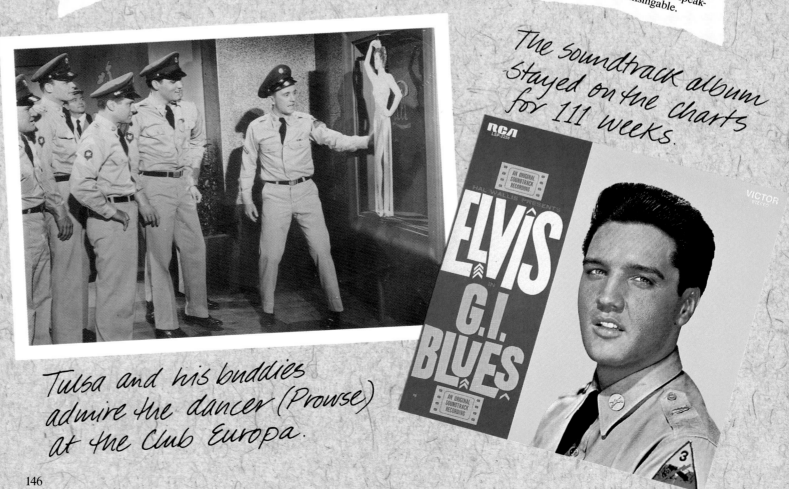

Tulsa and his buddies admire the dancer (Prowse) at the Club Europa.

The soundtrack album stayed on the charts for 111 weeks.

RCA LSP-2256

AN ORIGINAL SOUNDTRACK RECORDING

HAL WALLIS PRESENTS

ELVIS in **G.I. BLUES**

AN ORIGINAL SOUNDTRACK RECORDING

VICTOR

BEHIND THE SCENES:
Is This a 'New' Presley?

The twelve pretty starlets had been shooed away from the vicinity of the great man in the shower for fear they would be a disturbing influence. The shower had been started, with cold water that would not streak his make-up, and the fake steam had been turned on. Then the pre-recorded music began and, in the latest switch on Hollywood's famous star-in-the-bath scene, Elvis Presley started mouthing "What's She Really Like?"—one of the eleven songs he sings in Paramount's "G.I. Blues."

In his first movie after two Army years in Germany, ex-Sergeant Presley was playing, of all things, a soldier stationed in, of all places, Germany. The sideburns and 15 pounds of flesh were gone, but otherwise it was just like the old days—oceans of hubbub washing over the star who, as long as he wasn't singing, remained quiet, deferential, and serious.

After the shower scene, Elvis changed into uniform and walked toward his luxurious dressing room several blocks away, answering, "Yes, sir," or "No, sir" to the questions put to him by underlings along the way. He strolled through an anteroom where half a dozen young men lounged in sports clothes—some of the nine pals he had brought from Memphis to Hollywood in a private railroad car (the trip cost him $2,424). The friends were variously carried on the payroll as "valet," "security guard," and "accountant." ("He was a bookkeeper before he went in the Army," Elvis says defensively of this last functionary.)

"If you don't mind, sir, I'll just keep my hat on while I eat," Elvis said, glancing at the air conditioner in his dressing room. "I got to keep this hair in place and I might catch a chill after that shower."

Mum on Show Biz: He began munching an unbuttered roll ("A lunch makes me sleepy") as he was asked about his Army stint. "I learned a lot about people in the Army," he said. "There was all different types. I never lived with other people before and had a chance to find out how they think. It sure changed me, but I can't tell you offhand just how. . . ."

"I never griped. If I didn't like something, nobody knew, excepting me. Nothing bad happened. If I'd'a'been what they thought, I'd have got what was coming to me. But I never talked about show business. I went along."

He was asked about his future plans. "I'm ambitious to become a more serious actor, but I don't want to give up the music business by no means," he said. "I can't change my style, either. If I feel like moving around, I still move. As for the fans, they've changed some but they're still there, the same ones. The president of one fan club came to see me and I hardly recognized her. She's going to college now. I was surprised she looked me up. She was more mature, but she stopped by anyway."

Then the door burst open and a huge platter of tuna-fish sandwiches was borne in, followed eagerly by the pals.

Paper army hats were given away as promotional items.

NOW... AT YOUR FAVORITE THEATRE ELVIS in "G.I. Blues" A HAL WALLIS PRODUCTION-A PARAMOUNT PICTURE

Elvis relaxes between scenes.

Elvis sings "Wooden Heart" to a marionette.

NEW MUSICAL EXPRESS

PRESLEY CUTS TWO SONGS FROM 'FLAMING STAR': HIS ACTING SHOWS NEW DEPTH

From JONAH RUDDY

HOLLYWOOD.—I was the only newsman to see the preview of *Flaming Star* and I report to you that Elvis Presley is an actor with dramatic depth.

He did not want to sing four songs especially two ballads when he is on horseback.

Two songs therefore have been cut and he sings the title song over the credits and a ballad at the party "With A Cane And High Starched Collar."

The backing is by the Jordanaires.

The two songs cut, "Britches" and "Summer Kisses, Winter Tears," may be recorded and sent out by RCA to disc-jockeys, world-wide, as a special promotion.

Flaming Star is a good Western, originally written for Marlon Brando, who had agreed to play the half-breed five years ago.

Brando quarrelled with 20th Century-Fox; the story, then called *Flaming Arrow*, was shelved and revived and rewritten for Presley who comes through with flaming colors as an actor!

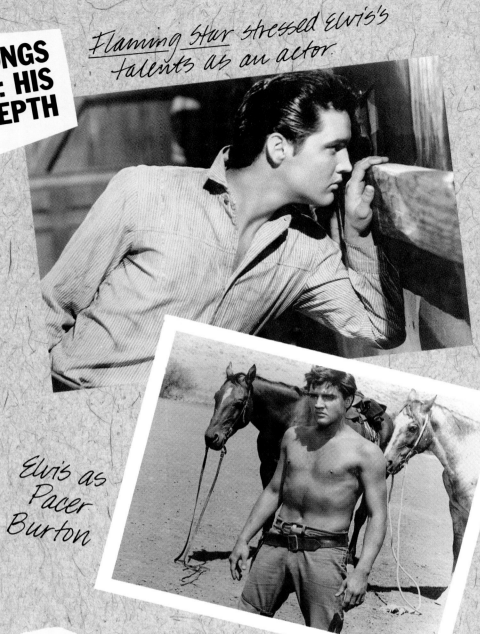

Flaming Star stressed Elvis's talents as an actor.

Elvis as Pacer Burton

Elvis did most of his own stunts for the film.

More About Elvis P. In 'Flaming Star'

BEHIND THE SCENES OF FLAMING STAR:

Elvis, 180 lbs. and fit, insisted on doing all the fight scenes himself. For a fight with a man who attempts to molest his mother, Elvis had **Charles Horvath** as opponent.

Horvath teaches judo and karate (the Japanese forms of self defense and attack) to the Marine Corps AND the FBI.

Elvis has made a study of these methods . . . so it was quite a battle.

Riding didn't come so easily for Mr. P for one reason. He couldn't ride!

So he had to learn, very quickly and the hard way. Result—one fall and one runaway!

Eyes Had It

ACCORDING to the rigid laws of heredity, Elvis, with a pure Indian mother, should have dark eyes in the film.

Dark, cosmetic contact lenses were made to cover up Elvis's blue ones. But his eyes are actually rather deeply recessed and, since he wears a stetson in most of the scenes, the lenses tended to rob his eyes of expression. So the lens idea was dropped — and Elvis has blue eyes.

"Let's say that there was a Spaniard back in his mother's family tree," said producer Wekisbart.

Compliments

ELVIS PRESLEY and DOLORES DEL RIO have a high regard for each other.

Dolores on Elvis: "My young black panther, he is a fine young man. He has the look of a Latin. He is dark and lithe. He moves like a cat. He is good actor and I even like his singing.

"I would like him for a son."

Elvis on Dolores: "Miss Del Rio is a fine actress. She helped me a lot through the film. I am grateful and proud that I am permitted to play with her."

The Dallas Morning News
Wednesday, December 21, 1960

SCREEN IN REVIEW:

Elvis Takes on Kiowas In Half Breed Role

Elvis Presley, who failed to get in any licks while serving a hitch in the army, takes on an entire Kiowa tribe in *Flaming Star* which opens Wednesday at the Majestic.

It is a two-fisted, bare-to-the-waist almost guitarless Presley this time around. Twentieth-Fox has cast him as a half-breed . . . caught in the crossfire of a bloody strife between settlers and [Native Americans] in Texas.

Pa Burton, portrayed by the veteran John McIntire, married a full-blooded Kiowa beauty—the ageless and lovely Dolores Del Rio. He had a son, Steve Forrest, by a previous marriage before settling in Texas.

While the latter offspring is accepted in the sparse community, there has always been a social barrier where Elvis was concerned. Ironically, even the Kiowas considered him somewhat of a social outcast—a problem which probably started the entire juvenile delinquency business back around 1878.

When the Kiowas elect a new chief, the old range wars are revived and the whites are slaughtered like deer during the current season. The settlers demand a quick decision from the Burtons, who ask only to be left alone.

CIRCUMSTANCES, including the murder of Ma Burton by a crazed neighbor, lead Elvis into the Kiowa camp. It is prefaced by a fight between the brothers and the best wishes of a weary father.

The Kiowa chieftain promises no raids against the Burton property or its inhabitants—a promise the warriors are quick to break when they kill Pa Burton down by the water hole with his cattle. Burton's white son spots Buffalo Horn, Elvis and his gang riding the trail and draws a bead on the chief. When the Kiowas go after his brother, Elvis gets the old "blood is thicker than water" feeling and shoots down half of the tribe. He pulls off a minor miracle in getting his brother to safety in the midst of the running battle.

The [racial] problem haunts the handsome half-breed to the bitter end. He refuses an 11th hour appeal from the white community to come die in their midst—choosing instead to wander into the hills in search of the proverbial happy hunting grounds.

IN A WORD: A surprisingly good acting effort from the king of the rock 'n' rollers. The opportunity to see Miss Del Rio again is worth the admission.

—TONY ZOPPI

lobby cards

Movie Poster

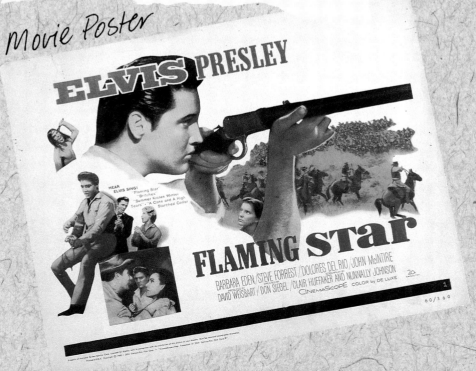

Soundtrack album

Memphis Commercial Appeal   February 26, 1961

Elvis Captures New Fans, Pours Profit Into Charity

Two Shows And Lunch Push Receipts Over Goal Of $50,000—
Singer Showered With Tokens Of Appreciation

By MALCOLM ADAMS

Elvis Presley ended a personal appearance "fast" of four years yesterday to recapture old fans and win new ones with two performances which netted Memphis charities $51,612.

Vowing he was nervous and "fighting butterflies in the stomach," Elvis quickly captured his big matinee audience. For 49 minutes he ran through some 20 songs and had the crowd shrieking for more.

The matinee and evening performances at Ellis Auditorium were high spots of Elvis Presley Day in Memphis.

Receipts from the shows and a $100-a-plate luncheon pushed the total receipts beyond the goal of $50,000.

Last night's crowd of 5,323 brought $19,622 into the box office. The matinee crowd of 3,999 made the total attendance of the two shows 9,211. The luncheon netted $17,200 with 172 persons attending. The matinee took in $11,580.

Receipts from the sale of pictures, program and refreshments added to the box office total of $48,402 to push the grand total beyond the $51,000 mark.

Twenty-seven charities have been designated by a local committee to share in the receipts. Not a penny was spent for staging the shows. All performers, including Elvis, donated their services and even bought tickets to get in the Auditorium.

Elvis and the Colonel helped many charities.

A familiar sight back stage before a big show like the Memphis Charity benefit is the Colonel giving his "boy" warm encouragement and wishes of good luck. The star Elvis, and his mentor make a hard-to-match showbiz team.

One of Elvis's first charities— Fans helped maintain the Elvis Presley Youth Center by sending in contributions.

Youth Center
Tupelo, Mississippi
January 22, 1964

Miss Sharon Fox, President
Elvis Presley Fan Club
5742 W. Giddings St.
Chicago 30, Illinois 60630.

Dear Sharon:

Thank you very much for the latest contribution of $1.00 to the Elvis Presley Youth Center, for which we enclose your receipt.

The last time you wrote to us, you were looking for a job. We are delighted to learn that you now have one, and certainly hope it is a nice one that will bring much satisfaction and feeling of accomplishment.

We hope you will be fortunate enough to see Elvis when he is next at home in Memphis. As for my personal opinion of him as a person, and not just as an entertainer, I couldn't have a higher opinion of anyone that I know. He is one of the finest people that I have ever met, and his high moral standards should certainly be an inspiration to all who know him. I am indeed proud to call him a friend.

Once again, thank you for your contribution and your interest. We hope to finish the Elvis Presley Youth Center in the summer of 1964, and then plan to undertake to build the "Elvis" Swimming Pool in his Park also.

Sincerely,

James L. Ballard
Mayor

JLB:es
Encl.

ELVIS REMEMBERS PEARL HARBOR

Spartanburg Herald   Monday, March 27, 1961

$52,000 Raised By Presley For Pearl Harbor Memorial

HONOLULU (AP)—Rock 'n' roll vocalist Elvis Presley raised $52,000 for the U.S. battleship *Arizona* memorial Saturday night before a screaming, stomping crowd of 5,500 at Pearl Harbor's Bloch Arena.

The audience was mostly teenagers.

Presley wore a gold lame sports coat with silver-sequin lapels and thumped a mother-of-pearl inlaid guitar.

It was announced that Presley and his manager, Col. Tom Parker, had contributed $5,000 of the $52,000.

The memorial will honor the 1,102 men entombed when the battleship *Arizona* was sunk by [Japanese airfighters] in the Pearl Harbor attack Dec. 7, 1941.

Elvis at the Pearl Harbor benefit

Hawaii Next Charity Stop

By DON WALKER

When a 26-year-old ex-GI named Elvis Presley pays $100 to climb up on stage in Honolulu next March, twenty long and silent years will have passed for 1,102 American seamen entombed in the hull of the valiant battleship *Arizona*.

The average age of those shipmates who died during the Pearl Harbor disaster was about the same as that of the guitar-strumming singer who seeks to raise at least $50,000 towards a giant memorial to the *Arizona* crew and all who died for freedom.

Symbol of Freedom

The benefit performance by Presley—only a lad of five at the time war broke out—is symbolic of a new generation of Americans who have not forgotten the price of freedom or how dearly it has been maintained.

Except for the colossal charity benefit in his home-town of Memphis Feb. 25, the Honolulu public appearance will be Presley's first since he played the Hawaiian city in 1957 just prior to entry in the Army.

Filling the 4,000 seats of Pearl Harbor's Bloch Arena for the show, sponsored by the Pacific War Memorial Commission, will be a host of other Americans who will have contributed to the *Arizona* Memorial with the purchase of their tickets.

All For Arizona

All proceeds from the show will be channeled directly to the fund. Presley plans to buy the first ticket. His will cost $100. Everyone—top Navy brass, commission members and even Col. Tom Parker, Presley's manager who arranged the benefit, will pay. Though ticket costs will be scaled to meet the pocketbooks of all, a number of ringsiders will also pay $100 for their seats. A second performance will be added if the demand is great enough, Col. Parker said.

Parker Answers Plea

A Los Angeles newspaper's plea for help in raising the $200,000 still needed to complete the Memorial prompted Col. Parker to fly to Honolulu several weeks ago to offer Presley's service on the condition—"Every penny of that taken in must go to the fund."

H. Tucker Gratz, chairman of the Pacific War Memorial Commission, said the $50,000 anticipated from the benefit performance will provide "bare essentials" to prepare for the official dedication ceremonies on Memorial Day May 30. Since March 15, 1958 when Congress authorized the construction of the memorial museum through contributions, $300,000 has been raised. It was hoped that the final construction of the building would be completed by May 30, 1961—20 years after the murderous attack in which more than 3,000 Americans lost their lives.

A Proper Tribute

Presley and the Colonel responded to the commission's cry that fund collections had slowed to a snail's pace and "today the *Arizona* is but a rusting tomb . . . (while) the proposed memorial will be a proper tribute."

The commission hopes the Presley show will not only raise money itself but will also serve as a stimulus for obtaining the rest of the $200,000 necessary before the museum can become a reality.

Film To Follow

Col. Parker said Presley will arrive in Honolulu March 25 for the filming of *Blue Hawaii*. It will begin on March 27, the day after the benefit.

The giant museum building will stand on pilings—equal to the height of an 18-story building—over the Pacific near the hulk of the *Arizona*. One entire wall or bulkhead has been designed for the Honor Roll of the *Arizona's* crew, who hailed from all 48 states which then comprised the Union.

Elvis and the Colonel personally donated $5,000 to the memorial.

FEUDING STARS

WHICH STORY IS TRUE?

by Roger Beck

PRESLEY and BOONE SLUG IT OUT
(Inside the battle of the year)

Hollywood, a town noted for its blasé attitude toward strange alliances, has been buzzing lately in puzzlement over the close friendship of two seemingly opposite individuals—Pat Boone and Elvis Presley. Aside from the fact that they have each achieved tremendous popularity in the same field and jointly occupy the top rung on the ladder of pop singing fame, there seems to be little that they have in common that could foster and nurture a friendship. "What," Hollywoodians ask each other, "could they possibly have to talk about? What interests could they share?" Even one of Pat's closest business associates has predicted that these two young men, as alike as they might be professionally, could never be close friends because there is nothing to draw them together. In fact, it seems that most everyone who knows either Pat or Elvis more than casually believes that this friendship can be nothing more than a light acquaintanceship—certainly nothing approaching a Damon and Pythias brotherhood. But these opinions, apparently, do not reflect the thinking of the principles themselves for Elvis and Pat can see nothing unique in their relationship. "I think Elvis is a great person," Pat told me. "Pat is a real nice guy, someone I admire," Elvis admitted in all sincerity.

The boyish-looking Pat would not go into detail on the subject.

"Elvis is very colorful, has a great sense of humor and I like him very much," was about all he would say, figuring that this summed it up pretty well. . . .

Juliet Prowse, Elvis and Pat Boone— Pat and Elvis engaged in friendly competition for many years.

OR FRIENDS?

BILL FURY talks about ELVIS

Nervous? You bet! But I needn't have been

I've just come back from America after meeting The Giant. Man, I'll tell you. I was dead nervous. But I needn't have been. Elvis Presley put me at ease right away. He's one of the nicest guys I've ever met.

This was one of the biggest things to happen to me since I started singing. It's wonderful to be able to look back on it all and to have shaken hands with Elvis.

My manager Larry Parnes and I went over to the States for a month, mainly for a holiday. But we wanted to meet up with Elvis and Larry wrote to Colonel Tom Parker, his manager, from here before we went. It was all laid on.

Chatted

I met Elvis on the Paramount Films set in Hollywood. I suppose I dried up a bit when one of his manager's assistants, Tom Diskin, introduced us to the world's biggest pop singer.

But we soon got chatting. We spoke for 20 minutes. He's a great character.

Really, I got quite a surprise. He knew a lot about the scene here. His first words to me when we said hello were: "Well, so we finally got to meet."

He obviously followed everything happening in Britain. He said a few things that proved it. He said he'd heard of me. To be honest, I couldn't believe it!

Around the film set he was very interesting to watch. Elvis moves about stealthily, almost like an animal! He's cool, man. Very relaxed. He's a quiet person, but nevertheless very self-assured.

But I got the impression he's the sort of person who has to keep himself occupied all the time. I got this feeling quite a lot while I watched him during the filming. . .

Great Song

Talking of his voice, I heard Elvis's record of "Follow that Dream" while I was in the States. It's from the picture of that title which was his last film.

I reckon this is one of Presley's very best. What a song!

This must go right up the charts here to No. 1. Incidentally, Elvis's two songwriters are composing a tune specially for me. I'm looking forward to that. It should be great.

Unfortunately, we missed meeting Colonel Parker, but he sounds (like) such a great guy I'd liked to have seen him.

He phoned us to say he hoped we got on all right. That's what Americans are like all around—so hospitable. I couldn't get over it.

Meeting Elvis was the biggest thing on the trip, of course, but Larry and I got around quite a bit.

Elvis's rivals on the pop scene

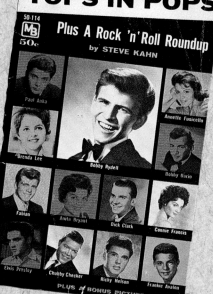

Pat Boone dons Elvis's famous gold suit for this album cover.

DLP 3501

NOTED PERSONALITIES

Las Vegas, Nev.: Harmony seems to reign as the country's top young singers, **Elvis Presley** (left) and **Bobby Darin**, compare notes at Las Vegas, Nev. Presley was on his way to Hollywood for a role in "Flaming Lance," while Darin was appearing at the Hotel Sahara in Las Vegas.

153

'Wild in the Country' Stars Elvis Presley

By Justin Gilbert

The intimation is becoming increasingly strong on our movie screens that rough-edged rebels and tough talkers can capture the heart of the least likely lady.

Why, it almost amounts to miscegenation.

In *Wild in the Country,* Jerry Wald's latest at Paramount, Elvis Presley is a sort of circumstance-stricken savage—a young Southern goop who steals and scraps and mires himself in trouble—but only because of domestic difficulties. Still, he reads.

"COMIC BOOKS?" asks the female social service worker (Hope Lange) in charge of his case.

But when she learns that he's a Bible scholar and a kid with his nose in all but the best by scriveners a cut above Grace Metalious, the dark suspicions disappear and a lovelight goes on in her eyes.

Then she learns he can write. Oskywowwow!

(Frank Sinatra was a hooligan of similar sorts, too, in Some Came Running. *And darned if he didn't aspire to write and eventually found a mentor in a girl named Martha Hyer.)*

Clifford Odets must have had his mind on a couple of other drastic-doings-in-Dixie stories, other than the J.R. Salamanca novel from which he's credited with writing the screenplay. The characters he's created are familiar sleazy trash or swamp angels (Millie Perkins appears as one of the latter) you find in the familiar potboilers about the peckerwoods.

Elvis, following his jam-ups, is paroled to an uncle (William Mims) who runs a snake oil store, where whisky is sold as a cancer cure. There he meets Miss Perkins' opposite number, a fast moving piece of fluff (Tuesday Weld) who's living with her father and illegitimate child.

Well, folks, which shall it be—the sociologist or the slut?

We already may have given you an indication of the ending—but don't let that bother you. There are enough improbabilities and impossibilities before then to keep you wondering whether Elvis, rather than being wild in the country, ought not to simmer down in the cinema.

Rafer Johnson, John Ireland and Gary Lockwood are also cast in the DeLuxe color film.

Elvis's single release of the title tune reached #26 on the charts.

Newspaper ads

WILD IN THE COUNTRY
20th; CinemaScope, De Luxe Color (Adult)

WHO'S IN IT? Elvis Presley, Tuesday Weld, Hope Lange, Millie Perkins.

WHAT'S IT ABOUT? A hard-luck Southern kid and three girls who love him.

WHAT'S SPECIAL? All the gorgeous, lingering closeups of Elvis in glorious color (even if they are stranded in the middle of a wide, empty screen) . . . five well-assorted songs (even if they don't fit comfortably into the story) . . . Tuesday's sleepy, sleazy, sexy, look.

WHAT'S THE VERDICT? Pretty silly—and pretty rough on poor Elvis, playing the male version of a soap-opera heroine.

William Mims, Tuesday Weld, and Elvis — Tuesday played one of Elvis's love interests.

DAILY NEWS, SATURDAY, JUNE 10, 1961

Elvis Sings Sweetly To Variety of Girls

By DOROTHY MASTERS

Elvis Presley is working himself up to a dramatic career in slow and easy stages. He's on screen for almost two hours at the Paramount, during which time his allotment is three songs and three romantic entanglements. It's a switch to have the swooned-over bachelor in pursuit of females, but that's the way the cooky crumbles in *Wild in the Country*.

The casting provides provocative stimulus. Elvis is tantalized by such variety as Hope Lange, Tuesday Weld and Millie Perkins. Twentieth Century-Fox takes extra-special care of the popular idol, too, with a generous production budget and veteran support in bit roles. Jason Robards, Sr., for instance, is too far down the list to rate cast-box mention.

For most of the footage Presley is a sulky rebel plagued by bitter memories and the sadism of his father and brother. After a violent outburst that lands him in court, his principal contacts are the venal uncle to whom he is paroled, the latter's sex-crazy daughter and a psychiatrist with troubles of her own. One of the town's rich boys also gives him a bad time.

A lot of what happens is unlikely, but the story gets completely out of hand during the last two reels.

Hope Lange costarred as another of Elvis's love interests.

Millie Perkins played Elvis's high-school sweetheart.

Tuesday Started Most Of Rumors About Self

While shooting Wild in the Country Elvis and Tuesday Weld were linked romantically.

Hollywood, Feb. 4 (AP)—Is it true what they say about Tuesday?

Eyebrows have been lifting and tongues wagging since petite, blond Tuesday Weld came to movieland in 1958, a full-blown 15.

Gossips have chronicled romance after romance, one with an actor nearly three times her age. They picture her as no stranger to liquor, tobacco, gay parties and late hours.

When a movie needs a girl to play a sexy teenager, Tuesday is thought of first. She's a living legend at 17—while her contemporaries are still in high school.

She gets more publicity than most of the screen's senior sirens—just about all of it bad.

But does Tuesday try to blow it down? She's more apt to fan it.

* * *

Ask her what she thinks of the tales they tell and she deplores only the ones that accent her tender years. One reason she doesn't knock the more lurid yarns is because many originated with her. Tuesday is not unaware of the value of publicity, good or bad, and admits she's the principle source of Tuesday Weld tales.

Tuesday is spending her time these days working with two actors whose names figure in the Weld legend: John Ireland and Elvis Presley. The three co-star in *Wild in the Country*. And Tuesday's the *Wild* of the script.

Tuesday dated Ireland when she was 15. He is 45. Her romance with Presley, 25, came later.

She says working with two ex-boyfriends in the same picture presents no problems. She and Presley are very friendly and wisecrack back and forth on the set.

She and Ireland are also friendly, but Tuesday says that's all—or all there ever was. Friends of Ireland say he once was so smitten with her that he wanted to marry her. Of that report, Tuesday flips:

"Well, it would have been a very friendly marriage because he was only a friend. I place no age limits on my friends. . . ."

Elvis and Hope Lange celebrate Elvis's birthday on the set.

You'd never recognize Elvis Presley as the singin' man of yore in this DeLuxe-colored saga of earthy Shenandoah Valley folklore. Without even a guitar he can call his own, Elvis does manage one wistful madrigal to a palpitating Tuesday Weld. The rest of the time Hope Lange, a psychiatrist, tries to bring out the best in Elvis, and Millie Perkins, ever on hand, just tries. It would appear, has additional talent for writing. Whether this gift will ever have a chance to burgeon despite all the conflict with relatives, a murder charge, a suicide, and various other distractions is not for a woman to say. Instead, Elvis' future rests with John Ireland. In this emotional obstacle course, Elvis, in exceptional physical condition, seems hardly winded at all. (20th Century-Fox.)

Millie Perkins remained aloof from Elvis during filming.

PHILADELPHIA DAILY NEWS   THURSDAY, DECEMBER 8, 1960

How Does It Feel To Smooch with Elvis?

HOLLYWOOD (UPI)—**Hope Lange** is the envy of millions of screaming teenagers who would bob their ponytails to be in her position —in Elvis Presley's arms.

So what's it like to smooch with Sir Swivel?

"He's like a great big teddy bear," the blonde actress said with a twinkle in her blue eyes.

"He's a cuddly type of man; the kind of person you want to hug, like you would a teddy bear. And I mean that to be complimentary."

Hope's romance with Elvis is limited to the screen and their co-starring roles in *Wild in the Country*. She never sees him anywhere but on the set at 20th Century-Fox studios where the movie is being filmed.

But in the love scenes, is there any personal relationship above and beyond the call of the script?

"No, I don't think so," Hope said. **Does she enjoy** kissing Elvis?

"Let's put it this way," she suggested, "the character I play enjoys the love scenes very much. And because you try to be as believable as possible, your own feelings don't enter into it.

"He compares very well in romantic scenes with the other actors I've worked with.

"If Elvis is given the right picture and director he can become a great dramatic actor. He hasn't fallen into the trap of dramatic training by forcing himself to be superficial. Elvis has terrific instincts which makes his performance absolutely real.

"You're never aware that he's acting."

Hope said she finds it necessary to check her own feelings while doing love scenes, with Elvis or anyone else.

"You go into the scene as yourself, but once the cameras are rolling you let the character's feelings and emotions take over," she explained.

"It can be quite impersonal. You really don't get to know people well when you're working on a film unless you play a great many scenes with them.

"Most of my scenes in this picture have been with Elvis, but I only see him during rehearsals and the actual shooting. I guess it does happen that performers work together and fall in love after playing love scenes.

"Emotional involvement is not uncommon, but most of the time it passes at the end of the picture.

"Just for the record, there is no personal emotional involvement between Elvis and me."

157

Elvis OK's Role as Beach Boy

Hollywood—Elvis Presley was invited to Hal Wallis' house to take a look at *GI Blues*. Both Hal and Elvis liked what they saw, so a new deal for another movie was made then and there.

Next spring, when the weather is good, guitar-playing-swivel-hips Elvis will star in *Hawaii Beach Boy*, by Allen Weiss, who was formerly on the Los Angeles Examiner.

Elvis will go to Honolulu before the film begins, to look over the tropical isle. If he doesn't like it he'll be the first one. Hal says Elvis will dance as well as sing in "Hawaii Beach Boy."

Elvis and his costars pose for publicity stills— Joan Blackman (left); Jennie Maxwell (right).

Elvis signs autographs for fans while on the set.

The original title for Blue Hawaii was Hawaii Beach Boy

Elvis Presley Sings 'Blue Hawaii'

Elvis Presley is chipper and Hawaiian scenery is gaily colorful in *Blue Hawaii*. This new lure for the Presley hordes is showing at neighborhood theaters, all over town.

Elvis sings at the slightest excuse or none at all. Before he is through he has rolled up no less than 17 songs.

He mixes them up ranging through rock 'n' roll, ballads, Italian and Austrian songs and, of course, lots of Hawaiian music, both folk and "The Bird of Paradise" variety.

The story does not amount to much, a slender fable about the rich boy who wants to make good on his own instead of stepping into readymade success in his father's pineapple plant. The humor is equally inconsequential, most of it based on foolish misunderstandings, often on the vulgar side.

Elvis has two pretty girls for his dalliance, Joan Blackman and Nancy Walters. Angela Lansbury pops up again as a snobbish clown.

Except for the Hawaiian scenery and music, there is nothing in this one to distinguish it from all the other Presley movies since his return from the Army.

Blue Hawaii, with Elvis Presley, Joan Blackman, Nancy Walters, Angela Lansbury, Roland Winters and John Archer. A Paramount film in color, directed by Norman Taurog, screen play by Ial Kanter, story by Allan Well. At neighborhood theaters. Running time: 1 hour, 41 minutes.

Newspaper ad

Promotional item

Elvis as Chad Gates

Looking at Hollywood

Angela Lansbury Quits Stage for Presley Film

By HEDDA HOPPER

Hollywood, May 15—An actress takes on mother roles when good parts run in that direction. Angela Lansbury, who spent seven months on Broadway in *Taste of Honey*, and quit the production to play Elvis Presley's mother in *Blue Hawaii*, says: "In *Honey* I was the mother of Joan Plowright, a girl of 17 in the play; whereas Elvis is 26 and I admit it's a jolt for a woman of 35 to be asked to play his mother. It sort of stopped me, from the point of vanity. I thought—Do they think I'm that old? But the role intrigued me, it's a kind of comedy I'd never done before, a sort of grown-up baby doll and it takes me out of the British things".... Except for stars in series, she thinks TV has done little for run of the mill actors beyond giving them money to pay their bills. "A star like Richard Boone can make a fortune, and Lloyd Bridges has come up for air to count his money now. Actors reach the point where they feel they must provide some long-range security; so they do a series. An episode in a series, such as Have Gun, may have a cast of 20, but all except top stars and regulars on show get only the minimum pay and can work a series only once...."

★ **Elvis Presley** told me about some of the kids in Hawaii during his location filming of *Blue Hawaii*. A few pretended to be mail messengers with registered letters that Elvis would have to sign for. Others got up the fire escape into his room. Elvis finally found peace behind a 24-hour-a-day guard. Co-star Joan Blackman told me of their rock-a-hula dance number—a combination of rock 'n' roll and hula gyrations. Can you see Elvis?

Lobby card with Jennie Maxwell and Elvis

Newspaper aa

ELVIS PRESLEY GUIDES YOU THROUGH A PARADISE OF SONG!

BLUE HAWAII

SEE ELVIS Sing & Dance THE ROCK-A-HULA TWIST!

HAL WALLIS Production TECHNICOLOR AND PANAVISION

14 TERRIFIC SONGS

From JOAN BLACKMAN · ANGELA LANSBURY · NANCY WALTERS

WEDNESDAY at PARAMOUNT

Elvis and Joan Blackman during "The Hawaiian Wedding Song"

BLUE HAWAII
Paramount: Technicolor: Director, Norman Taurog; Producer, Hal Willis (Family)

WHO'S IN IT? Elvis Presley, Joan Blackman, Angela Lansbury.
WHAT'S IT ABOUT? An ex-GI's career and marriage plans draw frowns from his snooty family, who are high in Hawaiian society.
WHAT'S THE VERDICT? If plenty of music can keep Presley fans happy, this picture fills the bill with fourteen numbers that give Elvis a chance to display a variety of styles: rock to ballad, Hawaiian to Calypso. In between the songs…well, the scenery is magnificent, filmed all around the new state.

Juliet Prowse was originally slated for Joan Blackman's role.

160

★ ★ ★ ★ ★ ★ ★
Elvis' 'Blue Hawaii' Likely To Top Judy

For more than two months the Judy Garland double record album, *Judy at Carnegie Hall*, has been the top selling LP in North America according to the surveys. It has also been the top LP seller in Toronto despite its high list price of $9.98 for monaural and $12.98 stereo.

However, if the survey predictions come true, *Judy* will slip out of the top spot this week. The new Elvis Presley LP *Blue Hawaii* is expected to top it.

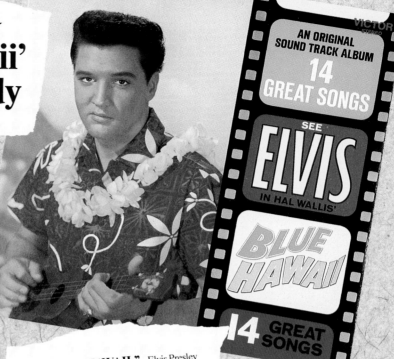
"BLUE HAWAII."— Elvis Presley is resting from serious acting in this colourful and unexceptional series of musical numbers, strung around an almost non-existent fantasy story, so his fans will know what to expect. He plays a soldier back from his National Service to Hawaii, with a perfunctory character point that he "doesn't know himself yet" and doesn't want to take advantage of all his parents' money and his mother's overpowering affection. That's right, he's a mixed-up ex-Serviceman. He also loves a rather delectable piece of local scenery, nicely played by Joan Blackman, and there is a likeable, but infuriating, grotesque of a mother, played by Angela Lansbury. He sings, he modestly wriggles and develops a pleasant showmanship— otherwise it's something for the fans.

Elvis Presley is the star of "Blue Hawaii," a colourful musical which makes agreeable light entertainment.

"Blue Hawaii" to Star Elvis

HOLLYWOOD—Elvis Presley sets a new record for his motion picture appearances by performing 13 songs in Hal Wallis' *Blue Hawaii*, technicolor comedy-with-music being filmed on location in the 50th state.

In addition to two "standards," the title song and "Hawaiian Wedding Song," new numbers especially written for Elvis include "Almost Always True," "No More," "I Can't Help Falling in Love," "Hawaiian Sunrise," "Rock-a-Hula Baby," "Moonlight Swim," "Hawaiian Sweetheart," "Playing With Fire," "Beach Boy Blues," "Island of Love" and "Slicin' Sand."

Presley will accompany himself on the ukelele in many of the musical numbers in the attraction, which costars Joan Blackman, Angela Lansbury and Nancy Walters. Norman Taurog directs.

Elvis and Joan dance to "Rock-a-Hula Baby," one of the 14 songs in the film.

Newspaper ad

All About Elvis . . .

Elvis couldn't really surf.

and 'Blue Hawaii'

Joan and Elvis clinch for the camera.

In Spanking Mood!

LET'S JUST SAY IT WASN'T JENNY MAXWELL'S DAY. IT ALL STARTED EARLY, WHEN SCENES FOR BLUE HAWAII CALLED FOR JENNY TO TRY TO DROWN HERSELF, BE RESCUED BY ELVIS PRESLEY, WHO THEN TURNS THE TINY 19-YEAR-OLD BLONDE OVER HIS KNEE AND GIVES HER A SOUND SPANKING!

For the long shots and close-ups, Jenny dunked herself thoroughly three times, was hauled out and spanked by Elvis, a total four times.

"He had to spank hard to make it look good," Jenny later conceded while rubbing the spanked area carefully, "but my skimpy costume was wet and there wasn't much between Elvis and what he was spanking, and it stung like anything."

Just then, director Norman Taurog called: "Now, let us get Jenny dried off and onto her horse!"

For the next three hours Jenny, Elvis and Joan Blackman did scenes on horseback over rough terrain, and if Jenny hovered somewhat gingerly above her saddle, everyone understood.

Then, after the final shot for the day, a gust of wind toppled a heavy reflector standard which hit the back of Jenny's foot. No bones were broken, but the doctor who treated the painful bruise has prescribed a cane between scenes for several days.

"The cane helps my sore foot," says "Hopalong" Maxwell, "but it doesn't do anything for the *seat* of my trouble!"

Costar Nancy Walters and Elvis

Prominent islanders who appear in the picture are "Hilo" Hattie, the popular television personality, who plays a lei seller, and "Lucky" Luck, the popular Honolulu disc jockey, who makes his debut on the screen as an airline passenger.

HIS HAPPIEST FILM:
With Happy People All Around Him

Elvis performs "No More" with his beach buddies.

Hawaii quickly became one of Elvis's favorite spots.

Walkie Talkie Solves Sound Problem

A sequence in *Blue Hawaii*, called for a quartet of beach-boys in an outrigger to sing a number as Elvis Presley swims out to meet their canoe while cameras grind from the nearby shore.

The problem was to synchronize the quartet's singing and rhythmic paddle strokes with the play-back on the beach—too far away for sound to carry above surf noises.

It was solved by choreographer Charles O'Curran and cable man Jerry DeVore, with two walkie-talkies, one suspended in front of the play-back loudspeaker, the other lashed out of sight inside the canoe, where it picked up the pre-recorded number perfectly.

THE LUCKY GAL WITH THE 14 SMOOCHES

PRETTY PAT FACKEN-THAL, 22, made her movie début recently in a torrid kissing scene with Elvis Presley for Blue Hawaii, *filming in Hawaii and Hollywood—and she has just about decided to quit while she is ahead!*

"The scene involved Elvis kissing me and then me kissing Elvis," Pat recalls blissfully. "We rehearsed it four times and they photographed it from three angles. That is 14 smooches any way you look at it. After that, anything I did in a movie career would be an anti-climactic."

Pat plays an airline stewardess, who responds ardently to Presley's embrace just as he leaves the plane in a prearranged plan to make his Sweetheart *(Joan Blackman)* jealous.

"Things like that aren't normally a part of the service," confided Pat, who was a real stewardess on the mainland for two years.

A striking statuesque blonde, Pat was "Miss Arizona" in the 1959 "Miss Universe" contest. [She] landed her first screen role on her first try when a friend told her Producer Wallis and Director Norman Taurog were auditioning several local people for roles in the picture.

Her home is in Phoenix, Arizona, and she went to Hawaii "for a week's vacation six weeks ago."

"I didn't believe it when they told me I had the part," she says. "I didn't meet Elvis until two minutes before we began rehearsing the kissing scene."

How does she rate the Presley brand of smooching?

"I think actors would consider that a professional secret," she said, adding quickly, "but it was a wonderful way to get acquainted."

Any plans for dating Elvis?

"Nothing very definite," she replied vaguely.

Asked the same question, Elvis tactfully evaded a direct reply. "Pat's a real pretty girl," he said. "*Real* pretty."

Friday, February 1, 1963

Famous film producer Joe Pasternak reveals plans for super musical

ELVIS MAY STAR WITH CLASSICAL ARTIST

"Elvis Presley is a wonderful performer, but I don't think the films he's made do enough for him. When I make a musical with Elvis for MGM it's going to be different, so different.

"I think I'll co-star him with some big classical artist—a concert pianist or a singer. That way we'll bring the popular and classical music fans together. And it will make for a better film."

The speaker was crew-cut Joe Pasternak, a friendly man who has produced a total of 77 films, including the new Doris Day musical, *Jumbo*. Even in his dramatic pictures he's featured plenty of music.

He says it himself. "Music is my life. It makes people happy. I suppose these heavy dramas are all right, but I like to stand outside a cinema and watch the audience coming with smiles on their faces."

Joe has worked with almost every major Hollywood star during his career, from Deanna Durbin to Connie Francis, Mario Lanza, Judy Garland, Esther Williams, Kathryn Grayson and many more.

Of **CONNIE** he says: "She's extremely pleasant to work with, though so far we've made only *Follow The Boys*. I found her very adaptable and talented—she picked things up very easily as we went along. I'd welcome the opportunity of doing another musical with Connie."

DORIS DAY is one of Joe's favourite musical comedy actresses. "She's wonderful, wonderful. I can't tell you how much it pleases me that she's back in a musical like *Jumbo*. It was a terrible thing when she started going dramatic.

"I'm not saying she isn't a good dramatic actress, but someone with such a talent for musical comedy shouldn't waste it."

Although he's in his late sixties, Joe has no plans for retirement. I asked him if he aimed to work until he reached his hundredth film and he said, "No. I'm going to carry on for as long as I can!"

That Presley film will be one of Joe's major commitments in the next two years.

"I never stop working," he says. "Making films is work and play to me. The big thing about the Presley film, though, is that I'm going to try and find a really great script. He's one of the world's top names in his field, and I figure he should have the very best.

"The only trouble is **finding** a script...." **KEN THOMSON**

After Blue Hawaii, Elvis was slated to star in several movies that never came off.

Hollywood

By Hedda Hopper

Hollywood, Jan. 30—**Elvis Presley's** first of four pictures for MGM will be *Mister, Will You Marry Me?* (just an old refrain for swivel hips) by **Frederick Rohner.** The producer will be **Jack Cummings,** and this is his welcome-home picture on his new Metro deal. You can bet Elvis will be singing, 'cause Jack's an old hand at turning out musicals. . . .

Elvis' MGM Pact Almost Finished

Never Say Yes will be Elvis Presley's next starring motion picture under his MGM contract. A mid-February starting date has been set for the romantic comedy.

Norman Taurog, who has directed more Elvis Presley features than any other director, will direct.

Never Say Yes will be Elvis' seventh motion picture for MGM, dating back to *Jailhouse Rock* in 1956. Presley has one more picture to go on his current contract.

Elvis and his chimp, Scatter, read one of the many scripts offered Elvis.

'Fastest Guitar In West': Elvis, Natch! Katzman Economy

Elvis Presley's next for MGM and producer Sam Katzman will be an original western story tagged *The Fastest Guitar In The West*. Robert Kent, now scripting *Girl Crazy* for the producer, will screenplay *Guitar*.

Katzman next week wraps up *Harem Holiday*, current Presley starrer for Metro. Budgeted at $2,400,000 film will have been shot in 18 days following three weeks rehearsal. Gene Nelson directs.

Finetooth preparation, according to Katzman, is the only way to compete against high filming costs. "A motion picture should be made in the office—so when you go on the stages you know what every move is going to be. Then there can be no alibis on anyone's part."

He reports new IATSE pact added $44,000 to *Harem*. Presley gets flat $1,000,000 fee, with $200,000 going to remainder of cast.

Katzman estimated production costs as rising at least 25% in last five years, and predicts another 5% increase over next five years. He is confident, however, that Hollywood will be able to make necessary adjustments and continue to make a buck. "While prices are up, the price of tickets is up, too," he shrugs, "so it's about a 50-50 split."

Katzman has little idea of how many pix he may have produced in his prolific career. But he remembers clearly that his first film, *His Private Secretary*, with John Wayne, was made for $96,000 with $25,000 in cash and the rest on deferred payments.

He reports that his current MGM release, *Your Cheatin' Heart*, will make back its negative cost—$850,000—in its southern playdates alone.

Presley A Sleuth in NGP 'Valentine'

Elvis Presley has been bottled in Bond-type role as star of Natl. General Prods. film, *That Jack Valentine*, which, per latest report, now will roll next summer. While role of a super-sleuth will be a new tangent for Presley, he will still sing some songs, enough, presumably, to fill another Victor album.

Paul Gaer's original *Jack* script will be filmed here, for Easter 1969, release by Natl. General Pictures Corp., distribution wing. Irving H. Levin, exec veepee of parent company heads production activities.

Movie Call Sheet
Presley Film on MGM Slate

Elvis Presley's next film, *You're Killing Me*, will be produced by Judd Bernard and Irwin Winkler for MGM. Filming will begin in June after Presley completes *Never Say Yes*, which begins shooting February 21. Joe Heims is writing the screenplay for *You're Killing Me* from an original story by Marc Brandell.

Presley to Star in 'Gumbo Ya-Ya'

Elvis Presley will report to producer Hall Wallis this spring for his next picture, *Gumbo Ya-Ya*, a romantic comedy with music to be filmed in New Orleans and nearby colorful Gulf Coast locations.

Gumbo Ya-Ya, a Creole expression meaning "Everybody talks at once," will have Elvis playing the skipper of a fishing boat, a young fellow whose yen for a craft of his own involves him with high adventure and any number of pretty girls.

Like *Blue Hawaii*, Wallis' current hit which is breaking all previous Presley box office records, *Gumbo Ya-Ya* will afford Elvis ample opportunity to sing, dance and romance in a vividly, beautiful setting.

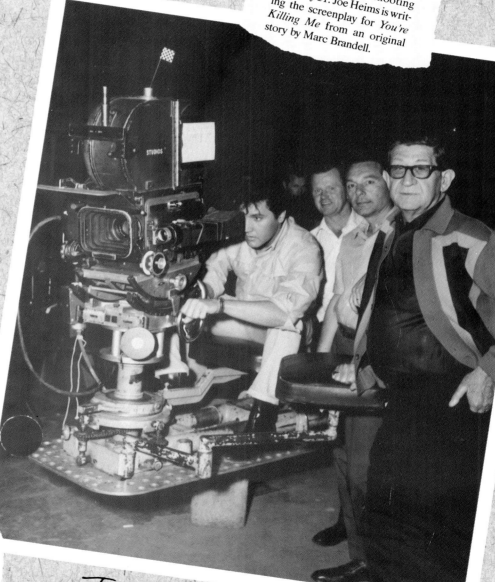

The crew lets Elvis take a peek through the camera.

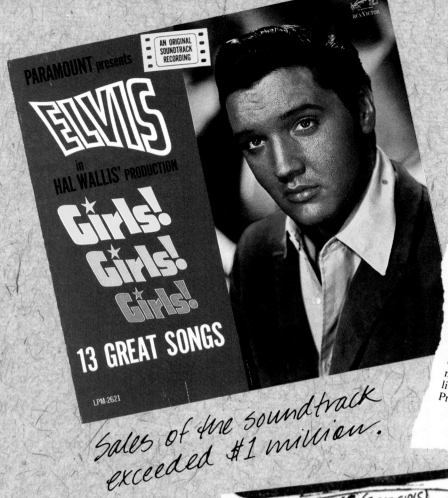

PARAMOUNT presents

AN ORIGINAL SOUNDTRACK RECORDING

ELVIS

in HAL WALLIS' PRODUCTION

Girls! Girls! Girls!

13 GREAT SONGS

LPM-2621

Sales of the soundtrack exceeded #1 million.

Newspaper ads

GIRLS! GIRLS! GIRLS!

Paramount; Technicolor; Director, Norman Taurog; Producer, Hall Wallis (Family)

WHO'S IN IT? Elvis Presley, Stella Stevens, Laura Goodwin, Jeremy Slate.

WHAT'S IT ABOUT? Two girls complicate a fisherman's struggle to earn the purchase price for a beloved sailboat.

WHAT'S THE VERDICT? If it's Presley songs you want, here's aplenty—in fact, a musical overload that threatens to sink the frail story. But there are laughs (mostly supplied by Jeremy, the genial villain) to keep this craft afloat. And Laurel comes across as a highly decorative newcomer with cheerful charm.

SHORTS and FILLERS

Elvis Presley sings to Laurel Goodwin in front of a gothic stone church for a scene in Hal Wallis' *Girls! Girls! Girls!* directed in Technicolor by Norman Taurog. Bing Crosby sang in front of the same church 20 years ago, for *Going My Way*. The Presley film is next at the [local] theatre.

In the face of movie tradition which says it's the villain who wears black, Elvis Presley wears black in several scenes while wooing Laurel Goodwin, in Hal Wallis' *Girls! Girls! Girls!*, a Paramount release directed in Technicolor by Norman Taurog—and Elvis is the hero. The motion picture opens next week.

The flamenco has taken the place of karate in the life of Elvis Presley, now that he has learned to dance the flamenco with Laurel Goodwin in Hal Wallis' *Girls! Girls! Girls!* which opens next week.

Although she is a good cook, screen newcomer Laurel Goodwin is afraid no young man will ever let her cook for him after seeing her burn the roast and boil over the soup while preparing dinner for Elvis Presley in a scene for Hal Wallis' *Girls! Girls! Girls!* The Technicolor romance opens next week.

First Nude in Hal Wallis Movie Seen in Presley Film

The first nude ever to appear in a Hal Wallis movie in all the years the producer has been making pictures will be seen in the new Elvis Presley starrer, *Girls! Girls! Girls!*, a Paramount Technicolor release due next at the [local] theatre. It was filmed at the small Kona Coast village of Milolii in Hawaii under Norman Taurog's direction.

However, neither Wallis nor Taurog anticipates any censor trouble with the scene, which called for Elvis and Laurel Goodwin to put ashore at a remote island hamlet. As they left their boat and walked down the tiny pier, they encountered a trio of small boys swimming. One four-year-old on the pier sans swim suit, quickly dived in as they approached. But Elvis added extra censor insurance by turning Miss Goodwin's head away from the scene.

Laurel Goodwin made her screen debut in Girls! Girls! Girls!

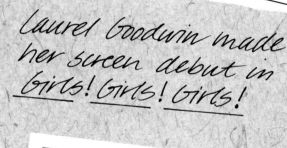

Elvis as Ross Carpenter

167

LOUELLA O. PARSONS

Comedy for Elvis One Spot of Peace

Hollywood—Gleefully, Harold Mirisch told me that he has Elvis Presley tied up for *Pioneer Go Home,* based on a book by Richard Powell. Harold said:

"It's a warm comedy, and Elvis will make it for us next spring. We have George Marshall set to direct."

It's going to be made here, which is good news. So many movies are being made abroad.

What lucky young lady will play opposite the popular Elvis has not yet been determined.

From the left: Arthur O'Connell, Elvis and Anne Helm

Follow That Dream was based on Pioneer, Go Home!

Joanna Moore and Elvis

This newspaper ad shows that the French title was Le Shérif de ces Dames.

FOLLOW THAT DREAM

WHO'S IN IT? Elvis Presley, Anne Helm, Arthur O'Connell, Joanna Moore.

WHAT'S IT ABOUT? As present-day homesteaders, a happy-go-lucky family has government authorities baffled.

WHAT'S THE VERDICT? Most of the way, it's a cheerful homespun comedy with easygoing songs and funny lines; so it can be forgiven for slowing to a near-standstill at the finish. Elvis, as a good-natured backwoods kid, and Anne, as a smart tomboy, make a romantic team that suits the picture's fresh approach.

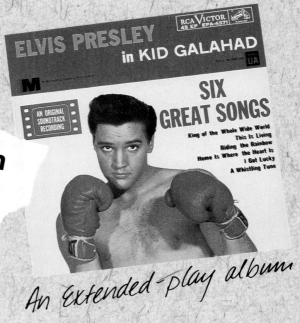

DISCS . . .
Presley in top form

Elvis Presley's latest film *Kid Galahad*, is a little disappointing but the songs are right on the ball and the six from the film have all been included on an RCA Victor EP.

My favourite is a pleasant ballad titled "Home Is Where The Heart Is," with Elvis serenading at his best.

Other titles are "King Of The Whole Wide World," "This Is Living," "Riding The Rainbow," "I Got Lucky," and "A Whistling Tune."

Good stuff!

An Extended-play album

Newspaper ad

Elvis and Joan Blackman

Can this really be Elvis?

Who is this young fellow with a black eye, split lip and bloody nose? It's Elvis Presley. And what I wonder, will his fans think of him as a prizefighter?

As *KID GALAHAD* (London Pavilion, tomorrow), he looks to me a bit too paunchy for a successful welter-weight. Not that he wants really to be a boxer. But he has this tremendous k.o. punch, you see. As soon as he has punched his way to enough money, however, he marries the girl and opens a garage.

Actually, it is quite a good film. Mr. Presley's singing gets more endurable as he gets older. He does not prance so much. And they will make an actor of him yet.

KID GALAHAD
UA; DeLuxe Color; Director, Phil Karlson; Producer, David Weisbart (Family)

WHO'S IN IT? Elvis Presley, Lola Albright, Gig Young, Joan Blackman

WHAT'S IT ABOUT? A new recruit to the fight game finds that his conniving manager is mixed up with racketeers.

WHAT'S THE VERDICT? Easy-going musical melodrama that plays down the fisticuffs and plays up the songs and the love stuff instead. It's pretty mild compared to the old movie of the same title, but at least Elvis' hero has a refreshing attitude, unimpressed by prize-ring glamour. Joan and Lola are quite likable co-heroines.

Former boxing champ Mushy Callahan coached Elvis for his fighting scenes.

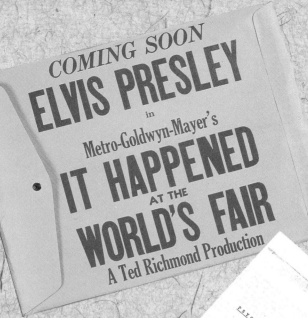

COMING SOON
ELVIS PRESLEY
in
Metro-Goldwyn-Mayer's
IT HAPPENED
AT THE
WORLD'S FAIR
A Ted Richmond Production

Psycho sticks were given out as promo items for this film

PSYCHO-STICK

A product of
S O P O T
A Junior Achievement Company
Counseled by
Pacific Electric Railway Company
(Southern Pacific Company)
521 East Green Street
Pasadena, California

Price
Sales Tax $.24
Total Price $.01
                 $.25

ELVIS PRESLEY and JOAN O'BRIEN
starring in M.G.M's
"IT HAPPENED AT THE ...
in Panavision ...

"It Happened at the World's Fair"

Co-starring JOAN O'BRIEN and GARY LOCKWOOD

A new formula appears to be emerging for film musicals—certainly those starring Elvis Presley. The action is set against colourful, natural backgrounds. After having filmed in such exotic locales as Hawaii, the Pacific and Florida, Elvis now turns up in Seattle to find the World's Fair in full swing.

The film is off to a flying start by introducing Elvis as Mike, singing "Beyond The Bend" from the cockpit of a plane he owns in partnership with his friend Danny (Gary Lockwood). They don't realize that beyond the bend is a sheriff with a writ impounding their aircraft as security for various debts.

The two grounded pilots hitch-hike in search of work to help them reclaim their plane, and are given a lift by a Chinese farmer driving to the Seattle World's Fair with his little niece Sue-Lin (Vicky Tiu).

At Seattle Mike finds he has two "fair" ladies: one is Sue-Lin whom he takes on a tour of the fair, and the other is a pretty nurse, Diane (Joan O'Brien) who works at the medical post to which he takes Sue-Lin when she has over-eaten.

Complications arise when Mike appoints himself Sue-Lin's guardian on her uncle's disappearance, and Sue-Lin is taken away from him by welfare people. To add to his frustrations, Sue-Lin runs away from the custody of the welfare people at the same time that his friend Danny is getting him involved in a smuggling deal. But as with all good musicals, there's a happy ending. In fact, there's a rousing finale called "Happy Ending" as Mike walks Diane through the fair grounds leading a military band.

Between the opening and closing numbers mentioned, there are eight others including "One Broken Heart For Sale" which was in the Top Twenty. All of them are sung on the long-playing record from the soundtrack—RCA VICTOR R.D. 7565 (33-1/3)—which Elvis fans will want to add to their collection of fifteen other LP's issued by RCA.

One of the big romantic tunes is "I'm Falling In Love Tonight" with which Elvis serenades Miss O'Brien in the revolving restaurant on top of the fair's big showpiece, the Space Needle. This and other attractions are breathtakingly photographed in Metrocolor and Panavision. I enjoyed the Seattle scenery, snappy songs and the scintillating stars, but for me one of the biggest features is also its smallest; this is little pigtailed Vicky Tiu whose two sisters appeared briefly with Elvis in *Girls! Girls! Girls!*

It was an ingenious move to use the exciting World's Fair as the background for a film and one could not wish for more entertaining escorts than Elvis and his friends.

Brian Swift

NEW WARDROBE FOR ELVIS

"We'll give Elvis a new wardrobe for this film, and have him look like a smart, well-dressed young business man. It's a switch from sports shirt and blue jeans and sports jackets," said the producer of *Take Me To The Fair* at Metro-Goldwyn-Mayer Studios, Mr. Presley's third movie for 1962.

Accordingly Sy Devore, the master-tailor of show business stars, was given the assignment of equipping Elvis with his new wardrobe.

For the last Presley film, *Girls! Girls! Girls!*, the Devore organization had provided Mr. Presley with three raw-silk jackets and several pairs of black silk trousers.

"It was decided to make this wardrobe as a sort of surprise for him," Sy Devore told me.

"I had his measurements, and I engaged an actor who is his exact size and weight to stand in for his fittings.

"We then took the wardrobe to the studio and all I can say is that Elvis flipped when he saw it. He looked marvelous in them and I'll tell you why. He has a natural flair for wearing well-fitting clothes."

Mr. Devore gave me the cost of the clothes in dollars, but to bring it to Savile Row standards, I've calculated the equivalent in guineas.

There were, therefore, ten suits at 100 guineas each; four sports coats at 75 guineas each; 30 specially designed shirts with a deep collar and narrowed cuffs, at eight guineas each; 15 pairs of slacks at 25 guineas a pair, and six dozen ties at three guineas each!

The trousers Elvis Presley wears have to be specially designed. It seems that he wears no underwear, not even briefs.

All his jackets have to be designed to allow for freedom of movement.

He wears boots, not shoes. They are of the short Wellington kind, called Continental Gaiters in Hollywood.

In *Take Me To The Fair*, Elvis plays a pilot who gets romantically involved with a lovely girl at the Seattle World's Fair.

So Mr. Devore designed a special black leather jacket which he wears while piloting his plane.

It is probably the world's most expensive leather jacket. It cost 80 guineas, and is entirely hand made.

Mr. Devore considers this film marks the beginning of a new era for Elvis Presley. "He will take his place amongst America's well-dressed men," he assured me. "I consider this is my greatest styling achievement since I persuaded Bing Crosby to give up his incredible chromatic sports shirts and trousers which didn't match at all."

The nice thing is that Sy Devore uses the finest British materials for his suits, jackets and trousers.

Thus Elvis is sporting fine suitings from Huddersfield, Bradford and the West of England in *Take Me To The Fair*.

Originally the title was <u>Take me to the Fair.</u>

MIKE EDWARDS

A young Kurt Russell kicks Elvis on the shin.

Gary Lockwood Come By His Scrapping Naturally

Elvis Presley and Gary Lockwood, playing his sidekick in Metro-Goldwyn-Mayer's *It Happened at the World's Fair*, fight on the same side in two spectacular free-for-all brawls in the action-filled comedy-drama.

It was not always thus.

In *Wild in the Country*, Elvis and Gary also appeared together and engaged in two realistic fist fights, but this time as opponents, and Gary lost both bouts.

The 175-pound six-footer hasn't always limited his scrapping to the screen. At UCLA, when he became involved in a fight into which he was provoked and didn't start, he was expelled from the university for a year.

It was during this enforced hiatus in his education that Lockwood became a movie stunt man, which ultimately led to his stardom as an actor.

Elvis Presley Stars in 'Fun in Acapulco'

Elvis is back on the screen after an absence of several months, and his devotees should be ecstatic. Presley's new picture, called *Fun In Acapulco*, screens citywide.

In this musical movie, the young star sings about 10 times, but only once throws himself into the free-wheeling style that used to bring loud squeals from female teeners. A new "image"?

While plot and performances in *Fun In Acapulco* are about as substantial as the film's title, one can't dismiss the fact that producer Hal Wallis undoubtedly has another box office success. Presley buffs should eat it up.

Writer Allan Weiss places his hero in Acapulco, Mexico's plush resort, where he has been dismissed as seaman on a private yacht after refusing to romance the owner's daughter.

The young fellow secures work as a night club singer and life guard. In the latter capacity he hopes to overcome acrophobia, or fear of heights, which developed when he was a member of an aerial act involved in a fatal accident.

A romantic entanglement brings Elvis to the point of testing his phobia by subbing for one of the famous Acapulco high divers.

Director Richard Thorpe has kept the film's pace swift, which helps to cover up a lack of character development and a routine plot.

Two Heroines

Romantic interest for Presley is handsomely furnished by Elsa Cardenas and Ursula Andress. Paul Lukas, as an ex-duke turned chef, plays for comedy. Young Larry Domasin gives a lively portrayal of a kid who attaches himself to Elvis.

Alejandro Rey, Robert Carricart, Teri Hope and others enact supporting roles.

Costar Elsa Cardenas and Elvis

PERFECT TIMING
But Elvis Wouldn't Stand Still

by Neil Rau

In a scene with Elvis Presley for *Fun at Acapulco*, Ursula Andress was called upon to throw a book at Elvis to establish the fact that they were about to fall in love. So property man Bob McCrillis set about it with customary thoroughness.

He chose a hard-cover edition of Homer's *Iliad* for Ursula to hurl, not for the book's title or literary content, but because the property department had several identical copies.

McCrillis' forebodings proved well-founded. In 13 hard throws for various camera angles, Ursula ruined four books beyond repair, and one valuable tropical plant that was a sort of innocent bystander.

Ursula's aim was wild, but her timing was perfect. Elvis escaped unscathed out the doorway each time, just as the book hit.

The soundtrack album — #3 on the charts

YOUR PASSPORT TO "Fun in ACAPULCO" 'U'

TECHNICOLOR®

A HAL WALLIS PRODUCTION · A PARAMOUNT RELEASE

483473

OLE! ELVIS

ACAPULCO TECHNICOLOR AND GIRLS!

Elvis Presley has a lot of **Fun in Acapulco** (at the Plaza) and sings not a few songs in the process of this, his latest cinematic extravaganza.

As usual, he mixes his numbers, including some beaty, some pleasantly subdued, and some quite frankly sloppy songs and routines, all delivered in the style which we can now adopt at the drop of a Mexican hat.

The story concerns a mixed-up, footloose trapeze artist (that's Elvis) on the run after a circus accident for which he believes himself responsible, and his eventual self-reappraisal on the sunny shores of Acapulco Bay. He meets, on the way back to the sawdust life, an Austrian emigre countess (Ursula Andress), a lady bullfighter (Elsa Cardenas), an unusually likeable shoeshine boy (Larry Domasin) and a rival for Miss Andress's hand (Alejandro Rey), with whom there is the eventual, inevitable punch-up.

Pleasingly innocuous "family entertainment," with a Latin beat and a glimpse of Latin weather that for most of us will only be realized on the screen. But still wait for a film in which Presley is given a chance to act! P.D.

Paramount printed passports as promo items.

Elvis sings "Vino, Dinero y Amor."

Elvis and Ursula Andress

Elsa Cardenas— Elvis's "Bossa Nova Baby"

173

Every Christmas Elvis gave to many charities.

Charities Presley Helped Last Year Again To Benefit

Colonel Tom Parker, who has managed Elvis Presley's rise to stardom, told Mayor Henry Loeb by telephone yesterday the singer wanted the 37 charities that shared in the money raised by the 1961 benefit show to receive shares of the $50,000 being given to Memphis this year.

Vernon Presley, the singer's father, and Mayor Loeb will take the list of charities which received donations last year with them to California on Monday. This list was increased from 37 to 50 but the names of the additional charities will not be released until the revised list is cleared with Colonel Parker today.

It was stressed last night that time does not permit additional requests to be considered.

The charities which received donations from the 1961 show included:
The Elvis Presley Youth Center at Tupelo, Miss.
The Commercial Appeal Fresh Air Fund.
The Memphis Press-Scimitar's Cynthia Milk Fund.
Ave Maria Guild.
Bethany Home.
Crippled Children's Hospital.
Convent of the Good Shepherd.
Duration Club.
Family Service.
Happy Acres.
Goodwill Industries.
Home for Incurables.
Jewish Community Center.
Les Passees.
Junior League.
L.S. Lawo Man Fund for Boys Club.
Little City of the Mid-South Inc.
Neighborhood House.
Orange Mound Day Nursery for Negroes.
Porter Leath Home.
St. Jude Hospital Foundation.
Lions School for Visually Handicapped Children.
Salvation Army.
Variety Club of Memphis.
Phoenix Club's Boys Club.
Goodwill Homes for Children, Inc.
Alpine Guild.
Boys Town.
Le Bonheur Club.
Jessie Mahan Day Care Center for Negro Children in the Dixie Homes area.
Marry Galloway Home.
Memphis and Shelby County Council of Retarded Children.
St. Gerard Hall.
Memphis Mothers Service.
Canteen of the YMCA.
Memphis Speech and Hearing Center.
The Abe Scharff Branch of the YMCA for Negroes.

Elvis family helps ease pair's grief

MEMPHIS, Tenn. (AP) — Elvis Presley's father and stepmother have helped ease the burdens of a Gleason [Tenn.] couple, beset by grief.

For seven weeks, Mr. and Mrs. Calvin Whitlow have kept a day-and-night vigil at a Memphis hospital where their 16-year-old son David, is ill with a brain tumor.

Monday, their home burned down, destroying their furniture, clothing and food.

Friday, Mr. and Mrs. Vernon Presley handed the Whitlows the keys to a station wagon crammed with food and clothing for them and six other children.

Mrs. Presley learned of the Whitlows and their ill son through a newspaper story and she visited them in the hospital.

"They told me then that their house burned down. I told Vernon and he ordered a turkey for the family for Thanksgiving."

Mrs. Presley also asked members of her church to help and they collected the food and clothing.

Vernon Presley bought the [brand-new] station wagon for the Whitlows so they could travel to Gleason to visit their other children.

Handing him the title to the vehicle, Presley said, "Here, Mr. Whitlow, good luck."

"May God bless Mr. Presley," Whitlow said.

PEOPLE

Presley Gives $68,000 To Charity in 3 Cities

'Twas two days before Christmas and all through the day celebrities were giving and getting. . .

Elvis Presley, who made a fortune exercising in public, donated $68,000 to charities in Memphis, Tenn., Los Angeles, and Omaha, Neb.—a Christmas tradition he has followed for the past four years.

The 29-year-old Presley said he could remember when he wasn't a millionaire, and wanted to share his success with the needy.

In Jan. 1964, Elvis purchased Franklin Roosevelt's yacht for charity.

Memphis Press-Scimitar — February 15, 1964

Presley's Big $55,000 Yacht Called White Elephant

That big yacht that Elvis Presley bought on the West Coast for $55,000 is a white elephant, according to news reports from the area. It's not likely Memphis will ever see it.

It's pretty far gone. It would be expensive to repair the ship and move it the 11,000 sea miles to Memphis. So the ship, the Potomac, used by the late President Roosevelt, will probably be scrapped and the money turned over to St. Jude hospital of Memphis. Elvis, a Memphian, gave the ship to St. Jude.

Of Icarus Class

The U.S. Coast Guard says the ship is an Icarus class cutter built in 1934. The cutters are 165 feet long with a beam of 25¼ feet and draw eight and a half feet of water. The ships had a top speed of 16½ knots and cruised at 10 knots. They were powered by Winston Diesel rated at 1300 h.p., and were of all-steel construction. They consumed about 300 gallons of diesel oil every 24 hours at cruising speed.

According to a survey inspection started on the vessel in 1963 by the Coast Guard's office of marine inspection at San Diego, the Potomac still has the original engines. Based on this figure, if the ship were moved to Memphis, it would cost about $6,000 for fuel. No one has said what it would cost to get this ship ready for sea. Elvis said that he would pay the transportation costs when the ship was first offered to the National Foundation. However, he has said nothing about paying the costs to Memphis.

The 1963 survey was never completed but permission was given to the Hydro Capital of Newport Beach, Cal., the owners then, to move the ship to Long Beach Harbor at Los Angeles. At that time her life boats were useless. One was in a leaking condition and the other had a hole in the port side. Neither had adequate provisions as specified by law.

In 1960, when the ship was owned by the Neptune Lines Inc. Canden, N.J., the Potomac was surveyed by the Coast Guard and the interior was found to be in good condition. Outside she had some badly pitted . . . plates that had to be replaced.

Hydro Capital said it invested $250,000 into the ship, including refitting.

Glen Roland, President of Hydro Capital, said today it would take between $5,000 and $10,000 to get the Potomac ready for sea. He said the ship was picked up by them in Barbados in the winter of 1962 and sailed to Los Angeles. At that time, all the navigation, fire control and other equipment was in first class condition.

Last August, the ship was in tip-top shape. With red carpets on the decks and beautifully finished interiors. In seven weeks time, 14,000 people went thru the ship, sightseeing. It was anchored at the King Harbor Marina and they had a contract with the City of Redondo Beach to show the Potomac. But the surf was bad during that period and the ship was in danger of being damaged by the surf breaking over the breakwater.

With the full approval of the harbor master, the ship was moved out in the harbor and anchored. The insurance carrier found out the boat had been moved and said it could not cover the ship while it was swinging on its own anchor.

Hydro Capital decided to get rid of the ship when it couldn't find a suitable location.

Ping Pong

Entertainer Danny Thomas, chief benefactor of St. Jude, accepted the yacht from Elvis Presley. Thomas said later, "It seems sad that we are playing ping pong with the memento of history."

He said he hopes the Potomac can be preserved as a historic shrine but also said it is doubtful that the ship would be moved to Memphis.

"It will probably be sold as scrap," he said.

If so, it appears the ship will bring less than Elvis paid for it.

Memphis Commercial Appeal — February 15, 1964

St. Jude Gets Elvis Yacht —Use In Memphis Possible

The yacht Potomac, bought by Elvis Presley for $55,000 on Jan. 30, might wind up at the end of a boardwalk from the bank of the Mississippi River in Memphis.

That's the only use a local official of St. Jude Hospital could think of when informed last night that the singer will give it the hospital today.

The Memphis entertainer bought the yacht at auction and tried to give it to the March of Dimes Foundation, but the officials did not think it proper to spend donated funds to maintain such a gift.

Then Elvis tried to give the yacht, which was President Franklin D. Roosevelt's floating White House before and during World War II, to a Coast Guard Auxiliary unit at Miami, Fla. Some Coast Guardsmen expressed doubts that it could make the trip from California to Miami and the Coast Guard prohibited the auxiliary unit from accepting the gift.

"The Miami group wanted to accept the yacht, sell it for scrap, and use the money to build a club house," said a Coast Guard spokesman. "This would be ranging pretty far from water safety and other purposes of a Coast Guard auxiliary unit so permission to accept the gift was refused."

After the plan to give the yacht to the Miami group blew up, a promotion group from North Carolina moved yesterday to acquire the Potomac.

They sent a wire to Elvis asking him to give them the yacht to be used "as a companion to the battleship North Carolina" which is berthed at Wilmington, N.C. as a war memorial.

Yesterday afternoon Tom Diskin, assistant to Col. Tom Parker, Elvis' manager, confirmed that several groups had asked for the yacht but said Elvis had decided to give it to St. Jude Hospital.

Entertainer Danny Thomas, founder of St. Jude Hospital, is scheduled to accept the yacht for the hospital in Los Angeles this afternoon.

"It doesn't surprise me that Elvis Presley is making this gracious contribution," said Mr. Thomas last night. "Elvis is a great humanitarian."

After accepting the yacht, Mr. Thomas will have the problem of finding a use for it.

. . . a member of the St. Jude board of governors, said last night he thought it could be made to "serve a humanitarian cause" by bringing it to Memphis and building a boardwalk so visitors could go aboard the vessel.

Such visitors, be indicated, could make contributions that would go for the support and maintenance of St. Jude Hospital.

So, it may end up in Memphis. We will see.

'Viva Las Vegas' Explosive

Viva Las Vegas, currently screening in multiple run throughout the Southland, has an explosive pair of dynamite performers in the persons of Elvis Presley and Ann-Margret. And the film has all the excitement and color of a Roman candle.

Presley and Ann-Margret do everything expected of a singing and a dancing dervish, respectively, and, in between their 10 top musical numbers, they do a bit of romancing and story-telling. *Viva Las Vegas* is as colorful as the town; as gay and flamboyant as its entertainment and the lush, plush desert spa was never showcased better.

Presley is seen as a race driver who gets stranded when his bankroll literally goes down the drain of a swimming pool, and luscious, lovely A-M is the swimming pool manager who makes his heart miss a beat and gets his motor racing. Presley becomes a waiter, wins a contest (against A-M) and love blossoms.

Actually, director George Sidney has put together one of the "true musicals" without resorting to a top Broadway production. In *Viva Las Vegas* he's got the big production numbers oozing with color; capturing the personality's best fortes and lavishing time on entertainment rather than the inherently weak (and most predictable) story. Sidney's direction is robust and sharp and there's few, if any, sluggish moments.

Presley must get the money for an engine in order to race his car in "The Las Vegas Grand Prix." At the last minute, he does, and, in as scorching, pulse-racing and exciting race as has ever been filmed, he comes out the winner and gets A-M as well. In some of the race scenes, the audience is in one of the cars and you'll get the same thrill as on a roller coaster as you zoom up and down the hills.

Cesare Danova is seen as an Italian count and racing champ who also has an eye for Ann-Margret's lovely chassis. Although he hardly plays a "villain," he doesn't deserve the horrible death in an auto race; one of the most ghastly ever filmed.

Among the tunes, and they're all good, that Elvis and A-M warble are the title tune, a real rouser, and "My Rival," which A-M puts over as a smash solo.

Elvis is a cinch to please the femme fans and any male who doesn't like Ann-Margret is a candidate for Siberia. *Viva Las Vegas* has humor, romance, songs, dances and excitement.

IT'S ANN-MARGRET AND ELVIS

Actress Ann-Margret has told reporters in London that she's going steady with singer Elvis Presley, but doesn't know yet if they will get married. She said they have lots of fun together, including rides on motor bikes and added: "I guess I'm in love." They are shown together last summer on a Hollywood movie set. (UPI)

Soundtrack album autographed by Ann-Margret

lobby card

176

Romance bloomed both on and off screen ...

... for Elvis and Ann-Margret.

Memphis Press-Scimitar August 8, 1963

It Looks Like Romance for Presley and Ann-Margret

But They Are Not Saying Anything

By BOB THOMAS

HOLLYWOOD—This is news to make the younger set flip—Elvis Presley and Ann-Margret are having a romance.

At least that's the way it looks. You can't always be sure about romances of costars in Hollywood. Sometimes they will flame while the movie is being made and released, then sputter out when all the publicity has been garnered.

That's why some Hollywood citizens are casting a dubious eye on the reports about Elvis and A-M. After all, they are appearing opposite each other in "Viva Las Vegas."

Behavior On Set

Well, seeing is believing. And their behavior on the film set might make you believe that something is brewing between the two. They hold hands. They disappear into his dressing room between shots. They lunch together in seclusion.

The other day they were filming a musical number at Culver City Memorial Auditorium across the street from MGM. The song was titled "Love You, Baby."

Between takes Elvis was available for one of his laconic conversations. What about this girl Ann-Margret?

"She's really got magnetism, that girl," he said.

He was speaking of her professional style and added that he had seen all of her movies. All except "Bye Bye Birdie." He'll get around to it some day, he said.

That's the musical about a singing idol's departure for the Army. Elvis admitted that he had seen an abbreviated version in Las Vegas. Did he recognize anyone in it? He grinned and replied, "No, not really."

That's about as personal as you can get with Elvis.

She's Evasive

Ann-M, fetching in a sheer, skin tight leotard, was evasive. When asked if a romance was blooming, she responded with a shake of her red tresses, "That's something I won't talk about."

She did admit to having been a Presley fan, tho, curiously, she never bought his records. "I listened to them on the radio," she explained.

"I love this kind of music," she added, referring to the Presley style of rock 'n' roll. "It's so free, so uninhibited. It's not the kind of music I have generally done. I've usually had the show-type song.

"But I can do all kinds. If it's show, I'll be showy. If it's a ballad, I'll be tender. If it's wild, I'll be wild."

It was "Birdie" that made Ann-Margret the hit of the teenagers, especially the prologue and epilogue in which she belted the title tune. The idea originated with the director, George Sidney, who is directing "Viva Las Vegas."

"The studio didn't want it, but Mr. Sidney insisted," she said. "It turned out to be the thing that most people remarked about when they came out of the picture. Which proves that you've got to fight for what you think is right."

177

Memphis Commercial Appeal   November 8, 1963

Elvis Wins Love Of Ann-Margret

LONDON, Nov. 7—(UPI)— Hollywood's Ann-Margret says she's going steady with Elvis Presley and "I guess I'm in love."

In London for the world premiere of the musical film "Bye Bye Birdie," the red-haired 22-year-old beauty said she doesn't know yet if they will get married.

"Nothing has been fixed," she said.

Ann-Margret said she and Elvis have lots of fun together riding motor bikes.

"I'm going steady with him and I guess I'm in love," she said. "But I cannot say when, or if, we will marry."

Added Ann-Margret: "He's a real man."

Ann-Margret played Rusty Martin to Elvis's Lucky Jackson.

ELVIS PRESLEY & ANN-MARGRET

SOME ROMANCES ARE SIMPLY TOO, TOO GOOD TO BE TRUE

Ann-M on Elvis: "He's a real man"

ANN-MARGRET AND ELVIS WED!

Hollywood's Wedding Of The Year for MOVIE LIFE's scene-of-the-month! Elvis and Ann-Margret merge in MGM's colorful *Viva Las Vegas*. It's a marriage between race-car driver and swim instructress for pic. But now the stars are talking of going steady—and turning fiction into FACT!

Ann-M's provocative dancing matched Elvis's intense performing style.

179

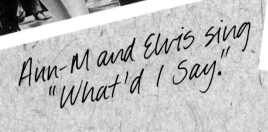

Ann-M and Elvis sing "What'd I Say."

Elvis croons "If You Think I Don't Love You."

He ended the relationship after she talked to the press.

THE END OF A FLUB AFFAIR

"I am going steady with Elvis and I guess I'm in love. . . . He's a real man."

Ann-Margret blurted out her feelings in London on a publicity jaunt. This rather lukewarm statement had the shocking effect of a tidal wave across the Atlantic! First because it's the only time since she's become a star that A-M's committed herself to one guy. And second, the truth is Elvis was certainly the last to know! He mooned over A-M when they filmed MGM's *Viva Las Vegas.* She dated him, but kept him guessing by dating others. Two days before she flew to England, Ann absolutely refused to see El, period. Pals say El was left with "egg on his face," was in the blackest of moods because of A-M's jilt. In short, he goofed. Then when the swingin' Swede is separated from her lover, she throws him this "We're going steady" bait. But if absence made Ann-Maggie's heart fonder—it caused Elvis' mind to wander. He picked up where he left off—squired around Hollywood Priscilla Beaulieu, the gal he met in the army, who'd been cooling her heels with El's folks, while Ann-M. played coy with El.

ELVIS' OWN STORY

DID THEY MAKE UP . . . OR BREAK UP

By Chris Kane

The question everyone wants to ask Elvis Presley is if he's going to marry Ann-Margret. If you remember, way back when displayed a diamond-supposed-engagement-ring, and the London paper quoted her as saying they were engaged. She also sported a charm bracelet with the appropriate words "I love you," which she didn't deny came from Elvis. Today, the talk is these two are married secretly, or are about to be married. Though Ann-Margret is now openly dating others, while Elvis hasn't been dating anyone else—the rumor is that it's all a smoke-blind—to preserve the privacy of their real feelings, to say nothing of their plans.

Well, 150,000,000 Elvis fans can relax. For Elvis, himself, on the set of *Roustabout* the new Hal Wallis Production at Paramount has set the record straight.

"She's a wonderful girl, but we don't have any plans," Elvis said. Elvis is known to be honest in replying to any questions. The only trouble is that no one can get to him to give a reply. This fact has long discouraged the average Hollywood newsman from asking for an interview. "By the time you go through all of the advance guard, the studio, the producer, Colonel Parker and the rest, you get 'no' anyway. The Presley sets are always closed, so why bother?"

Elvis cares a lot about what's said about him. He likes the truth. And the truth is he has no plans with Ann-Margret or any other girl.

"I'm not in the frame of mind nowadays to get married. I don't know why, but it's the farthest thing from my thoughts," he said point blank., "Eventually I hope the right girl comes along and I fall in love with her. And she falls in love with me and we get married. I love kids and I want a family. But right now—I'm not anxious. And how many times can I say it. . . .'

The Way-Out West

Viva Las Vegas has the wholesome, mindless spontaneity it takes to create a successful Elvis Presley movie. This one gambles on hips, not chips. Chorus girls scamper through such neon fleshpots as the Stardust, Flamingo, Tropicana and Sahara, and Elvis himself, as wrinkleproof an example of modern packaging as anyone has yet produced, sings, dances, swims, water-skis, flies a helicopter and finally enters his baby-blue racing car in a big, exciting race referred to as the Las Vegas Grand Prix.

First, though, he meets Ann-Margret, who wriggles by the garage to coo: "I'd like you to check my motor." Once her motor turns over, it seldom stops. Neither does the movie, mostly because Ann-Margret—whose scanty wardrobe suggests that she draws her energy directly from the sun—gyrates with a stem-to-stern fury that makes Presley's pelvis r.p.m.'s seem powered by a flashlight battery. Ann-Margret isn't worried about his sacrum, she is afraid he'll break his neck in the Grand Prix. But no. They enter a talent contest and tie for first prize—a prepaid honeymoon in Las Vegas. Since they are already there, the picture ends in a hurry.

181

ELVIS PRESLEY
Kissin' Cousins

There's no getting anywhere near Big Smokey Mountain without getting a hail of buckshot in the seat of your pants, because although hillbilly moonshine-liquor-maker Pappy Tatum (*Arthur O'Connell*) owns the mountain, he's always scared the Inland Revenue men will move in and confiscate his illicit still. Along with his wife Ma Tatum (*Glenda Farrell*), his two daughters Selena (*Pam Austin*) and Azalea (*Yvonne Craig*), and his nephew Jody (*Elvis Presley*), he wards off the "revenoors"—and every other stranger who ventures into Big Smokey territory.

Pappy's uncompromising hostility to all comers makes things decidedly awkward for the United States Air Force, who are anxious to build a missile base on top of the mountain but find it impossible to approach the explosive Pappy. Presently they hit upon the idea of using a go-between—a man born and raised within 15 miles of Big Smokey. He is 2nd Lieut. Josh Morgan (also played by *Elvis Presley*), who along with Capt. Salbo (*Jack Albertson*), is given seven days in which to get Pappy's signature on the lease.

Arriving in the Big Smokey region, Josh allows himself to be captured by the prowling Tatums so that he can get near enough to Pappy to explain what the government has in mind. Everyone is amazed to notice that apart from the colour of their hair, Josh and Jody are exactly alike. Josh says this is probably because his great-great-great aunt married a Tatum which makes them all 'kissin' cousins.'

Naturally, Selena and Azalea are delighted to welcome Josh and they soon make it clear that they regard him as an attractive matrimonial possibility. They are somewhat frustrated in their romantic endeavours, however, by the intermittent appearance of the Kittyhawks—a predation of love-sick mountain maidens who roam the hills in search of romance.

Meanwhile Salbo sends Josh back to the air base with a requisition for a typist. The Lieutenant returns with Midge Reilly (*Cynthia Pepper*), a beautiful WAC whom Jody immediately decides is the girl of his dreams. In time the boys and girls sort themselves out and even the Kittyhawks find their dreams unexpectedly coming true with so many G.I.s on the mountain. The remaining and biggest obstacle is Pappy's pig-headedness in the matter of signing the lease.

Kissin' Cousins can be summed-up in the phrase 'Elvis does it again'—which is a different way of saying that this film is another of those gay, colourful, romantic, fast-moving musicals which have consistently put Presley movies among the top box-office hits ever since *Blue Hawaii*. *Kissin' Cousins* is perhaps funnier than the others, with strong comedy performances by Arthur O'Connell and Glenda Farrell. Elvis demonstrates his versatility in the dual roles of smart young Air Force officer Josh, and lubberly hillbilly Jody. By playing a dual role he is able to woo and win two young lovelies, Cynthia Pepper and Yvonne Craig—the latter being the curvaceous brunette whose brief scene with Elvis in *It Happened At The World's Fair* resulted in a flood of letters to Metro-Goldwyn-Mayer to "bring her back!"

Ten sparkling numbers make a superb musical background to this fab film. They are "Smokey Mountain Boy," "Once is Enough," "Anyone," "It Hurts Me," "Kissin' Cousins," "One Boy, Two Little Girls," "Tender Feeling," "Catchin' on Fast," "There's Gold in the Mountains" and "Barefoot Ballad." *Kissin' Cousins*—that's what's buzzin' cousin!

Elvis plays a dual role.

KISSIN' COUSINS
M-G-M; Metrocolor; Director: Gene Nelson; Producer, Sam Katzman (Family)

WHO'S IN IT? Elvis Presley, Yvonne Craig, Arthur O'Connell, Glenda Farrell
WHAT'S IT ABOUT? Southern hillbillies raise a ruckus when the Air Force wants to lease their land for a missile base.
WHAT'S THE VERDICT? Fans who can't get enough of Elvis may now have a double helping: He plays both a trim officer and a shaggy mountain boy in a bright-colored musical that's put together with no particular grace, except in too-brief dances. Costuming Daisy Mae types in bikinis (of bashful cut) is a big mistake.

Despite this newspaper ad, Elvis didn't really play twins.

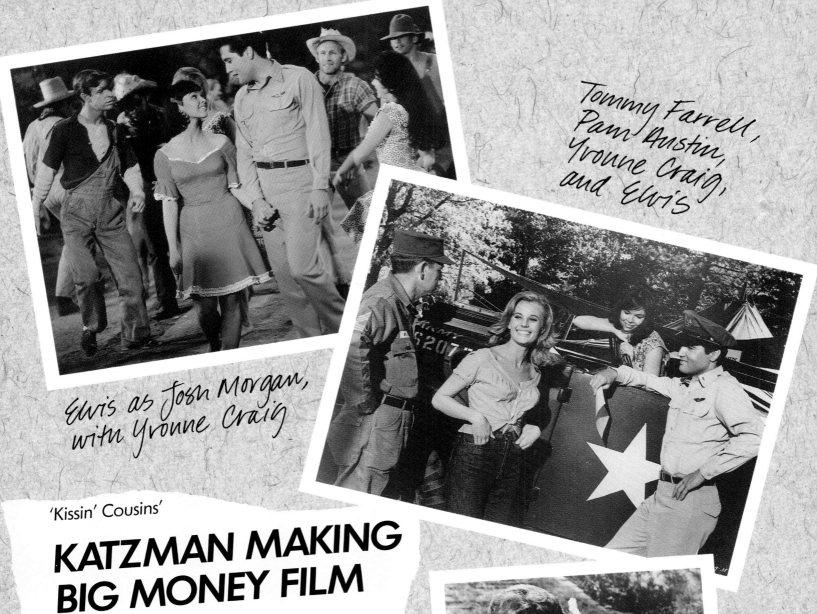

Tommy Farrell, Pam Austin, Yvonne Craig, and Elvis

Elvis as Josh Morgan, with Yvonne Craig

'Kissin' Cousins'

KATZMAN MAKING BIG MONEY FILM

By Bob Thomas

Hollywood (AP)—"Look— I'm a Woolworth guy, not a Tiffany man," said Sam Katzman, explaining his worried look.

What worried Sam, master of the quickie? He is shooting an Elvis Presley picture for $1.7 million.

"A lot of money," he said, shaking his bald head. "Elvis himself costs $500,000, plus $100,000 studio overhead on salary—don't ask me why. Then you've got $300,000 to $400,000 overhead on production costs, which means I got to make the picture for $700,000. Listen, I can do it.

Sam was sitting hard by the set of *Kissin' Cousins*, as always.

"I'm here from the first shot in the morning until the last one at night," he said. "Got to keep things moving along. Okay, let's shoot it!"

He shouted the last suggestion to the film crew, and director Gene Nelson lined up a shot of Elvis (playing a dual role in a blond wig) and a flock of curvy mountain girls.

"See that forest scene," said Sam. "Most producers would have shot it on location, where they'd run into bad weather and sit around all day. Me, I shoot at Lake Arrowhead and the rest here at the studio, where I can control things.

"We've been shooting four and a half weeks and we finish tomorrow."

"We're two hours behind schedule, and I'm worried. But we'll make it up before we're finished. Let's get moving!"

Katzman gave some hints of his operation in between nudging the film crew.

"I keep an eye on all the record charts, hunting for the latest rage," he said. "Rock 'n' Roll, The Twist—that's my meat. *Rock Around the Clock* was a good one; made it for $300,000 and it grossed $4 million.

"I had a script all ready for the Bossa Nova—put $15,000 in it. Still, I held back; it didn't seem right to me. So I took the same script and changed it to a Hootenanny."

Elvis as Jody Tatum, with Glenda Farrell

183

ELVIS, THE COLONEL...

by Henry Cris

"I'll tell you about the Colonel," said Elvis. "Last week his car broke down and Allan had the flu, so I drove him home and he invited me in. This was the first time I'd been to his house in all the years we've been in Hollywood."

"That's nothing," said the Colonel, full name Col. Tom Parker. "Last week I had a paper for Elvis to sign and I needed it in a hurry so I went up to his house, over in Bel Air.

"This was the second time in six years that I had been to Elvis' home. The other time was back in Memphis."

"I guess," said Elvis, and grinned, "We aren't the visiting kind." Elvis Presley was in Hollywood completing his latest picture, *Fun in Acapulco*, when I came to see him. The picture is his thirteenth since he stepped off the rock 'n' roll stage for his movie debut in *Love Me Tender*. he said with a good-natured chuckle, "I had a nervous twitch? Did you know," he said with a good-natured chuckle, "I had a nervous twitch? My mouth was crooked throughout the whole picture, I was that scared."

But today Elvis is neither scared nor nervous, and at 28 he is at his handsomest best. At 28, too, he has settled down to making movies with a vengeance, one following the other off the assembly line. It seems that this is the latest movie decided upon by the Colonel who thus far has called all the shots in mapping the Presley career: movies instead of personal appearances.

Somehow, the Colonel must have added up the dollars (no cents) of each operation to arrive at the conclusion that, at this time, at least, movies are much more profitable. Thus Elvis hasn't been seen on television in many a moon, and won't be by the Colonel's orders until TV networks meet his demand of 150,000 dollars a television appearance.

On the other hand, a Presley movie, rarely requiring more than four weeks of shooting, can yield for its star as much as 600,000 dollars or 150,000 dollars per week, or 3,750 dollars per hour of work. This is the current maximum and the Colonel knows he'll never be able to get more. So, he makes hay while the sun shines. But not every Presley movie brings in that much. There is only one man on the face of this earth who has outsmarted the Colonel, and he is film producer Hal Wallis, who signed Presley to his original 1956 contract...

...Tom Parker's colourful life [which] he dislikes to dwell on included a long stretch with the circus. For a while he worked for a quack doctor selling all-purpose medicine. From this he advanced to promotions of larger and wilder schemes, and so became the man responsible for the "Hadacol" craze in America a dozen years ago.

Parker was the genius of advertising for the all-purpose "medicine" which was said to be a cure-all. Parker proved his genius by never making any claims, publicly, in writing or on "Hadacol" labels. A million dollar enterprise, it was eventually sold, and Parker went on to new horizons.

The new road he took was an old one for him—hillbilly shows. America's south and south-west rely on these traveling shows for their cultural entertainment and enlightenment, in lieu of concerts and theatres. The humble folk of such States as Tennessee, Florida, Louisiana, Arkansas and Texas would rather spend an evening in a Town Hall listening to them there hillbillies sing and strum the guitar than take in a Heifetz or a Cliburn. Their admiration for a good hillbilly singer has made the shows a profitable operation with a modus operandi of one-night stands. Parker became the advance man of such a show, he being the man traveling ahead of the troupe, getting plugs from disc jockeys of local radio stations, putting up the posters.

It was in the town of Texarkana on the border of Texas and Arkansas that Parker first heard a Presley record, actually his first, on a jukebox in a roadhouse cafe. This led to the two meeting in Nashville, Mecca of the hillbillies, a month later and the Colonel making a mental note to make use of the lad whenever he got a show of his own together....

...And through all these years of triumph Elvis has been following the Colonel's orders as obediently as an army private facing his platoon sergeant. In fact, the only other person allowed to tell Elvis what to do or not to do was his late mother whom he worshipped. Strangely, even though the Colonel won't admit it, Elvis will listen to the Colonel rather than to his father whom he truly loves and respects but in a very different way. The Colonel is really "dad" but Parker is shrewd enough to insist that he has no influence on Elvis.

But don't you believe him...

"Elvis is big enough to lead his own life," the Colonel said that day from behind the giant desk in his private inner sanctum at Paramount Studios in Hollywood. The desk, in L-shape, offers him a least 12 lineal feet of table space. Elvis was occupying one of the brown vistors' chairs next to a giant stuffed Koala bear, a gift for the Colonel from Australia," Elvis said diplomatically.

"The Colonel always knows what he is talking about," said Elvis.

"If there is such a thing as a Presley image," said Colonel, "it's all Elvis' own doing. I just run the business side..."

Elvis smiled, said nothing.

"I guess we agreed on a number of things early in the game," the Colonel went on, "but that was quite a few years ago. Ever since I let Mr. Presley live his life the way he wants to, and maybe that's why I've made a point not to call on him at home. Ever."

Col. Parker was a shrewd manager and tough negotiator. After 1955, Elvis was his only client.

Tough Old Col. Parker Gets Elvis a Raise

BY HEDDA HOPPER

Hollywood, Jan. 24—Col. Parker keeps saying, "I've had a barrel of rice waiting in my office for years. I'm sure I'd be the first to know if Elvis got married. He'd want a better deal because he'd need more money to support a wife." The wheeling, dealing colonel has just closed a contract with United Artists for two pictures in '65 for $1,3000,000. One producer told him Elvis' films weren't doing so good and he'd better cut his price. "I'd better go up," said Parker. Next day the producer signed Presley for more dough. "If they're happy losing money," said the colonel, "I don't want to disappoint them."

• • •

Sometime ago another producer gave the colonel the script and said: "If Elvis does this, he'll win an Oscar. But he'd have to cut his price to $50,000." "Tell you what," said the colonel. "You pay our fee—$350,000—and if Elvis wins, I'll refund your money."

Memphis Press-Scimitar

Hedda Says Elvis Still The King In Hollywood

By HEDDA HOPPER

HOLLYWOOD—By the standards of its golden era, Hollywood has only one real capital-letter Movie Star left, and Hollywood hardly knows him. Valentino and Garbo had cults of worshipers around the globe; they could not appear in public without police on hand to prevent a riot.

And that's a pair of shoes that fits nobody in town today except the man an international community of the young calls "Elvis the King."

Elvis Presley was 30 this month, but nobody's worried. Norman Taurog, who has just directed him in "Tickle Me," their fifth picture together, reasons: "Being young today is an attitude; it's like being in a secret society…

Square Peg

He may be the kingpin, but in Hollywood he's like a square peg. Hollywood, except for a girl here and there, hardly knows him because he has managed to make 18 pictures over a nine-year period while studiously keeping Hollywood at arm's length.

He has never set foot in any of its restaurants or night clubs. He never goes to its parties or attends the premieres. He rents a house while making a picture and there gives small dinner parties seldom attended by guests whose names you see in lights or headlines. When the picture is over, he goes back to Graceland, his Memphis estate.

There he holes up with the nine young cronies who accompany him everywhere, including Hollywood. They have their own dates at his dinner parties, play touch football with him, run errands, attend to his every want and jealously seal him off from all intruders. Hollywood facetiously calls them the "Tennessee Mafia," and he couldn't be safer behind the Notre Dame line. The world of Elvis Presley is, in fact, a closed circuit.…

Elvis was injured playing football with the Memphis Mafia.

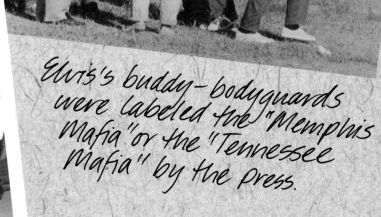

Elvis's buddy-bodyguards were labeled the "Memphis Mafia" or the "Tennessee Mafia" by the press.

Elvis and close pal Red West practice Karate.

Elvis Presley Stars in 'Roustabout,' a Movie About Carnivals

The Cast

Roustabout, screenplay by Anthony Lawrence and Allan Weiss; directed by John Rich; produced by Hal Wallis for Paramount. At the Forum Theater, Broadway and 46th Street, and other theaters. Running time: 101 minutes.

Charlie Rogers	Elvis Presley
Maggie Morgan	Barbara Stanwyck
Cathy Lean	Joan Freeman
Joe Lean	Leif Erickson
Mijanou	Sue Ane Langdon
Harry Carver	Pat Buttram
Margie	Joan Staley
Little Egypt	Wilda Taylor

There are worse things than an Elvis Presley movie—far worse. By now the producer Hal Wallis and his Memphis Percolator have a reasonably workable formula down pat, and, we might add, painless. Take one Presley, add pretty girls, pretty color and a picturesque background and mix in plenty of tunes.

Roustabout, arriving yesterday at the Forum and other theaters (with the latter also showing a Western, *Stage to Thunder Rock*) isn't nearly so trim a package as, say, *Fun in Acapulco* or *Viva, Las Vegas.* Unfortunately, the very thinnest of stories has been extracted from the world of the carnival. The picture simply ambles around in a circle, getting nowhere.

It has three assets. One is Mr. Presley, perfectly cast and perfectly at ease, as a knockabout, leathery young derelict who links up with a small-time transient midway. It also has, as the carnival owner, the professional seasoning of Barbara Stanwyck. Welcome back, Miss Stanwyck, and where on earth have you been? And while the carnival canvas yields little in the way of dramatic substance, it does cue in 11 songs. Most of them, arriving thick and fast, are dandy.

The plot? Well, Elvis can't get along with Leif Erickson as the foaming show manager, or with Joan Freeman as his comely daughter. The young roustabout takes his guitar to a rival show, but comes back just in time to save Miss Stanwyck's outfit from financial ruin. That's about it. The gristly dialogue and flavorsome atmosphere add up to nothing.

However, Presley fans shouldn't mind. The man from Memphis is on the screen every minute and surprisingly convincing in his role, whether whizzing over the roads on his motorcycle, haggling over money or belting out the music. The songs, composed by Joseph J. Lilley, are right up his alley. "One-Track Heart" and "Big Love" are a pair of nifties. The cleverest, cueing in a sinuous burlesque dance by some cuties of the Nile, is a rock 'n' roll parody titled "Little Egypt."

Roustabout is tuneful and colorful, yes. But it's mighty, mighty light considering the meat of such a background.

HOWARD THOMPSON

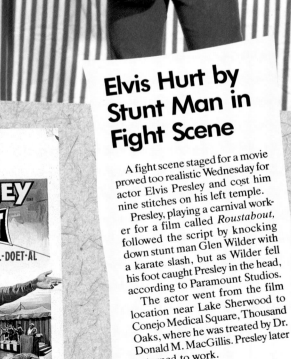

Elvis sang 11 tunes in Roustabout.

Elvis Hurt by Stunt Man in Fight Scene

A fight scene staged for a movie proved too realistic Wednesday for actor Elvis Presley and cost him nine stitches on his left temple.

Presley, playing a carnival worker for a film called *Roustabout,* followed the script by knocking down stunt man Glen Wilder with a karate slash, but as Wilder fell his foot caught Presley in the head, according to Paramount Studios.

The actor went from the film location near Lake Sherwood to Conejo Medical Square, Thousand Oaks, where he was treated by Dr. Donald M. MacGillis. Presley later returned to work.

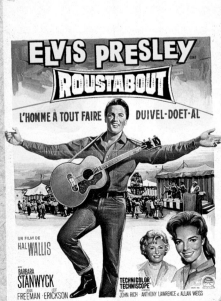

French poster for the film

Elvis and Joan Freeman – the new generation; Barbara Stanwyck and Leif Erickson – stars from Hollywood's golden age

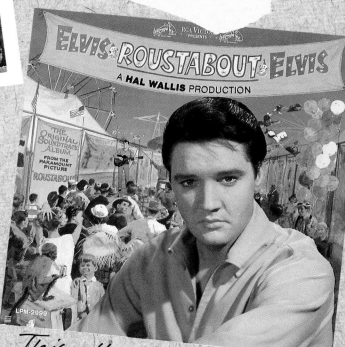

LPM-2999

Magazine ads

This album reached #1 on the charts.

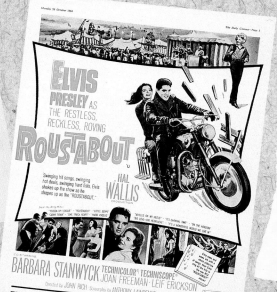

187

Memphis Press-Scimitar   September 7, 1965

Elvi$ Pre$ley Now The Biggest $tar

By EDWIN HOWARD

Nobody, but nobody, in show business will earn more this year than Elvis Presley. And that's the gospel truth; it comes from Variety, the bible of show business.

Variety estimates Elvis's income from all sources for 1965, at between $4 and $5 million. Even more astonishing, Elvis's salary from movies alone during 1965 will amount to at least $2,700,000. That's just basic salary, without the percentage of net profits which he also gets on all his film deals. And that's for only about 20 weeks' work. Liz Taylor, Cary Grant, Audrey Hepburn and a few others may get $1 million per film, plus a percentage of the profits, but they make only one, or at the most, two films a year. Elvis is moving into the million dollar class, and he is finishing up his fourth film for the year.

Elvis's income from the four films, according to Variety, breaks down this way:

Allied Artists' *Tickle Me* (made the first of the year and released in the spring)—$750,000 plus 50 per cent of the net profits.

MGM's *Harum Scarum* (made in the spring and scheduled for release at Thanksgiving)—$1,000,000 plus 40 per cent of the net.

United Artists' *Frankie and Johnny* (made this summer and due for release early in 1966)—$650,000 plus 50 per cent of the net.

Paramount Has a Bargain

Paramount's *Hawaiian Paradise* (now being completed in Hawaii)—about $300,000. This is an estimate based on the fact that Elvis's contract with producer Hal Wallis was made some time ago, before his price went so high. This is his last picture under his current contract with Wallis, and if a new contract is negotiated, the price will undoubtedly be considerably higher.

The $2,700,000 total, remember does not include the percentages. On a film that cost $1.5 million and grossed $5,000,000, which is about average for a Presley picture, the net would be about $500,000, of which Elvis, under most contracts, would get half, or $250,000.

On top of his movie income, Elvis gets his record royalties, publishing royalties (most of his songs are published by his own music publishing companies), BMI (Broadcast Music Inc.) performance royalties, residuals from tv showings of his earlier movies, and income from Elvis Presley merchandise and personal investments. Variety's estimate of $4 to $5 million total income for the year doesn't seem at all excessive. . . .

IS ELVIS WORTH $1,000,000 ???

To those who actually believe that the Beatles, or any of the top groups really compare with Elvis Presley's fame these days — we wonder if they know that now El gets the same money as Liz Taylor—a million dollars per picture!

As for Liz, she insists that she wants to check over the scripts of future movies and then she will approve or disapprove, but Elvis says, "If someone wants to pay me a million dollars, I jus' have faith enough to know they aren't going to pick out something that isn't great."

Not long ago this magazine asked you readers whether or not you still felt El is King—well we knew he was all the time —but we didn't know that the King had so much power! The letters poured and poured into our office until the postmen were traveling in shifts and we barely had room for all the ballots you sent—and every one said YES—ELVIS IS STILL KING!

Elvis himself was one of the happiest people on this Green Earth when we told him and his manager, Colonel Parker, about how faithful you fans were and how much you still cared about him. About all Elvis could say on the phone was, "Golly . . . . they are wonderful fans. Please tell them I love them all."

There's no doubt about it—ELVIS PRESLEY is worth a million dollars to us and to the people he works for and we are as happy as you are that he's getting it. Why? Simply because El donates such a large amount of his earnings to the poor, to charities, to people who need it. LONG MAY HE BE KING!

TEEN SCRAP BOOK

IS ELVIS PRESLEY REALLY WORTH A MILLION DOLLARS?

TRINI LOPEZ: HIS SECRET WEAPON

ANNETTE and HER FRIENDS: "WHAT WE THINK ABOUT PAJAMA PARTIES!"

THOSE SHINDIG GALS

GETTING PERSONAL WITH SANDRA DEE

CLINT EASTWOOD TALKS ON BLIND DATING

In 1965, Elvis earned more than any other film star.

Mop-Haired Rivals Come and Go, But He Stays

Elvis—Bigger Than Ever

By Dick Kleiner

Will the Beatles threaten Elvis's popularity?

HOLLYWOOD—It begins to look as though Elvis Presley, Old Man Rhythm, will just keep on rock 'n' rolling along.

(Elvis is presently at his Graceland home in Whitehaven. He is expected to return to Hollywood next month.)

Presley, 30, has just finished his 21st feature film, *Paradise Hawaiian Style.* There is no reason to believe the results will be any different from the previous 20—most of the critics will dismiss it as drivel. But it will make enormous profits.

There are few sure things in the movie business, but a Presley film appears to be that rarity. His pictures cost relatively little to make but are inevitably huge profit makers.

NINE DEALS

Consequently, Presley—or, rather, his molder-manipulator-manager, Col. Tom Parker—can predictably write his own ticket. Every major studio wants Presley and currently there are nine deals outstanding for films.

For the recent *Tickle Me,* Presley received a salary of $750,000. plus 50 percent of the profits—and the profits will probably run around $5 million. For another of his latest movies, *Harum Scarum,* Presley was paid $1 million, plus a reported 50 per cent of the profits.

RCA'S KING

What's more, Presley is still RCA's top record seller. As of the beginning of this year, 66 Presley singles had sold more than one million copies each. Total record sales are considerably more than 100 million. One record—"Hound Dog" has sold 6½ million copies.

A breakdown of his 1965 income alone staggers the mind:
- Salary for *Harum Scarum*—$1,000,000.
- Salary for *Frankie and Johnny*—$650,000.
- Salary for *Paradise Hawaiian Style*—$350,000.
- Percentage of profits for *Tickle Me*—$850,000.
- Percentage of profits for *Girl Happy*—$850,000.
- RCA record royalties—$1,125,000.
- Music publishing company royalties—$400,000.
- Merchandise product royalties—$60,000.

This comes roughly to $5½ million, a figure sources close to Presley estimate as "reasonably accurate." But the tax bite is enormous—even with Col. Parker's careful paring.

BIG PAYROLL

And his expenses are no small potatoes, since there are believed to be some 33 people on his payroll.

Happily, however, Presley seems virtually unaware of his power. He lives a quiet, almost uneventful life (for a Hollywood star). Because of his enormous wealth, there is little he cannot do or buy. And yet most people who have come to know him wind up feeling a little sorry for him.

His life is insulated. He exists in a kind of mink-lined cocoon. Whether at home in Graceland, his estate in Memphis; or in his rented home in the Bel Air section of Los Angeles; or in his fancy dressing room at one of the studios, he wants for nothing.

His dressing room at Paramount, for example, has two refrigerators—one exclusively for ice cream. There is a soda bar (Presley neither smokes nor drinks). Behind a big mirror, there is a hidden bedroom and bath. The dressing room even has its own barber chair.

FLEET OF CARS

He has a fleet of Cadillacs and Lincoln Continentals. He still keeps the pink Cadillac he bought for his mother. She died in '58 and he was devoted to her, so he kept the car.

Presley seldom goes out. His fun revolves around his coterie of friends. There are 12 of them on his payroll. Word is that they each make $10,000 a year. Recently he bought them all motorcycles, at $1,000 per bike. With Presley on his Harley-Davidson, they make up a group they call El's Angels.

STAYS HOME

Still, Presley says he is reluctant to go out often because of his overwhelming popularity.

Perhaps that feeling is justified. He has been burned in the past.

In New Orleans once, six girls bound and gagged an elevator operator and captured Elvis. They held him prisoner between floors on the elevator for an hour. On one trip to Hawaii, he had to walk 50 feet from the hotel to a car. In that distance, the waiting crowd took his shirt, watch, ring and wallet.

But unlike some stars, Presley is not bitter.

They tell a story in Hawaii about his generosity. Some years ago, he did a show to help raise money for the USS Arizona Memorial. The show brought in $67,000. Elvis wrote out a matching check.

* * * *

Elvis gave $35,000 to Memphis charities this year as Christmas gifts, a check for $1,000 going to each organization. This includes the Press-Scimitar's Cynthia Milk Fund and the Goodfellows.

He also remembered a number of charities in Mississippi, Los Angeles and Omaha, Nebraska for a grand total of $101,350.

Fanzines from around the world think so.

Shelley Fabares and Elvis

Gary Crosby, Elvis, Joby Baker, and Jimmy Hawkins

Newspaper ad

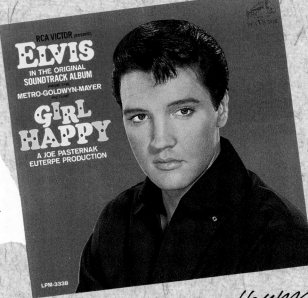

Soundtrack album

Elvis' Chinese New Year

MGM's *Girl Happy*, starring Elvis Presley, has broken all house records in its world premiere engagement at the Lee and Princess theatres in Hong Kong. Released in Hong Kong as a Chinese New Year's attraction, *Girl Happy* grossed $46,436 in first nine days at the two theatres, approximately 20% over the previous Presley record holder, *Viva Las Vegas*.

★★★★★★★★★★★★★★
MOVIE SLANTS
A REVIEW OF FILMS CURRENT AND RECENT

TICKLE ME

The plots of Elvis Presley pictures are so predictable these days that one could almost write a "blind" review. As usual, Elvis is a swaggering stud who wanders into a girl-filled milieu, causes a plethora of jealous feelings and a minimum of intelligent behavior, gets his girls (this time it's toothsome Jocelyn Lane) and wins the admiration of a mature woman (Julie Adams) who owns the expensive dude ranch into which guitar-twanging rodeo-rider Elvis has wandered. Need we tell you more? Yes, there are songs; yes, there are the stock romantic situations and banal conflicts and infantile dialogues that we have come to expect in Presley films. It is, of course, sacrilege to suggest it, but Elvis at 30 ought to make up his mind that he can't go on this way forever; his admirers keep claiming he can act, but he will never get a chance to prove it in this eternal succession of tripey films that he chooses to walk through rather than act. He is his usual pouting, half-sneering self here, projecting those negative, animalistic, pseudo-sexed qualities that the immature think attractive. But maybe—just maybe—he can act. So why doesn't he try?

Costar Jocelyn Lane and Elvis

Elvis swings to "Dirty, Dirty Feeling."

Memphis Press-Scimitar   November 7, 1964

Brigitte May Be Elvis' Co-Star

by EDWIN HOWARD

While Elvis Presley is lounging around the *Tickle Me* set in Hollywood with 12 (count 'em) bikinied beauties (tickle whom, I wonder), producer Joe Pasternak is preparing to go to Paris. If all goes well, he'll bring back Elvis a present that any red-blooded American boy would like to have, and I don't mean a miniature of the Eiffel Tower.

Pasternak takes off Monday for Paris to talk to Brigitte Bardot about co-starring with Elvis in *The Kiss That Set the World on Fire.* (That ought to tickle him, by golly!) It will be Elvis's second film for Pasternak. The first, *Girl Happy,* is set for spring release. But first will come *Roustabout,* in which Elvis has veteran Barbara Stanwyck as his co-star. It opens Nov. 25 at the Malco.

I suggested a year or so ago in The Front Row that it was time to start pairing Elvis on the screen with other big names, and now it looks as if the producers are having the same idea.

Magazine and Newspaper ads

191

ELVIS SWINGS IN— STILL ON TOP

...After 10 years Elvis Presley is a classical figure in rock 'n'roll, a respected institution—and still a howling success. Here, as a sheik, he swings into a harem in his new film, *Harem Holiday*. For 18 days' work in the movie he got $1 million plus 50% of profits. At 30, he is the highest paid actor in the world. In his decade at the top, Elvis has sold 100 million records, more than any other singer. He makes four single records a year and none sell less than 1,000,000....

The costumes and sets for Harum Scarum were leftovers from other movies.

Elvis strikes a pose reminiscent of Valentino.

Teenage Supplement to Personality, February 3, 1966

ELVIS'S CORNER

English critics slam new Elvis film—is it because the "King" wants to meet the Queen?

by Don Macfarlane

Is England taking revenge on Elvis? A few weeks ago Colonel Tom Parker received his umpteenth request for "his boy" to appear in England. After 10 years at the top and after selling millions of records in the British Isles, Elvis has never visited England. When he was serving in the American Forces in 1958-1960 he spent two years in Europe, but England never saw him. Since then he has received all kinds of offers to appear there and the fees offered have reached astronomical proportions.

The latest request for a personal appearance by Elvis came from a charitable organization, which offered Elvis half a million dollars for one show. Col. Parker turned it down, pleading that Elvis was far too busy making pictures.

But then the Colonel (unfortunately) happened to mention that, if Queen Elizabeth would consent to meet Elvis, such a visit might be considered. The English Press apparently did not like this. When he was about to start work on his newest film for M-G-M, tentatively titled *Never Say Yes* and to be produced by "musical king" Joe Pasternak, Elvis's other M-G-M offering, *Harem Holiday*, had just been released in England.

And then the critics pounced.

Never before has a Presley picture been given such a thorough and merciless hammering by the British Press. Here are a few examples:

"Elvis's worst film yet!"

"Audiences are going to laugh in the wrong places. Even Presley's appearance in baggy, Sinbad-the-Sailor-type pants and a turban is laughable."

His acting is stilted and the love scenes pathetic.

"Nothing good can possibly be said about this B-type effort. The standard is so bad that some parts defy description!"

"Presley has three facial expressions. In *Harem Holiday* he uses them endlessly."

"Why someone in Presley's undisputed position allows himself to be associated with this sort of poor film, I will never know."

"Bad lighting, poor dubbing and jerky editing that occasionally seems to send Elvis twitching across the screen."

"All if this would be excusable if the songs were worth hearing. But most of them have mediocre tunes. They're old-fashioned items like 'My Desert Serenade' and 'Kismet.'"

"Technically poor. . . ."

"I nominate this as the worst picture he has ever made."

Now we know that Elvis has seldom found favour with professional film critics as such. Ever since his career began with *Love Me Tender* (that film in particular seemed to rouse reviewers into using words not normally found in newspaper reviews!) he has been the butt of attacks.

But nothing such as the reviews that were printed after *Harem Holiday* was screened for the Press in London's Regal Theatre have ever appeared before. Why? Can it be a result of Colonel Parker's demand that the Queen meet Elvis?

Could be! . . .

Elvis Gets 3-Film Deal on Birthday

'In My Harem' First Picture Under His New Metro Pact

BY HEDDA HOPPER

Elvis Presley got a beautiful birthday present (he was 30 last Friday)—a three-picture deal with Metro. Colonel Tom Parker couldn't give out the exact figures—other stars get jealous you know—but for one of his recent films Elvis got $750,000 plus 50% of the profits, and he's not cutting his price. His first under the new deal will be *In My Harem*. I asked the Colonel what that was about.

"I don't read scripts," he said. "If those studios aren't smart enough to come up with a good story, I can't help 'em. For the kind of money they're paying us, we can leave the problem of making pictures to them. All Elvis has to do is be there on time. He is. We just take the money as we work. We give the government its full share, and we've never had it so good...."

The film was first titled In My Harem, then Harem Holiday, then Harem Scarum, and finally Harum Scarum.

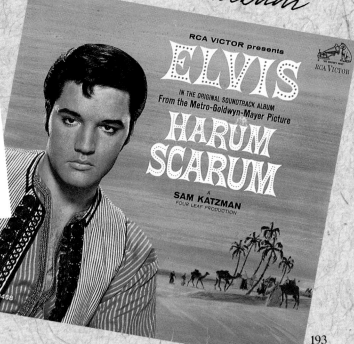

Soundtrack album

Elvis croons "Mirage" to a harem of exotic women.

The Girls He Left Behind Him

Since he first burst into song several years ago, Elvis Presley has expressed his sentiments towards the opposite sex in scores of lyrics.

"I will spend my whole life through—Loving You," he throbbed on one occasion, and sang the same vow in different words in "For just as long as I live—I'm Yours."

He has insisted in song that "I want you, I need you, I love you," and "I can't help falling in love with you"; and he has suffered several painful states of loving set to music, such as "I got stung," "I'm all shook up," "All I could do was stand—paralysed," and "I'm going to stick like glue because I'm stuck on you."

In his eleven movies, however, Elvis hasn't been "stuck on" any girl more than two films. He has behaved, in fact, more according to the intentions he voiced in an early song: "Got a lot o' livin' to do, whole lot o' lovin' to do."

We have just seen him surrounded by half a gross of girls in *Girls! Girls! Girls!*, though he was romantically affected only by two of them, **Laurel Goodwin** and **Stella Stevens**—both new to Presley pictures and the latest in a long line of co-stars.

Let us recall the other girls he's left behind in films.

Debra Paget was his first girl friend, in *Love Me Tender*.

In *Loving You*, **Lizabeth Scott** and **Dolores Hart** clashed for his affections, but Dolores won—and fell for him all over again two pictures later in *King Creole*, this time in competition with **Carolyn Jones**.

In between, **Judy Tyler** was the girl he implored to "Treat Me Nice" in *Jailhouse Rock*, and then—after army service—he met **Juliet Prowse** in *G. I. Blues*.

Barbara Eden nursed an unrequited love for him in *Flaming Star*, and in *Wild In The Country* he had to choose between **Hope Lange, Tuesday Weld** and **Millie Perkins**.

More girls than ever found their way into *Blue Hawaii*, in which he enjoyed the job of showing them round the island. **Joan Blackman** was the "Hawaiian Sweetheart" of his choice and Joan recently ousted **Lola Albright** and clinched him again in *Kid Galahad*. Before his spell in the boxing ring, however, he had discovered that **Anne Helm** was his "Angel" in *Follow That Dream*.

As for Elvis in real life, his attitude so far can be summed up in another song he sang in *Follow That Dream:* "I'm Not The Marrying Kind," which he caps with "I Don't Wanna Be Tied" in *Girls! Girls! Girls!*

And that's the girl situation at this moment . . . .

With Debra Paget...

... Juliet Prowse...

...Joan Blackman...

... and Barbara Eden

With Laurel Goodwin

ELVIS PRESLEY'S NEW GIRLFRIENDS

During the past ten years the romantic linking of Elvis Presley's name with his leading ladies, and countless other female stars and starlets around Hollywood, has become the most popular game in the film city since gin rummy.

SINATRA TELLS ELVIS HOW TO REALLY SWING

The image is preposterous. Sinatra even wanting to give Presley advice—on anything! Why he wouldn't waste his time! And Presley—how much do you want to bet El would listen? He'd be polite because he's always polite, but he wouldn't necessarily sit and take it for more than a few minutes.

It's a toss up as to who sells more records, but at this writing we have to admit it's El all the way—as far as selling records internationally he's the winner (except for Bing Crosby in total sales). Then why—you ask—you under the hair dryers or at the soda fountains or in your frilly little bedrooms—why the speculation? the query? the statement? Sinatra tells Elvis how to really swing??

Well—because it's an intriguing thought. Take Sinatra—once a scrawny kid from the Italian slums of Hoboken—now at 50 he's presumably older and a little wiser than El so he could show him a few things—give him a few tips.

Like how he got to be where he is. One of the most powerful figures in the entertainment industry today. Plus being one of the most romantic and mystical figures no matter how you slice it—as a former girlfriend said wistfully. "He made me love him. I didn't want to do it . . . it's like this—his eyes, plus his mouth, plus his voice, plus his attitude equal a sex appeal so earth shattering there's no point in fighting it. . . ."

. . . Sinatra is world famous as a swinger and great lover; his exploits are too numerous to go into now—let's just say the last one was pretty tempestuous. It ended abruptly and sadly for both parties. Now Mia is in Rome nursing her wounds with Mike Nichols and the Burtons are giving her advice. She's probably a more womanly girl for this experience. But Sinatra won't be telling. It's his code and most famous men behave in like fashion—they never talk about it afterwards—it ain't gentlemanly to tattle.

And El would agree on that score. Although this soft faced lad has not tried marriage yet, he's been awfully close to it. He too keeps his mouth shut about romance. "I can't discuss it," he grinned several years ago when a reporter asked him if he wanted to get married. "I haven't found a girl I'm sure I'm right for," was his modest statement.

El has diligently kept out of the spotlight for several years now causing his fans to love him even more. Mystery breeds interest and El has certainly been mysterious about love. If and when he marries it'll be a big surprise—maybe even to him!

So—Sinatra and he wouldn't trade secrets of the boudoir—perish the thought! . . .

Elvis, Priscilla Beaulieu, Jerry Schilling, and Jerry's date

The Girl Elvis Marries . . .

Elvis Presley announced recently that the girl he marries will have to like his kind of life. That means no fancy restaurants, no first-nighter scenes, and no late nights. Elvis never goes out on the town, and you can't really blame him. Every time he ventures out he gets mobbed. If you're lucky enough to date Elvis, here's what you'll probably be doing. You'll have a fabulous dinner at his place, shoot a game or two of billiards, watch the latest movie or perhaps television.

The girl who's come closest to becoming Mrs. Elvis is 22-year-old Priscilla Beaulieu, the daughter of an Army officer. Elvis has bought her a diamond and a home. There are two places that Elvis calls "home", a mansion in Hollywood and a lavish home in Memphis called Graceland. Elvis doesn't smoke or drink, calls his elders "sir" or "ma-am," and has never been involved in any scandal. After 10 years of making records, Elvis is still King. . . .

Elvis and mystery girl Priscilla

TROUBLE IN HIS PARADISE?

**From:
derek hunter
in hollywood**

☐ "Whatever's the matter with Elvis Presley?" is a question that's been heard frequently around Hollywood these days.

Elvis, long cited as one of Hollywood's most co-operative and least "difficult" stars, has lately been reported as having turned on some surprising outbursts of temperament. He even held up shooting on one recent movie, adding to the cost of the picture.

This was the soon-to-be-released *Paradise, Hawaiian-Style*, which turned out to be anything but a paradise for Elvis—and his co-workers!

The trouble started even before Elvis set out for location shooting in Hawaiian islands. A mystery illness caused several days' delay, when Elvis was too sick to present himself at the studio for wardrobe fittings.

Elvis eventually arrived in Hawaii, but without his usual smiling face. And he promptly shut himself away from everyone—including his gang of pals, bodyguards, so-called "Memphis Mafia."

The only person he would see was a "mystery" visitor from Hollywood—a 19-year-old blonde whom he did not even introduce to the rest of the film company.

Although he must have known that filming was at a standstill because the picture could not proceed without him, Elvis remained incommunicado in his hotel suite or his oak-panelled, red-carpeted luxury portable dressing-room, with its own three-stool bar and refrigerator stocked with his favourite ice cream.

When after two days of Elvis' self-imposed isolation, crew members ventured to approach his sanctuary, Elvis sharply rebuked them. "I'm resting", he said tersely. "I said I didn't want to see anyone, and I mean it. I didn't think you were ready for me to start shooting just yet. Now I'm not ready for YOU!"

When Elvis finally went to work in front of the cameras, he was not his usual patient and polite self. He continually grumbled about the way his privacy was always being disturbed. He beefed about the circus that always surrounds him, and how he'd hoped to be able to get away from it all in Hawaii.

Members of the crew—who usually sing the praises of Presley—shook their heads in disapproval of his odd behaviour, which caused friction in the company.

Blonde singer, Brenda Martell, who knows Elvis very well, confirmed reports of his recent strangeness when I talked to her. Miss Martell, noted for her "Day In, Day Out" record, told me Elvis had shut himself up in his private room of his 22-room Bel Air mansion just before going to Hawaii.

"And it was the same in Hawaii," she said. "The boys told me Elvis wanted to be alone much of the time there, although he had his 'mystery' guest for company...."

Magazine and newspaper ads

The Soundtrack peaked at # 15.

Memphis Commercial Appeal June 10, 1966

Elvis Acting Still Limps After 10 Years, 12 Movies

By John Knott

Ten years ago, I reviewed Elvis Presley's first movie, *Love Me Tender.* Yesterday I reviewed his latest, *Paradise, Hawaiian Style,* which opened at the Malco.

In that first review, I complained mildly over the fact that he couldn't act so well, but he was new at it then, and there wasn't much plot.

A lot of film has gone through the camera in 10 years. Elvis now makes something like $13,000 every day, holidays and all. He's been in the service, had a dozen or so films behind him, and gotten a little bit jowly.

His movies haven't changed. Not much acting, not much plot.

This is just a comment. The producers quite probably would say: "So what? You want Jill St. John should cook?"

And they're right...If you like this kind of movie, you'll like this movie. And this kind of movie is liked. Reviewing movies in the afternoon on a summer day is usually kind of lonesome; you may be one of three or four in the huge emporium.

There was a line of people outside the Malco waiting to get in yesterday. The movie will make money; that's one of the sure things that exists in show business. Any Elvis Presley movie will make money, all of them always do.

The movie is about a fly-by-night pilot who can't keep the girls away from him and loses his job. So he becomes partners with an old friend in a helicopter tourist service. So he enlists some of his many girl friends who just happen to work for airlines and tourist agencies and hotels to help him. And they're all strong for him. But there's this girl that works in the office, who pretends she's married to fend him off, and suddenly she doesn't want to fend him off....

There are some gorgeous scenes of Hawaii that should increase travel from here to there, the girls are equally gorgeous and a little girl named Donna Butterworth who plays the young daughter of his partner is an absolute doll. She sings along in one of the nine songs Elvis sings in the film.

Actress Hill Unimpressed by Presley

By EARL WILSON

New York — There are people brave enough to think and mostly they are young... and one is 21-year-old Marianna Hill who plays Elvis Presley's leading lady in a film but cannot be induced to say that Elvis is a great acting talent.

And many of the so-called "in" people and places are "frauds," "wasteful," and "dissipating," alleges she.

Long-haired Marianna, grandniece of New Jersey police boss Norman Schwarzkopf, has recently filmed *Paradise, Hawaiian Style,* with Presley.

"They kept asking me," Marianna says, "'Hasn't he got talent?' That was when the picture was starting.

"I said, 'He's a show business phenomenon.'

"Did you ever have a date with Elvis?" I asked Marianna.

"No," she squirmed. "You see, he's got his entourage, and they go over to his house and eat popcorn and watch television...."

197

FRANKIE AND JOHNNY

U.A.; Technicolor; Director, Frederick de Cordova; Producer, Edward Small (Family)

WHO'S IN IT? Elvis Presley, Donna Douglas, Nancy Kovack, Harry Morgan.

WHAT'S IT ABOUT? On an old-time riverboat, a singer's gambling mania enrages his partner-sweetheart.

WHAT'S THE VERDICT? Don't let the title throw you. The gamy American folk song has been cleaned up and prettified to serve only as a musical number in a lazy sort of movie that is quite proper—even for Elvis' youngest fans. Ballads with no wiggling, Gay Nineties air allow him though some do have an early-jazz beat. Good fare for the kids.

Donna Douglas and Elvis as Frankie and Johnny

ELVIS PRESLEY: "FRANKIE AND JOHNNY" (RCA Victor). The Soundtrack album of the Edward Small production of *Frankie and Johnny* presents Elvis Presley on another bright musical session, this one marked by the de-emphasis on the rocking beat. Instead there's a reversion to an old-timey Dixie and ragtime beat, which Presley also handles very well. Standout numbers are the title song, recorded specially for the LP, and the pretty ballad "Please Don't Stop Loving Me."

The French title means A Lucky Redhead.

PRESLEY'S LATEST

At the turn of the century, an obscure minstrel in New Orleans started playing a narrative blues song titled "Frankie and Johnny." Since that time the song has become one of the best-loved folk songs in the history of musical Americana and has been the basis for literature, drama and ballet. Despite the tremendous world-wide popularity of the poignant love story, "Frankie and Johnny" has never been made into a film. Until now, that is—for the cameras started rolling recently with Elvis Presley starring in the title role of Johnny. The old folk song has been expanded and, as with all Presley pictures, many lavish musical numbers have been added.

Johnny has been written as a charming wastrel with a great set of vocal chords and a nimble pair of legs and a doer of wrong. Frankie, the girl whom he did wrong, the girl at the trigger end of a six-shooter, is played by Donna Douglas, who will be familiar to *Beverly Hillbillies* fans. The comedy role of Nellie Bly is well filled by shapely young beauty Nancy Kovak.

Frankie and Johnny is probably Elvis's most spectacular movie in his ten year career as one of the top-ten box office stars. Among the sets built to encompass the eleven song and dance numbers are a Mississippi River Showboat complete with theatre and gambling saloon, a New Orleans mansion's grand ballroom, various streets and shops in turn of the century New Orleans and a Southern riverside glade, complete with flowing river.

One of the most interesting points about *Frankie and Johnny* will be seeing whether or not Hollywood has baulked at the killing-off of Johnny.

Spinout and the fanzines

Title Changes For The King

Those Elvis people are getting to be as bad as those Herman people when it comes to deciding titles for movies.

After numerous title changes, we think that Herman's movie, if it's ever released (we believe they said the first part of the year), seems to have settled at *Hold On*.

But Elvis' latest has gone from *Never Say No* to *Never Say Yes* and then that idea was tossed out altogether. Now they say they're going to call it *Spinout*.

Anyway, no matter what it's called, appearing with El will be Shelley Fabares, Diane McBain, Deborah Walley, and Dodie Marshall.

And, even though they haven't yet finished this one, those Presley people have already announced the title of his next movie.

It's a romantic musical called *A Girl In Every Port* and should begin filming this summer.

The story is based on an original screenplay by Allan Weiss and Anthony Lawrence, who also wrote *Paradise, Hawaiian Style* and *Roustabout*.

ELVIS PRESLEY (RCA LPM 3702)

Elvis has been producing some fantastic albums of late. This one's a winner all the way. The first track, "Stop Look And Listen," is a knock-out. In fact to pinch a phrase, stop look and listen to this album, then you'll spinout too. This album is, of course, the sound track from his latest film, California Holiday. Best tracks include "Stop Look and Listen," "Spinout" and "Am I Ready." Other tracks include "Adam And Evil," "All That I Am," "Beach Shack" and "I'll Be Back."

Soundtrack album

Elvis and Shelley Fabares—Spinout was originally titled California Holiday.

Magazine ad

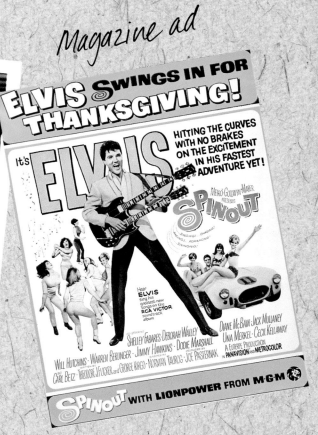

WHAT FANS THINK OF ELVIS

ELVIS PRESLEY BLAZERS
This certifies that
Sharon Fox
is a member in good standing
Motto—" Always Faithful to ELVIS"
Date *February 20, 1963*
ELVIS PRESLEY
Honorary Pres.
President—Rudonna Bruck
1105 Forrest Avenue
Fort Payne, Alabama

I am a
loyal Elvis Fan

I collect all of his
records and pictures
and see all of
his movies

signature *Sharon Fox*

Anybody who doesn't like Elvis should
see a doctor, because something must be
wrong with them.

"Elvis Fan,"
Tarram, Vic.

If Elvis is a "has-been," why is it he wins
the pop polls?

"The King Forever,"
Kilkivan, Qld.

If Elvis is a "has-been," how come he is
so popular? I have heard of groups and
singers whom people have said would last
for years—but where are they now?

"Elvis Fan,"
Redwood Park, S.A.

Elvis Presley's
Golden Platters Fan Club

Sharon Fox
IS A MEMBER IN GOOD STANDING
Motto: *"A Golden Voice - A Golden Platter"*
Aim: *"We Aim to Keep' Em Golden"*
January 1964
DATE
Mildred Eaton
INTERNATIONAL
PRESIDENT

Fan club membership cards

I am an Elvis fan, always have been and
always will be. At least he is always well
dressed, with none of this long-haired
sissy look.

"Angry Fredi,"
Adelaide City.

In reply to "Anti-Elvis," I say Elvis is the
best performer on the pop scene today.
His recordings are much more original
and exciting than the Beatle-copiers, who
comprise most of today's artists. His list of
hits from 1956 to 1967 is a phenomenal
one, which probably won't be equalled in
our time.

"Another Teenager,"
Brisbane.

Elvis didn't need a gimmick like long
hair to make him popular. He had—and
still has—a style of his own. His popularity
inevitably is shown in the number of films
and recordings he has made.
"King of Kings Fan"
Reservoir, Vic.

Elvis is one pop star the whole family
can enjoy.
"Elvis Forever,"
(a married woman),
Ballarat, Vic.

Elvis always made time
for his fans.

ELVIS ECHO   Vol. 1 No. 1

ACTOR, SINGER OR HANDSOME MAN NO ONE FILLS IT LIKE ELVIS CAN !!

ELVIS IS "KING OF KINGS" LONG MAY HE REIGN !

THE ELVIS ECHO

APRIL 1964

VOL. 1 NO. 1

INTRODUCTION
By Mildred Eaton

It has been a cherished and treasured dream in the mind and hearts of many, many fans to see an ALL-ELVIS newspaper edited, published and made available in our own United States of America, the country that gave the world the great entertainer of all times — Elvis Aron Presley.

By the hard work, the love in their hearts, and the will not to become discouraged had to be overcome, the FOREVER FAITHFUL ELVIS PRESLEY FAN CLUB OF Yonkers, New York, with its capable and efficient president, Paulette Sansone, has made this dream a reality.

In the pages of this great new publication you will be caught in the spellbound magic of the ever-growing unique world of a KING who rules the universe of entertainment.

This ALL-ELVIS newspaper, with its news, stories, contests, salutes to great Elvis disk jockeys, pictures, crossword puzzle and comic, will capture the interest and fancy of the entire world!

IT'S ALL ABOUT ELVIS — A NEWSPAPER YOU WILL TAKE TO YOUR HEART!

DEDICATED IN LOVING MEMORY OF GLADYS PRESLEY
By Sharon Goetzinger

Gladys!
The mother of our lover who shared him with the world!

From her life of poverty to her life of riches, she kept up her smile, a smile of happiness and pride. For the happiness that her son was happy, Pride because he was her son!

A woman so great, so grand, so kind! Great as a Queen, Grand as a Duchess, Kind as kindness-can be!

She was all a woman could ever be! But in the eyes of her fans she was more than just a woman. She was and still is the Queen of Hearts and Laughter!

Her heart was bigger than a mountain, a mountain of warmness, joy, and love over running stream of kindness! Always a smile on her face, a face of love and gentleness!

A wonderful mother to her, wonderful wife to her son and only wife to her one and only husband. As a wonderful hostess. Everyone she met—

Gladys!

If you could only hear us now! How much we say, how much we do and how much we appreciate what you did for your family and your family's friends and fans!

While you're away, we'll take care of your family. As each of us seen our part — a part of your family!

Now there Is a part of her, Shelby Presley, left in her son. Her smile, when he smiles. His kindness was a part of her one. And a part of her taught him when he was growing up to be her big boy, our big boy. Our Man!

Although it is not visible, she wears a crown! A crown given to her by her friends, and unknown friends, the crown for the best woman of us all! A woman with dignity, kindness, gentleness, and love! A woman with a pure heart of righteousness! So Elvis,

We, our fans, are trying to tell you how much we appreciate your mother. Her kindness and gentleness. Her times she helped you when you needed her, when we needed you!

ELVIS WINS CIVIC AWARD

Miami Herald, March 11th — Memphis — (AP) — A Memphis and Shelby County named ELVIS ARON PRESLEY as winner of its first annual AMERICANISM AWARD. The super-movie was unanimously selected over Memphis and Shelby County business and civic leaders.

The Elks said Elvis "typifies the American way of life in which anyone may rise above a lowly station to any heights in which mankind to lift him. He has retained in make measure the american attributes of DECENCY, HONESTY, FAIRPLAY and has constantly in his personal life been a flawless example of American youth."

FLASH! While doing a fight scene for his movie now in production, "Roustabout," Elvis was accidentally kicked in the head. It took from 6 to 9 stitches to close the gash over his eye.

EDITORIAL

Webster defines unity as the state of being one. Well, several months ago, I had a dream that maybe someday all of Elvis' fans could know and experience the true meaning of this word. I had visions of an all-Elvis newspaper which would one day serve as our central source of information, thus uniting us all in our common goal ... to support, boost and defend Elvis and keep him King forever!

Now I am seeing that dream become a reality, and I owe it all to you, to each and every one of you, who had enough faith in Elvis to subscribe to this publication. I don't know how to begin to express my gratitude for your understanding, patience and support, without which this paper would still be a dream.

The name ELVIS ECHO was chosen because it appropriately describes what we hope to accomplish through this paper. We shall try to keep you informed on all of Elvis' latest activities and on what you, as a fan, can do to help spread his goodness and popularity throughout the world. It must serve as your voice ... your means of expressing your opinions, your beliefs, your dreams and your ideas relating to Elvis. You are the heart of this paper, and, therefore you must supply it with the materials needed if it is to survive. Please join with us, and by us I'm referring to all of Elvis' club presidents and countless fans who have already pledged their support, and help us to make this newspaper a success. I hope you will understand that we have never attempted anything like this before, and there is much we must learn. So please send us your stories and suggestions ... let us know what you would like us to feature and omit in the future issues. Only with your support can we add more pages, more pictures, and in summation, MORE ELVIS!

We may not be professionals when it comes to writing and expressing our thoughts, but NO ONE can top us when it comes to supporting and defending the man we all love.

Echoing for Elvis,
Paulette Sansone, editor

Some fan publications look professional...

Happy Holidays

God bless you this Christmas; Elvis Presley's Golden Platters

...others look more personal.

ELVIS THE ENTERTAINER ELVIS THE PERSON CANNOT BE DUPLICATED THAT'S FOR CERTAIN !!

Xmas card from Elvis

ESPECIALLY FOR ELVIS PURPOSELY FOR PRESLEY

Seasons' Greetings
ELVIS
and the Colonel

I WOULD DIE FOR ELVIS

Elvis sticker

For Presley the grass is greener

From James Bradford in Hollywood

Three Memphis, Tennessee, teenagers are cashing in on their fellow Elvis Presley fans' worship of the ground their idol walks on.

The enterprising three have found the grass grows greener in their own neighborhood.

So they pick it from the lush lawns of Graceland, the Presley mansion in Memphis, and sell it, a blade at a time, to Elvis fans.

The teenagers, Pat Murphy, Connie McKnight and Betty Morrison, thought up the gimmick when they had to attend an out-of-town convention of young ladies, and were told to bring something "representative" of their hometown.

They decided nothing was more "representative" of Memphis today than Mr. Presley himself.

Since they could hardly bring him, they hit on the gimmick of the grass, picked some samples, put them in glass vials, and found they were the most popular young ladies at the convention.

Elated with their success, they sought out Presley's father on their return and asked permission to go on picking the grass over which Presley may have walked at some time.

When Presley heard of their plea, he instantly gave his consent, flattered and amused and pleased to learn some of his favorite charities were to benefit from the sale of the grass.

Within days there was a staggering demand for the grass vials and, pushing the gimmick for all it was worth, the three girls advertised in a teenagers magazine.

This time the response surpassed their wildest dreams. They were overwhelmed with orders, some coming from as far away as Japan and Germany, and not only from individuals but from stores as well.

The single blades sell at 50 cents a piece, and continue to sell at a brisk pace.

Since the success of the girls' venture, along has come a sharp businessman, who has tied up all the rights to the leaves that fall from the Graceland trees.

It would hardly be surprising now if someone were to go a step further and introduce the idea of bottling the Graceland air.

Elvis, who was lingering in Hollywood only long enough to pose for a few publicity stills in connection with the *Frankie and Johnny* and *Paradise, Hawaiian-Style* pictures he recently completed, admitted he was quite stunned by the extreme limits of his fans' adoration.

"I am indeed a lucky guy," he said.

He is lucky, too, to be the highest-paid entertainer in the whole of show business, again to reap fortunes from his *Frankie and Johnny* and *Paradise, Hawaiian-Style* soundtrack albums.

The industry is tremendously excited over the potential blockbusting revenues envisaged from the advance word-of-mouth raves for the scores of these two pictures.

Elvis is quite accustomed now to finding dozens of girls waiting outside the studio gates each day when he leaves work, most carrying his albums in the hope that he will stop and autograph them.

Despite his grueling schedules on *Paradise, Hawaiian-Style*, he did have his car stop at the studio gate on a number of occasions, handing out small colored photographs of himself —all autographed.

Following the completion of *Frankie and Johnny*, Presley gave away the very first guitar he had owned, to be auctioned for charity.

The original 300 dollar guitar brought a top bid of 21,000 dollars.

Elvis plays the guitar in *Paradise, Hawaiian-Style*, among a variety of other instruments, mostly Hawaiian.

He admits that he actually is not a good guitar player, more or less playing it along with his singing just to get a good beat.

The actual guitar sound is carried and properly played by his accompanying musicians.

DJ dj on the air
Do you know how much I care?
Please play Elvis every day
and next to my radio I will stay.

KING OF KINGS

We Who Love Him
ELVIS PRESLEY FAN CLUB
is one who loves Elvis
SHARON FOX, President

INTERNATIONAL ELVIS PRESLEY FAN CLUB

Fan club publications

VOLUME 1
No. 4 issue
MAY

ELVIS MONTHLY

ELVIS'S BIG YEAR
December

ELVIS MONTHLY

G.I. BLUES FILM SPECIAL

Elvis greets some ecstatic fans.

A typical fan's room c. 1960s

An Elvis souvenir

Elvis Grabs Cab, But First . . .

'I Touched Him,' Squeals Teener

HOLLYWOOD, April 21 (UPI)— It was a scene to warm the heart of the most hardened publicity man. Five-hundred squealing, giggling, sighing fans including a 72-year-old woman lined up last night to greet the return of their idol, singer Elvis Presley.

They gathered at Union Station hours before Mr. Presley and his entourage of nine friends were due to arrive aboard a private railroad car and patiently milled around when the train was almost an hour late.

'I TOUCHED HIM'

Although most of the fans were bypassed when Elvis' car was pulled to a siding where the young singer immediately boarded a taxi, one girl briefly touched him as he climbed into the cab.

"I touched him. . . . I touched him," she screamed as she dashed after the cab taking him to a hotel.

The 72-year-old fan who stood with the predominantly teenage crowd, identified herself as Mrs. Christine Rosen of Chicago and Los Angeles.

"I'm a fan of Elvis'," she said, tugging at the shawl around her shoulders. "But I don't dance rock and roll. . . ."

Elvis obliges a lucky fan.

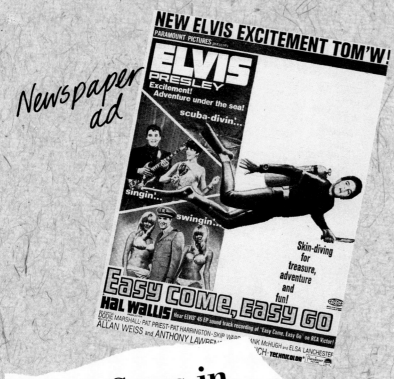

NEW ELVIS EXCITEMENT TOM'W!

PARAMOUNT PICTURES presents

ELVIS PRESLEY
Excitement!
Adventure under the sea!
scuba-divin'...
singin'...
swingin'...

Skin-diving for treasure, adventure and fun!

Easy come, Easy go

HAL WALLIS

Hear ELVIS' 45 EP sound track recording of "Easy Come, Easy Go" on RCA Victor!

DODIE MARSHALL·PAT PRIEST·PAT HARRINGTON·SKIP WARD·FRANK McHUGH and ELSA LANCHESTER
ALLAN WEISS and ANTHONY LAWRENCE ··· ···RICH·TEKNIKOLOR· Paramount

ELVIS AT HIS BEST

By Glenn Hawkins

Easy Come, Easy Go, Hal Wallis' production screening citywide, is one of Elvis Presley's best pictures.

There is a noticeable difference in this pleasant little Presley romp: He isn't called upon to warble affectatiously in every other scene as he has been in previous efforts.

The story is emphasized more. There's less strain on the ears.

He sings only a half dozen songs (at reasonable moments) to sell the picture to his legions of fans and then he holds them to their seats with a good action-adventure yarn.

Elvis (a darn good actor) plays a young Naval officer about to be mustered out of service. His last duty as an underwater demolition expert is to disarm an old mine. He discovers a sunken frigate carrying a treasure chest in the vicinity of the mine.

Curvaceous Dodie Marshall tells him that the treasure chest was carrying Spanish pieces-of-eight at the time the ship sank.

With the help of Dodie, their beatnik buddy Pat Harrington, Jr. and lovable Frank McHugh who rents diving equipment, Elvis goes after the sunken treasure.

Trouble, however, intervenes disguised in a bikini. Pat Priest, a rich girl with a Sunday-morning face and Saturday-night ideas, is out looking for kicks and Elvis is swiftest with one.

Skip Ward is ready to battle for her favor. He learns of Presley's treasure. Together, Pat and Skip try to abscond with the chest before Elvis can finish a chorus.

There's plenty of excitement above and below the water when Elvis and Skip clash. Action fans will be pleased.

Pat Harrington, Jr. is fun in a semi-comedy role. Elsa Lanchester as a yogi gets off some funny lines and joins Elvis in a duet.

But it's Frank McHugh who very nearly steals the picture, and with Elvis that's not easy. He plays a sea-sick captain of a kiddie TV show. The others are fine in their roles.

John Rich, who directed Elvis in *Roustabout*, skippers the Technicolor adventure written by Allan Weiss and Anthony Lawrence.

Elvis Stars in 'Easy Come, Go'

Easy Come, Easy Go, the latest Elvis Presley picture, is aptly summed up in its title: easy to take, easy to forget. Always pleasant, occasionally just plain hokey, it sticks to the familiar Presley formula of songs, pretty girls and a slight plot.

This time Presley plays a Navy demolitions specialist who discovers an underwater treasure trove—and Dodie Marshall, a beachnik whose grandfather owned the sunken ship containing the booty. Before Presley and his partner (Pat Harrington) can recover the pieces of eight they run afoul of heavies Pat Priest and her boyfriend Skip Ward. Naturally, all ends well.

Along the way Presley comes across two especially colorful characters: Miss Marshall's yoga teacher and a one-time captain of a TV kiddie show who's never been to sea. Elsa Lanchester, who shares a delightful duet with Elvis, "Yoga Is as Yoga Does," and Frank McHugh make the most of these parts.

Indeed, everyone excels under the smooth, well-paced direction of John Rich, who was working from an Allan Weiss-Anthony Lawrence script that is sound but a bit square in its delineation of Miss Marshall's hippy set. All told, however, Presley fans shouldn't be disappointed.

Dodie Marshall and Elvis

Elsa Lanchester and Elvis

Memphis Press-Scimitar   June 2, 1967

Best of Elvis' Recent Outings: Park's 'Double Trouble'

By Edwin Howard

A pair of fledgling producers, Judd Bernard and Irwin Winkler, have doubled up to produce the pleasantest Elvis Presley picture in the past year or so. It's called *Double Trouble*, and it opened yesterday at the Park.

Novelty and imagination don't exactly run rampant—they have Elvis doing just about what he always does—but the songs are better, the plot more intriguing, and the comic touch a soupcon lighter.

The story has Elvis, as Guy Lambert, an American rock 'n' roll singer, barnstorming European discotheques. In London, he falls for one of his fans, a red-haired, blue-eyed teen-ager named Jill (Annette Day) who rebuffs his advances but follows him on tour.

An exotic brunette beauty (Yvonne Romain) follows him, too, as do a pair of British types played by Australian Chips Rafferty and Englishman Norman Rossington.

The plot quickens as mysterious perils come within inches of injuring or killing Guy and Jill. But there is always time for a song, of course, and Elvis sings nine of them, including the title tune and "Long-Legged Girl With the Short Dress On," which seemed to me the best of the lot.

Norman Taurog's direction maintains a snappy pace, and although the film was made in MGM's Culver City studios, the European backgrounds are slickly worked in through rear screen projection and various other trick processes.

Miss Day, a newcomer allegedly plucked by producer Bernard out of her father's antique stall on London's Portobello Road, is as bright as a freshly-minted thrupence and performs more capably than one would expect of a fledgling.

Elvis, who has always had a knack for comedy, has never employed it better. Rafferty and Rossington make an amusingly bunglesome pair of thieves, and the Wiere Bros. provide their characteristic brand of slapstick as a trio of inept detectives.

Double Trouble is strictly for Presley fans, but it should double their pleasure, double their fun, and isn't hard to take even if you don't happen to be one.

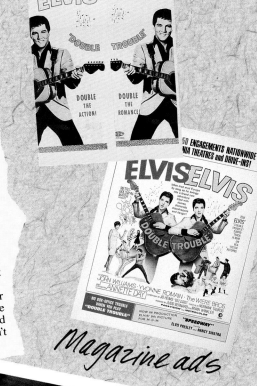

Magazine ads

Elvis croons to a Belgian Beauty.

Annette Day costars in Elvis' Musical Mystery.

On the MGM set of *Double Trouble*, 18-year-old Annette Day has been talking with Elvis Presley about buying a car and learning to drive. Elvis is just the boy to talk to about cars—at last count he owned one of each model, or just about.

Early this week Elvis said to his little English leading lady, "Come with me" and he took her by the hand right up to a brand new blue and white Mustang parked outside the stage.

It was all wrapped up in cellophane and bore the card, "Start learning to drive. Love and kisses, Elvis." You can bet not every star in Hollywood is this thoughtful nor this extravagant.

205

I SAY ELVIS IS MARRIED

—Walter Rainbird

There are 6,000,000 Elvis Presley fans in the States and uncounted millions elsewhere who want a straight answer to a simple question: Is Elvis married?

So when I ask him in New York with his entourage, which included, as usual pretty Priscilla Beaulieu, I put the question to him.

"Search the records," said Elvis, a little sharply.

Maybe it was simply because he was tired after the journey from his home in Memphis, Tennessee.

Earlier I had asked Colonel Tom Parker, Elvis's mentor, manager, financial advisor and close companion.

"Ah nevah meddle in mah boy Elvis's private life," he said.

But a good source down South had told me that Elvis and Priscilla slipped into Northern Mississippi sometime last spring and got hitched.

Colonel Tom just grunted. So I set off to search the records —and discovered an amazing fact.

There is hardly a key county job in Northern Mississippi that is not filled by Elvis's kinfolk. I never knew a man could have so many cousins.

UNWELCOME

If Elvis did get married, his country cousins are not showing the records to any "furriners."

Mississippi has a way of making outsiders feel unwelcome, especially if they ask questions, and most especially if they come from north of the Mason-Dixon line. . . .

ONLY CHILD

Elvis vows that married life is the only life.

"I was an only child. I was raised strictly by the most wonderful mother a guy ever had.

"For the first 16 years of my life, my mother and I were inseparable.

"And when she died, two weeks before I went into the army, I can't tell you what an emotional shock that was . . . what an emotional loss."

Proof of Elvis's devotion to his mother still exists today. In one of his living rooms at Graceland lies a Christmas tree on its side. It was knocked down when his mother collapsed shortly before she died. And it still lies there . . .

"My mother always taught me to behave, to have good manners, to help people, not harm them, to work hard and never give up, and make it on my own.

"She and my father were very happy —and extremely good parents.

"I want the kind of life they had together. It is the only way of life."

In that case, if Elvis is married, he will be wanting to start a family any day now . . . Then the truth will have to come out.

Elvis lives by his mother's teachings. He has an entourage like any other big star, but his are not the usual Hollywood hangers-on. They are buddies from his school days in Memphis, or else friends he made in the army.

He is completely loyal to them, and they to him.

They do all his odd jobs, like driving his Rolls Royces—he has two—or one of several Cadillacs.

MAD MOMENT

I asked him: "Just suppose, for one mad moment, you were to marry.

"Would you pick a girl like Priscilla?"

Elvis smiled. "You sure don't give up, do you?" Then seriously, he added: "She has everything a man could want in a wife."

Was 31 a good age to get married?

"Almost any age is good if you have the right girl," said Elvis.

He gave Priscilla a knowing wink. This time Priscilla smiled. If she's not "the right girl" then there just isn't one.

Fanzines speculate that Elvis and Priscilla are secretly married.

Elvis with grandmother Minnie Mae Presley and Priscilla

Memphis Commercial Appeal   May 2, 1967

Wedding Is Typically Elvis— Quick, Quiet And In Style

By Thomas F. BeVier

The private Lear jet carrying Elvis Presley and his bride-to-be thundered down from the sky before dawn yesterday to Las Vegas, a desert playground where the marriage license bureau rocks all night long.

From McCarrun Airport, Elvis Aron Presley, first of the millionaire rock and rollers, and Priscilla Ann Beaulieu, the gray-eyed, brown-haired beauty he met in 1959 during his army career in Germany went to the Clark County Courthouse.

"It was 3 a.m. (5 a.m. Memphis time) when they got here," said Mrs. Blanche Murphy, supervisor of marriage license clerks. "It was during our graveyard shift—a tough one to pull.

"The clerks couldn't remember how Elvis and Miss Beaulieu were dressed but they were impressed with what a pretty girl she was."

Both Elvis and Miss Beaulieu gave their home as Memphis. He gave his age as 32. She gave hers as 21. It was the first marriage for each.

"We ask a minimum of information here," said Mrs. Murphy. "There are no blood tests and no waiting period."

The couple paid the $15 fee—it would have been $5 if they'd gotten it between 8 a.m. and 5 p.m.—and left with an entourage of six for the Aladdin Hotel, a 400-room hostelry of English Tudor architecture across the street from Caesar's Palace.

Apparently, the couple rested for several hours until 11:41 a.m., Memphis time, when the ceremony began. It took only eight minutes for Nevada Supreme Court Justice David Zenoff, a short (5-foot-7), distinguished looking man, to marry them.

The marriage took place in the second floor private suite of Milton Prell, principal owner of the Aladdin, and longtime friend of Elvis' manager, Col. Tom Parker. There was a bridal arch and altar decorated with white chrysanthemums and roses. It was a double-ring ceremony. Elvis slipped on his bride's finger a 20-diamond ring which featured a four-carat centerstone. . . .

Elvis marries Priscilla Beaulieu on May 1, 1967.

A Tenderized Elvis Weds Longtime Gal Pal

Las Vegas, May 1 (AP)—Elvis Presley, the Mississippi boy who helped to popularize rock 'n' roll music and became a millionaire in the process, ended a reign as one of show business' most eligible bachelors today by marrying his longtime girl friend.

Presley, 32, and Priscilla Beaulieu, 22, took their vows before 14 friends in a hotel suite, then entertained 100 guests at a champagne breakfast. They said they will honeymoon for a month, probably somewhere in the United States.

Presley, who started in Memphis, Tenn., as a guitar-twanging, hip-wiggling singer, whose style has been widely imitated, has concentrated in recent years on movies. He came here from Palm Springs, Calif., for the ceremony.

Hotel Suite Ceremony

Nevada Supreme Court Justice David Zenoff performed the ceremony in the suite of Milton Prell, owner of the Aladdin Hotel. Best men were Presley's secretaries, Joe Esposito of Chicago and Marty Lacker of Memphis.

Presley wore a tuxedo. The bride, whose maid of honor was her sister, Michelle, wore a white chiffon gown embroidered with tiny pearls and full chiffon veil. Bodice and sleeves of her long train dress were of lace. She wore a 20-carat diamond ring with a three-carat centerstone, and carried a white Bible. The marriage was the first for both. Asked why he waited so long, Presley said: "Well, I guess it was about time. With the life I had, I decided it would be best to wait. You know, all of the shows and record engagements. . . ."

An English fanzine breaks the news abroad.

THE INSIDE STORY OF ELVIS' WEDDING

The whole world now knows that Elvis had been waiting for Priscilla to grow up . . . When she did, he was the last to realize that he'd loved her all along!

Elvis and Priscilla might just as well have been married. She went home in a high dudgeon to Mama, after a bitter argument.

Furthermore, the beauteous Priscilla blew her top and flew off over a matter she has meekly accepted up until recently. Elvis' frequently leaving her behind in Memphis while he goes gaily off to Hollywood.

It was all very simple—or so Elvis thought. He merely told Priscilla he wanted her to stay behind in Memphis for a month. While he and his cronies traveled across the continent for Elvis to film his latest picture, *Clambake,* for United Artists.

That was all. And it was nothing unusual. For, oftentimes in the past half dozen years or so that Elvis and Priscilla have been sweethearts, Elvis has "suggested" that Priscilla absent herself from his presence for varying lengths of time. . .

. . . So—all unsuspecting the storm he was about to set off, Elvis made his not-unusual "suggestion" to Priscilla. And almost fell off his chair in surprise when, without a moment's hesitation, she flatly, firmly refused to accede to his wishes.

It was a real donnybrook, according to our informant. Once he recovered from the shock, Elvis was not so courteous in his statements. They were no longer mere suggestions; they became orders. Delivered in a loud, angry, no-nonsense voice. A tone that went ringing through the halls of Graceland with enough volume for everyone there to hear. . . .

. . . After a few minutes of this sort of thing, Priscilla suddenly turned on her heel, stamped off upstairs and slammed her bedroom door behind her. Leaving Elvis a bit nonplussed, but confidently relieved that the brawl was over and everything settled.

It certainly was—but not the way Elvis envisioned. For, in a remarkably short time, Priscilla head high, chin firm, came back downstairs carrying a suitcase. And before Elvis could do more than catch his breath, Priscilla announced "Good-bye. I'm going home to Mother. . . ."

. . . Every chance he got, at whatever hour, Elvis was on the telephone, begging the lovely girl who'd loved him so long to recant, to return. No one knows exactly what promises he made, what vows he swore, but whatever they were, they finally worked. Perhaps then he promised to marry her and change his wayward ways.

For, finally—after several weeks—Priscilla got on another plane, and returned to Elvis. Returned to him in Hollywood, which was what she had wanted in the first place. And had Elvis not tried to leave her in Memphis, the whole ho-ha would never have happened.

All this had every earmark of the spat of a married couple. And many people in Hollywood believed fully that Elvis and Priscilla were married, secretly. Others hold just the opposite viewpoint. They point out that Elvis always had said that when he married, it would be such a happy day that he would want to shout it to the whole world. And he certainly did no shouting about Priscilla until now. . . .

. . . So something had changed. Perhaps Priscilla earned the respect of Elvis by standing up to him. Perhaps also, Elvis, for the first time realized he could lose Priscilla. In any case, her independence paid off—for now they are wed.

A Spanish fanzine

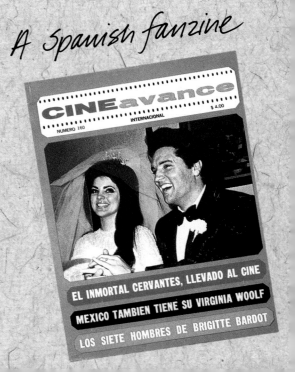

208

Memphis Press-Scimitar   May 19, 1967

Parker's Wedding Gift for Presley: A 24-Carat Ring of Security

by Dick Kleiner

HOLLYWOOD—If Elvis Presley's manager, Col. Tom Parker, ever tires of the show business game, he could always make a nice living as a spy. The security net around Elvis' wedding was tighter than around your average nuclear explosion.

The wedding in Las Vegas was actually planned a couple of weeks ahead of time. But the colonel put on his cloak-and-dagger outfit and misled everybody. He did everything but write the invitations in invisible ink.

He reserved some rooms in Yuma, Ariz. That shook off some. He made all the preparations in Las Vegas under different names at different hotels. When Elvis flew from Palm Springs to Las Vegas, the limousine that met him whisked him to one hotel and then he went out a back door into another car to take him to the Aladdin.

The Aladdin's chef made a wedding cake—but left the names blank. As the guests arrived, he hastily iced in "Elvis" and "Priscilla."

Even the bride was in on the espionage act. She had flown up from San Francisco to shop for her wedding gown—and bought it there under an assumed name. Later she did some remodeling on it herself.

The guests—60 old business associates—got calls Sunday afternoon, the day before the wedding. They were booked into several different hotels and none of them knew why they had been summoned. Late Sunday night, they received mysterious messages which told them to be in the Aladdin lobby at 5:30 a.m., Monday morning.

Then they were rounded up and whisked to a room and told about the wedding. They had to stay in the room until the ceremony.

Thus, Elvis Presley became a bridegroom. I'd like to see Col. Parker head up the CIA.

The photo that broke a million hearts

The couple were married in Las Vegas amid much secrecy.

O Happy Wedding Day

*T*his is a time as ageless as Eden,
  A bliss as newborn as a leaf-bud in spring.
This is a moment to treasure forever,
  No matter what joys all the future may bring.
Here's the first print for a family album:
  "Cloud 9" come to life in chiffon and pearls—
A beautiful bride with the one man beside her
  and knowing herself the luckiest of girls!

*D*id the master chef know what a tale he was telling,
  Creating this cake with frosting and fire?
Wee childlike hearts of the whitest and purest
  Spun-sugar roses as red as desire . . .
Tiny bells fit for a fairyland wedding
  Chiming an unheard but haunting refrain . . .
Oh, what a shame to put knife to such beauty!
  Six tiers soar skyward like some castle in Spain—

*O*r six wonder-filled years since the day they first parted,
  Her own heart quite sure at the age of sixteen.
(But will he remember? Will her Prince Charming
  Ever return to make her his queen?)
For this is a "piper" too potent for Hamelin—
  He plucks many hearts, just strumming the strings.
A world full of girls weave their love-dreams around him!
  (Can it be just for her that this troubadour sings?)

*B*ut reunion is sweet, and Elvis remembers.
  His family accept her as closest of kin.
He is devoted (away from the spotlight) . . .
  This wedding's the crown of all that has been.
(It never struck twelve for this Cinderella,
  Although she might wish she were back at the ball
To dance with prince where the whole court could see her—
  And never say, "Goodnight, my sweetheart," at all!)

A storybook ending is just the beginning,
  "Ever after" a promise to last all your life.
If doubts ever plague you, young home-girl Priscilla,
  Just look at his eyes as he calls you "my wife."
If ever you wonder, "Was all this just dreaming?"
  Then open your album to this page again:
Fill your eyes with the sight of a radiant bridegroom
  Who obviously knows he's the luckiest of men!

Cutting the cake

A fan magazine honors Elvis's wedding with a poem.

Memphis Press-Scimitar   May 1967

Elvis' Popularity Puzzling to Hollywood 'Insiders'

HOLLYWOOD (AP)—Elvis Presley emerged this week from the seclusion of his private life. He celebrated his marriage to Priscilla Ann Beaulieu at a lavish Las Vegas reception then resumed the role of near recluse. He slipped quietly into Memphis, his home town, yesterday.

The wedding apparently caused no wave of consternation among the Presley fans. Most of the girls who screamed at his gyrations 10 years ago are now wives and mothers. While many of them remain fiercely loyal to their hero, they appear sympathetic to his acquiring a wife.

The loyalty of the Presley fans puzzles Hollywood insiders. Unlike some popular favorites who are willing to share their personal lives with the public, Elvis has led an almost Garbo-like existence in recent years.

He makes no personal appearances, gives only perfunctory interviews on movie sets. His records and movies are his only exposure to the public. While his record sales have been overshadowed by the Beatles and other more recent favorites, he is still a top seller. And he can still earn $1 million apiece for the three films he makes annually.

During the past year, his fellow movie workers thought Elvis was inclining toward matrimony, especially since several of his close followers were marrying and starting families. More evidence appeared when he bought his own Bel Air mansion a year ago, then a $560,000 house in Palm Springs.

And so on Monday Elvis married Priscilla, and posed nervously for press photographers. Then the honeymooners disappeared behind the walls of his Palm Springs house. The reason for his secrecy?

"Elvis is shy, anyway," says a close observer, "and he feels like a country boy in the sophisticated world of Hollywood. That's why he stays away from the movie crowd. But most of all, he was scared by all that clamor in his early career. When you've nearly been torn limb from limb by mobs of screaming girls, you become wary about showing your face in public."

The newlyweds head for a Palm Springs Honeymoon.

Mrs. Presley meets the press at a media reception following the ceremony.

PRESLEY'S 'CLAMBAKE'

By Archer Winsten

Elvis Presley's *Clambake,* at Showcase theaters, gives us the singer-athlete as the son of a wealthy Texas oilman who hates all that money. Poor Elvis can't figure out whether girls like him for himself or his money.

So . . . arriving in Florida in his red Corvette, he trades names and places with Tom Wilson, Will Hutchins, a poor boy who has to teach water skiing for a living, ride a motorcycle and try to pick up girls who won't give him a tumble.

Not so with Elvis. Very soon he's putting together a wrecked racing boat for defeated Sam Burton (Gary Merrill), water skiing with professional skill, and competing with a nasty boat-racing millionaire, James Jamison III (Bill Bixby) for both the racing championship and The Girl, Dianne Carter (Shelley Fabares).

This girl, you should be told, came down to Florida to pick up a billionaire herself. Now you have to guess for yourself whether she falls in love with the poor but talented Elvis and whether he falls for her and whether they live happily forever after among money, oil, autos, water skis, racing boats and songs, lots of songs. Old Elvis can still sing 'em even if he does refuse to wiggle now that so many kids can.

'Clambake'

A United Artists release. Produced by Jules Levey-Arthur Gardner-Arnold Laven. Directed by Arthur H. Nadel. Screenplay by Arthur Browne, Jr. The cast: Elvis Presley, Shelley Fabares, Will Hutchins, Bill Bixby, Gary Merrill and James Gregory. 97 minutes.

Elvis played Scott Hayward in Clambake.

Memphis Press-Scimitar   December 31, 1967

Off-Beat Title Awaits Presley Film

There may be similarity in all Elvis Presley movies, but when he goes to work on No. 28 a few months hence, one distinction will be apparent at the start.

None of his previous 27 has borne as off-beat a title as this one: *Kiss My Firm But Pliant Lips.* (Colonel Parker, where are you now that we need you?)

It is, mercifully, a comedy and is based on a novel by Dan Greenburg. Filming is to begin in March at M-G-M, with Douglas Laurence producer and Norman Taurog director.

It will be the ninth teaming for Elvis and Taurog, and Elvis' 11th film for M-G-M. Laurence also produced the unreleased Presley pictures, *Speedway* and *Stay Away, Joe,* filmed within a five-month period and both scheduled for release in 1968. M-G-M is reportedly undecided on order of release.

Speedway, the auto-racing story with Nancy Sinatra, was completed first. Principal photography on *Stay Away* was finished just before Elvis arrived for Christmas at Graceland.

Stay Away has in its cast Joan Blondell, Katy Jurado and Burgess Meredith. Likely release dates will be Easter and June.

Tabbed for summer production is *That Jack Valentine!* in which Elvis will be a singing super spy.

In the meantime, the blessed event for the Presleys is due around Feb. 8 and presumably at Graceland.

Reports filtering out from that Presley principality indicate that Elvis and Priscilla's firstborn will be delivered there rather than at a hospital. The idea is to avoid the excitement and disruption of hospital routine which almost certainly would be stirred up by

an event of such public interest.

Elvis has done little location work in his movie career because of the problems of coping with the throng of spectators who would be attracted. Virtually all his scenes have been shot under studio conditions.

This has on occasion given a touch of unintentional humor to his films, as in the current *Clambake.* In a sequence where Elvis is supposed to be driving Shelly Fabares to the Miami airport, a not overly close examination of the scene will reveal unmistakable mountains in the background. In Florida yet!

Students of Elvis' movies doubtless recall Dolores Hart, a promising actress of the late 1950s who appeared with him in such as *Loving You* (1957) and *King Creole* (1958). She recently completed her fifth year as a nun, Sister Judith, in a New England convent.

IS ELVIS WORTH AN OSCAR?

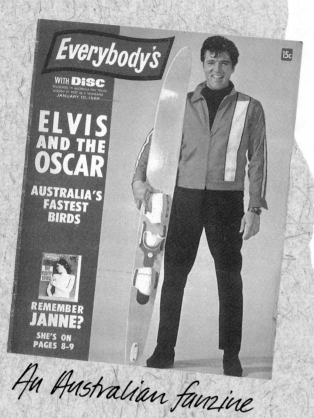

An Australian fanzine

From Alan Hunter in Hollywood

"One of these days Elvis is going to be nominated for an Academy Award." Now, that is a sweeping statement—one which some people would scoff at. But it didn't come from someone with little knowledge of the business of film-making; it came from Norman Taurog, a director, who has spent 50 years in the game.

Taurog has directed Elvis in eight movies now, including *Speedway*, which could be the last of his lightweight efforts.

Elvis himself told me recently: "I have to go on to something different. I want more serious roles; I want to go out and face new challenges . . ."

. . . It was during the final days shooting of *Clambake*, another not-too-demanding outing, that he wed his Priscilla. This film is an up-dated version of the timeless *Prince and the Pauper* tale, with Elvis as a Texas oil heir who yearns to make his own mark in the world.

So the heir trades identities with a poor water-ski instructor in colorful Miami Beach setting.

The emphasis is on action as much as singing, as Hollywood explores the thrill-a-second world of ski-boat racing.

Again, though, he is surrounded by beautiful leading ladies, Shelley Fabares, in her third outing with Elvis, plays a poor rich girl on the prowl for a rich mate.

Also on hand are Will Hutchins, of TV's *Sugarfoot* and *Hey Landlord* series, and Bill Bixby.

When I asked Elvis about the film he said he had enjoyed making it. He water-skis himself.

Immediately after the film he was off to Memphis, Tennessee, for a honeymoon. That's where his family is; that's where he goes to relax, that's where he unwinds . . . and maybe that's where he did some serious thinking about his work.

Elvis doesn't have to spend another minute of his life at work if he doesn't want to. But he wants to. . . .

. . . "I have much to gain in myself if I can take on characterizations that demand more emotion and depth.

"Other singers, like Sinatra and Dean Martin, have accomplished this; and I know the time will come when I must give it a try, too.

"I only hope my fans will approve of it."

Shelley Fabares stars in her third Elvis Film.

Elvis and costar Will Hutchins

Memphis Press-Scimitar   February 5, 1968

'She's Too Much,' Says Elvis; 'She's Perfect,' Says Wife

By Bill Evans

Elvis Presley left Baptist Hospital at 1:55 p.m. today with his wife Priscilla and their newborn daughter, Lisa Marie.

Climbing into a long black Cadillac, Presley commented, "Oh, man, she's too much," when asked how he liked his daughter.

He said he was "still a little shaky," echoing his earlier comment when he brought his wife to the hospital Thursday.

Mrs. Presley, dressed in a pink dress and with long, flowing hairdo, was pretty pleased with her daughter herself.

"She's perfect, she couldn't be any better," she told a reporter.

The proud grandfather, Vernon Presley, said he liked his new role fine. "I think it's going to be great," he said.

About 75 fans, including a number of Baptist Hospital student nurses, gathered outside the hospital entrance awaiting the singing star's departure.

Many more persons watched through hospital and nearby office building windows, including three construction workmen on the hospital roof.

One hospital administrator said: "Today is the only day we've really had any trouble. I can't keep my girls at work."

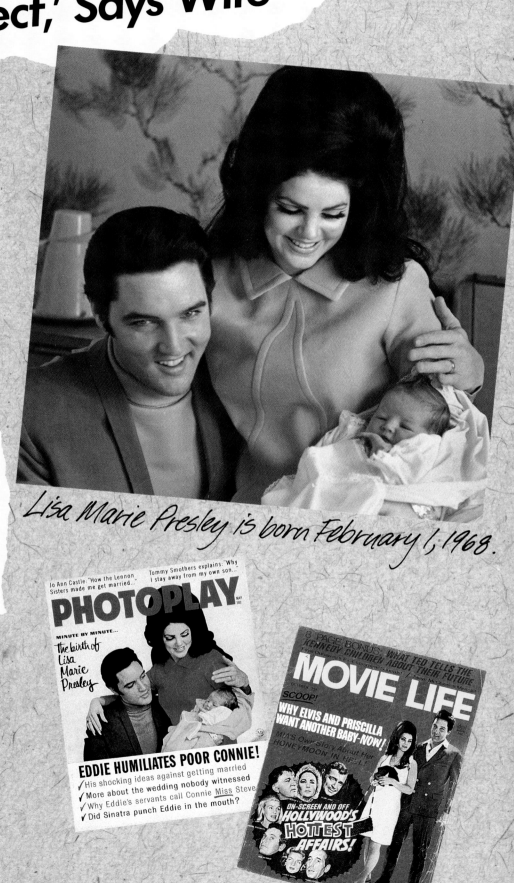

Lisa Marie Presley is born February 1, 1968.

English fanzine

GIRL BORN TO PRESLEYS IN MEMPHIS

by HARRISON CARROLL

It's a baby girl for film star Elvis Presley and his wife Priscilla Beaulieu.

The child was born at 5:01 p.m. yesterday in a Memphis hospital. She weighed 6-pounds 14-ounces. Both mother and child are doing fine.

According to Elvis they still haven't picked a name for the baby. Presley is due back here in March to report to MGM for his next picture *Kiss My Firm But Pliant Lips*.

BIRTHS

Mr. and Mrs. Elvis Presley, daughter, 6 lbs. 15 oz., in Memphis yesterday. Father is the singer-actor, mother non-pro.

DAUGHTER BORN TO PRESLEY'S WIFE

MEMPHIS—Rock 'n' Roll star Elvis Presley became a father Thursday with the birth of a 6-pound 15-ounce girl Lisa Marie.

The baby was born at 5:01 p.m., 6 hours and 19 minutes after her attractive, brunette mother checked into Baptist Hospital. A hospital spokesman described Presley as "a pretty typical first-time father."

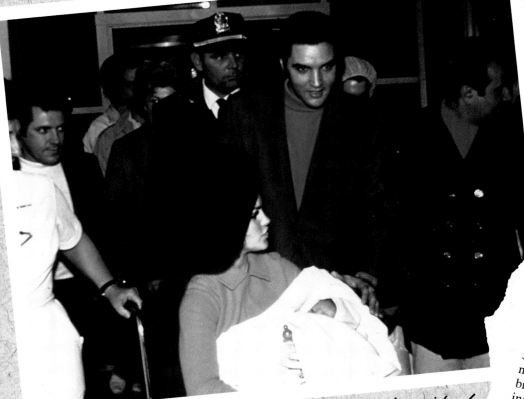

The Presley family leaves the Hospital.

Soundtrack album

SPEEDWAY

Speedway is the latest release of one of the current top ten favorites, **Elvis Presley,** and the 26th film of his fantastic 11-year career. It is also his eighth for M-G-M who this time present him with two special gifts. One is sensational singing star **Nancy Sinatra** as his leading lady, and the other is an exciting story set in the daredevil world of stock car racing.

Elvis plays a top racing champ whose irresponsibility puts him heavily in debt with the income tax people. Nancy is an Internal Revenue agent assigned to follow Elvis around and get her hands on his money before he starts being rash with it. When the two are not involved in comedy, romance and racing, they share a series of tender ballads and fast-paced dance songs.

Racing sequences were shot at a famous speedway in North Carolina, and provide suspenseful spinouts and frightening crashes. More frenzied action takes place in a discotheque called The Hangout where the booths are made from cars. All in all, *Speedway* should please the Presley fans, of whom there are still many millions.

BRIAN SWIFT

Elvis and costar Bill Bixby emote for the cameras.

ELVIS PRESLEY FEATURED IN 'SPEEDWAY' CITYWIDE

Speedway (playing citywide) has a script that ran out of gas before Elvis Presley was born. Presley pictures can be unpretentious fun, but this one is both uninspired and too much of an imitation of too many of his previous movies.

At any rate, stock car racer Presley and partner Bill Bixby, an ingenious lecher, are so generous and extravagant that Internal Revenue agent Nancy Sinatra is out to get them.

There aren't even very many songs to break up developments too predictable to outline here.

There are a couple of well-photographed racing sequences, but their authenticity serves only to underline the movie's over-all set-bound look. Indeed, this picture is so out of touch with reality it seems embalmed. Don't let the stars' Mod attire fool you; they're really being required to do Jack Oakie and Toby Wing.

As usual, there's a nice rapport between Presley and his most frequent director, Norman Taurog, who does the best that probably can be expected under the circumstances. Elvis is amiable as always, especially in some scenes with Victoria Meyerink and some other little girls, but the picture belongs to Bixby, an excellent comedian. What precious few good lines and gags there are go to him, and he more than makes the most of them.

Very blond and very sexy, Miss Sinatra unfortunately sings but one song, the high point of the picture. Although she has found an effective style as a singer she is not yet an actress. Most welcome is Gale Gordon's dry wit as her boss, and Miss Meyerink's ne'er-do-well but fecund father is nicely played by William Schalert.

WILL NANCY SINATRA STEAL ELVIS FROM PRISCILLA?

HOW CAN ELVIS RESIST HIS SEXY CO-STAR?

What happens when two irresistible forces meet one immovable object? Pretty dangerous odds, right? Well this is just what happened when the man himself met the woman herself. What man? None other than the flamboyant Elvis Presley! What woman? One of the most sensation-causing women to hit the screen in many moons... Miss Nancy Sinatra!

Now we all know that El is married to his long-time sweetheart, Priscilla, and that they are planning a large family.

While Pris, sweet and lovely, has stolen the number one love away from so many wailing women, and managed to do what no other could—trap him with the fatal words "I do," she is still a long way from being safe and secure.

When one gorgeous, voluptuous, absolutely mind-blowing girl like Nancy walks up to Elvis on the set of *Speedway*, Elvis' newest flick with Nancy as his romance, and says, I've idolized two people in my lifetime, my father and Elvis Presley, we know there's nothing but trouble ahead! Now let's face it, what man in his right mind would raise an eyebrow and say oh, yeah? With just about every male in the world foaming at the mouth just to see Nancy... can you imagine how a guy feels to not only meet her face to face, but on top of it find out that she has always idolized him? Instant insanity...

...So, dear readers, what do you think? Can Priscilla withstand another siege? Will she come out on top as always? I wonder how stiff the competition really is. On one side we have a very tantalizing woman and on the other a wife and mother with much love in her heart for her husband. How do those odds stack up? Will Nancy steal Elvis from Priscilla? How do you vote?

THE END

Newspaper ad

Fanzines cooked up a romance between Elvis and Nancy Sinatra (left of Elvis).

217

The Colonel, Mrs. Parker (?), Elvis, and Priscilla on the set

Elvis as Joe Lightcloud in Stay Away Joe

Elvis's buddy Bronc Hoverty was played by L.Q. Jones (left of Elvis).

THE NEW ELVIS

A completely different image for Elvis Presley is seen in his new MGM picture, *Stay Away, Joe*.

He plays an irresponsible half-breed Indian cowboy, who chases girls and sings only three numbers in the picture.

As I arrive on the set, director Peter Tewksbury is shooting a scene in a desert beer joint where everybody is dancing wildly and where Elvis is on the fast make for Quentin Dean, daughter of saloon owner Joan Blondell, with whom he has been having an affair.

The music is loud, the dancing is frantic. Finally, I get Elvis away from the camera for a minute.

"Hard to visualize you in a night club," I laugh. "Have you ever been in one in Hollywood?"

"Believe it or not, I have," he laughs back, "I was at the Red Velvet a few times, also at The Trip."

They whisk Elvis away so I grab onto Katy Jurado, who plays his disapproving stepmother in the picture, wife of his Navajo father, Burgess Meredith.

Katy looks plumper than when I saw her last.

"You're not kidding," she says, "I gained 20 pounds for this picture. It is my first comedy in 25 years of acting."

I ask her how she likes working with Elvis.

"He's shy," she exclaims, "but he is a beautiful person, so considerate of everybody. And, now that he is about to become a father, I think he is coming out of his shell a little."

This really is a different movie for Elvis.

He has tricked Joan Blondell out of town so he can make a play for her daughter. And he is doing all right. In the middle of the dance, Quentin takes him by the hands and leads him into the bedroom behind the bar.

Presley pranks

Stay Away, Joe turns out to be sound advice to the public, though it's actually the title of the latest Elvis Presley movie which is by far the weakest he's made for some time.

The assumption seems to be that Presley doesn't need a story or much in the way of songs any more. Just gather a gang of pretty girls, rowdy men, and a few slapstick comedians, get out the color cameras, and let Presley strut through a few reels of wild parties and juvenile pranks. The result is a flat, forced collection of scenes that looks like the rejects from some other, better film.

Presley is the irresponsible son of a American Indian family who returns to the dilapidated homestead with a herd of government-supplied heifers and a bull. From the moment the welcome-home party begins (and it goes on for more than half an hour), it's clear that any plot considerations have been discarded in favor of a series of loosely related gags of the kind that used to be described as "zany hi-jinks."

The Indians are depicted as a grubby, shiftless lot, the performances of Burgess Meredith, Joan Blondell, Katy Jurado and Thomas Gomez are desperately antic, and Presley doesn't bother to act at all, he's just there.

The picture is just about as awful as a movie can get. One searches in vain for some redeeming feature but there is absolutely nothing to recommend.

J. M. I.

Memphis Commercial Appeal   March 3, 1968

Swinger Is Elvis' 21st Leading Lady

by John Knott

Michele Carey, who plays a swinging chick in *The Sweet Ride*, will be Elvis Presley's 21st leading lady in *Live a Little, Love A Little*, a comedy.

Let us add that *The Sweet Ride* is latter-day *Where The Boys Are* and *Where The Boys Are* was blah.

In the new Elvis number, she has the role "of a beautiful and wildly kooky girl in relentless pursuit of a reluctant Presley." A reluctant Presley in the romance department—something new, eh?

The new film is being taken from a book called *Kiss My Firm But Pliant Lips.*

Miss Carey is what you could call a "NOW" girl in *The Sweet Ride* and very generously displays much of her extensive charms in various costumes.

Dick Sargent, Michele Carey, and Elvis

Live a Little, Love a Little had only 4 songs.

A DIFFERENT ELVIS?

Live a Little, Love a Little, MGM's latest Elvis Presley film, is, to say the least, a distinct departure for the former king of rock and roll.

For starters, Elvis sings just four songs. He's allowed to us a not inconsiderable comedic talent for the first time since *Follow That Dream*, and *Little* has a plot that serves as more than a device to change the scenery for the next production number.

The biggest surprise of all, though, is Michelle Carey, Elvis' co-star, nearly stealing the picture with a canny portrayal of Bernice, one of the kookiest girls ever put on film.

Part farce, part fantasy, *Little* now citywide, concerns a beach-dwelling, man-loving Miss Carey who isn't above sicking her dog on recalcitrant boyfriends.

The kind of girl who changes her name to suit her mood, she traps Elvis in her beach house, causes him to lose his job as a photo-journalist and moves him out of his home into one she likes better.

Thoroughly bewildered by her zany behavior, Elvis talks his way into two new full-time jobs with firms in the same building.

One is a sedate advertising outfit, the other a Playboy-type magazine. To keep both jobs, he scampers up and down a back stairway changing costume en route.

Desperately trying to make it with Bernice, but continually interrupted by either the dog or an old boy friend, Elvis gives up in frustration only to find Bernice not willing to give up on him.

He tries to date another girl but Bernice decides it's time to crack her head on a coffee table and confines herself to his bed. From there the film winds its way to an inevitable happy ending.

The supporting cast includes Don Porter, very funny in a take-off on Hugh Hefner's Playboy Philosophy; Rudy Vallee, injecting the correct amount of starch in his role as an advertising executive; Dick Sargent as Michelle Carey's boyfriend... and Joan Shawlee as a house wife who sees a potential molester behind every doorbell.

Little is extremely well-photographed, the special effects are finely executed and Billy Strange's score is Elvis's best.

Screenplayed by Michael A. Hoey and Dan Greenburg from Greenburg's novel, *Kiss My Firm But Pliant Lips. Live A Little, Love a Little* may just be the picture to finally break Elvis out of his static rock and roll mold.

Elvis's films were popular in France.

219

'NEW' ELVIS BACK WITH OLD MAGIC

Souvenir ad

TUESDAY/DECEMBER 3

Singer Presents Elvis (9:00-10:00) Elvis Presley singing some of the songs that made him famous…Elvis offering a Gospel medley …Elvis heading a production number about the rise of a young entertainer. His first TV appearance in eight years also marks Elvis' debut as the star of his own television special.

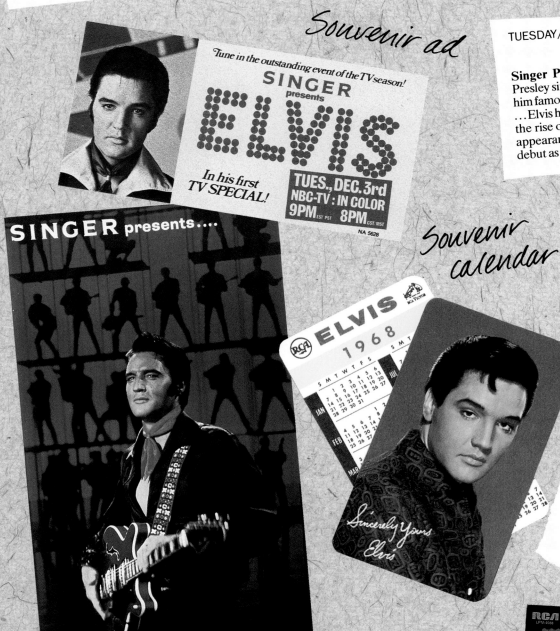

Souvenir calendar

TV Guide
Tuesday December 3, 1968

ELVIS
9:00 [4] [20]

Special Color Surrounded by musicians and adoring fans Elvis Presley headlines his first TV special.

The fans are up and screaming as Elvis rocks through a nostalgic medley of his hits: "Heartbreak Hotel," "Hound Dog," "All Shook Up," "Can't Help Falling in Love with You," "Jailhouse Rock," and "Love Me Tender." He also sings "Memories" and his seasonal hit "Blue Christmas."

The Blossoms vocal group and dancer-choreographer Claude Thompson open a gospel medley with "Sometimes I Feel like a Motherless Child," and Elvis joins them for "Where Could I Go but to the Lord?" "Up Above My Head" and "Saved!"

A rocking production number stars Elvis as a traveling musician (singing "Guitar Man") who leaves a dull job ("Nothingsville") for an amusement park ("Big Boss Man") and modest night-club success ("Trouble"). Finale: "If I Can Dream," written for Elvis by vocal arranger Earl Brown. (60 min.)

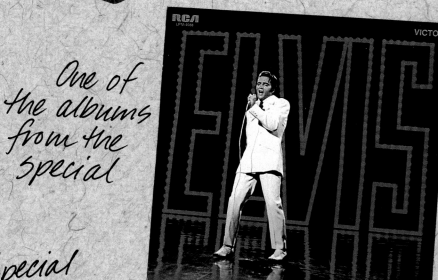

One of the albums from the special

Poster for Elvis's TV special

ELVIS THE ELDER STATESMAN, STILL TURNS PEOPLE ON

By Dorothy Collin

UNLIKE THE BRITISH Empire, the sun seemingly really will never set on Elvis Presley.

The side-burned boy with pouting mouth and sexy hips who started it all is now 33. He lives the most private of lives with his wife and baby daughter. He hasn't made a personal appearance in years. His first TV show in 8 years will appear Dec. 3.

Yet, the latest in his string of technicolor, starlet-filled movies is bound to make money, as have the other 30 he has made. He is making more money for himself and his recording company, RCA-Victor, now than he did during his "Hound Dog" heyday. And, his fans can be just as wildly enthused as they ever were.

The latest example of devotion to Elvis came during the 4-day taping of his TV special, "Singer Presents Elvis." Women of varying ages lurked around the gates of NBC in beautiful downtown Burbank, attempting to outsmart the extra security guards hired by the network for the festivities.

WHEN FANS with tickets were admitted to the taping sessions, several got carried away just like in the good old days and charged the stage only to be subdued by the guards.

In order to halt invasions by passionate ladies, Elvis' manager and NBC issued special color-coded tags labeled "Elvis."

But the incredible thing about Mr. Presley is not really that he is still popular 15 years after he wriggled onto the pop record scene. What is almost astounding is that the one-time southern "hood" youth who was denounced as a moral threat to the world's young people is now a respected sort of elder statesman.

…THE LATE HEDDA HOPPER nearly blew her top off one of her fruit salad hats on the subject of Elvis: "I applaud parents of teen-agers who work to get the blood and horror gangster stories off TV. They should work harder against the new alleged singer." About 8 years and several million records later, Hedda apologized.

And, finally, from England came the ultimate work from music critic Tom Richardson: "This man is dangerous."

To all this the young Elvis replied: "Those folks who accuse me of bein' vulgar, they just don't understand. "If that was true, I'd be in some kinda institution as some kinda sex maniac. The thing is that I've got an act. I sing—not like Sinatra, not like Crosby, but like Elvis Presley."

And as it turned out singing like Elvis Presley made him the biggest record seller of all time [though the Beatles are pushing him]. According to RCA, Elvis has sold "well in excess" of 200 million records.

THE INTRIGUING thing about RCA's figures, however, is that Presley is a big seller in tape decks—the status way to listen for young, with-it professionals.

How has Elvis, the southern country-boy, managed to attract these fans in addition to keeping the ever-faithful rural and small town people?

For one thing, anyone on the underside of 30 grew up with him. He's like Mom and apple pie.

For another, he is historic. The pop entertainment business today on all levels owes itself to Presley. He was the breakthru, the original for-teens-only idol.

…AND THEN, Presley is a good entertainer, especially now that the eyes of the beholders are used to him. Attitudes and standards have changed in the 15 years since Elvis recorded his first record. Men who hesitated to put him on TV now refer to his upcoming show, which features a medley of his hits plus a gospel singing session, as "great."

The times, they indeed have changed. Elvis doesn't have to tell anyone not to step on his blue suede shoes these days.

Elvis performs live for the studio audience.

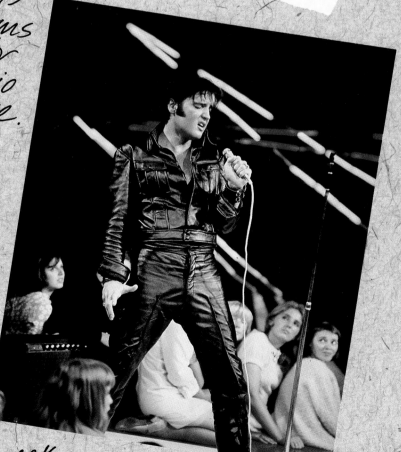

Elvis's TV special was the highest-rated show that week.

221

Elvis Will Make More Personal Appearances

One of the production numbers from the special

by John Knott

With 29 movies and 50 gold records behind him, Elvis has decided that he ought to get more exposure.

"It's been too long since I've done anything but make movies and cut records," he told the Commercial Appeal Chicago Daily News Service in Los Angeles last week. "I want to make some personal appearance tours. I want to see some new places and get back where the audience is."

This is rather tenuous at the moment, but can you imagine what the scene would be if he should schedule a personal appearance at the Mid-South Coliseum? Probably attendance records would fall.

It would be good for Elvis to get before the public since it's a brand new public from the one that idolized him 12 years ago when he made occasional appearances before live audiences, just as he was starting his movie career.

The little girls who screamed and carried on over Elvis have daughters of their own now.

A few more television appearances like the one coming up Tuesday wouldn't hurt either. This is more a television generation than it is a movie generation and there are millions who haven't seen him. His most recent movies, while successful, don't draw nearly as well as his earlier ones, which saw throngs lined up outside movie houses....

Elvis Skips Gyrations but Still Generates Heat

So much rock 'n' roll has been performed in the past dozen years that Elvis Presley's doing his first special on TV Tuesday night somehow seemed anti-climactic—even though he was one of the pioneers in the field.

ELVIS

Elvis Presley in a musical special. Executive producer Bob Finkel. Producer-director Steve Binder. Writers Allan Bive, Chris Beard. Musical production Bones Howe. Musical direction and arrangements William Goldberg. Special lyrics and vocal arrangements Earl Brown. Choreographer Jamie Rogers, Claude Thompson. NBC Tuesday, 9 p.m.

The Elvis hour on NBC was virtually a one-man show with the star doing most of his numbers on a small square stage surrounded by a studio audience which had some screamers in it. But according to executive producer Bob Finkel, none of them were hand-picked. They just simply loved Elvis.

Although he didn't indulge in the dynamic physical gyrations which made him so controversial that we saw only the top half of him on an Ed Sullivan Show many years ago, Elvis still generates considerable heat with his singing.

His repertoire included many of his recorded hits such as "Hound Dog," "Jailhouse Rock" and "Love Me Tender." Producer-director Steve Binder employed lots of camera closeups and two-camera superimposed shots, which were effective, except for those closeups showing Elvis sweating. I don't think many viewers care to see singers sweat on TV.

Moving away from the small stage and studio audience, Elvis did two impressive production numbers. One was a gospel song with dancers and singers; the other opened on a carnival midway and progressed from his singing in a joint to better-class night-clubs.

The show closed with him in a white suit standing in front of the huge lit letters spelling E-L-V-I-S which opened the proceedings, and he sang "If I Can Dream."

Except for TV runs of his old movies, this marked Elvis' first TV appearance since he did a guest shot on a Frank Sinatra special in 1960, so it was an event in that sense and Elvis managed to sustain the hour very well.

Even so, as I said at the beginning, there was the feeling of anti-climax. Some of the magic was gone, diminished by the fact that this type of music has progressed and hotter names have come along since Elvis to perform it.

—HAL HUMPHREY

ONE MAN, ALL MUSIC

"I'm doing a television special now because we figure the time is right and today's music is right," said Elvis Presley.

Presley stars in his first television special in eight years, at 9 p.m. Tuesday, Ch. 4.

"Also, I though I ought to do this special before I got too old," Elvis said, grinning and implying that work on a television show might require a somewhat faster pace than working on a motion picture.

Admitting that he had worked hard on the special (a full month of strenuous rehearsals—four 12-to-16 hour days of taping) Elvis continued:

"TELEVISION is a different world from movies. It does something to you... it demands more of you."

One difference was that Elvis performed before a live audience for the first time since he decided to forego concert and supper club appearances in favor of a full-time motion picture and recording career.

"I want you to know that I was scared to death, sir, when I did my first number for that studio audience," Elvis reported.

"Let me tell you my knees were shaking, and it wasn't just from keeping time with the music.

"It's just been so long since I worked before a live audience," said Presley, who made his last live appearance 12 years ago at the Hawaiian premiere for his *Blue Hawaii* film. He last appeared on television as a guest star on a Frank Sinatra special in 1960.

"But then it all came back to me and it was just like when I was doing one-night stands in the old days," he continued.

OBVIOUSLY relaxed during the interview, Elvis pulled thoughtfully on a slender German cigar. When did he start smoking?

"Just since I've been working on this special," he laughed, then added: "Actually, this is just a prop. I don't inhale."

Is he planning another television special soon after the Dec. 3 program?

"I don't think I'll do another one right away," he answered emphatically. "Son,

I lost 10 pounds doing this show.

"It's been too long since I've done anything except make movies (20 to date) and cut records (earning some 50 gold records, each indicating sales of one million).

"Now I want to make some personal appearance tours," Presley continued. "I'll probably start out there in this country and then play some concerts abroad.

"I want to see some places I haven't seen before and I want to get back where the audiences is . . . I miss the personal contact with audiences."

IN ADDITION, Presley plans some changes in his movies.

"We're looking for better scripts; trying to do more mature movies. I want to do some straight dramatic stories as well as musicals and comedies."

Along this line, Presley recently completed his latest motion picture, a Western entitled *Charro,* and he doesn't sing a song in it.

"I play a gunfighter, and I just couldn't see a singing gunfighter," Elvis explained.

"I'm getting more and more interested in acting. I'd like to become a contemporary actor, not just a singer."

Why, after 15 years of success is Elvis opting for a change?

"My audience is changing . . . they don't move as fast as they used to," he laughed, pointing out that his fans of a decade ago are now young married couples, many with families of their own.

"And I think young people generally are a lot smarter and more open-minded than they were 10 yrs ago. They expect more of you."

The television special, too, is an indication of a new Elvis. In addition to singing several of his best-known songs (such as "Hound Dog" and "Blue Suede Shoes"), Elvis essays several modern numbers which he may not have touched with a 10-foot slab of Tennessee cornpone 10 years ago.

"Soundwise, musicians and engineers have improved the sound of music over the years." Elvis volunteered. "That means I have to improve, too."

Elvis closed the program with "If I can Dream," a song written especially for him.

223

ELVIS PLAYS 'CHARRO' SANS SONGS

By Dale Munroe

Elvis Presley proves in National General's Western, *Charro,* that there's nothing like a song when the going gets tough—would that he had some.

The only commendable thing about this Panavision-color movie is its title tune penned by Hugo Montenegro, with lyrics by Alan and Marilyn Bergman. If only a half-dozen more tunes for Elvis to warble.

The storyline is almost non-existent in this poorly constructed, badly edited Western directed by Charles Marquis Warren.

Presley portrays Jess Wade, a reformed badman forced to come to the aid of a town terrorized by his former gang.

There is this gold-plated Mexican cannon, once used by Maximillian, that the gang has stolen and turned on the town to enforce their demands. Of course, Presley-Wade saves the town.

The acting is uniformly pedestrian. Victor French portrays the gang leader; Ina Balin, Presley's dancehall girlfriend; and Lynn Kellogg, one of Miss Balin's girls, who provides the feminine interest in this boondoggling attempt at a straight acting role for Presley.

Solomon Sturges, son of the late filmmaker Preston Sturges, takes a crack at enacting the emotionally unbalanced younger brother of the gang leader.

James Almanzar as the sheriff rambles throughout his chores.

Charro is now on screens all over Los Angeles.

The film was based on this book.

Newspaper ad

Charro!, a serious western, was a departure for Elvis.

CHARRO (National General). Personally I enjoyed the film. It gives Elvis a chance to show he can do more acting than he has been allowed to. But Colonel Parker should start using his head again and refuse to allow such *terrible* scripts to be approved. It is very badly written and the directing isn't great. But Elvis is good and the film is worth seeing. (El lost quite a bit of weight for this—and he *does* look good!)

A NEW ROLE FOR ELVIS

APACHELAND, Ariz.—Under a blazing desert sun where afternoon temperatures reach 120 degrees, Elvis Presley, the former boy wonder of the folk-rock world is toiling at his 29th motion picture role in little over a decade, National General's *Charro!*

Under the eye of old western hand producer-director Charles Marquis Warren (*The Virginian, Rawhide*, etc.) Elvis, deprived of his guitar and the use of his undulating hips, is going through his paces as a "sometimes" sheriff dressed in the grimy garb of cowpoke of the 1870's and sporting a beard which he started growing just before shooting began.

Tanned and serious, it's an Elvis the folks in Nashville might not recognize.

Ads emphasized how different Charro! was from Elvis's usual film fare.

The film resembles an Italian western.

The only song in Charro! was sung over the credits.

Elvis as chautauqua owner Walter Hale

Elvis and Marlyn Mason

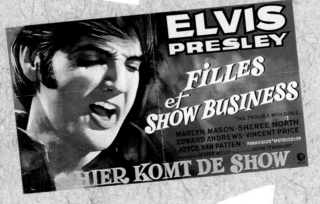

The French changed the title of The Trouble with Girls.

PRESLEY HAS GIRL TROUBLE

★ ★

Elvis Presley is supposed to have trouble with girls in *The Trouble With Girls,* double-billed with *Flareup* at Loew's 83rd St. and other Showcase Theatres. But the real trouble is with his acting. As usual, he is at his best only when singing; he can put over the most trivial song.

As the manager of a traveling tent show, called a chautauqua in the 1920's, Presley has to contend with labor problems, ambitious local talent and a murder.

"The Trouble With Girls" a Metro-Goldwyn-Mayer release in Panavision and Technicolor. Produced by Lester Welch and directed by Peter Tewksbury from a screenplay by Arnold and Lois Peyser based on the novel by Day Keen and Dwight Babcock. Presented at Loew's 83rd St. and other Showcase theaters. Running time: 1 hour, 45 minutes. MPAA rating: G (suggested for general audiences).

THE CAST	
Walter Hale	Elvis Presley
Charlene	Marlyn Mason
Betty	Nicole Jaffe
Nita	Sheree North
Johnny	Edward Andrews
Mr. Drewcolt	John Carradine
Carol	Anissa Jones
Mr. Morality	Vincent Price
Maude	Joyce Van Patten

VARIETY ACTS, fireworks and cameos by Vincent Price and John Carradine are added to liven up things but nothing really works. Not even a cute moppet, Anissa Jones, is able to save the picture the way Shirley Temple did in her heyday.

Marlyn Mason as Presley's assistant and romantic interest tries hard for comedy, as does Nicole Jaffe, playing a manchaser. But the script is too obvious. Sheree North has some good sequences as a shady lady until director Peter Tewksbury allows her to carry on overlong in her drunk scenes.

★ ★ ★ ★ ★ ★ ★ ★ ★ ★ ★ ★ ★ ★

MOVIE SCENE

by Frances Herridge

NEW PRESLEY MOVIE AT SHOWCASES

Elvis Presley's new film, *The Trouble With Girls,* has a lot more trouble than it seems to realize. You can't blame the cast, even the girls—though they're pretty bad. The main fault is the script.

It's a bland hodgepodge that mixes a seedy murder with tedious goings-on in a 1927 Chautauqua tent show. Presley as the show's manager is beset with problems—like whether to give the mayor's untalented daughter the lead in the children's pageant, how to deal with a pretty assistant who keeps bugging him about union rules, how to avoid an unfunny comedienne who pursues him, how to get his card player out of jail when he is accused of killing the town's villain.

These loose ends are sloppily tied together by one of those improvised stage shows which must keep going until the real murderer sobers up enough to confess. Seems forever.

THE TROUBLE WITH GIRLS

An MGM release. Produced by Lester Welch. Directed by Peter Tewksbury. Screenplay by Arnold and Lois Peyser from novel by Day Keen and Dwight Babcock. Cast includes Elvis Presley, Marlyn Mason, Nicole Jaffe, Sheree North, Edward Andrews and Vincent Price. 105 minutes.

There's nothing wrong with Presley. He wisely underacts, and sings pleasantly. But why doesn't he find better scripts—at least ones that give him more than three so-so songs.

The film is at showcase theaters with *Flare Up*—another loser.

ELVIS STARS IN 'CHANGE OF HABIT'

★ ★ ★

Universal's *Change of Habit* is said to be based on the story of Sister Mary Olivia Gibson and her work with speech-handicapped children. Whether or not the film tells it like it is does not matter too much, for the light comedy-drama manages to hold interest all the way because it entertains.

The feature is doubled with *House of Cards* at Loew's Victoria and other Showcase Theaters. **ONE WOULD HARDLY** expect Elvis Presley to figure in such a story, but he portrays a doctor in a ghetto clinic and somehow fits the role quite well. He sings only four songs this time, with smooth effect as usual.

"Change of Habit" a Universal Pictures release in Technicolor. Produced by Joe Connelly and directed by William Graham from a screenplay by James Lee, S.S. Schweitzer and Eric Bercovici based on a story by John Joseph and Richard Morris. Presented at Loew's Victoria and other Showcase Theaters. Running time: 1 hour, 37 minutes. MPAA rating: G (For general audiences).

THE CAST:

Dr. John Carpenter	Elvis Presley
Sister Michelle	Mary Tyler Moore
Sister Irene	Barbara McNair
Sister Barbara	Jane Elliot
Mother Joseph	Leora Dana
Lt. Moretti	Edward Asner
Father Gibson	Regis Toomey
Rose	Doro Merande
Lily	Ruth McDevitt
Bishop Finley	Richard Carlson

Mary Tyler Moore, Barbara McNair and Jane Elliot appear as Catholic nuns who go out into the world. They exchange their traditional habits for modern dress in order to become more quickly involved with people and their problems. They certainly do.

Miss Moore as the speech therapist meets with success as far as her patients are concerned, but finds herself attracted to the doctor. For Miss McNair, it is a return to an environment from which she wanted to escape. Miss Elliot finds herself committed to social causes.

Doro Merande and Ruth McDevitt lend some light moments as busybody spinsters. Regis Toomey plays a priest of the old school.

Under William Graham's direction, modern confrontations are skimmed but meaning is not lost. The whole thing contrives to provide a bit of thought to a large dose of general entertainment.

Elvis and Mary Tyler Moore

3 NUNS VISIT A SLUM IN 'CHANGE OF HABIT'

The story of *Change of Habit* doubling at the showcases with *House of Cards,* is its own severest criticism as well as source of humanitarian-racist religious commentary.

Three nuns, Sister Michelle (Mary Tyler Moore), Sister Irene (Barbara McNair) and Sister Barbara (Jane Elliot) have been sent to a Negro-Puerto Rican slum to see what they can do to help a charitable doctor with an ear for music, Dr. John Carpenter (hold your breath: Elvis Presley).

They don't wear their habits, which makes them incognito to the general public to whom they resemble handsome chicks. Only the local priest knows—Father Gibbons (Regis Toomey)—and he hates their modern ways. Street bums accost them. Street girls get jealous. Gangsters feel they're muscling in as indeed they are on the loan shark racket.

The girls get themselves into troubles of the sort that can only be corrected by the united efforts of Elvis Presley who fights off a rapist and a couple of Black Panthers who fight off muscle men of the loan shark banker.

As you can readily understand, there's a lot of warm feeling engendered for sweet good-looking young women who want to do so much good. The only trouble is, can you believe any little bit of it? Believers, as usual, will love it. The rest of us, I guess, again as usual, will just have to lump it.

Newspaper ad

Elvis plays a doctor in this musical drama.

THE FILMS OF ELVIS PRESLEY

by Richard Meltzer

DEATH TAKES A HOLOCAUST . . . In Patti Duke's first four celluloid efforts she didn't get killed a single goddam time. Ditto for Ernie Kovacs's first four and Buster Crabbe as well. Even James Dean didn't leave the planet, for even a second, in *his* first quatre (needed "real life" to accomplish the feat—no mean one to say the least, but all he could come up with in that regard was a lousy *once*). ELVIS GOT TO CROAK *TWICE* IN HIS FIRST FOUR PITCHERS!!!

Love Me Tender (November '56) and *King Creole* (May '58). Former of which was even his very first venture into the land of sprockets ever and whadda they do, they kill him off, jeez . . .

. . . 'Cause one thing you gotta realize is that of all the singers-turned-moviestar, there never were NONE of 'em ever made as many stinkers as Elvis. Pat Boone was getting there for awhile, but at least he had the sense to stop—or maybe the industry finally had the sense to pull him out. Fred Astaire—in this movie crit's mind one of the all-time overrated cinematic nobodies—reached his all-time nadir with *Silk Stockings* (which happened to be Peter Lorre's worst one too, and who was Peter but the original incarnation of Elvis-competitor Sal Mineo who, to this day, hasn't done one that bad: which partially demonstrates what I mean about the *a priori* infallibility of '50s teenstars) but when you get down to it *Silk Stockings* was about as good as Elvis' best (excluding the one factor that Elvis still had while he had it, namely PRESENCE. 'cause if you wanna get down to it, Elvis' first moment in his first folly of a film—him plowing or something out in the fields *way in the distance* in *Love Me Tender,* greeted by sufficient shrieks right there in theaters to indicate that his actual hysteria potential was *at least* as big as Valentino's—was, in context, far more powerful of course than every second that Fred Astaire has ever lived and breathed put together times 50, but let's confirm it to the filmic side of his turkeys for awhile, in which case it is true that etc.). In fact, few others in the entire biz—Jerry Lewis, Glenn Ford, Doris Day, Bob Hope?—have individually been in a greater number of nowhere movies than he. No mean feat, considering Elvis 1. youth, and 2. total superiority to all of 'em put together times a million. And all of 'em, *including* Elvis, get to be shown all the time on the 4:30 TV movie in most big cities, and his pictures are the absolute worst even in that time slot without exception (only he's the only worth-a-damn person at all who gets shown in that time slot without exception (only reason you get to see him is he's been wholesomed to death, but who wants to see him under those circumstances except your mommy?) . . .

. . . So anyway, the question that oughta be dealt with to get this over with is did the Pelvis really *sell out* at all? Like was it a matter of this was the path of least resistance, e-z way to make a buck and all of that? Not really, 'cause he really hadda bust his hump workwise, and the only thing that sold the movies was him in 'em, not the ease or cheapness with which they mighta been made or even their simple-dimple family entertainment ambience. They coulda done *anything* with him back in the days when these movies were selling like hotcakes, and they still woulda sold like wheatcakes. Classical sellout thus wasn't necessary until later, but at any time it woulda consisted, at most, of maybe a few more exploitation themes: more leg, an occasional R or even PG, something about Vietnam or hippies, etc.

. . . Wholesome, and he was gonna shove it down the public's throat whether they wanted it or not. I mean like he can't expect to out-Disney Disney for all these years (extending back to even before Walt himself has ventured very far into non-animated territory—*Shaggy Dog* with Annette Funicello was just about the official first pre-60's step—which means that Elvis and the Colonel were the *real* original pioneers of the whole family entertainment genre *per se* as we know it, since in those days fam. ent. usually consisted only of *South Pacific* type *epics,* not B&W meager . . .) and not be seen for his sinister motives: . . . Hicks wanna hickify the world or something . . .

. . . Time may have eroded this writeboy's memory 'cause now it occurs to me that coulda been Carolyn Jones who died in *King Creole* instead of Elvis. But so what. . . .

END

Elvis is attacked in print for the poor quality of his films.

Memphis Commercial Appeal February 18, 1968

Maybe Elvis Could Use A Bit More Exposure?

By John Knott

Two conversations recently led to some mental wool-gathering about the city's No. 1 entertainer.

First, a discussion with Shee Yovan, manager of the State Theater, about the Daytona International auto race he will show on closed circuit TV next Sunday brought up an interesting comparison:

Marat-Sade, the wild production about a bunch of lunatics telling about Marat's assassination, and *Ulysses,* the controversial film version of James Joyce's classic, drew almost as well as Elvis Presley's latest film *Clambake.*

That is rather interesting because it shows that Elvis doesn't do what he did in past years, particularly in the film line. His first film 12 years ago, *Love Me Tender,* had long lines of eager sweet young things waiting eagerly to get in.

Now he's a ho-hum draw—ranking with a couple of renditions of classics, art films almost.

Most of the sweet young things are probably mothers now with daughters coming up who quite probably aren't familiar at all with the squire of Graceland. Why? Lack of exposure.

Another conversation was with Jim Stewart, brilliant young president of Stax-Volt Records who is the foremost of those who have developed the "Memphis Sound."

I mused that some of his top stars—say Carla Thomas, Sam and Dave, and others—had a built-in reception for new records.

"That isn't the case at all. We're always pushing, always trying hard to top the last effort. Sure, a not-too-good record can automatically come out and sell, say, 100,000. But then it stops, bang. And it may hurt the artist's next record, too. You just don't count on, can't trust that built-in acceptance."

Maybe a great deal more exposure of Elvis via television wouldn't hurt at all. Wily old Col. Tom Parker has arranged for one TV appearance—and the network will probably only give him a couple of skyscrapers for the show—sometime this year.

But when he's on a par with Marat-Sade and James Joyce—some people he probably hasn't heard of—then he possibly could use a bit more exposure so the lines will return to his films.

Elvis as he exists in legend...

... vs. the actual Elvis, who suffers from a decline in album sales and at the box office.

229

The Concert Years

1969-1977

"At 9:15, Elvis appeared, materialized, in a white suit of lights, shining with gold appliques, the shirt front slashed to show his chest. Around his shoulders was a cape lined in a cloth of gold, its collar faced with scarlet. It was anything you wanted to call it, gaudy, vulgar, magnificent."

Donna Muir
The New York Times

At last the King is set loose!

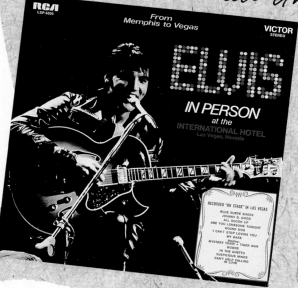

Recorded live in Vegas in '69

Record Mirror reports, Elvis' first 'live' appearance in 7 years . . .

The swivel hips of the greatest rock and roller in history swung again on Thursday, July 31, after seven years without a wiggle. Elvis Presley leapt on stage at America's gigantic International Hotel Show Room, lifted the mike like a hot bull whip and swiftly reinstated himself as one of the most polished performers of all time.

Since long before the invitation-only opening night performance, seething Las Vegas has been alight with signs proclaiming the return of the King and all shows to August 28 have been booked solid. For years, fans all over the world have been relentless in their support and faith that eventually Elvis would step out of the many film sets back on to the stage to rejuvenate the unsteady structure of the rock and roll empire he built, and he has proven it to be as young and amazingly healthy as he himself. At 34 years old, there is little change in the floppy black hair, shiny white teeth and smooth tanned complexion. The Pelvis wore a brightly coloured karate suit with scarves when he walked on stage to a hero's welcome for the first of his lengthy series at the hotel. The audience ranged from middle aged ladies who had grown up screaming for the Elvis of old, to young men and women who have inherited the affection from their elders.

It was a young night as Presley, like a wild beast, roared through a long list of the songs that made him famous, "Hound Dog," "Don't Be Cruel," "One Night," "Blue Suede Shoes" and many more brought him massive ovations and closed the long gap that had frustrated rockers the world over. His strenuous gyrations and virile voicing caused a tumult of uproar from the screaming patronage as ladies lost years and threw themselves at the feet of their leader in frenzied glory. The King jerked and twisted, coaxing the response from the audience. He had to be sure it was all right. There was confidence in every drop of sweat that rolled down his face, but he had to hear it from them—and they told him. Better and more powerful than ever before, Elvis had reunited fans with their idol, a movement with its leader.

This was Presley's first live appearance since he wailed through the 1962 charity benefit at Memphis. It is no longer Elvis and Country Cats, but Elvis the accomplished cabaret artiste—the supreme stylist—the Elvis that retains intact, all the feeling that went into his emotional songs. His backing group consisted of musicians he has been recording with in California and who proved to be worthy of setting his repertoire afire. The outfit included Larry Muhoberac on piano, James Burton and John Wilkinson on guitars, Ronnie Tutt on drums and some beaty bass work by Jerry Scher. Larry Muhoberac was present at the Memphis sessions for Elvis' last LP. Behind the rhythm section was the hotel's 30-piece staff band, conducted by ex-Tony Martin drummer, Bobby Morris.

Over 12,000 fans have already paid up to £20 a ticket to see the first six shows and there is 80% of capacity reserved for the remainder of the season. Pat O'Neill, of the publicity staff, said: "It is one of the biggest advance reservations requests I have ever heard of." His well known manager, Col. Tom Parker, said Elvis had worked very hard for this show and that he was one of the most dedicated performers around. Parker spent a lot of time at the roulette table between organising the show.

Elvis himself explained that he really wanted to go to Britain. He admitted he had said it before, but this time he was genuinely going to make the effort. He said there would probably be a lapse in his film career as he prepared to do more live shows.

Married and with a family, Elvis has shown that nothing was lost in the years he spent in the background. If anything, his ghostly absence has served more to heighten expectation for his new arrival and the reception clearly demonstrates that the young lion has been unleashed with twice the power and lustre of the legendary teenager from the South with the unruly sideboards and the beat-up guitar.

By our correspondent.

Elvis Ponders Tour of World

By JAMES KINGSLEY
Staff Writer

LAS VEGAS, Nev., Aug. 1. —Elvis Presley announced yesterday tentative plans for a world-wide tour following the enthusiastic reception here to his first personal appearance since 1962.

England, the far East and Australia may be included in the tour, the popular Tennessee singer said.

Elvis opened at the International Hotel Thursday night and received a standing ovation from a crowd of nearly 2,000.

"Man they knocked me out," Elvis said after the show. "I was a little nervous for the first three songs, but then I thought 'what the heck, get with it man or you might be out of a job tomorrow.' So I did and things just seemed to rock along and fall into place."

All the gyrations remembered from Presley's 1956 launching of rock and roll and of himself were there—his legs spread apart, shaking his left leg, shaking his head, rotating the guitar.

The tall, dark-haired singer proved that seven years away from live audiences had not affected his stance, timing and virile style of blasting forth with a hot blues tune or a warm enticing ballad. He only looked back at his quintet and the 30-piece International Hotel band once. That was when he walked on stage wearing a black karate tuxedo, black sash, Italian boots with gold tips and picked up a guitar from his friend Charlie Hodges and opened with "Blue Suede Shoes."

He followed with "I Got a Woman," "One Night," "Love Me Tender," "Don't Be Cruel," "Jailhouse Rock," "In the Ghetto," "Suspicious Minds," "Can't Help Falling in Love," "Yesterday," "Hey Jude," "Johnny B. Goode," "Mystery Train," "Tiger Man" and "What'd I Say."

He said he was returning to stage performance because he had missed live audiences. "It was getting harder and harder to perform to a movie-camera."

Memphis Commercial Appeal   August 10, 1969

Elvis Turns Down Contract For Five Million In Las Vegas

By JAMES KINGSLEY

Aug. 9—Elvis Presley, playing to standing-room-only crowds twice nightly at the International Hotel here, has turned down a proposed contract that would assure him an estimated five million dollars during the next decade.

The Commercial Appeal Saturday learned the proposed contract was from one of Nevada's largest hotels. It would require Elvis to appear in Las Vegas for four weeks annually.

The contract reportedly would give Elvis the option of selecting dates and possibly splitting his appearance into two weeks at a time, instead of a four-week stay.

Elvis' manager, Col. Tom Parker, when approached about the contract would only wipe his brow, grin and say: "We are very happy with what is happening at the moment. Looking into the future 10 years is a long time. In fact, I don't know what we might be doing 10 years from now."

Elvis has had packed houses in the 2,000 seat Internationale Showroom of the International Hotel since he opened July 31. His scheduled shows at 8:15 p.m. and midnight have been running about 30 minutes late for each show because of seating problems.

A hotel spokesman, Pat O'Neal, said, "We are having to put extra tables for each performance. It takes time and we try to have as many of the tables cleared as possible before the 8:15 dinner show goes on each night.

However, Elvis quietly notified the hotel the noise of rattling dishes, clinking glasses or flashing camera bulbs does not bother his act, in an effort to help relieve the hotel of the pressure.

"This is where it is, right before the audience. They make me feel good and I don't mind a little noise," Elvis said.

He shouldn't. He is losing several apache ties nightly to female fans as he lets them wipe his forehead or as he sips water from their glasses.

"We are here for a show; the audience wants a show, and we are trying to give them each one show," said Colonel Parker. Ready for number 2?

In 1969, Elvis gave his first live performance in 8 years in Vegas.

Rock Music

Elvis: An Artistic Renaissance

LAS VEGAS—Elvis is back. He had been away.

Good music seems to be one thing that's left after life has moved on. Elvis Presley is a good musician, a great singer, and—quite possibly—the most magnetic performer in the history of (what's commonly called) show biz.

If there had never been an Elvis Presley, certainly no one could have invented him.

The emotional reaction to his first live appearance in nine years is akin to the way a St. Petersburg reporter described the chaotic aftermath of a Presley concert back in 1956: "The Pied Piper of rock 'n roll, a swivel-hipped, leg-lashing entertainment bomb, blasted the downtown area into chaos all day yesterday.

"Screaming, fainting teenagers lined the streets early to catch a glimpse of Elvis Presley, a rock-a-billy gyrating singer who's shattered show business with his sultry style. He hit St. Petersburg with the effect of a small H-bomb, sending fans into mass hysteria and receiving an ovation rarely seen on the Suncoast."

Elvis was the symbol of anti-establishment behavior before Mario Savio had left grade-school. Some suggested he was a Communist plot.

But for better or worse, he fathered a new art form in popular music called rock 'n roll.

Back in 1956, Presley was studying to be an electrician. But, he remembers, "I got wired the wrong way."

He caused a major squirmish when he appeared on the Ed Sullivan show. Then he went to Hollywood.

"My first movie ('Love Me Tender') was kind of weird." But he persevered. "I made four more movies and then I got drafted."

When Elvis returned from the service, something had changed. The taut, casually sinister figure had rounded out. The exuberant spirit seemed to have atrophied. And his singing had become too jello-smooth for its own good. He went through an artistic Dark Age.

In his own words, "I got hung up in Hollywood, making pictures and got away from the people."

But now he is back.

Same swivel-hips. Same gyrations. Same emotional strangle-hold.

His victims are now 30-plus. Hardened waitresses, who just recently struggled through the ennuied debut of the Divine Barbara, were visibly swooning. A well-attired matron scrambled on stage without once breaking stride and corralled the shy Presley.

And his artistry is undiminished. In fact, it seems even enhanced when compared to the rather-trendy impulse by some "to return to the roots of rock 'n roll."

When Elvis swings into "Blue Suede Shows," and "I Got a Woman," and "All Shook Up," and all the others he is where it is at. That's one of the few truths in pop music.

NEWSWEEK   August 11, 1969

. . . Shaking, gyrating, and quivering, he again proved himself worthy of his nickname, the Pelvis. Though nervousness caused him to sing "Love my, me tender" for "Love me tender," the pasty-faced enchanter quickly settled down to work his oleaginous charms, backed by a 30-piece orchestra, a five-man combo and a chorus of seven. Oozing the sullen sexuality that threw America into a state of shock in the '50s, he groaned and swiveled through a medley of "Jailhouse Rock," "Don't Be Cruel," "Heartbreak Hotel," "All Shook Up" and "Hound Dog." It was hard to believe he was 34 and no longer 19 years old . . .

Elvis Helps Push Memphis Sound

Elvis's first critically acclaimed album in years

sheet music

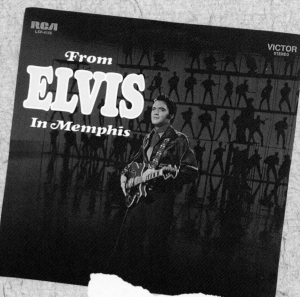

Voice Saves 'Elvis in Memphis'

• "From Elvis in Memphis" (RCA LSP-4155) is a partial concession to those who have been wishing that Presley would return to his rockin' and rollin' ways.

Although it pleases me more than any album he has released in the 1960s, it is not quite the album I had hoped for and really has little to do with the Memphis Sound.

Elvis Presley's recording career began in the mid-50s in Memphis, where he was discovered by Sam Phillips of Sun Records.

Sun Records prospered through an original mixture of country and western music and rhythm and blues belted out by a stable of artists which included Jerry Lee Lewis, Johnny Cash, Carl Perkins and Roy Orbison.

Rhythmic Base

Presley was the most perfect practitioner of this kind of music. His voice could generate the intense power of blues but still project its subtle nuances and he was grounded enough in both country music and R&B to fuse them into a new kind of rock 'n' roll.

The predominant elements of the Memphis Sound then were a heavy rhythmic base which barreled along relatively simple lines and an echoey wailing vocal. No horns, no back-up female chorus and (naturally) no string section, just lead, rhythm and bass guitars, an occasional pumping piano and drums.

The Memphis Sound now is exemplified by Stax Records (Booker T and the MGs, Carla Thomas, Albert King and—in association with Atlantic Records—Otis Redding, Wilson Pickett and Sam and Dave).

Little Inspiration

Its hallmark is still a heavy rhythmic base (furnished on about 80% of the Stax sessions by Booker T and the MGs), but Stax has added a distinctive horn section, which replaces the ubiquitous rhythm and blues girls chorus. The instrumental component of a typical Stax record is still ultra-simple (in contrast to Motown which goes for elaborate arrangements).

"From Elvis in Memphis" owes little inspiration either to Sun Records or to Stax. The rhythm section used on the album rarely gets off the ground, horns are scarce and generally insipid, the musical arrangements are Hollywoodish and the few simply-structured performances seem to spring more from laziness than deliberation on the part of the producer and arranger.

What saves the album, though, is Elvis' voice, which has gotten back down to grittiness. Elvis Presley is capable of being a great singer and the move to Memphis seems to have freed him of the crooner image which has dulled many of his records.

His current hit, "In the Ghetto," is the stand-out track, followed by "Long Black Limousine" and a nice (but a bit fast) remake of Chuck Jackson's "Any Day Now."

The remainder of the album is worth hearing because of his voice, which seems to have arrived in Memphis even if no one else concerned with the LP did.

Elvis Home— Cuts 16 Sides

MEMPHIS—Elvis Presley and a contingent of RCA recording technicians quietly slipped in here last week and recorded a 16-tune session at American Record Studios. In the only recording studio interview granted by Presley since he joined RCA he said, "This is where it all started for me. It feels good to be back in Memphis recording."

American, headed by Chips Moman, is regarded as one of the "hottest" studios today and responsible for such hits as "Hooked on a Feeling," by B.J. Thomas and "Son of a Preacher Man," by Dusty Springfield.

The session, from which an LP and singles will be produced, utilized American's studio band, a symphony orchestra string section, local brass men and a chorus.

Here from RCA's Nashville studios were Felton Jarvis, Al Pachuki and Roy Shockley. Harry Jenkins, vice-president, RCA's record division, New York, was also here.

Moman, co-owner of the studio with Bob Crews, manned the control board. Presley and Jarvis teamed with Moman in producing the session.

Presley said the session, his first since recording here on Sun Records in 1954, was the first that did not also involve motion pictures. "This is especially refreshing," he said.

234

Elvis's guard had it rough

"If you wanted to get through you'd better have a badge and a gun." Pete Kimbrel was a tired, tired man Sunday night. What he needed was to take a warm bath and forget the week end, but what he did was go to work as a Houston police dispatcher.

KIMBREL HAD JUST SPENT two days, his days off, guarding the most recent super-idol on the Houston scene: Elvis. Elvis Presley, that is.

He spent those two days watching out for the singing star, standing between him and the ogling, happy, occasionally screaming crowds that just wanted to touch him. And just tear the clothes from his back.

"The teeny-boppers were everywhere," Kimbrel said wearily. "Elvis has his own bodyguards, but he wanted the Houston police too—the local police can move him around better."

Kimbrel and about 100 other policemen guarded Presley at his hotel—"He had the whole eighth floor"—escorted him to the Domed Stadium for his rodeo appearances, and stood guard around him there while he sang.

"At the Saturday matinee a man got through and started running toward the stand," Kimbrel said. He patted his stomach and smiled, shaking his head.

"I told another officer, 'Go get him, Rabbit.' You never saw such bulldogging in your life."

IN THE SHADOW OF A JUMPING, swinging guitar, the man was wrestled to the ground, shouting "He's my idol. He's my idol."

At the hotel, fans tried desperately to get through for an autograph or a little peek at Elvis.

"At one of the press conferences, I saw a rope start coming down from a balcony," Kimbrel said. "They were trying to get to him that way—they had jumped across from another roof."

Gray hairs speck Kimbrel's head. It's been a while since he got very excited over a singing star.

"He didn't do much for me," he grinned. "He didn't turn me on, but those little teeny-boppers . . . wow!"

Elvis returned to the road in 1970...

...and every concert was a sell-out.

THE LAS VEGAS SCENE

Sinatras, Presley Headline Summer Fete

LAS VEGAS—Probably the summer season's most gala events take place tomorrow and Monday nights when Nancy Sinatra—with a little help from her famous father—ushers in Caesar's Palace's fourth anniversary and Elvis Presley respectively.

Miss Sinatra's bow, along with The Osmond Brothers and The Blossoms, will launch a three-day celebration capped by the opening of a new 14-story high-rise addition and a black-tie affair Saturday night hosted by Frank Sinatra.

Included in the new addition are 222 suites, a Japanese steak house, Cleopatra's Floating Barge, a European cuisine restaurant and the circular Discus Bar.

[Elvis' stint at the] International is being billed as the "Elvis Summer Festival" and will feature the filming of the release by RCA of a four-record album containing all 50 of his million-sellers entitled, "Elvis' World-wide 50 Gold Award Hits, Vol. 1."

It will be Presley's 33rd movie for MGM over a 13-year period, and according to a source close to the entertainer, "by far the most exciting." During Elvis' last stay he recorded an "On Stage" album which has passed the million mark in sales bringing his number of Gold Record albums to 14, 4 of them within the past year.

Comedian Sammy Shore, the Imperials and the Sweet Inspirations, plus five of his personal musicians augmenting the International Hotel orchestra, will again be the supporting bill.

Other openings this week find Marty Robbins returning tomorrow night at the Fremont with comedian Sid Gould featured. Saturday night Joey Bishop makes his initial club appearance in four years at the Sands. Co-billed with Bishop is the comedy team of Al Fisher and Lou Marks, singer Carolyn Blakey, The People Tree and Mel Bishop.

Elvis and Priscilla enjoy Vegas.

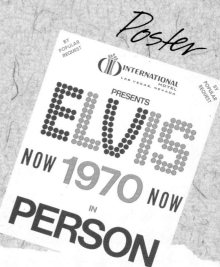

Poster

BY POPULAR REQUEST

INTERNATIONAL HOTEL
LAS VEGAS, NEVADA
PRESENTS

ELVIS

NOW 1970 NOW

IN

PERSON

BY POPULAR REQUEST

A LEGEND THAT LIVES

By FRANK LIEBERMAN

LAS VEGAS—At the airport, the International Hotel's towering marquee simply reads "ELVIS."

The cab drivers ask, "Are you going to see Elvis?"

Patrons at every hotel are talking about seeing or trying to see Elvis.

Elvis Presley, now a legend, is alive.

He's the ghost who walks on the stage of the International showroom twice nightly to capacity throngs of 2000-plus per show. Never in the annals of Las Vegas show business has an entertainer caused such a clamor.

But there has never been another Elvis Presley.

Few guests, if any, leave the International disappointed. Presley's life-long ambition is to make people happy, to entertain them, to become a friend. He would like to get out and meet them all.

Elvis Presley, to the people, is "The King."

Presley's nine-year hiatus from clubs ended last August. It gave his fans a new chance to view their idol. What so many people don't realize is that it did more for the man himself.

"It gave me a new life. I was human again," Presley said in his International dressing room. "There was hope for the future. New things, new ways. It wasn't the same old movies, the same type of songs. I was able to give some feeling, put some expression into my work.

"And it gave me a chance to do what I do best, sing," added Elvis, with a smiling, friendly "let's cut out that bragging," look.

Presley is 35 now, and happily married, despite rumors to the contrary. His 6-foot plus thin frame stands tall and his pitch-black hair is still long. But the shyness and self-conscious slouch that always were associated with the younger Presley are gone.

On his fingers are four rings, all gleaming despite the lack of light in the dressing quarters.

Presley's clothes are "in," but not outlandish. On stage he wore white. Relaxing, he wore black.

The country boy image has vanished. His coterie has been reduced to four or five instead of the old 10 to 13. And those left are friends and workers. The body-guard front is no longer.

His words are clear and precise, the old cornpone accent barely discernible. His return to the stage is a giant step forward.

Following his first engagement, Presley returned to this city as a tourist. He was seen kissing admirers, signing autographs, playing blackjack, and doing the things ordinary people do.

His newest movie, "Change of Habit," came and went, just as the star was doing from hotel to hotel. It didn't matter, for Elvis was doing what he wanted. He wasn't hiding and sneaking about. No walks through kitchens, up back elevators. He was Elvis Presley, a human being . . . .

Seattle Post-Intelligencer, May 7, 1970

If Elvis Is in It, Film Outlook Good

NEW YORK—(AP)—A movie shown on television has the best chance for success if:

A. It stars Elvis Presley. B. It is either a comedy or a drama. C. It is in color. D. It runs longer than two hours.

It also helps if the film runs against weak competition and has a strong lead-in, according to a study made of movies shown between September 1961 and September 1969.

During that period Elvis Presley appeared in seven high-rated movies, almost twice as much as his nearest competitors, Rock Hudson and Doris Day. They had four each. John Wayne, Cary Grant, Jerry Lewis, Jack Lemmon and Shirley MacLaine each had three.

Comedy and drama fared equally well with 24 top-ranked films each, but comedy was slightly ahead in percentage. Over-all, drama pushed comedy completely out of the top 10 for the period. Science-fiction and biography did the poorest of all types of films, with only two each receiving a rating higher than 25.

The survey showed that NBC had the most winners, followed by CBS and ABC.

The top 10 films for the period are:

"The Birds," "Bridge Over the River Kwai," "Cat on a Hot Tin Roof," "Great Escape" Part 2, "McClintock," "Great Escape" Part 1, "The Robe," "Lilies of the Field," "Your Cheatin' Heart" and "Something of Value." "The Birds," pulled in a whopping 38.9 rating, and "Bridge" had 38.3. The lowest rated in the top 10, "Something of Value," had 29.6.

In this past season "My Sweet Charlie," a movie made for television, ran 31.7 rating, which would make it the fourth highest-rated movie behind "Cat on a Hot Tin Roof." "The Ballad of Josie," shown in September, got a 31.1 rating, which gives it a tie with "The Great Escape" Part 1. It also gives Doris Day one more top picture and puts her just behind Elvis Presley with five.

"Born Free" ran up a 34.2 rating, but it was shown Feb. 16 by CBS as a special and outside of its regular movie nights.

Elvis Presley Returns to International

Elvis Presley, whose two earlier Las Vegas appearances established him as the resort city's all-time top entertainment attraction, returns to the International Hotel's main showroom Aug. 10 to launch a four-week engagement being billed as the "Elvis Summer Festival".

The special billing comes in conjunction with a spectacular innovation for Las Vegas—the filming of a two-hour "Elvis festival" type motion picture by MGM, scheduled for world-wide theatre release.

It will be Elvis's 33rd movie for MGM over a period of 13 years with the major portion of the new film centered around his performance in the 2,000-seat Showroom Internationale.

It was just a year ago that Elvis made his International Hotel debut, his first public appearance in eight years. In the ensuing 12 months he has seen three new recordings achieve Gold Record status, representing sales of over one million each. This brings to 50 the number of Presley Gold Record single releases, unprecedented in the recording industry, and adding further strength to the RCA claim that he has one of the most heard voices in the history of mankind. RCA is marking the event with the release of a special four-record album containing all 50 million-sellers to coincide with his Las Vegas opening.

Elvis's special "On Stage" album, recorded live at the International during his second engagement in February, has already passed the million mark in sales, bringing his number of Gold Record albums to 14, four of them within the last 12 months.

He will bring with him the same lineup of supporting stars as in past performances including comic Sammy Shore, the Imperials and the Sweet Inspirations, plus five of his personal musicians to augment the 30-member International Orchestra.

Elvis will do two performances every evening at 8:00 p.m. and midnight through Labor Day. Pearl Bailey and Louis Armstrong will follow him into the Showroom Internationale.

Presley Rebooked In 'Vegas

Elvis Presley, who made his first public appearance in a decade at the International Hotel in Las Vegas, returns to the International on Monday for another four weeks of Elvismania.

The entertainer attracted over 100,000 fans into the posh hotel's huge showroom during his 29-day run last summer, breaking every existing Las Vegas attendance record.

He brings with him again the same lineup of supporting stars including comic Sammy Shore, the Imperials and the Sweet Inspirations, plus five of his personal musicians to augment the 30-member International Orchestra.

Like last time, Elvis is again expected to give International audiences exactly what they ask for—a full sampling from the Presley catalogue of golden hits ranging "Hound Dog" to "Suspicious Minds" with plenty of others including "Blue Suede Shoes," "Love Me Tender," "I Got a Woman," "In the Ghetto" and "All Shook Up" tossed in. All are performed with the swinging gyrations that helped him alter the entire course of popular music just 14 years ago this month with his first recording, "Heartbreak Hotel."

Elvis will do two shows every night at 8 p.m. and midnight through Feb. 23.

After 1970, jumpsuits became Elvis's trademark.

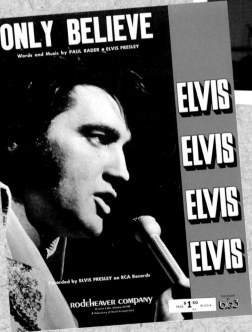

ONLY BELIEVE
Words and Music by PAUL RADER • ELVIS PRESLEY

ELVIS
ELVIS
ELVIS
ELVIS

Recorded by ELVIS PRESLEY on RCA Records

RODEHEAVER COMPANY

Sheet music

This album was a slapdash mix of tunes from Elvis's movies and songs recorded in Memphis in 1969.

Concert album

February, 1970
ON STAGE
RCA
LSP-4362
VICTOR
STEREO

Bill Belew designed most of Elvis's jumpsuits.

Seattle Post-Intelligencer, October 13, 1970

Elvis Can Pack Pistol

MEMPHIS, Tenn.—(UPI)—Entertainer Elvis Presley has been commissioned a special Shelby County deputy sheriff, an act that will allow the singing star to carry a pistol.

Sheriff Roy C. Nixon confirmed yesterday the commission ceremony was held privately in his office Saturday. He said Presley had been an "honorary" deputy for several years.

The sheriff said the change in status was requested by Presley's office. In addition to allowing him to carry a pistol, it provided him with identification papers.

Nixon said he has no plans to call his new special deputy for any law enforcement duties.

Memphis Commercial Appeal

Morris Is Driving Elvis' Stocking-Stuffer

Former Shelby County Sheriff William N. Morris Jr. last night called 1970 "a good year for cars", after receiving a sleek Mercedes-Benz as a Christmas present from Elvis Presley.

The $9,000 gift joins a 1970 Pontiac in Mr. Morris' driveway. The Pontiac was a going away present from sheriff's deputies and well-wishers when Mr. Morris left office last August. The Pontiac was priced at $4,500.

Mr. Morris said he and his family spent Christmas Eve with the singer at his Graceland mansion. He said Elvis called him outside the mansion and gave him the car keys.

"I've enjoyed Elvis' friendship for about 12 years, I guess. My wife was graduated with him from Humes High School in 1953," he said.

"It's some kinda car—makes us a three-car family now."

Mr. Morris said Elvis apparently bought several of the German-made cars and gave them to other close friends as Christmas gifts.

"I'm still speechless, and you can bet it'll be a while before my son has a chance to drive it," Mr. Morris said of the shiny burgundy-color four-door auto.

The former sheriff said he had no idea of the value of the Mercedes-Benz but a salesman said last night that a fully equipped 280 SL model would cost about $9,000.

Mr. Morris said he did not know how many cars the entertainer bought or to whom he gave them. Elvis could not be reached for comment last night.

Meanwhile, yesterday, the singer's father, Vernon Presley, said Elvis has not let his hair grow to shoulder length.

It had been reported that Elvis visited central police headquarters early Christmas Day with shoulder-length hair.

TWO FORUM CONCERTS

Capacity Gatherings Welcome Presley

It had been 13 years since Presley had performed in Los Angeles at the Pan Pacific. That night—according to a teenager now in his late 20s—was "outa sight. The girls and even the guys were hysterical. Every gyration brought screams and you could hardly hear him sing. It truly was an unforgettable experience."

So was Saturday.

Presley was greeted by 37,398 fans for two performances at the Forum that grossed $313,464. He was welcomed with screams and a constant barrage of flash bulbs popping, but there was respect and an overwhelming desire to listen, to watch, to appreciate the magical world Elvis Presley had created during the past 15 years.

I doubt if anyone left disappointed. The many sides of Presley were revealed to the audience that made a sell-out of the evening in just nine hours last month. There was also a share of uncharacteristic comments about record sales and magazine stories. Presley felt he was among friends and that the Los Angeles crowd was special. "He was more excited and nervous about this date than any on the tour," said a member of his entourage.

He appeared after intermission and the first half of the show that featured his Las Vegas opening acts—comedian Sammy Shore, The Sweet Inspirations and The Imperials. Presley wore a white jump suit—"bought especially for tonight"—with a high back collar, bell bottoms, gold embroidery and cape-like wings with floor-length fringe.

"Damn fringe," Presley kept commenting as it continually got tangled in the mike chord, guitar strings and Elvis. "They seemed like a good idea at the time," he noted. (The picture above shows how the fringe affected the performance. They were a nice addition to Elvis' swirling, twisting and karate-type poses.)

With every move the audience screamed. The shrills equalled those heard at any hard-rock concert, yet the crowd was much older, many of them had grown-up with Presley. Along with his tunes Presley noted his record sales. "I've sold over 200 million records, that's more than Jones (Tom) and the Beatles and a few others combined." The audience loved it.

Vocally, Presley was dynamic. His deep rich, powerful voice sounded magnificent over the huge Forum speakers. He wailed on a funky tune and handled a ballad in a simple, sensitive manner.

His repertoire included a retrospective of his hits—"Suspicious Minds," "Wonder of You," "Love Me Tender"—and other top chart songs. As it did Las Vegas, his rendition of "Bridge Over Troubled Waters" brought oohs and ahs, with much of the audience not realizing the unlimited potential and surefire handling of Presley and a "deep" song.

Presley had the lights turned up toward the end of the show to look at the audience. He greeted many fans with a congenial smile and thanked them for attending. He plugged his upcoming MGM feature entitled "ELVIS, that's the way it is," saying that it's the "best one I've made in 10 years."

Adding another dimension to the distinctive concert were Presley's personal musicians and a superb orchestra under the direction of Joe Guercio.

The members of Presley's entourage included Glen D. Hardin on piano, Jerry Schiff on guitar, Charlie Hodge on guitar (he is also Presley's water boy), Ronnie Tutt on drums, James Burton on lead guitar and John Wilkinson on bass guitar.

Australian Magazine

Both of these albums were released in Nov. 1970.

Elvis Makes 'Quiet Visit' To Tupelo

Singer Elvis Presley made what was described as a "quiet visit" to Tupelo, Miss., his birthplace, and received a plaque from some friends for being "a good neighbor."

Two couples—Mr. and Mrs. Roy McComb and Mr. and Mrs. James Farrar—had the plaque made and presented it to Elvis in Tupelo yesterday.

It was titled "Impossible Dream," and Elvis remarked it was "quite a coincidence" since his next record will be titled that. The words describe how a "boy-next-door" type becomes a nationally known entertainer.

Elvis also visited Police Sgt. Guy Harris, who once attended school with him, and Lee County Sheriff Bill Mitchell at the Tupelo county jail, and the Elvis Presley Youth Center, a facility in east Tupelo.

Elvis brought the plaque back with him to his Whitehaven home, Graceland.

Metro-Goldwyn-Mayer

ELVIS
"That's the way it is"
PANAVISION — METROCOLOR

MGM

soundtrack album

RCA
LSP-4445
Elvis That's The Way It Is Elvis
VICTOR
STEREO

Elvis- That's the Way It Is is a documentary about Elvis's preparations for a Vegas appearance.

Stamps Four Planning Elvis Movie

NASHVILLE—J.D. Sumner and the Stamps Quartet will leave Nashville this week to film a special documentary movie with Elvis Presley before beginning their April tour.

Presley had booked the group for the tour before learning of the special documentary that will be made of him. They had just completed a five-week engagement at the International Hotel in Las Vegas.

According to Sumner, the movie will contain Presley and the Stamps rehearsing for a recording session, in an actual session at RCA in Hollywood and then portions of the April tour.

The Stamps record for Heartwarming, and are booked through Sumar Talent Inc., here.

ELVIS— HE'S BACK!

Elvis Presley has starred in 31 motion pictures. Number 32 is both a unique project for ·Presley and an unusual approach to movie entertainment. For the first time Elvis is seen on film as he really is, portrayed as an artist and as a phenomenon.

MGM's "Elvis . . . That's The Way It Is" was directed by two-time Academy Award-winner Denis Sanders, who explains, "The subject is Elvis and the core of the picture is Elvis on stage in Las Vegas performing his incredible, record-breaking act."

Sanders continues, "However, we went much further with the cameras. We attempted to capture the ups and downs he experiences putting his show together, showing the man as a musician. We filmed both sides of the lights, exploring what he feels and the emotions he creates in others."

Pursuing that goal, the director photographed his subject in private rehearsals at MGM Studios, further rehearsals in Las Vegas and then on stage in the Showroom Internationale of Las Vegas' International Hotel. MGM cameras were also on hand in Phoenix, September 9, for the opening of the star's first concert tour in thirteen years.

To gain insight into Presley's following, certainly the largest and most varied group of fans in entertainment, Sanders interviewed businessmen, students, housewives and a bride, among others, in settings ranging from living rooms to churches, talking with a variety of people who have literally devoted varying proportions of their existence to the former teenage truck driver named Elvis Presley. Additionally, he travelled to Europe to capture the Fifth Annual Elvis Presley Appreciation Society Convention, attended by up to 4,000 people of all ages each year in Luxembourg.

More rehearsals

The film covered each stage of the rehearsals .

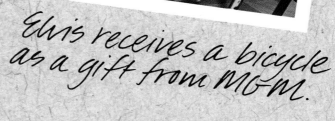

Elvis receives a bicycle as a gift from MGM.

241

Jaycees Urged To Get In Arena

A hectic day of Jaycee activities yesterday was highlighted by a luncheon speech from United Nations Ambassador-appointee George Bush and last night by the organization's awards ceremony honoring the Ten Outstanding Young Men in America.

The slender, Texas oil millionaire, whom many believe was President Nixon's United Nations choice because he ran gamely but unsuccessfully for the Senate seat held by Ralph Yarborough, spoke to an estimated 1,100 at the Holiday Inn-Rivermont.

He praised his audience as "men who have thought new thoughts and rejected old dogmas. But to guarantee this country never accepts the violent answer," our people must be willing to work "within the system," he said.

He complimented the Jaycees on their "Top Ten" selection and told Memphis politicians to "watch out" if entertainer Elvis Presley ever decided to enter politics. "They would have to regroup their forces," he said.

Last night at the awards ceremony the entertainer had a few words for the 2,000 persons at the Auditorium.

"I've always been a dreamer. When I was young I used to read comic books and go to movies, and I was the hero.

"My dreams have come true a 100 times over. These men here," he said, pointing to the nine other award winners, "they care. You stop to think, and they're building the kingdom of heaven."

Dressed in a modest black tuxedo, Elvis closed by saying that without a song the day never ends. "So I just keep singing a song," he said as tears rushed to his eyes.

The singer had one hand too few as he accepted the award from the United States Jaycee President Gordon Thomas. Shaking Mr. Thomas' hand and taking the Outstanding Man trophy in the other, Elvis had no place to hold his yellow "Easy Rider" sunglasses.

Each of the Outstanding Men made a short speech prior to receiving their awards.

Thomas Atkins, Boston's first black councilman, called on Jaycees throughout the country to donate one dollar per year for four years to advance the ideals of the late Dr. Martin Luther King.

"I appeal to you to lift this country from the quicksand of racism to the solid rock of human dignity," Mr. Atkins said.

Wendell Cherry, president of Extendicare Nursing Corp., in his address said the American system will continue to work as long as people such as the Jaycees continue to involve themselves in community life.

"We must temper our urge to overcome with compassion and patience," he said. Then quoting Tennyson, he closed with, "Come my friend, 'tis not too late to seek a newer world."

Comic strip artist Al Capp, was scheduled to be master of ceremonies at the awards ceremony but did not appear.

"He wasn't able to come due to a last minute breakdown in communications," said Ken Scrivner, public relations director of the Jaycees. He declined to elaborate on Mr. Capp's absence.

Ron Zeigler, White House press secretary, paid tribute to the Jaycees for accepting "the high adventure of being Americans.

"This nation has a history of striving, stretching, doing and caring. We have refused to believe that things are impossible," he said.

Others honored were Dr. Mario Capecchi, a biophysicist at Harvard Medical School; Dr. George Todaro, researcher for the National Cancer Institute; Capt. Paul William Bucha, professor at West Point; Walter J. Humann, corporation executive; Jim Goetz, radio station owner; and Thomas Edward Coll, founder of a private volunteer service.

Mr. Bush earlier praised Presley's comments at the morning forum, closed to the press, in which Jaycees attending the 33rd congress were permitted to question the honorees.

In that forum, Elvis "held his own" with his more "learned colleagues," said George Cajoleas, president of the Bradenton, Fla., Jaycees.

"He was forthright in his answers and didn't stumble. The guy came off looking very good, although he seemed very humble. I felt he was very impressed with the men around him in terms of their contributions to social advancement."

The honorees were asked if they made a religious commitment before undertaking their life's work.

"Six or seven of the men said they didn't belong to a church and felt a certain hypocrisy about organized religion. But Elvis seemed to feel religion was very important in his life, not in the organized sense, but in the sense that he had called on God many times for strength. I think he also quoted some scripture," said Mr. Cajoleas.

Presley said after the luncheon that he didn't quote scripture but had "commented that God is a living presence in all of us."

MEMPHIS, Tenn., Jan. 16—PRESLEY AND WIFE AT PRAYER BREAKFAST—Elvis Presley and his wife stand for their introduction Saturday morning at a U. S. Jaycees prayer breakfast. Presley is one of Ten Outstanding Young Men being honored here by the Jaycees. The Memphis entertainer wore a fur suit for the breakfast and later appeared at a forum with the other winners. Award ceremonies were Saturday night.

Reservations Up for Elvis Shows

LAS VEGAS—Despite the economic slump that has cut severely into attendance at most showrooms here, advance reservations for Elvis Presley's fourth International Hotel engagement are running as strong as ever.

During each of his other four-week stands, Presley acknowledged to be the city's most powerful showroom attraction, drew more than 100,000 persons into the hotel's 2,000-seat Showroom Internationale.

"It's remarkable," an International Hotel spokesman said. "Every time Presley comes back, the demand for reservations gets stronger. The economy hasn't apparently had any impact on his drawing power." The engagement opens Tuesday and runs through Feb. 23.

As usual, Col. Tom Parker, Presley's manager, has arranged for a special piece of promotion to tie-in to the International engagement. Last August, MGM made a documentary film ("Elvis—That's The Way It Is") of Presley's opening at the International. This time, RCA has released a new album. Titled "Elvis Country," it is Presley's first all-country album. It contains 12 songs all connected by a gospel-flavored "I'm 10,000 Years Old" song that gives the album something of a live concert feel.

No Stranger to Country Music

While it is Presley's first "official" country album, he is, of course, no stranger to country music. Before he was a rock idol, Presley was a fast rising country music star. His Sun recording of "I Forgot to Remember to Forget" was on the country charts for nearly a year in his pre-"Heartbreak Hotel," pre-television, pre-Hollywood days.

On the early Sun records, Presley not only demonstrated a strong voice that was suited to both country and blues material, he did some exciting musical experimentation. Eliminating the traditional steel guitar and fiddle in country music, he would put a bluegrass tune (Bill Monroe's "Blue Moon of Kentucky") on one side of a record and a blues number (Arthur "Big Boy" Crudup's "That's All Right") on the other side.

Though there have been some exceptions, Presley's best work has tended to be on the songs closest to root (country, particularly, and blues) forms. It shouldn't be surprising, then, to find Presley does some of his best vocals on "Elvis Country." It is, in many ways, one of his most interesting non-concert albums.

Presley's version of Willie Nelson's "Funny How Time Slips Away," for instance, is one of the finest things he's ever done on record. It has a great bluesy feeling, backed by an excellent arrangement. Similarly, Presley's vocals on the album's other ballads (including "I Really Don't Want to Know," "Faded Love" and "Tomorrow Never Comes") are consistently strong.

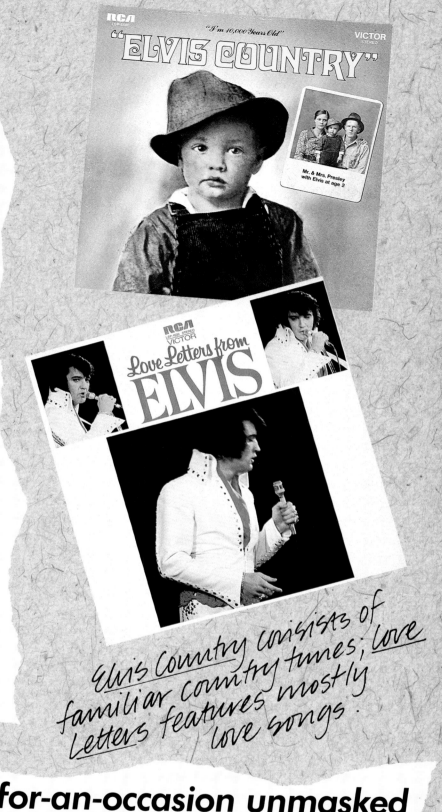

Elvis Country consists of familiar country tunes; Love Letters features mostly love songs.

Elvis-for-an-occasion unmasked

LONDON (UPI)—The white-suited guitar-carrying young man with the dark hair and long sideburns stepped from the jetliner onto the runway at London's Heathrow Airport and said in a Southern drawl: "I'm overwhelmed—this is great."

"Elvis! Elvis! Elvis!" screamed several dozen girls. Flashbulbs popped and Heathrow's VIP greeter, Ross Chaffer, stepped forward Sunday to shake the hand of the man he thought was Elvis Presley.

Chaffer and everyone else —including the British Broadcasting Corp. and British Press Assn.—was the victim of a hoax.

"Elvis," said a customs officer after the young man had roared off in a Rolls Royce limousine, was a far less well known American pop singer, Eli Culbertson, 23.

"I was phoned and told to go to the airport to meet Elvis Presley," greeter Chaffer said afterward. "I was convinced it was Elvis."

The real Elvis was appearing at Lake Tahoe, Nev.

A newsman who was asked to verify that sent this message to the London bureau of United Press International: "He is scheduled to do two shows today. If he can fit the trip to Europe between them he is a better man than Gunga Din."

Memphis Press-Scimitar March 9, 1971

Fans Cheer Screen

They came in "hot pants" and long pants, floor-length dresses and mini skirts.

They were in mod suits and conservative suits, tee-shirts and blue jeans.

They came to see, "The Fight."

They came to two screens set up in each hall of the building.

Archie was there. And so was Elvis.

Ancient Ellis Auditorium was packed. It was a complete sellout. Scalpers had a field day. One man bought three tickets for $65. Singles were going for as much as $25 or $30 apiece.

About half the crowd was for the champ, Joe Frazier. But those pulling for Muhammad Ali, the deposed champion, were louder. Except at the end. Then they were just like their hero. Silent.

It may not have been Madison Square Garden, but it was the next best thing. It may have been just a screen on the Auditorium stage, but the 6,700 fans screamed words of encouragement at it for 15 rounds. There were screams of ecstasy when Frazier threw that devastating left hook in the 15th round and Ali went down. But there were also groans, curse words and utter shock.

A few thought afterwards that Ali had won. Most thought the decision was right, but hardly anyone agreed with judge Bill Recht's card, 11 rounds for Frazier, four for Ali.

It was a racially-mixed crowd, though there may have been a few more whites than blacks. Most whites were for Frazier, most blacks for Ali. But not all.

"I don't like Clay," said one Negro man. "He talks too much. But Smokin' Joe shut him up but good."

A white man, dressed in an expensive, stylish mod suit, seemed crestfallen that Ali lost. "I couldn't believe it when he went down, I just couldn't believe it," he muttered, shaking his head. "I love that man. He's my hero. He stands up for what he believes in. But Frazier's fists knocked him down, flat down, man."

Archie Manning drove up from Oxford with two of his Ole Miss teammates, Skip Jernigan and Billy VanDevender. "I'm for Frazier," said the legendary Ole Miss Rebel quarterback before the bout, "but I think you ought to realize that I know a whole lot more about football than I do about boxing."

Elvis Presley and about 10 of his friends, including former sheriff William Morris, entered the Music Hall from a side door about five minutes before the first round. Elvis' party sat in the orchestra pit. Many people sitting nearby recognized Memphis' famed singer, but for one of the few times in Elvis' adult life he was all but ignored. People were too interested in the main attraction and on this night Ali and Frazier, not Elvis held the center stage.

Afterwards Elvis said he has always been a fight fan, but added he didn't have a particular favorite in the championship bout.

If that's true, he was probably the only unemotional fan in the building.

Elvis and Priscilla attend a simulcast of the Ali-Frazier fight.

Though fans thought him a sex symbol, Elvis also had a keen sense of humor.

Memphis Commercial Appeal, December 1971

Elvis Plays Santa Claus —With Sly Grin On Face

By JAMES KINGSLEY

Elvis Presley, the multimillionaire squire of Graceland, is well known as the "practical joker."

He pulled off one of his best at his annual Christmas Eve get-together when he usually hands out envelopes 'stuffed with money and sometimes gold-plated automobile keys to employees and friends.

Everyone remembered that last year some of his gifts included expensive Mercedes-Benz automobiles and the usual cash gifts that he likes to share.

As Elvis began to play Santa Claus this year he was in a happy-go-lucky mood as everyone gathered in his den and living room expecting the usual gifts and maybe a "little something special."

With a sly grin on his face, the singer turned to his father, Vernon Presley, and asked: "Where are the envelopes please?"

Vernon reached into his coat pocket and produced the envelopes.

"Well, it's been a mighty lean year," said Elvis, whose income probably exceeded four million dollars in 1971 with two appearances at the Las Vegas Hilton International Hotel, two tours of the country, and record royalties.

He had built them up for the kill. He knew inside the envelopes was a gift that would be worth a hamburger, french fries and a soft drink.

As the envelopes began to be opened the room fell silent.

His special gift for 1971 was a 50-cent gift certificate to McDonald's Hamburgers.

His joke over, Elvis later distributed his real gifts which included envelopes stuffed with cash for his employees.

POINTS WEST—Hello again! **Elvis Presley** opened his engagement at the Las Vegas Hilton last week to fanatic SRO crowds. Elvis' show, from all reports, is one of his most unusual in a career that spans the beginnings of rock and roll through motion pictures, and a superstardom that defies the ravages of time! The performer held no rehearsals for the engagement. A container set up at the entrance to the showroom was put into use, and patrons dropped names of songs they wanted Elvis to sing on stage. The container was put on stage and Elvis picked the songs out at random, often conversing with the donors in the audience. Obviously no show can be the same under this arrangement, and Elvis' attitude and on-stage responsiveness are at the most positive point in years, as he joked freely with the crowd and reached back for some incredible high notes. The "pelvis" will come to L.A. to record his new RCA album in September. Rocket Records artist **Neil Sedaka** was on hand at the opening night show and although each artist has had great respect for one another through the years, this was the first occasion of their meeting. Elvis introduced Sedaka to the crowd and they played piano and sang together backstage. Reportedly, Neil was asked by Presley to compose a song for Elvis' new LP. Reports that Elvis is considering hanging it up? "A bunch of bull," replies Elvis. He reportedly is enjoying his work more than ever and has already scheduled more tours for later this year. Elvis is back!

This souvenir booklet Commemorates one of Elvis's concert tours.

Souvenir Photo Album

On the road: Elvis obliges some lucky fans with kisses and snapshots.

Elvis Again World's Top Male Singer

LONDON (AP)—For the 12th time in 13 years, Elvis Presley has been named the world's top male singer in the annual New Musical Express poll.

The 35-year-old king of pop also was named world's top musical personality in 1970. Britain's Cliff Richard was runner-up in both categories.

Readers of the New Musical Express, which claims 300,000 circulation, elected the American Creedence Clearwater Revival as the top world group.

That title last went to the Beatles, who were placed second this time, although they have said they are no longer a group. The Beatles kept their title as top British group, however, and their "Let It Be" was chosen as the best album of 1970.

The title of world's most popular singer went to Diana Ross.

245

'Burning Love'

IN THE MORE THAN 15 years Elvis Presley's been in the recording biz, he's managed to shake and sing up a storm of statistics that keep spelling success. Worldwide, more than 250 million Presley platters have been sold since 1956, with "Hound Dog" accounting for 7 million alone. So far, those sales have translated into 47 gold records for million-selling singles and 10 goldies for albums, including a couple of soundtracks from Elvis' 32 movies. Sales of "Blue Hawaii" recently reached the 3 million mark and "G.I. Blues" has been taken into the hearts and homes of nearly 2 million Elvis fans. Probably the most impressive statistic of all, tho, is the fact that after all those years, Ol' El is still going strong. These days, the big thing in his life is "Burning Love" . . . .

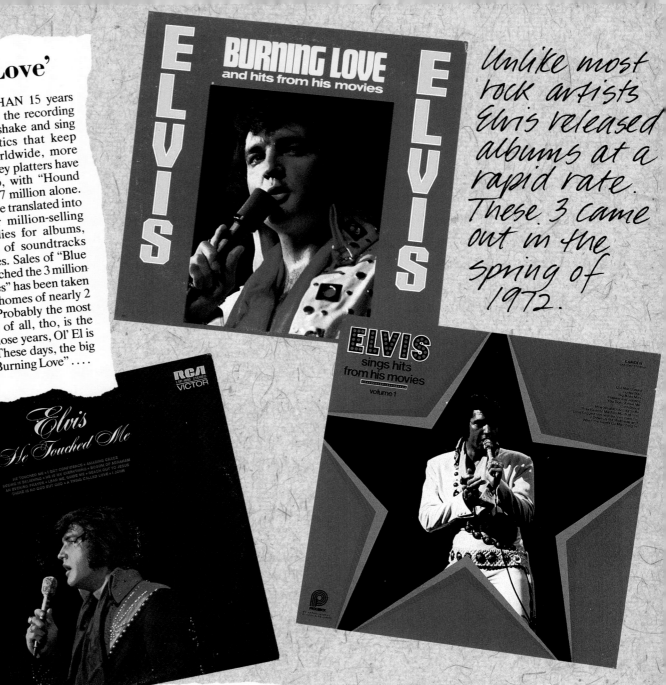

Unlike most rock artists Elvis released albums at a rapid rate. These 3 came out in the spring of 1972.

HE TOUCHED ME   Elvis Presley

RCA (LSP-4690)

. . . But fortunately, *Elvis Now* is not Elvis now. Elvis now is *He Touched Me*, a beautiful LP, Elvis' first sacred release since 1967.

Both of Elvis' previous spiritual lps were lovely, very exciting records. Each made it plain that this particular type of music was and remains today Elvis' favorite. That this new lp is not quite as good as either *His Hand In Mine* (1960, in my opinion one of Elvis' best lps of any sort) or *How Great Thou Art* is fortunately not the result of any lack of commitment or waning of ability on Elvis' part. Rather, a couple of spots suffer from the lapses in taste which will occasionally mar his regular releases. For example: "Seeing Is Believing" and "There Is No God But God" are too pop to be taken seriously in an lp which features the real stuff. Also, "An Evening Prayer" never really becomes a song, while "He Is My Everything" is an unconvincing rewrite of a good country hit, "There Goes My Everything."

Beyond this, I would say that the eight remaining tracks comprise a very strong set, the most exciting Elvis has put together in a couple years. The material, both traditional and new, is excellent, the production never over-develops into something obtuse. But most of all, Elvis dug it; he cared and he's magnificent.

Also, for a spiritual record the selection of material is refreshingly diverse. From the inspired beauty of such tracks as "He Touched Me," "Reach Out to Jesus" and "Lead Me, Guide Me," Elvis easily crosses into the country-funk of "I've Got Confidence" and "A Thing Called Love" (a really great cut, a great arrangement of his recent hit for Johnny Cash). It's also good to hear him take a more traditional approach to "Amazing Grace," following that song's recent success in the folk and country fields.

However, most inspiring of all the tracks (and not so much in terms of God as in terms of Elvis' status as the unleashed wail from the sticks) are "Bosom Of Abraham" and "I, John," two tracks on which the King sounds uncannily as he had so many years ago. Even the Imperials, Elvis' back-up quartet of the past few years, finally manage to get it on and bounce it all around the way the Jordanaires once did. Never getting in the way, but complementing his every vocal thrust, they allow Elvis to once again be the storm that follows the calm.

In all, despite the couple of minor shortcomings as to material, *He Touched Me* is a joyous and uniquely satisfying Elvis lp. It's one I'd recommend without hesitation, not only to his fans but also to anyone who might enjoy a momentary involvement with the tenacious roots of what was to become rock 'n roll.

Presley's career still going strong

United Press International

NEW YORK—Elvis Presley said yesterday his gyrating performances of 15 years ago, which shocked thousands of parents and got him censored below the waist on television, were "tame compared to what they're doing now."

"All I did was jiggle," Presley, now 37, said during one of his rare news conferences.

Appearing with his father, Vernon, Presley was greeted by the usual feminine screams on the eve of his first appearance in New York City.

"I love you, Elvis," shouted an attractive woman reporter in her mid-20s. "Thank you, dear," replied Presley.

Asked about the screams which started more than 15 years and 30 gold records ago, Presley said, "I got used to them. I'd miss it now if it didn't happen. To me, it's part of the business and I accept it."

Wearing a baby blue coat with a long, flowing dark blue cape, Presley was asked the reason for the length of his career. "I take Vitamin E," he quipped.

But he added, "I don't know. I enjoy the business.

"I'd like to think I've improved over the last 15 years," he said. "But I don't want to take away from my early hits. I'm not the least bit ashamed of 'Hound Dog' and 'Heartbreak Hotel.'"

Presley, whose weekend appearances at Madison Square Garden reportedly were sold out in record time, also was asked his views on Vietnam and politics.

"Honey," he replied to the female reporter asking the questions, "I'd just as soon keep my personal opinions to myself. I'm just an entertainer."

Silver-haired Vernon Presley then got into the act. He was asked by another woman reporter what he thought of his son's success.

"Kinda hard to say," replied the elder Presley, "Happened so fast—boom—in 1956 after the first (Ed) Sullivan Show."

Elvis

You say you attended the recent Elvis Presley concert and you wish you could experience again that night of rapture? Now, for you, thru the magic of rush releasing—and even before your photos get back from the drugstore—RCA presents "Elvis—As Recorded at Madison Square Garden." The Garden performance was part of the same tour that brought Presley to Chicago, and the shows were essentially the same, from the "Also Sprach Zarathustra" intro to the encore-stifling "Elvis has left the building." In between, El does a healthy 47 minutes or so of oldies like "Heartbreak Hotel" and newies like "American Trilogy."

The Garden concert, incidentally, was held on June 10. The record was ready about two weeks later. Pretty soon, folks, they'll have 'em on sale as you file out the door.

LPs from the Garden concerts.

ELVIS: His first & only press conference

RCA VICTOR — ELVIS AS RECORDED AT madison square garden

Elvis appears at a press conference before his 1972 Madison Square Garden engagement.

Later, Elvis would throw this scarf into the audience.

Elvis's concerts at the Garden constituted his first live appearances in New York City.

N.Y. fans mob box office
Out at dawn for Elvis

By Betty Flynn *Our New York Correspondent*

NEW YORK—More than 2,000 persons mobbed the front of Madison Square Garden before dawn Monday clamoring for tickets to rock singer Elvis Presley's first New York City concerts, June 9 and 10.

Police erected barricades to maintain order and the box office was forced to open two hours early to handle the crush.

The first ticket-buyers, Becky Tewell, 24 and Christine Snell, 20 had been in line since Saturday morning, when they arrived after an all-night drive from Columbus, Ohio.

Becky, a blond secretary, was adorned with photographs of Elvis pasted onto her red T-shirt.

"Elvis is the most handsome ever," squealed Mrs. Joanne Varnekas, a New Jersey housewife. She said her husband was jealous because she arose at 5 a.m. to get into New York to wait in line to buy 13 tickets at the top ticket price of $10.

Presley will get $300,000 for the three New York concerts.

He is scheduled to appear in three concerts at the Chicago Stadium June 16-17.

Teen Screams Greet Elvis At His 1st Concert in N.Y.

NEW YORK (AP)—Elvis Presley, the first king—and still king—of rock n' roll, gave the first New York City concert of his 16-year career Friday night to an audience of hard-core Presley fans who came to scream, listen and move to the music.

Presley came on in a gold-studded white suit with a deep V front, in which he wore a gold scarf; a white cape lined in gold, a wide gold belt and white boots. The audience didn't care that he was 37 or that he dyes his prematurely gray hair jet black. He has sold more recordings, over 400 million, than any other person or group in history, and he could do no wrong.

Every time he made one hand into a fist and jerked his arm like a cheerleader, there was screaming; every time he turned to the people sitting behind the stage, those fans screamed. The stage was set up at one end of the bowl-shaped 21,000 seat Madison Square Garden. Flash bulbs popped constantly.

Presley went quickly from one song to another, cutting off the applause for the last one by starting another. He sang some of his hits—51 of his single records have sold more than a million copies—and a lot of songs that were hits for other people.

Most of the audience appeared to be in their teens and 20s, the same age as any rock concert audience.

Presley began with the first song he ever recorded commercially, "That's All Right, Mama." Then he sang "Proud Mary," a hit for Creedence Clearwater; 3 Dog Night's "Never Been to Spain;" Dusty Springfield's "You Don't Have To Say You Love Me;" "You've Lost that Lovin' Feelin'," a hit by the Righteous Brothers.

Then he went into "Early Elvis," which he sang even better than before, but with less pelvis action this time. "All Shook Up," "Heartbreak Hotel," "Don't Be Cruel," "Love Me Tender," "Blue Suede Shoes," and the one he called "my message song for tonight," "Hound Dog."

Then he returned to more recent songs.

He threw two or three scarves into the audience, causing an eruption of screams each time, and a couple of handkerchiefs with which he had mopped his face, causing more screams. A girl jumped from the loge onto the corner of the stage beside the 20-piece orchestra backing Presley and was quickly escorted out.

Presley went on a 14-city, 14-day tour last fall with all concerts sold out. He now is starting another tour with four concerts in Madison Square Garden, the first three sold out. The fourth, on Sunday, will probably be sold out by then.

PRESLEY'S NEW YORK DEBUT

In the star spangled, legendary career of Elvis Presley the impossible has become an accomplishment at every turn. Yet in the 17 odd years that his career has raged he had not, until a few weeks ago played in the largest city of the U.S.—New York.

Presley made his New York debut at Madison Square Garden. Outside that concrete colosseum there were traffic jams that caused half of New York to grind to a halt. Inside, there were guys selling Elvis posters, Elvis buttons, Elvis LP's and Elvis everythings.

The orchestra played "2001: Space Odyssey" and Presley ran on stage accompanied to the edge by four bodyguards. His suit was white with a red stripe down each side of the trouser legs.

He opened with "That's Alright," then "Proud Mary," "You Don't Have to Say You Love Me," and "Believe Me." The Sweet Inspirations were there as backing chorus, plus a group and the orchestra—they all suffered from technical difficulties. No-one on that vast stage really got it together.

"Polk Salad Annie," "I've Never Been to Heaven," "Love Me Tender," "Heartbreak Hotel," "All Shook Up"—the crowd reactions varied from song to song but the biggest explosion was for "Hound Dog." In this, Elvis started real slow, building to its normal fast tempo with the full beat, gyrations and all.

A single from the concert

Elvis took a hefty bite out of the Big Apple!

PRESLEY'S GLORY HALLELUJAH

Last week's column included a report on Elvis Presley's Concert at Madison Square Garden. It will be recalled that the finale to that concert included "Battle Hymn Of The Republic."

This week this finale has been released on a single in New Zealand as recorded at the concert. It is called "An American Trilogy" and is complete with 'Glory Hallelujahs'. The flip is 'The First Time Ever I Saw Your Face.' An album of the Madison Square Concert was rush released in the United States last week and will be available here in the very near future.

Elvis moves hips—

Screams fill Chicago Stadium

THE ALL-TIME KING of rock and roll made his second appearance in history in Chicago last night and all passed peacefully.

Elvis Presley, now 37, stepped out on the stage of the Chicago Stadium to an ocean of screams and a fantastic explosion of flash bulbs from 20,000 fans who had gathered to hear him sing oldies and newies and watch him swivel those hips.

The crowd ranged from infants to grandmothers. Most were conventionally dressed. A large contingent of Andy Frain ushers were on hand and Presley's own traveling security force patrolled the fringes of the stage, which was set up on the west side of the stadium floor. But there was no trouble.

THREE TIMES DURING the performance, Presley made sojourns to the three sides of the stage, touching arms and tossing his gold scarves to the crowd. At one point, a brassiere was thrown at his feet. He picked it up, regarded it tenderly and placed it on his head before throwing it to the floor.

Fans continued to throw handkerchiefs, pictures, candy and keys to the stage, but Presley ignored the barrage and performed his nonstop, nearly hour-long act.

PRESLEY'S FANS have changed in the years since his 1957 appearance here in the International Amphitheater, but his appeal has endured. Girls who were not yet born at that time, screamed and jumped on their seats throughout the concert.

"My God," one young lady said as Presley swung into his old hit, "Heartbreak Hotel," "I was two when he recorded that."

Tickets for the concert, the first of three in two days here, ranged from $10 down. The box office receipts were estimated at upwards of $150,000 for last night's concert. Tonight's affair is sold out.

CHICAGO TODAY readers who had won tickets for the concert, screamed and applauded from their stage-front seats, armed with pennants ($1) and posters ($2 and up).

Presley, who first broke onto the music scene in 1955, has been one of America's most consistently popular performers. He has sold millions of records and has starred in more than two dozen films. The musical *Bye Bye Birdie* was inspired by the pandemonium among teen-agers when he was drafted into the Army in 1958.

Most recently, Presley has confined his personal appearances to two yearly month-long engagements in the Las Vegas Hilton Hotel where he holds a record for show attendance, and an annual summer tour of 10 cities. He still lives in Memphis, which has just renamed a main street Elvis Presley Boulevard.

Vernon Presley (left) and Red West (right) escort Elvis safely to the stage.

20,000 all shook up

Newspaper ad

AMUSEMENTS — AMUSEMENTS — AMUSEMENTS

IN PERSON **ELVIS** IN PERSON

NOW NOW

ELVIS ELVIS

CHICAGO STADIUM
3 BIG SHOWS

| FRIDAY JUNE 16th 8:30 P.M. | SATURDAY JUNE 17th 2:30 P.M. | SATURDAY JUNE 17th 8:30 P.M. |

TICKETS ON SALE NOW: Stadium Box Office & All Ticketron Outlets
FOR INFORMATION CALL 733-5300
MAIL ORDERS: Send certified check or Money Orders with stamped, self-addressed envelope to Chicago Stadium.

$10.00 — $7.50 — $5.00

HEAR ELVIS ON RCA RECORDS AND TAPES

Elvis played Vegas twice a year and toured the country the remaining months.

ELVIS PRESLEY . . . goes on concert tour again next month starting with Madison Square Garden on June 9 and 10 [and maybe the 11th]. And here is the rest of Elvis' schedule: June 12, Fort Wayne, Ind.; June 13, Evansville, Ind.; June 14 and 15, Milwaukee; June 16 and 17, Chicago Stadium; June 18, Fort Worth; June 19, Wichita, Kas. and June 20, Tulsa, Okla.

Sammy Davis Jr. and Elvis clown around in Las Vegas.

Presley show impresses even the celebrities

LAS VEGAS—Sammy Davis describes it better than anybody.

"You've got to see the Elvis Presley Show," Sammy said, opening his own show at the Sands. "We were there last night, and he opens with that "Space Odyssey" theme—bummm, bahh, bahhh—you think it's the second coming.

"Then you get a spotlight just on his leg. The spot doesn't even open up. His whole first number is just shaking his leg. Then he sings 'Proud Mary' and gives it that karate chop. I give it that, and people think, 'Hmmm.' And I'm straight."

If Elvis can turn on a showman like Sammy you know it's a good show. Davis hasn't missed being ringside for the last two Presley openings at the Las Vegas Hilton.

KOOL Radio's Dan Coffey was there, sporting an Elvis look-alike white suit with shirt front slashed to the navel.

Mary Sue McCarty, president of the International Love Me Tender Elvis Presley Fan Club from Monroe, La., made it again opening night and planned to see every show for a week.

A 40-ish blonde giggled like a teenager throughout the show, huge 7x50 binoculars trained on her idol. Paul Anka was there, Chill Wills was signing autographs as fast as he could write between gulps of champagne and the hotel was sold out despite the summer heat.

Elvis got a superstar's welcome. Every spare pillar had a poster on it and all the help sported straw skimmers advertising the Elvis Presley Summer Festival.

The King will be here until Labor Day and indications are that he will be sold out most of the time.

If you saw his show here last spring you'll recognize much of the material. He opens with "C.C. Ryder" and closes with the moving, hymnlike "American Trilogy," a blending of "Dixie," "Battle Hymn of the Republic" and "All My Trials."

Jackie Kahane even tells the same jokes.

But for some reason, the show had more impact opening night than his last Las Vegas appearance. One of the reasons Sammy Davis comes to Elvis' openings, one suspects, is because, like Sammy himself, Presley puts everything he has into a show.

The skin-tight jumpsuit was gone this time, replaced by a white suit and the ever-present cape, his shaggy black hair hanging well below the collar. He shucked the coat immediately, revealing an open-necked shirt covered with big blue swirls. A white belt with silver and turquoise emblems was slung low around his hips and a macrame sash hung down to his knee.

One girl in the audience whispered he wears a girdle now.

Elvis had several jokes about his apparel and his single status.

"Sorry I kept you waiting but I couldn't get into these clothes," he grinned. "But you see how quick I got out of them."

He struck up the opening words of "Love Me Tender" and moved along the stage kissing girls.

Turning his back to the audience, a single spotlight making the beads of perspiration in his hair sparkle, he drew out the words to "You've Got That Loving Feeling," one of his best of the evening. The songs came in rapid succession, easily, with a sureness which wrapped his audience in the mood.

An elbow, a knee, a twist of the pelvis drove home the beat.

"This is my message song for the evening," he said, down on one knee. You ain't . . ."

A dozen girls screamed approval.

"Hang on, baby, you don't know what's coming yet."

More screams.

"I'll be with you later. I'm free, you know."

His fans didn't seem to mind that Elvis and his wife had separated recently. Mary Sue and her mother, two generations of Elvis fan club leadership, said afterward a couple of his moody songs indicated a wistfulness that wasn't there before.

But it seemed that the song he really enjoyed singing most was "My Way." He almost got a standing ovation for it and the applause lasted more than a minute.

His finale, backed by the 30-piece orchestra and a superb flute solo ended the show. Presley doesn't mess around with curtain calls and encores. He gives everything he has, says goodnight and walks off.

"Is it over already?" A girl said incredulously. "But he just started."

Presley had been on stage almost two hours.

Elvis's jumpsuits often featured mythical birds or karate symbols.

251

Report Presleys Have Split

July 27, 1972

Discordant note for Elvis?

A Memphis newspaper reports that millionaire singer Elvis Presley and his wife Priscilla have separated. She reportedly has left the Memphis mansion and moved to Los Angeles with their 4-year-old daughter.

Elvis Sues Wife for Divorce

LOS ANGELES, Aug. 19 (AP) —Entertainer Elvis Presley sued his wife of five years for divorce Friday, citing irreconcilable differences.

The suit, filed by one of Mr. Presley's attorneys in Santa Monica Superior Court, conceded that his wife, Priscilla, 24, will have custody of the couple's daughter, Lisa, 4.

In the suit, Mr. Presley said a major reason for the divorce was the pressure of his traveling half the year.

Mr. Presley, 37, and his wife were reported to have reached agreement on a property settlement, but the terms have not been made public.

After five years of marriage Elvis and Priscilla separated.

Presleys split

Priscilla Presley and her husband Elvis have been living in separate homes in California since the singer's birthday last Jan. 8, the Memphis Commercial Appeal says. However, the couple is reported to have been trying for a reconciliation. (AP)

Presley files for divorce

Elvis Presley, 37, has filed for divorce in Santa Monica, Calif., from wife of five years, Priscilla, 24. She will get custody of their 4-year-old daughter, Lisa.

Lisa Marie was four when her parents split up.

Could she be part of Elvis's job pressure?

Star Elvis Presley Sues for Divorce; Blames Job Pressure

SANTA MONICA, Cal., Aug. 18 [UPI]—Elvis Presley sued his wife of five years for divorce today, blaming the pressures of his traveling half the year for the breakup.

The hip-swinging singer and his wife Priscilla separated last Feb. 23.

Presley's lawyer, E. Gregory Hookstratten, said: "Elvis and Priscilla have agreed to terminate their marriage, they parted amicably.

6 Months on Road

"I'm sad to say the reason for the divorce is that Elvis has been spending six months a year on the road, which puts a tremendous strain on the marriage."

The filing was made without appearance of either of the principals. The legal action was not contested.

Hookstratten listed "irreconcilable differences," which is sole legal grounds in California.

A property settlement has already been agreed on by both parties. Terms were not made public.

Elvis in Las Vegas

Presley, 37, is appearing at the Hilton International in Las Vegas, Nev. Mrs. Presley, 26, is in Hawaii.

Presley first met his wife in Germany when he was an enlisted man in the Army; Priscilla's father was an officer. They were married in Las Vegas, May 1, 1967.

Mrs. Presley will have custody of the couple's daughter, Lisa, 4.

Who's afraid of Elvis' bodyguards?

HOLLYWOOD—As first reported here, Priscilla Presley left Elvis for karate expert Mike Stone. Elvis, in turn, grabbed off Sandra Zancan, an attractive singer-dancer in the road company of "No, No, Nanette." And Presley's grab sent Sandra's boy friend, who was traveling with her and show, on a very fast flight from Hollywood.

Sandra's ex-beau Jim Hall, a 6-foot-2-inch weight lifter, called me from Oklahoma City, where he's sales representative for European Health Spas, to say: "I want to make one thing clear. I never met Elvis or his bodyguards, and I've never received a direct threat. But you can say I am cautious. And you can say that's part of the reason I moved from L.A."

Jim says he and Sandra had known each other for 18 months. They were planning to marry and go to Italy on a honeymoon. Then Elvis invited some of the girls from "Nanette," including Sandra, to Palm Springs for a party. Jim was on a business trip in San Francisco. When he got back, after only a week, Miss Zancan already had the white Datsun sports car and ruby ring that Elvis gave her. Jim says Sandra told him "that Elvis is a lonely man and he liked to cry on her shoulder."

Jim told Sandra he would still marry her if she gave back the car. While he was in her apartment, she received a call from Elvis: "Sandra suggested to me that I be careful . . . because of Elvis' bodyguards. I thought she was being melodramatic . . . But I don't know. I may be moving to Florida or Boston or maybe even South Africa. I don't know yet. Just say I'm in transit."

Soon after the break up, Elvis recorded "Separate Ways."

ELVIS' WIFE DATES KARATE CHAMP

A space-age first for Elvis

HOLLYWOOD—On Jan. 14, at 1 a.m., Elvis Presley, in all his fluorescent finery, will be beamed live from a Honolulu concert hall via Globcom Satellite into a network of Far Eastern countries in a television broadcasting first. A few days later, that program will be aired throughout Europe as well, thanks to satellite transmission.

Leave it to Presley to be the forerunner of such space-age entertainment specials. Spokesmen for RCA, who not only own the satellite but the disc label for which Presley records as well, report only one previous broadcast of an entertainment nature, and of this stature, has been undertaken—a Muhammad Ali fight last year.

The Presley special, which will air over NBC in the U.S. in late February, will mark the dynamic singer's only return to the air since his first—and only—special broadcast by NBC in 1969.

THE AUDIENCE RESPONSE to that program was overwhelming.

And Presley often has admitted the taping of the show—his first encounter with a live audience in many years—convinced him to return to the concert stage and was the inspiration that sent him into Las Vegas and around the country on tours.

Next Wednesday in Lubbock, Tex., Presley will begin a tour of one-nighters which will end on Nov. 18 in Honolulu. At that time, Presley and his associates will finalize the details of the January telecast.

In the meantime, in theaters across the nation, a deep, introspective look into the life of the entertainer who has borne the title of "idol" for the better part of 20 years, has opened in movie form.

"Elvis on Tour," an M-G-M documentary film which takes a factual look at the singer, was filmed by veteran music movie makers Robert Abel and Pierre Adidge ["In Concert: Credence Clearwater Revival," and "Joe Cocker: Mad Dogs and Englishmen,"] during the spring concert tour this year.

IN THE FILM, Presley talks about the drumbeat of life that dictates his gait. He recollects his childhood days. He talks about his friends, and his surprise at his own success.

"For Elvis, every show he does is like a kid's dream coming true," says producer-director Abel. "It's the fulfillment of his childhood longings. He's brought the gospel music into the act because of his love of it from childhood. He has the big orchestra backing him, and believe it or not, he does the conducting. It's a subtle, discreet thing. But the cameras have picked it all up—the signals and the rapport he shares with his musicians. The orchestra, too, is a part of the dream."

As a youngster, the Tupelo [Miss.]-born Presley would attend concerts at Memphis' outdoor shell [where he was to later make his own smash debut]. "I watched the conductor, listened to the music for hours. I was fascinated by the fact that these guys could play for hours," he admits on film.

PRESLEY HAS NEVER ceased to amaze both the public and the industry which spawned him. He squirmed on stage before rock 'n' roll, more specifically hard rock, made it acceptable to palpitate and groan publicly. He outraged the sentimental older generation of the '50s, titillated the youth and sold millions of records. He also has appeared in 32 movies—most of which were shallow and plastic exploitation films. He considers them a blow to his professional pride, but they have nearly always made money.

Socially, Presley withdrew from the spotlight years ago. He was intimidated by adoring fans who forced their way into his homelife. For the most part, his personal life was left to speculation —with a few noteworthy exceptions: the 2-year-old paternity suit brought against the singer by waitress Patricia Parker, which still is in the courts, and the failure of his six-year-old marriage to Priscilla Beaulieu, currently in the divorce court.

Through it all, two things seem constant: Presley's ability to pack in audiences, and his love of his work.

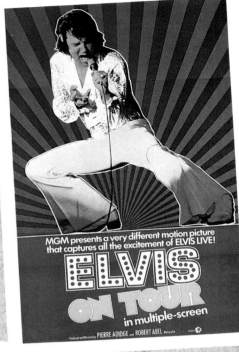

MGM presents a very different motion picture that captures all the excitement of ELVIS LIVE!

ELVIS ON TOUR in multiple-screen

Produced and Directed by PIERRE ADIDGE and ROBERT ABEL

Elvis on Tour documented the Spring '72 tour.

The film combines concert footage with Elvis's reminiscences.

MOVIE REVIEW

'Tour': Super Version of Elvis Concert

ENTERTAINMENT

Whatever its claims, MGM's new movie "Elvis On Tour" drops no veils. It is a contribution to the myth of the performer, not an investigation of the nature of the man.

The film by Pierre Adidge and Robert Abel (who made "Joe Cocker Mad Dogs and Englishmen") is essentially a super version of an Elvis concert, showcasing the star more expertly and artistically than any mere stage show could. The major portion of the film records on-stage appearances during an extensive 15-day, 15-city tour last April centered mainly in the South where Elvis adulation reaches the ultimate.

Off stage the cameras discover little we did not know before. The close-ups are not prying but reflect the adoration in the eyes of his fans and associates.

The most impressive element of the movie is the atmosphere it captures—the ecstasy of the audience and the protective, high-keyed, semi-panic as Elvis is rushed by his bodyguards to and from the concert as though fleeing for his life.

Most of all the film projects awareness of that magic distance which separates Elvis from his admirers so that even the girls who surge forward to kiss him never really seem quite sure that contact was more than a dream.

The excellent photography by Robert Thomas has been cleverly edited by Ken Zemke. Split screen and montage dominate but remain controlled, tied to the music and not overwhelming it.

It is the performer's real feeling for his music which remains the lasting impression of the film—his unrestrained urge to sing. One important sequence has Elvis and his musicians relaxing after the show by singing Southern gospel songs and Elvis on stage urging his audience to listen with him to his backup group, J. D. Sumner and the Stamps Quartet, singing of the spirit yet barely being able to restrain himself from joining in. A religious passion for the power of song emerges.

Additional footage includes a montage sequence of the cities visited by the tour, clips from the family album and early performances including excerpts from The Ed Sullivan Show and amusing snippets from the slap-stick romance of his inane movies sung to "Love Me Tender."

A movie for fans who expect the best, and if only Elvis didn't look so overweight they'd have nothing at all to complain about.

"Elvis On Tour" produced and directed by Pierre Adidge and Robert Abel for MGM, is playing citywide. Rated G.

Elvis stirs up nets

HOLLYWOOD—This must be a first: an entertainment special that will be aired on NBC considered so important, news teams from both competing networks are requesting permission to cover its production.

The special event is the Elvis Presley concert that's going to be beamed live from Honolulu via GlobCom satellite on Jan. 14 to countries around the world, and recorded by NBC for American viewing in February.

What's creating all the interest is not the fact that this will mark Elvis' first turn on the tube since 1969—but that it will be the first entertainment show ever to utilize satellite transmission.

Even M-G-M is attempting to cash in on the publicity the broadcasting first is generating.

The studio, in conjunction with producers Bob Abel and Pierre Adige, has pulled the "Elvis on Tour" documentary out of its theatrical run, and is planning its re-release to coincide with Presley's concert-by-satellite.

"Elvis on Tour" already has recouped its negative cost with limited playdates in the South and a few Midwestern states, so it's clear profits from here on in — particularly healthy profits, they figure.

T.V. GUIDE   MARCH 31-APRIL 6, 1973

ELVIS: ALOHA FROM HAWAII
8:30 ③

Special: Elvis Presley is in top form for this Hawaiian concert.

Backed by shifting light patterns and scenes of lush Oahu, Elvis delivers 90 minutes of songs including his hits "Blue Suede Shoes," "Hound Dog," "Blue Hawaii," "Can't Help Falling in Love," "Suspicious Minds," "All Shook Up," and "Burning Love."

Highlighting the rest of the concert: "Early Morning Rain," "My Way," "Fever," "I'll Remember You," "Welcome to My World," "I'm So Lonesome I Could Cry," "Johnny B. Goode," "C.C. Rider," "What Now, My Love?" and a medley of patriotic songs.

The musical backing is by J.D. Sumner and the Stamps, Kathy Westmoreland, Sweet Inspirations and the Joe Guercio Orchestra. The program was taped in January at the Honolulu International Center.

Elvis: Aloha from Hawaii was eventually seen by 1.5 billion people.

The TV special was actually a benefit for the Kui-Lee Cancer fund.

Yes, Elvis, 1.5 Billion

Tonight on NBC the world will hear and see (scream!!) Elvis (EEEEEEEE!!!) Presley (flash bulb! flash bulb!) sing "C.C. Rider," "Burning Love," "Early Morning Rain," "Blue Suede Shoes," "I'm So Lonesome I Could Cry," "Hound Dog," "Fever," "Hawaiian Wedding Song," "Long Tall Sally," "All Shook Up," "Dixie," "Battle Hymn of the Republic," "Big Hunk of Love," "I Can't Help Falling in Love With You" and others.

When I write that "the world" will hear and see this, I mean it. The show's producer-director, Marty Pasetta, told me that more than 1.5 billion(!) people will see the show.

In a slightly hushed voice, Pasetta added, "That's nearly every third person on this Earth."

It is an awesome thing to contemplate.

The program was seen live on Jan. 14 in the Far East (Japan, the Philippines, Hong Kong, Vietnam, etc.). We didn't see it then because, in our time period, it would have been broadcast live in the middle of the night.

In Africa, where there are few television sets, the concert will be shown in film form. The rest of the world will see it by satellite.

Pasetta revealed to me that this was "basically an unrehearsed show." And everything you'll see in the show was videotaped during a single performance.

It is easy to see why Elvis is so sheltered from his fans. At one point, he reaches down into the audience and his female fans slash at his hands with their nails to get his rings off his fingers.

Pasetta explained, "Presley's fans are older these days, and stronger. They get wiry as they get older."

Elvis' 'Aloha From Hawaii' Is First Number One Quad Album

NEW YORK— The Elvis Presley RCA album, "Elvis, Aloha from Hawaii-Via Satellite," hit number one on the charts last week, thus becoming the first compatible quad record ever to become a nationwide number one hit, less than a year after RCA's entry into the quad market.

The two-record album, of which almost one million sets have been sold in America alone, previously had become the first quad album ever to be certified as a million-dollar gold Album by the Recording Industry Association of America . . . .

Concert album

Elvis's threw his cape and belt into the audience.

behind the scenes
fans battle over belt

Idiot cards and an argument were among the behind-the-scenes "seens" at yesterday's Elvis Presley "Aloha from Hawaii" concert at the H.I.C. Arena.

The idiot cards—also known as cue cards, common in the world of television—were used by Presley during a couple of his tunes. The cards, with handwritten song lyrics, were flashed to Presley from beneath the pair of centrally located NBC-TV cameras, on the Arena's main floor.

The argument involved two women fans of Presley, who fought for possession of the belt he hurled to them. One claimed she got it, the other disagreed, and some hot words were exchanged—all while the show was going on.

OTHER SIDELIGHTS:

Prior to showtime, City Auditoriums Director Matt Esposito said the Kui-Lee Cancer Fund was $1,000 richer—thanks to a check received from E. A. Presley. The singer himself, of course.

Presley collected about a half-dozen leis during the telecast. Two disappointed would-be lei presenters were two daughters of the late Kui-Lee, who tried to signal Presley's attention from the shadows of the stage.

A bearded fellow sat on the huge stage all night with an important mission at hand—to wind up or uncoil the microphone cord for Presley.

Zulu was one of the scores of fans who contributed large sums to the Lee fund—in return for posters, pictures and other Presley mementos.

Mayor and Mrs. Frank F. Fasi had front-row-center seats, just below the central platform stage, but opted for a seat further back, for better perspective on the show.

While Presley performed, another Presley watched. The singer's dad, Vernon, was in the audience.

As a husband, Elvis was out of sight, Priscilla says

Elvis Presley, wife end marriage on friendly note

Elvis Presley and his 28-year-old wife, Priscilla, have ended their marriage with a friendly kiss and a property settlement making her a millionaire.

Presley, 38, was granted his divorce yesterday in Santa Monica, Calif. The couple, married six years, agreed on property settlement involving 1.5 million.

In seeking the divorce, the singer cited irreconcilable differences because of pressure from constant traveling.

The Presleys were married in Las Vegas in May, 1967, after a courtship that began in Germany. She was the daughter of an Army officer and he was the world's best-known tank-driving corporal.

Under the settlement, Presley will pay $725,000 in cash outright and another $720,000 at $6,000 a month over a 10-year period.

She also will receive half the proceeds from the intended sale of their Beverly Hills home; 5 per cent of the outstanding stock in Elvis Presley Music, Inc., and White Haven Music, Inc.: $4,200 a month for her additional support for a year, and $4,200-a-month support for their 5-year-old daughter, Lisa.

Memphis Press-Scimitar   October 10, 1973

Elvis and Priscilla were officially divorced on Oct. 9, 1973. Their parting was amicable however, and the two left the courthouse arm in arm.

Priscilla Presley Gets a Kiss and a $1.5 Million Settlement

SANTA MONICA, Calif.—(AP) —Singer Elvis Presley and his 28-year-old wife Priscilla have ended their marriage with a friendly kiss and a property settlement making her a millionaire.

Presley, 38, was granted his divorce Tuesday in Los Angeles County Superior Court. The couple, married six years, agreed on a modified property settlement involving $1.5 million.

In seeking the divorce, the singer cited irreconcilable differences because of the pressure from constant traveling. The hearing was closed to the public.

The Presleys were married in Las Vegas, Nev., in May 1967 after a courtship that began in Germany. She was the daughter of an Army officer and he was the world's best known tank-driving corporal.

Under the settlement, Presley will pay $725,000 in cash outright and another $720,000 at $6,000 a month over a 10-year period.

She also will receive half the proceeds from the intended sale of their Beverly Hills home; five per cent of the outstanding stock in Elvis Presley Music, Inc. and Whitehaven Music, Inc.; $4,200 a month for her additional support for a year, and $4,200 a month support for their 5-year-old daughter Lisa.

Presley paid $400,000 for the multi-leveled Beverly Hills home shortly after his marriage.

The original agreement had been $100,000 "and a couple of cars," said Harry Fain, a Presley attorney.

"This man agreed to pay her without any contest because he wanted to be generous and make her happy," Fain said. "I never met a man so unselfish."

Presley has been a regular headliner at Las Vegas casino shows.

The daughter's custody will be shared between the father and mother but she will live with Priscilla, who currently resides in the Marina del Rey area of Los Angeles.

SIX-YEAR MARRIAGE ENDED

Elvis Presley leaves Santa Monica, Calif., Superior Court after being granted a divorce from his wife, Priscilla. The couple appeared friendly as they left the courtroom.

Elvis Presley in Hospital Here

Memphis Press-Scimitar October 15, 1973

Elvis Presley is listed in good condition at Baptist Hospital after being admitted this morning for what his doctor calls a "persistent case of recurrent pneumonia."

The Memphis entertainer was taken to the hospital from his home in Whitehaven at 11:10 a.m. by a Fire Department ambulance, said Maurice Elliot, public relations director of the hospital.

Elliot said Presley's condition involved no real danger. "The doctor (Dr. George Nichopoulos) just felt that the situation could best be handled in a hospital," he added. "All Elvis requires is a few tests and about a week of rest."

Elvis' stepmother and father and his personal secretary Joe Esposito, were waiting for Elvis at Baptist, but few others knew of his arrival.

The hospital is withholding the room number to allow Elvis the necessary rest.

Well Again, Elvis Quits Hospital

Memphis Press-Scimitar November 2, 1973

Singer Elvis Presley was discharged from Baptist Hospital at 10:50 last night after a "complete recovery" from recurrent pneumonia, his physician said.

Dr. George Nichopoulos said Elvis was "so eager to get back home that I decided to discharge him last night and avoid the crowds." He had been at Baptist since October 15.

Nichopoulos said earlier he would release Elvis Saturday.

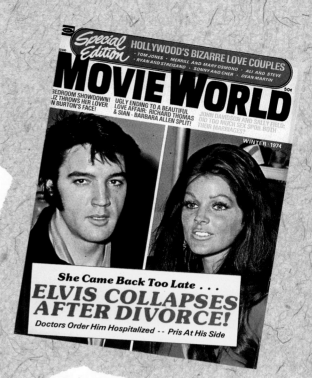

Special Edition

MOVIE WORLD 50¢

HOLLYWOOD'S BIZARRE LOVE COUPLES
· TOM JONES · MERRILL AND MARY OSMOND · ALI AND STEVE
· RYAN AND STREISAND · SONNY AND CHER · DEAN MARTIN

BEDROOM SHOWDOWN! LIZ THROWS HER LOVER IN BURTON'S FACE!
UGLY ENDING TO A BEAUTIFUL LOVE AFFAIR: RICHARD THOMAS & SIAN - BARBARA ALLEN SPLIT!
JOHN DAVIDSON AND SALLY FIELD: DID TOO MUCH SEX SPOIL BOTH THEIR MARRIAGES?

WINTER · 1974

She Came Back Too Late . . .
ELVIS COLLAPSES AFTER DIVORCE!
Doctors Order Him Hospitalized -- Pris At His Side

ELVIS PRESLEY ILLNESS REVEALED

"Elvis is neither looking good nor sounding good . . . overweight, puffy, white-faced and blinking against the light, he appears ill. The voice sounds weak; delivery is flabby and occasional dynamic gestures seem performed with great effort . . . ending in weak self-parody." So read the review in the show business Bible, Variety, when Presley opened at the Sahara Tahoe, his last job.

Hollywood was shocked! Could this be the same superstar who made critics look up glowing adjectives and who got standing ovations nightly? There must be a reason. There was! I'm reliably informed Elvis has been a very sick man the past few weeks. Being a trouper, he insisted "the show must go on" against doctor's advice and despite the fact he was suffering great pain from pleurisy and tendinitis. His bloated, swollen appearance was due to cortisone, a medication used to combat inflammation.

Thirty-eight year old Elvis has been blessed with good health all his life. But the past year hasn't been easy. Working hard on tours, he was under great emotional strain brought about by the break-up of his five year marriage to Priscilla and compounded by his heartbreak over not seeing much of their little girl, Lisa, whom he adores.

At the moment the rockabilly star is resting at his Trousdale mansion surrounded by his usual entourage. The Vegas Hilton announced that he is opening there on Aug. 6, but when I checked with Col. Tom Parker's office, I was told the engagement in Vegas is not definite.

Like everything else at the moment, Elvis' romance with Miss Tennessee, Linda Thompson, seems to be in limbo.

Shortly after the divorce, Elvis was hospitalized for recurrent pneumonia.

Elvis and girlfriend Linda Thompson dodge the press.

Rona Barrett's Gossip

Elvis Presley & Lynda Thompson—What Are They "Engaged" In?

"No matter what our problems might be . . . I'll never divorce Priscilla!"

Just returned from a concert tour, it was then November, 1970, and Elvis Presley had just spoken (officially) to reporters in an attempt to stifle the rumors that he and Priscilla were undergoing "marital difficulties."

Now, four years later, the "King" is ruling his kingdom without the aid of his wife. Since his divorce from "Pris," Elvis has been reported to have literally thrown himself into his career—more so than he had during his seven-year marriage. Ironically, it was due to "career pressures" and his constant traveling that Priscilla said was to blame for the union failing. But, then again, things do change and "things" aren't always what they appear to be . . .

. . . When their divorce was declared official in Santa Monica Courts, some sources said that if Priscilla had Mike Stone to console her, Elvis had an equally sympathetic shoulder to cry on that belonged to lovely Lynda Thompson. The beautiful Miss Thompson is a former Miss Tennessee, having competed in the Miss World Beauty Pageant in 1972. Like Priscilla, Lynda has light brown hair and a willowy beauty. Unlike Priscilla, though, she is apparently accustomed to publicity and, at the same time,

already appears to be following Elvis' tradition of keeping his "private life my private life!"

Rumors now have it that the vacancy at the Presley mansion may just be filled with Lynda's presence as the next Mrs. Presley. It is common knowledge that Elvis and Lynda have been seeing each other fairly "steadily" since they first met two years ago. However, one source says that the two people were already on a dating basis before Priscilla even filed for a divorce! Whether that is true or not remains to be seen. What can be seen, however, is the luxurious Mercedes that Elvis bought for Lynda not too long ago. Always known for his extravagant and impulsive generosity, Elvis' friends weren't particularly surprised when he bestowed the fancy automobile on Lynda. After all, he has also been known to have ordered a dozen motorcycles by phone one day ". . . to be delivered to his friends because it was a nice day to go motorcycling." It seemed "typical" of Elvis, then, to buy Lynda a suitable present.

Lynda, who has become generally accepted as the woman in Elvis' life, has also shown that she is as adept as her boyfriend is at dodging any questions aimed at her personal affairs . . . .

260

The EX-Mrs. Elvis Presley seems happy in her new "pursuits" while the FUTURE Mrs. Elvis Presley is pursuing more than just "friendship" with The KING!!!

Linda began dating Elvis in 1972.

How close did Elvis and Linda come to marriage?

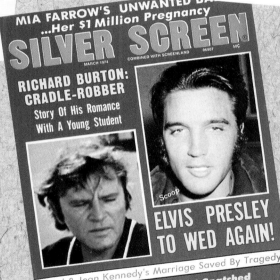

MIA FARROW'S UNWANTED BA...
...Her $1 Million Pregnancy

SILVER SCREEN
MARCH 1974   COMBINED WITH SCREENLAND   06807   50¢

RICHARD BURTON: CRADLE-ROBBER
Story Of His Romance With A Young Student

Scoop

ELVIS PRESLEY TO WED AGAIN!

Ted & Joan Kennedy's Marriage Saved By Tragedy

The Holy Mi... That Snatched
Raymond Burr Fr... Death

Rona Barrett's
GOSSIP
MOVIES PARTIES TELEVISION
SEP...N 1974   ...SEVENTY-FIVE CENTS

PRISCILLA

LYNDA

ELVIS TO MARRY LYNDA THOMPSON—
WHAT DOES HE SEE IN HER?

SONNY & CHER'S CUSTODY BATTLE OVER CHASTITY— WHY *NOBODY* WILL WIN!

INTRODUCING...
HENRY "FONZIE" WINKLER OF TV'S "HAPPY DAYS"

"THE WAY THEY WERE" WITH GENE HACKMAN

Memphis Press-Scimitar   March 18, 1974

Hucksters, 49,200 Elvisites Whoop It Up

By JANE SANDERSON

It could well be the Coliseum in Rome in the ceremonious days of Julius Caesar.

Instead, it is our own Mid-South Coliseum, filled with a cheering crowd welcoming an emperor of another sort—King of Rock Music Elvis Presley.

One wonders what Caesar and Presley could possibly have in common, and decides it must be a flair for flamboyant entrances. Where the Roman emperor brought forth wild cheering whenever putting his sandaled foot forward, Presley does the same by stepping into a spotlight. Both responses are products of strategic planning.

Blaring of trumpets, rolling of drums, beating of kettles, flashing of lights, and the ruler of rock arrives. Momentum propels to such heights that first glimpse of Presley sends the audience into a frenzy.

Like a streak of white lightning, Presley darts on stage. He is dramatically clad in all-white which sparkles with jewels and nailheads with a jacket slit to the waist and a diamond cross hanging from his neck. He nods approval to the overwhelming hometown reception, and he begins to sing.

It's "Si, Si" something or other. Little matter. The crowd goes wild. They scream, yell, cry, clap and do their best to drown out what they came to hear. The King is amused, but he goes on. Cameras flash everywhere.

They push in clusters toward the stage and are pushed back by security guards. They stretch hands upward to catch scarves flung periodically toward front rows by their idol, and they call his name in every key over and over.

Elvis laughs in the middle of songs, at himself and at the audience, but drops his head to gain repose. He rolls his eyes, jerks his head, thrusts his shoulder forward, points to pretty girls, slaps his guitar, and, of course shakes his hips. Screams get louder, and the audience, in Presley's own musical terms, seems "All Shook Up."

"He's a boomer," blurts out one small spectator who watches in awe as he throws the microphone and guitar around.

Presley Tour 'A Sellout'

LOS ANGELES—The first Elvis Presley tour of 1974 is a whirlwind 24 shows in 20 consecutive days, with all dates sold out, according to Col. Tom Parker, Presley's mentor, except for March 3rd's two shows at the Astrodome, Houston, which are a private promotion in conjunction with the Livestock Show and Rodeo. These dates are not a Presley-supervised promotion.

Tickets, as usual, are staggered from $5 to $10 for all sites. Itinerary includes; Oral Roberts University, Tulsa, March 1 and 2; Houston, 3; Civic Center, Monroe, La., 4, 7-8; Coliseum, Auburn, Ala., 5; Coliseum, Montgomery, 6; Coliseum, Charlotte, 9; Civic Center, Roanoke, 10; Coliseum, Hampton, Va., 11; Coliseum, Richmond, 12 and 18; Coliseum, Greensboro, 13; Center, Murfreesboro, Tenn., 14 and 19; Coliseum, Memphis, 16, 17 and 20.

Presley will be carrying an entourage of approximately 50 singers and musicians.

In a departure from the gleaming white jumpsuits, Elvis dons baby blue.

By 1974, Elvis had incorporated some unusual moves into his act

Talent in Action

ELVIS PRESLEY

Roanoke Civic Center, Roanoke, VA.

"Virginia is for Elvis Lovers," read the assorted banners hanging throughout the SRO, 10,000 seat plus arena. Elvis was back home, playing before the white, middle class southern folk, not unlike those who first bought his early Sun recordings nearly 20 years ago. Roanoke was the sixth stop on a 14-city, three-week March tour of the South, winding up in his hometown of Memphis.

The Roanoke show was customary for Presley. Official Elvis merchandise littered the hall, more readily available than food and drink. A standup comic, the Sweet Inspirations and an intermission mixed with anticipation set the mood. Soon, in a blaze of blinking flashcubes and with a blast of fanfare, RCA's White Knight mounted the stage, guitar slung over the shoulder of his jewel-studded jumpsuit. Elvis was in fine voice and good spirits, joking often and looking well, if a bit beefy. Songs were tossed off as rapidly as his scarves. Girls lunged at their idol's feet. With Presley, half the show is on stage and half is off.

It appears Elvis has put aside his notorious pelvic gyrations for good, but resurrected a little bit of the old hip wiggle for "Fever," poking fun at himself, and he even danced some on "Polk Salad Annie." That Presley is now apparently walking through his show had no adverse effect on this audience, most of whom have never seen him before in person. Hysteria greeted everything he did, much more than the most rambunctious of his northern audiences.

Elvis' versatility as a singer was represented in his selection of material. From his rock past came "Teddy Bear/Don't Be Cruel," "All Shook Up," "Love Me Tender," and a surprisingly effective "Tryin' to Get to You." Country tunes included "I Can't Stop Lovin' You," "Funny (How Time Slips Away)" and the recent Olivia Newton-John hit, "Let Me Be There." But best were the inspirational songs "Help Me" and Kristofferson's "Why Me, Lord." Backed by J. D. Sumner and the Stamps Quartet with the Nashville trio, Voices, each [song] displayed Presley's inner feeling for the music credited to be his most vital influence. Elvis crooned "Can't Help Falling in Love" and it was on to Richmond.

Rolling Stone, April 11, 1974

Elvis Anthology: From Memphis to Myth

**Elvis—
A Legendary Performer
Elvis Presley
RCA CPL1-0341**

By Jim Miller

Elvis Presley remains the quintessential American pop star: gaudy, garish, compromised in his middle age by commercial considerations, yet gifted with an enormous talent and a charismatic appeal beyond mere nostalgia. Presley remains a true American artist—one of the greatest in American popular music, a singer of native brilliance and a performer of magnetic dimensions. . . .

Enclosed: Illustrated memory log with 4-color picture suitable for framing

Another LP that combined past recordings with current ones

Elvis's concerts ranged from one to two hours.

Memphis Commercial Appeal   March 17, 1974

The King Delights His Subjects

Elvis Presley performed in Memphis for the first time in 13 years yesterday, with two shows at the Mid-South Coliseum drawing full houses of fiercely partisan devotees. The King was on for more than a hour, treating Memphians to something they have been able to enjoy only via movies or televisions for a long, long time. . . .

20 Years Later, Elvis Still a Superstar

On April 25, a Thursday, The Journal ran a four paragraph story on page 15 of the first section under the headline, "Elvis to Be Here June 28." A one column head shot of Elvis Presley ran with the story, which said that tickets for his appearance, selling at $10, $7.50 and $5, could be obtained by mail order from the Arena box office, 500 W. Kilbourn Ave.

That was the only announcement. No printed ads. No TV commercials.

Well, 900 letters arrived at the Arena box office the next day, and 1,600 the day after, and another 1,600 or so the following Monday. The average number of ticket requests per letter was three.

Altogether, 4,500 letters were received, of which 1,400 had to be turned down. The 11,800 seat house was sold out two months in advance, on the basis of a four paragraph story on an inside page of a weekday newspaper.

Status Evidence

Which is some indication of the superstar status of the 39 year old former truck driver who started out his singing carer 20 years ago under the name of Hillbilly Cat.

And tonight he's here at the Arena to stomp, shout and croon before an adoring audience that has followed every move of his twitching legs and rolling pelvis since "Heartbreak Hotel" and "Hound Dog" broke into national consciousness in the mid-1950s.

The audience, in fact, ought to be as interesting as the fabled performer on the stage. A good many of them may have caught their first sight of Elvis on the old Ed Sullivan show and the Jackie Gleason series, when the network censors cut him off at his writhing hips to prevent the wholesale destruction of morals in America's living rooms.

Still Their Hero

Those high school youngsters of the Eisenhower era practiced the Elvis leer in the bathroom mirror and slapped lanolin on their scalps with abandon in emulation of their hero with the smoldering eyes and curling lip.

And now they're respectable young parents and home makers —traffic managers, bank tellers, car salesmen, morticians—but Elvis is still their guy. Not even Crosby or Sinatra or the Beatles have magnetized so many for so long a time.

It was actor Richard Burton, not exactly a minor luminary himself, who summed it up best a number of years ago. He got out of a limousine in some public place and immediately was surrounded by a horde of celebrity seekers.

"My God," said Burton, "I feel like Elvis Presley!"

$100,000 Take

The way the tickets are scaled for tonight's performance—75% of the seats at $10, 15% at $7.50, and 10% at $5—the box office gross should be well above $100,000. When Elvis made his first appearance at the Arena two years ago, his manager, Col. Tom Parker, insisted on paying a flat rental rate for the house instead of the alternative 10% of the gross.

With good reason. Although the flat rate was higher than usual for the occasion, it was still considerably less than the 10% of the gross for the two nights, which came out to around $190,000. . . .

Memphis Commercial Appeal   September 24, 1974

Salesman's Killing at Schilling

Elvis Presley made a car salesman's dream come true when he walked in and bought five new Continental Mark IVs Saturday and Sunday. Raymond Surber, a salesman at Schilling on Union at 987 Union, said he was surprised by five visits from Elvis between 4:30 p.m. Saturday and 7 p.m. Sunday. The entertainer bought the dealer's entire stock of Mark IVs totaling more than $60,000. Surber said the cars were aqua, red, silver, blue and black, two of which had sunroofs. He said Elvis was buying the cars for friends and that none were in his name. "I've only been a salesman for two years, but I believe this is every salesman's dream," said Surber. Surber declined to reveal the amount of commission he received, but automotive sources placed it at about $4,000.

Presley rejects $1 million job

SYDNEY—(UPI)—Elvis Presley, the king of rock 'n' roll, has turned down a $1 million offer by an Australian promoter for two shows, according to a Sydney newspaper.

The Daily Telegraph reported a spokesman for the promoter, Bob Pritchard, said the reply from Presley's agents in Hollywood was: "Thank you, but if ever we need a million bucks that badly, we'll give you a ring."

Elvis Knocks A Visitor Off Stage

LAS VEGAS, Nev.—(AP) —Singer Elvis Presley got a standing ovation during a show here—but it wasn't for his singing.

Presley was on stage at the Las Vegas Hilton when four men climbed out of the crowd of 1,750, interrupting his act. A hotel spokesman said Presley used a karate-like chop to knock one of the men from the stage. A band member tackled another, and the remaining two left quickly.

The men were booked for investigation of drunkenness, but Clark County sheriff's deputies said Presley did not press charges. No injuries were reported.

Concert albums

Souvenir program

In the 1970's, Elvis performed before fans of all ages.

Elvis at 40: criticism that he is over-the-hill is defied by the fans' loyalty.

Memphis Press-Scimitar   January 18, 1975

'Hounds' in Crate for Elvis Didn't Bark, But Coeds Did

By DAVID HOGAN

"My grandmother's going to kill me," said a drowsy 17-year-old Greenville Miss., coed today at Elvis Presley's Graceland Mansion in Whitehaven.

This seemed to be the main concern of Areecia (Honeybee) Benson. She was one of the four Mississippi Delta Junior College coeds who unsuccessfully tried yesterday to make a special delivery of a crate, containing Honeybee and her friend Patsy Haynes, to the Presley residence.

Honeybee spent the night at the Presley mansion guardhouse and has vowed to stay until Sunday night in hopes of seeing Elvis.

Honeybee said she's "not really in love with Elvis or anything like that," but that she "only wants to see him to talk to him a while."

Honeybee and Patsy, 19, both adorned with ribbon, arrived at the Presley home at 4:30 yesterday afternoon inside a wooden crate delivered by an REA Express truck. The girls had disguised themselves as a birthday gift to Presley, and REA Express had been told that the package contained two Russian Wolfhounds.

But when REA Express driver Sam Delisi delivered the package to Presley, he was informed that Elvis did not need any dogs, and to return the package to the senders.

Patsy and Honeybee said they got scared at this point.

"We heard them kicking the box and saying something about 'Just dump 'em' and we thought they were going to shoot the crate and dump it in the river," said Honeybee.

As the delivery truck pulled away from Graceland, the two girls clawed their way out of the crate and tried to get the attention of the truck driver in the cab.

"We kept tapping and hollering, 'Sir, sir, sir,' but he just looked around real confused like," said Honeybee. "When he saw us he was in a state of shock for about five minutes."

The driver returned them to Graceland where the girls were met by classmates and fellow conspirators Debby Black and Joan Thigpen.

FOR ELVIS, FUN BEGINS AT 40

SHIMMERING and sparkling in his outrageous black and sky-blue sequinned costume, rings flashing, Elvis Presley belted out the songs and burlesqued his own sexy image with humor.

He wiggled his hips, shook a leg, paused while the girls went bananas, grinned and wiggled again.

This wasn't the Elvis I had expected. They told me he was 40, over the hill, sulky. A spoilt star who wanted to be alone, whose Memphis Mafia of bodyguards smashed up photographers and kept the fans away. A sex symbol who was no longer sexy. Gone to fat, they said.

You could have fooled me. I saw him in Asheville, N.C., last stop of his nation-wide summer tour, and every gal in town was praying that Elvis Presley would pick her.

Maybe he is a little huskier than he was, but he hasn't lost his elasticity. Every move of that India rubber body sent his audience into a frenzy. . . .

266

Memphis Commercial Appeal   January 9, 1975

Secluded Elvis Hailed As Best

By SCOTT WARE

"You are my best rockin roll singer," wrote 8-year-old Staci. "You are sexy to be 40 years old. To bad I'm not 35."

With this assurance, and thousands of others like it, singer Elvis Presley privately observed his 40th birthday yesterday in self-imposed seclusion at his Graceland Mansion on Elvis Presley Boulevard.

Yet despite the entertainer's isolation and low-key attitude, the city of Memphis, his adopted home, and friends and admirers from all over the world made certain the occasion would not go overlooked.

Letters have poured in at the rate of 600 per day for the past week, and hundreds of telegrams have been delivered regularly to the Presley estate. An estimated two-thirds of the letters were from Germany, where Elvis served in the Army in the late 1950s, while telegrams were received from all parts of the world.

Memphians like Staci were allowed to deliver their cards, letters and greetings personally to a special "Happy Birthday, Elvis" box set up at the gate at Graceland. But the guards made sure well-wishers did not approach the mansion.

Radio stations, the medium through which Elvis initially rose to fame two decades ago, played Elvis hits in Memphis throughout the day, gave away birthday cakes and Elvis albums every hour and conducted interviews with longtime Presley friends and associates.

Elvis remained shut up in his home. He slept until about 3 p.m., when his uncle, Vester Presley, phoned in his birthday greetings from the guard house at the gate.

Vester, who has worked as a security guard at Graceland since 1957 and has not seen his nephew since Christmas, said Elvis "talked like he was feeling pretty good.

"He said he was resting up and trying to get in shape to go on the road again," Vester said. "He doesn't plan to leave the house, although from the way he talked it would not surprise me if he had a small, private party tonight."

The reference to getting in shape came amid growing press reports that Elvis is "fat and 40." Actually, Elvis watchers say the entertainer has always had a weight problem, which is no better or worse this year. If he gains a few pounds he gets puffy looking, which is a no-no for the movie cameras. He apparently will slim down as he always does by dieting and practicing karate.

For the Elvis fans lingering at the gate, Vester's phone call was the closest they came to making contact with their idol.

By the end of the day more than 2,000 persons had stopped, with admirers from as far away as Holland, Connecticut and Wyoming paying their respects. A man identifying himself as "from the Pentagon" personally delivered one letter, saying he feared it would never be received if sent through the mail.

One family traveled all the way from Florida just for Elvis' birthday. Another man drove from Bristol, Va.

But it did not disturb most that Presley refused to appear publicly. They seemed content just being outside his home.

"I just wanted him to know that I was thinking about him," one young woman said. "Sure, I'd give anything to see him, but I don't really blame him for staying inside. I don't care if he is 40. I still love him. I'll be 40 someday."

Souvenir calendar

The kiss that made Elvis split his pants

CHUBBY Elvis Presley is still too big for his britches.

The 40 year-old singing idol, said to have lost more than 10 pounds at a fat farm, proved it in front of 12,000 hometown fans in Memphis, Tenn.

Elvis split his pants as he bent forward to kiss a girl. Clearly all shook up, he looked over his shoulder and asked the band: "Is it bad?"

"No" they told him, but Elvis with one hand covering his embarrassment stood knock-kneed for several moments before he regained his composure.

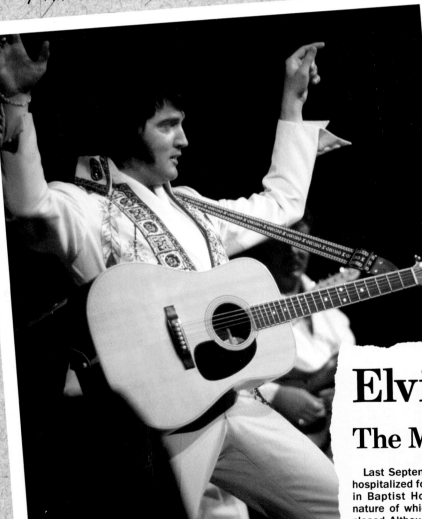

Elvis, Jerry Schilling, and Sonny West had once visited Nixon in the White House.

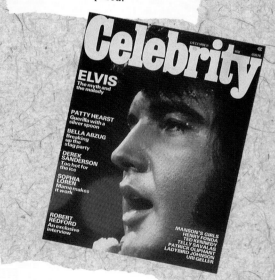

Still ailing, Elvis returned to the road.

Elvis Presley

The Myth and the Malady

Last September, Elvis Presley was hospitalized for a "recurrent ailment" in Baptist Hospital, Memphis—the nature of which was never fully disclosed. Although after his release Elvis was seen briefly by TV audiences riding a motor scooter, the disturbing rumor persisted that the life of the King of Rock 'n' Roll, one of the greatest single music personalities of all time, was in grave danger.

It was terribly ironic—even grotesque —that at the youthful age of 40, with every financial aid at his command, Elvis Presley, who throughout his spectacular career never smoked, nor drank, nor used any drugs because of his sound religious upbringing, should succumb to some mysterious weakness of the flesh that neither medical science nor clean living could conquer. . . .

THE KING 'COMES BACK'

Fighting a Bulging Waistline, He Says of His Fans: "I Owe Those People For Everything I've Got."

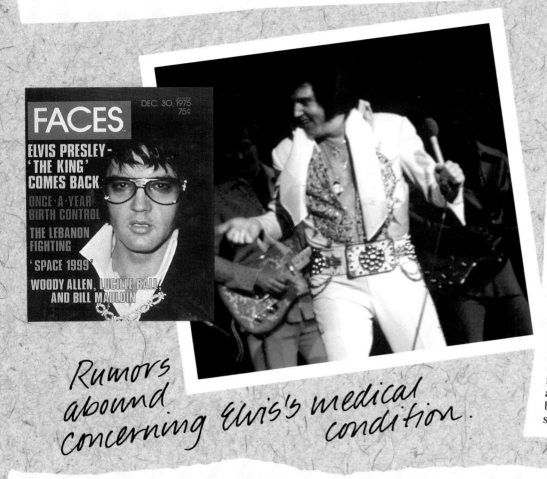

Rumors abound concerning Elvis's medical condition.

According to close associates, Elvis Presley is like a stranger in a foreign land and he's anxious to get back to familiar ground. But, they say, he knows he has a challenging task before him because he's making a comeback.

True, during the advent of popular musical groups such as the Beatles in the early Sixties, Elvis found himself in obscurity. But the circumstances at the time were not something he could control. The public's taste in music had changed drastically and a single artist was not a popular commodity. Still, when the trend changed, there was Elvis again, right on top.

Now, however, it's different. The root of many of his main problems is not the result of any outside influences. Elvis has suddenly become fat.

There are few people, men or women, with bulging waistlines who are accepted by the public as idols. Elvis has found he is no exception. When he was forced to cut short his scheduled two-week stand at the Hilton International Hotel this past summer, there were cries of disappointment not only from fans who didn't see him but also from some who saw him and felt they had been short-changed by seeing an overweight, sluggish Elvis. . . .

Memphis Press-Scimitar   March 14, 1975

Presley Carries More Weight At Opening Night in Las Vegas

LAS VEGAS, Nev.—(UPI)— Elvis Presley, the heartthrob of millions in the 1950s who thrilled audiences again in the 1970s, returned to the entertainment capital with his old flourish and a little more paunch.

The swivel-hipped, 40-year-old singer, whose gyrations earned him the nickname "Elvis the Pelvis," opened his show wearing cream-colored slacks and a loosely cut jacket-style shirt, different from his usual skin tight, metal studded shirts and trousers that emphasize his movements.

"You should have seen me a month ago when I got out of the hospital—I looked like Mama Cass," the entertainer joked during his opening night performance Tuesday at the Las Vegas Hilton.

Presley sang more than a dozen selections, with tunes ranging from "C.C.. Rider" to "I Got a Woman" and "Take My Hand," his closing number. Gone from his repertoire were such hits as "Hound Dog," "Blue Suede Shoes" and "All Shook Up."

In his first show since his release from the hospital in February, Presley gave away the traditional neck scarves and kisses to front row fans. He said it was the first time in five years that he had performed without his father in the audience.

Vernon Presley was hospitalized in Memphis Feb 5 following a heart attack. The entertainer himself entered the Baptist Hospital Jan 29. Doctors said he had an internal blockage and there were reports he suffered from a liver ailment.

One source said Presley had entered the hospital in an attempt to lose weight. He was scheduled to open here last month, but that appearance was canceled again because of reports of him being overweight.

Elvis Escapes Breakup Blame

By ALICE FULBRIGHT

One of the friendliest legal separations ever is the one between Dee and Vernon Presley, according to Dee.

The stepmother of Elvis Presley, blond Dee is attracting attention these days as she drives around Memphis in a baby blue Cadillac Eldorado convertible with white upholstery, one of many gifts from her estranged husband.

"I don't really think that Elvis feels like he broke up our marriage," she said in protest about a recent article in Photoplay. The magazine article was headlined, "Did My Career Ruin My Father's Marriage?" And the article claimed that Elvis was heartbroken over the possibility.

"If Elvis feels that way, he shouldn't," Dee said gently. "He was devoted to his mother but he never resented me.

"He's given me a lot of things like a jade necklace, an autumn haze mink coat, and special things like a diamond bracelet. He's generous, just like his father."

The article dwelled on the possible reasons for the break-up of the 14-year-old marriage of Dee and Vernon.

"What went wrong? Did Vernon grow restless because of her new-found independence (as a song-writer and record producer)? Or was it all the days and the nights that Vernon spent on the road with Elvis during concert tours and Las Vegas engagements?" the article asked.

In a talk in her Germantown apartment, Dee said cautiously that she never resented her husband's travels with his son. "It wouldn't have occurred to me to ask him to quit the road—Elvis needs him."

The public "owns" not only Elvis but his father, she said. "That's only natural and I never resented it.

"Until Vernon had his heart attack (in February), he handled Elvis' business out of his office at Graceland. We lived there for the first two years when we were married. He was gone a lot, of course. Elvis' tour now is the first one in five years that Vernon has missed being with him."

She said her husband's heart attack, which hospitalized him twice, was a serious one. "More serious than I was told at the time."

"But I see him frequently and talk to him on the phone almost every day. He's recuperating well and slowly."

Home is always where Elvis is to members of his family, and even divorce doesn't change that fact, Dee claimed. . . .

. . . She said she was busy getting settled in her apartment in Germantown, selling furniture from her Whitehaven house—and decorating her new lakeside home at Hickory Valley, Tenn.

"My lake house is only 45 minutes from here. It has four bedrooms and two baths, and I've already added a family room.

"It certainly isn't the house I was going to build. I meant to build a round glass house, with plenty of sunshine, I have nothing to hide. . . ."

. . . Dee's three sons—Bill Stanley Jr., 21, Rickey, 20, and David Stanley, 19—have an apartment in Memphis. "Vernon and I moved from Graceland because of the boys—so they could have their own home," Dee said. "They love and respect Vernon."

While she served her favorite drink, coffee and honey, she talked about her song-writing career. "I have two songs in albums, and three months ago I opened my own publishing company, called Dee's Music and Dee's Melodies.

"I'm also writing a book, called 'My Lonely Heart.' I've written a song by the same name that's in a Stax album. . . ."

. . . Her bright smile faded as she looked around her bedroom, which has been decorated in yellow. "The house in Whitehaven bothers me. It seems like when I sold Vernon the house, I was breaking ties."

The smile flashed again, "But that's not true and it's never going to be true. The ties are too strong. . . ."

. . . Relaxing on a huge, low sofa, she said, "I really don't know why Vernon and I are separated. But it got so we seldom saw each other—we just bumped into each other once in a while. And frankly," she took a deep breath and examined her bejeweled hands, "he's involved with someone else.

"But there never will be a divorce, and he's never asked for one.

"Elvis has been beautiful and my relationship with the family is the same. You'd hardly know what has happened except that we're apart.

"Well, my door is open. I never close a door that can't be opened."

Saturday, June 7, 1975

ELVIS GETS $3.5M OFFER

ELVIS PRESLEY has been offered $3.5 million to do one concert in London—and he is expected to reject the offer.

Last year "The King" turned down a $1.7 million offer for one show in Britain, despite desperate pleas from thousands of fans.

Promoter Arthur Howes, who made the two offers, says: "Every man has his price. And maybe $3.5 million is his."

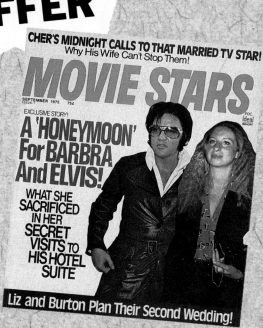

CHER'S MIDNIGHT CALLS TO THAT MARRIED TV STAR!
Why His Wife Can't Stop Them!

MOVIE STARS

SEPTEMBER 1975 75¢

EXCLUSIVE STORY!
A 'HONEYMOON' For BARBRA And ELVIS!

WHAT SHE SACRIFICED IN HER SECRET VISITS TO HIS HOTEL SUITE

Liz and Burton Plan Their Second Wedding!

Dee Stanley Presley

Barbra Streisand offered Elvis the lead in A Star Is Born, but Col. Parker turned her down.

Elvis bought a jet from Delta Air lines...

...and named it <u>Lisa Marie</u>

Memphis Press-Scimitar

Elvis Adds 'Lisa Marie' To His Fleet of Planes

By Orville Hancock
Press-Scimitar Staff Writer

Elvis Presley's fabulous new plane, the Lisa Marie, has arrived at Memphis International Airport after undergoing finishing touches in Texas and California.

The converted Delta Air Lines Convair 880, with a new white paint job on the outside and luxurious furnishings on the inside arrived at Memphis Aero late Monday night.

The plane seems destined to draw a lot of attention, even without trying.

When the ramp attendant at Memphis Aero was guiding the huge jet to a mooring, he guided it to a white line and allowed the pilot to park the plane about six feet off the line.

As a result, one wing yesterday extended about six feet beyond a taxi ramp and over a taxiway on the Memphis Aero side of the airport.

Parked alongside the Convair 880 is Elvis' Jet Star, looking like a frog beside an elephant in size comparison.

Pilot for the plane was called yesterday about the wing tip sticking out on the taxiway and he moved it. There was plenty of room for small planes to taxi past, but to keep things according to guidelines at the airport, the big jet was moved six feet.

The Convair 880 has a range of approximately 3,000 miles and is one of the fastest jetliners around. The Convair 880 holds several speed records for airliners.

Cruising speed is about 600 miles per hour and the plane is designed to fly above 40,000 feet.

When Delta used Convairs, the planes seated 99 persons.

Delta sold its Convairs at about $5 million each, thus, Elvis has a bundle of money in his Convair, after purchase and new configuration.

The Convair is the fourth in Elvis' fleet. He has a Gulfstream and a Jet Commander, both of which are up for sale. One is in Maryland and the other in Florida.

The name of Elvis' daughter, Lisa Marie, is painted on the nose of the big jet and TCB on the tail. The TCB are initials for Elvis' company, Taking Care of Business.

The giant jet looks ordinary enough on the outside, but when you step inside, that's something else.

Lavish carpeting greets the passenger. There are several seats and then the plane is divided into several rooms, partitioned.

There's a plush lounge and a fancy bathroom.

Elvis has an office in the plane and one for his secretary. There is a conference room also. And there is a king size bed for Elvis.

1975 LP releases

Memphis Commercial Appeal   July 27, 1975

Elvis Buys Manager $1.2-Million Plane

By JAMES KINGSLEY

Elvis Presley bought a $1.2-million turboprop for his long-time manager, Col. Tom Parker, and had it flown to Las Vegas yesterday to surprise the cigar-chomping promotional wizard, The Commercial Appeal learned yesterday.

"You've got to be kidding," said Parker, who was telephoned in Las Vegas before the plane arrived.

"I can't believe it and won't 'til I see it."

The white Grumman Gulfstream G-1 with blue trim left Memphis about 9 a.m. yesterday headed to Las Vegas. Elvis, who could not be reached for comment, remained at his Graceland mansion, sources said.

An airport executive in Vicksburg, Miss., said Elvis began negotiating with Cappaert Enterprises there for the luxury jet "sight unseen" about two weeks ago.

He said the twin-engine plane, which cruises at speeds of 450 to 600 mph, was flown to Memphis 10 days ago and then to Asheville, N.C., where Elvis was performing, so he could look at it before completing the deal.

Officials of Cappaert Enterprises could not be reached for comment yesterday.

The plane has a gold-carpeted interior with a stereo system, flight phone and bar. It will seat up to 22 persons and "is as nice as any you'll ever find," the source said.

Another source said the bar will probably not be used since Parker does not drink.

The source close to Elvis said Parker does not like to fly in big planes. He said Elvis decided to buy the plane after it took four leased aircraft to carry his touring company to his last concert.

Elvis bought himself a 109-passenger airplane last month for a reported $1 million. It is being refurbished in Fort Worth. The Convair 880 was formerly used by Delta Airlines, Inc.

After it is refurbished, it will seat 32, be equipped with two bedrooms and an office. It is not expected to be ready until September.

January 15, 1976

Elvis Gives Away 5 More Automobiles

Entertainer Elvis Presley took time out from skiing in Vail, Colo., yesterday to give away five more automobiles, three Cadillacs and two Continental Mark IVs.

The Rocky Mountain News said the Mark IVs were given to Denver Police Capt. Jerry Kennedy, who has handled security for a number of Presley appearances, and Dr. Gerald Starkey, Denver's police medical coordinator.

Det. Ronald Pietrafeso, who has also worked Presley concerts, received a Cadillac.

The other two Cadillacs were given to two unidentified women the newspaper said.

The two Continentals are valued at about $27,000 and Pietrafeso's Cadillac at $13,000, the News said.

Denver Police Chief Art Dill said he would allow Kennedy, Starkey and Pietrafeso to keep their cars because they were off duty when they performed services for Presley.

Presley has given away as many as 10 automobiles at a time on several previous occasions in Memphis and Hollywood.

Elvis was best man at bodyguard Sonny West's wedding. What was the flashlight for?

Memphis Press-Scimitar   January 16, 1976

3 Denver Officers, 2 Others Benefit From Elvis' Whim

DENVER—(AP)—Bob Surber says he was skeptical at first when someone called to say Elvis Presley would be around to buy some cars.

"We were all a little bit excited," said Surber as he described Presley's visit to the auto salesroom Wednesday night to buy new Lincoln Mark IVs for a Denver police officer and a police doctor, and a Cadillac for a Denver detective.

They weren't the only examples of Presley's largesse. The singer also bought luxury cars for two persons vacationing with him in the Colorado mountains.

Total tab: about $70,000.

Presley has given new cars as gifts in the past. Last summer, he bought several Cadillacs for people in Memphis. At least one of the recipients then was a stranger.

Surber said he learned of Presley's plans late Wednesday in a telephone call from Vail, Colo., where Presley's party was staying.

When Presley's party arrived, the singer told Capt. Jerry Kennedy, head of the Denver Police vice squad, and Dr. Gerald Starkey, a Denver police physician, to choose the cars they wanted.

Presley met Starkey in Las Vegas, Nev., in 1970. Kennedy met the singer at about the same time and had served as a security man on Presley's subsequent trips to Colorado.

Starkey, sitting in his brown-on-brown Mark IV and listening to Presley tapes, said the singer had called him for medication to treat an itch caused by a ski mask he'd been wearing to keep from drawing crowds.

By the time he arrived, Kennedy and Detective Ron Pietrafeso, who met Presley through Kennedy and also acts as a security man for the singer, had picked out their cars, Starkey said.

Police Chief Art Dill said it was all right for the men to accept the automobiles. "They were off duty at the time (of their services to Presley) and not acting in an official capacity," said Dill.

Surber said Presley paid for the Lincolns with two checks, one personal and one drawn on a company account.

Elvis Shows Generosity Again: Shiny New Car Is 'Fairy Tale' Come True

Mennie Person shows off the El Dorado Elvis gave her.

Memphis Commercial Appeal   July 29, 1975

Elvis' Whim Caters To Car Shopper's Fancy

By ROBERT KELLETT

A bank teller who was "just looking" on the lot of a downtown automobile agency Sunday night suddenly became a beneficiary of entertainer Elvis Presley's latest outburst of generosity and yesterday was driving a Cadillac El Dorado.

Mrs. Mennie L. Person of 1868 Meadowhill said she was admiring Presley's custom-made limousine about 9:30 p.m. when he apparently was on a Cadillac-buying spree.

"I had my head over in it looking at it and he came out of the back parking lot and asked if I liked it," Mrs. Person said.

"You don't expect to find him on a car lot that time of night."

Mrs. Person said she was "still standing there with my mouth open" but managed to compliment the star's personal vehicle.

"He said, 'That one's mine, but I'll buy you one,'" Mrs. Person said.

"He caught me back by the arm and carried me back to the parking lot where he had come from and told me to 'pick one out.'"

The vehicle which the woman decided on was a gold and white El Dorado which lists for about $11,500.

Presley told an officer of the auto agency to "put it on the list" and continued talking to Mrs. Person—learning among other things that her birthday is today.

Mrs. Person said that when he handed her the keys to the car he wished her "happy birthday" and told an aide to write her a check "to buy some clothes to go with

the car." She did not disclose the amount of the check.

Presley's gifts of automobiles over the years have constituted one of the more flamboyant aspects of his closely guarded private life and have included expensive vehicles given to friends, professional associates and in at least one case a politician—former Sheriff William N. Morris, Jr.

Officers of the company would not say how many vehicles Presley bought during his Sunday shopping spree, who received them or how much they cost. All questions were referred to "the Presley family." Family members were not immediately available for comment.

During the past weekend, Presley had a turboprop jet airplane

valued at about $1.2 million delivered to Las Vegas as a gift to his manager, Col. Tom Parker.

Mrs. Person, who has been a teller at the First National Bank's North Memphis branch for about five years, and her husband, Troy Person, a tile setter, were not exactly hurting for transportation before stumbling into their good fortune.

The couple drove onto the car lot in a 1974 Cadillac Coupe DeVille after going to dinner with their two children.

"He (Presley) told me to keep it," said Mrs. Person. "He told me to give it to my husband or whatever we wanted to do."

273

Gold-Spangled Elvis:

Hollywood's real 'fat cats'

. . . **AND OF COURSE**, there are those like Elvis Presley (who seems like a blown-up caricature of his once slim 'n' sexy self) who are living proof that diet pills can be more harm than help . . . .

Fans called this jumpsuit "the Peacock"!

Concert tickets

Jan. 2, 1976

Presley does a split, leaves crowd panting

Middle-age spread. Elvis Presley, whose swiveling hips have acquired a rolling motion, ripped his pants during the opening minutes of a New Year's Eve show in Pontiac, Mich. Presley, who has developed a little paunch and shades of a second chin, had to take a break after the first few numbers and get into something a little more comfortable.

Bootleg albums issued in 1976

Flashes of the Old Fire

One night for Elvis here

FOR THE RECORD: Elvis Presley will do one concert in the Chicago Stadium on Oct. 15 . . . as of this writing. Tickets go on sale Tuesday . . . not Monday. On Oct. 11, Elvis will be recording for RCA. A lot of Elvis' fans told us they will be waiting in line all night to buy tickets. Some fans are bringing campers, folding chairs, etc. Elvis . . . ever the legend.

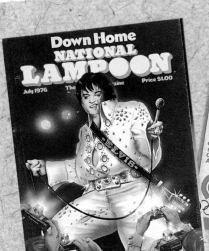

The press continued to hound Elvis about his weight.

He acts like an indifferent idol

A fat Elvis can still make female fans squeal

Elvis lives.

Louise Houser sits in the front row of the Capital Centre clutching a white teddy bear. She is dressed to kill in a spiffy denim outfit and her masses of black hair hang in curls around her neck. She is thrilled. Thrilled because she has managed to procure two front-row seats to the Elvis concert on a recent Sunday afternoon. Her husband, Raymond, sits next to her. "I bought from a friend," she allows, proudly. "I bought the set for $250. This has been my life's ambition—to sit in the front row of an Elvis concert. I feel like my life is complete now."

Well, uh, what exactly is it about Elvis that she loves so much.

"He's so sexy," she says matter-of-factly.

Sexier than Raymond here?

Incredulous, she looks up. "Why do you think I married my husband? Because he looks like Elvis."

She's right. Raymond, in a similar denim outfit with bell bottom trousers, a natty cap and sideburns looks exactly like Elvis.

Raymond grins.

It is intermission and Elvis has yet to appear. Down the row Kim Matheson, 16, gasps for breath. Her chest heaves up and down in the sequinned Elvis T-shirt she made herself. To it she clutches what looks like a guitar. It is a cake shaped like a guitar. Her aunt made it. She has driven 450 miles from North Carolina to present it to Elvis. "Oh man," she manages to get out as her excitement escalates, "He's just the greatest thing. I love him, I love him, I love him . . ."

Further on in the front row sit Linda and George Athans from New Jersey, 26- and 28-years-old members of an Elvis fan club, the Elvis Presley Association. They were in Rhode Island Saturday night and drove down for the concert as they do for all of Elvis' concerts. Eight hours' drive that night. When they have to take time from work, they take vacation time. They had driven down once before, to stand in line all night in order to get front-row tickets.

"That's nothing," says Linda. "In Philly we waited in line two nights to get tickets . . ."

. . . Now, this is going to annoy a lot of Elvis fans, about 38,000 to be exact, but it's just got to be said here.

Elvis is fat. Not only is he fat, his stomach hangs over his belt, his jowls hang over his collar and his hair hangs over his eyes . . .

. . . Dressed in his baby blue Bicentennial costume with the red, white and blue sequinned presidential seal and other patriotic insignia, he looks more like Siegfried in "Der Ring Des Nibelungen" than the great sex god of America.

His performance seems appallingly perfunctory to someone who had once been an Elvis idolizer and who had secretly expected to swoon when he went into his rendition of "Love Me Tender." But nothing happens. He is so busy being the idol, passing out Elvis scarves to the semi-hysterical women who occasionally will erupt into cries of "Elvis" from any given part of the Centre at any time that he barely concentrates on his singing.

The scarf routine is particularly disconcerting because as he sings, a draper drapes the silk scarves over his neck, he wipes the sweat off his neck with the scarves, the girls scream, he throws the sweaty scarves to them, they faint and collapse and are pushed away by the guards or led away by their friends. For the higher rungs of the stadium he has an ejector of sorts that shoots the scarves up into the seats . . .

. . . It is not understandable. The women all say they think he is sexy. They say they like his charisma. They say he is a humanitarian and is good to his mother. But they really don't understand what it is they like themselves . . . .

Reaching to touch the King

Memphis Press-Scimitar   September 7, 1976

'Fat' and Forty— But Also Sold Out

SYRACUSE, N.Y.—(AP)— Elvis Presley a has-been? Not in Syracuse.

Dale Rise, a reporter for the Syracuse Post-Standard, reviewed the singer's first performance here this week and wrote "Elvis is fat, and there's no hiding it. His cheeks are puffy and he has a double chin . . . To many, Elvis must only embody a remembrance of things past. Musically, the performance was mediocre."

Angry readers responded with many letters and telephone calls.

"Hundred of phone calls hit the Post-Standard offices. One call after another arrived at my home. They questioned. They shouted. And they swore," Rice reported.

Elvis gave another show, and like the first performance, it was sold out.

Fans do more gyrating than Elvis, but he's still tops

King Elvis writhes a rousing page of history

My ticket—the one I had called all over the country to find, a main-floor, not-bad-at-all ticket—was given to a photographer. He scored—for $35, a seat for me in the second balcony. If I had misgivings before, I was so steamed now that I barely remembered walking up the endless flights of stairs it takes to get to the second balcony.

I sat down with a decidedly angry scowl. There was a little boy with his mother on one side of me. He was excited, and his mother, watching him adoringly throughout, was happy to see him sharing her excitement. On the other side was a woman who had come along with four busloads of persons from Moline, Ill. Her childlike glee ("Oh, God, I can't believe he's here! I can't believe I'm here! Oh, God!") began to cheer me up.

More nerves followed intermission. I helped my friend from Moline decide whether to have a cigarette and how to keep her Elvis poster from being smashed. She was literally quivering in her jeans. I was beginning to.

After a 15-minute intermission that felt like years, to the opening buzz of "Also Sprach Zarathustra"—or as this crowd called it "The Theme from 2001"—out came Elvis!

Not since the Beatles have I seen the blackness pulsate with light from thousands of cameras. If he grunted in one direction, a battery of bulbs went off, and a wave of tense bodies strained forward. All night he created havoc, just glancing over his shoulder to various sections of the crowd. At first, just this had me fascinated. That and the rather large bra that hit the stage.

But then I borrowed my Moline pal's binoculars for a closer look at the perpetrator of this mania. I discovered what several gasping females had—he's balding on top. And from the stiffness of his calculated bumps and grinds, the extra poundage has slowed him down some. Once a seeming seething volcano of hot emotions, he is now slower, he sort of . . . smolders. He seemed tired, or perhaps just not very enthusiastic.

But. One lovely miss with Farrah Fawcett-Majors hair in a tight jumpsuit approached the stage, bouquet in hand. He squatted down, slowly, ever so slowly—you could hear every female's heart thumping as he got closer and closer to her. He gave her that smooth, sexy leer that every impressionist in the world has tried to do and in that voice that comes from someplace down in his belly he muttered, "Honey, whatchoo got on your mind?" It dripped suggestion. And then came the grudging, teasing smile. "Naw, I cain't do that—there's children in here, honey," he said. And then he laid a kiss on her, and the unanimous heartthrobs erupted into one huge groan from all corners of the stadium. This guy doesn't have to move. He just oozes cool.

He's the original. He sang all the legendary songs. By the time he got around to "Jailhouse Rock" I was clapping along, too. He did torchy songs—a hip-tossing "Fever" that set them screaming with every twitch—hot songs like "I'm All Shook Up," all of them, too many to list.

And all the while he caused near riots, tossing scarves to the audience. One Frain was nearly choked to death when a scarf landed around his neck, and thousands of hands went for a piece of it. Elvis gave that neck, and thousands of hands went for a piece of it. Elvis gave that smirking smile and coolly tossed another. The dude is smooth.

He proved with "I'm Hurt" that he still can make the rafters ring, and jerk tears out of the hardest of us, and he did it on purpose, as he did everything else. If that seems calculated and cold, I guess maybe it was.

But we had come for a sideshow. And he managed to give us instead a reminder that he is history, he is a legend and he is the King. And he can carry it off, now, balding, and more than 40, just as well as he did back when Ed Sullivan's censors cut him off at the waist to keep the shaking to a visual minimum.

He's moving slowly. He's got a paunch. He's not the fireball he was. He even—gasp—sweats. And a lot of persons no doubt are asking, "But, was it a good show? How did he sound? Was it musically right?"

To them I say: Hey, back off. When it's history, and it's Elvis, who cares?

Memphis Press-Scimitar   December 10, 1976

Rumors Fly Along As Girl's Family Goes to See Elvis

Fueling rumors of a pending marriage between Elvis Presley and a 20-year-old Memphis beauty queen, the entertainer today was flying the family of his new girlfriend to Las Vegas to view the 41-year-old Presley's show there tonight.

The family of Ginger Alden, who is the current Miss Mid-South Fair and first runner-up in February's Miss Tennessee Universe Pageant, was being flown to Las Vegas in Presley's private jet and being lodged for the weekend at a Las Vegas hotel.

Mrs. Walter Alden, Ginger's mother, said: "We've been invited out there to see Elvis Presley's concert, but I don't know anything about them getting married."

She said reports of a pending marriage were started as a rumor by an Elvis fan club in California, "I haven't heard anything about it," she said. "It's just a rumor."

Mrs. Alden said, however, that Elvis recently gave her daughter a new Lincoln Continental as a gift, although she said she doesn't think it was an engagement gift.

Ginger, a tall young woman with brunette hair worn shoulder length, has appeared in several television commercials and is a student at Memphis Academy of Arts.

Making the trip to Las Vegas are Mr. and Mrs. Alden, Terry, and their other two children, Rosemary and Michael. The family home is at 4152 Royal Crest Place.

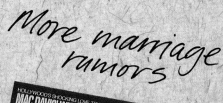

More marriage rumors

MAC DAVIS' WIFE MOVES IN WITH GLEN CAMPBELL

MOVIE STARS

ELVIS TELLS DAUGHTER SHE'LL HAVE A 'NEW MOTHER'

THE MYSTERY BEHIND THE GIRL... WHY HIS FAMILY ARRANGED THE MARRIAGE

LIZ AND DICK TO BECOME 'PARENTS'!

BURT'S 'TEENAGE LOVE' REVEALS THEIR PLANS TO WED! How Dinah Played Cupid!

SCOOP! Marie Osmond's Sexual Awakening! The Rock Star She Adores!

TV STAR PARADE

'SECRET MARRIAGE' FOR PRISCILLA & ELVIS!

'Second child' brings them together!

THE 'OTHER MAN' IN LEE MAJORS' MARRIAGE! The baby plans Farrah hides from her husband!

PAUL GLASER AND LINDSAY WAGNER TELL THEIR BEDROOM SECRETS! "SEX IS BEST WHEN YOU'RE IN LOVE!"

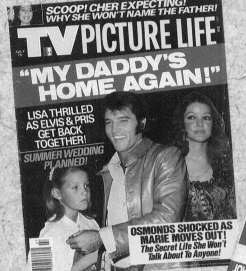

SCOOP! CHER EXPECTING! WHY SHE WON'T NAME THE FATHER!

TV PICTURE LIFE

"MY DADDY'S HOME AGAIN!"

LISA THRILLED AS ELVIS & PRIS GET BACK TOGETHER! SUMMER WEDDING PLANNED!

OSMONDS SHOCKED AS MARIE MOVES OUT! The Secret Life She Won't Talk About To Anyone!

FIRST TIME! FONZIE'S KISS AND TELL SWEETHEART TALKS

TV STAR PARADE

PRISCILLA & ELVIS REUNITED AS WITNESSES HEAR NEW VOWS! Honeymoon Site Revealed!

JOHN TRAVOLTA & MARIE OSMOND: FORCED TO DATE IN SECRET- The love and heartbreak they share!

LEE & FARRAH MAJORS REVEAL BABY PLANS: "We'll have six in a row!"

Ginger Alden became Elvis's girl in 1976.

Memphis Press-Scimitar   July 12, 1976

Elvis Fans Caught By Wedding Hoax

By CHARLES GOODMAN

Vernon Presley, father of Elvis, said he checked with Elvis, resting in Palm Springs, on the rumor the rock star is marrying actress Alexis Skylar today in Las Vegas and "It's totally a rumor."

"Elvis said he doesn't even know the girl," said Vernon Presley. "It's like the girl in Alabama a few months ago who announced she was going to marry Elvis. Just a rumor."

News services reported last night that Elvis was marrying the actress today at a Las Vegas Chapel. They said a man identified as a vice president of RCA Records made the wedding announcement. RCA Records said today that they have no such person working with them. The news service withdrew the story.

Right Up an Elvis Presley Fan's Street

MEMPHIS, Tenn.—(UPI) A funny thing happened to Mrs. E. P. Inderbitzen of Memphis on her way to take a young out-of-town friend to see Elvis Presley's Graceland mansion.

She honked her car horn and to her surprise a guard opened the gates to the singer's home.

"I couldn't believe it. I was dumbfounded," she said.

When the gates opened, Mrs. Inderbitzen and her companion, Nancy Booker, 18, of Bowling Green, Ky., drove right up to the singer's back door.

"We knocked on the door, which was open, and when nobody answered, we went in," she said.

"Some maids in the kitchen saw us and immediately asked, 'Who are you?' We told them we just wanted to see Elvis, but they told us he was asleep.

"I have been living here for years and I've passed Elvis' house many times, but I'd never tried to see it."

Mrs. Inderbitzen learned later that the gates were opened because her car is exactly like one owned by one of Presley's employees.

Fan Finds Elvis Gem of a Guy

MOBILE, Ala. (AP)— Tommy Milham waited in line 20 hours for tickets to the Elvis Presley show, and his persistence was rewarded with a startling gift. Elvis handed him a diamond ring.

"He gave it to me as a reward for my patience," the 33-year-old Milham said Friday.

He said a jeweler appraised the ring at $2,000, and added, "I don't care if the value is $2,000 or $200,000—it is not for sale."

The news is filled with stories of Elvis's strange bursts of generosity.

ELVIS IS SANTA AGAIN
Gives away two Mark IVs

Presley donates $1,000 to policeman in need

Elvis Presley heard over an L.A. radio station recently that a Torrance police motorcycle officer with nine children lost a leg, and sent a $1,000 check to the officer through KNBC newscaster Kelly Lange. Officer James Farquhar lost the leg in a vehicle accident but hopes to rejoin the police department after rehabilitation with an artificial limb.

"Elvis' office contacted me and sent the $1,000 check," Lange explained. "I understand he wanted to be a police officer at one time and that now he wants to give money directly where he sees a need instead of going through an organized charity."

MEMPHIS COMMERCIAL APPEAL

Presley Gives Land For Tourist Safety

Elvis Presley is trying to make it easier and safer for tourists to visit his Graceland Mansion, by donating to the city a piece of property in front of the mansion.

Nathan Ficklin, city traffic engineer, said yesterday that Presley has donated to the city 12,530 square feet of land in front of his Whitehaven property for construction of a "turn-out" lane for motorists trying to visit the popular tourist attraction.

Ficklin said the proposed viewing lane is part of an overall city plan to make the area around the singer's home safe for sightseers. He said the limited space in front of Graceland Mansion now makes it difficult and even dangerous for motorists and pedestrians to view the home.

Two years ago, a Kentucky mother and her child were struck and killed by a car while crossing Elvis Presley [Blvd.] after visiting the Presley home. Ficklin said the police report indicated the victims were returning to their car parked across the street. He said the accident was the impetus for the proposed improvements around the home.

The turn-out lane in front of the mansion will have 12 parallel parking spaces for northbound traffic. The city also plans to widen Elvis Presley [Blvd.] at two points in the area around Graceland Mansion and Graceland Christian Church at 3734 Elvis Presley [Blvd.] next door to the mansion.

Ficklin said the street widening proposals would permit the city to add a third traffic lane from north of the Presley mansion to Winchester for motorists heading north on Elvis Presley [Blvd.], and an additional left turn on the boulevard from Winchester to Craft.

"It's a real winner," Ficklin said of the proposed improvements. "It's one of those things you just fall into sometime."

Funds for the project have already been approved by the City Council, Ficklin said. He estimated the cost of the project at about $64,000, and said construction should begin within a month.

Elvis swings into action —but without his guitar

MADISON, Wis. [UPI]—"That was Elvis, no doubt about it," the young service station attendant said. "He was overweight and had jet-black hair."

Two youths were ganging up on the attendant, Keith Lowry Jr., about 1 a.m. Friday when rock star Elvis Presley strode up to the service station like it was a Hollywood set.

"All right, I'll take you on," Presley told one of Lowry's attackers.

PRESLEY, 42, finished a concert in Des Moines Thursday night and flew to Madison for a show Friday night. His limousine was en route from the airport to a hotel when he saw the fist fight.

Presley surprised his parents, managers, and three bodyguards when he joined the fight. The swivel-hipped singer was still wearing the blue jumpsuit from the Des Moines concert.

Though it has been said he is skilled in martial arts, the 42-year-old Presley never threw a punch. The fight broke up when Lowry and the two youths recognized him.

LOWRY'S FATHER owns the east side station, and one of the youths apparently had lost his job pumping gas. Presley did not leave until tempers were cool.

Bruce Frey witnessed Presley's biggest brawl since the movie *Jailhouse Rock* and said, "Elvis asked: 'Is everything settled now?'"

"He was willing to fight," said Thomas McCarthy, one of several police officers providing Presley with security. "That's the bad part."

Presley shook hands and posed for several pictures. He seemed amused by the whole episode as he got back into the limousine.

Memphis Press-Scimitar   February 2, 1977

1977 LP releases

Elvis Presley No-Shows RCA Recording Session

Taking care of business, Elvis Presley didn't win any friends or influence any people during a recent three-day stay in Nashville during which he was to record a new album at a south Nashville studio, but reportedly never left his room at the motel.

Nashville Banner columnist Bill Hance set out Presley's stay in his column, "Wax Fax." Following is a capsule of Hance's comments:

"Presley came to town last week to record. He needed some hits. He was here three days and never left his motel room.

"They say Presley is afraid to record because of recent disappointing record releases."

Elvis was scheduled in Nashville on a Wednesday, but didn't arrive until the next day, said Hance. His recording sessions were scheduled for eight straight nights. He never showed.

"We're going to write Presley off," said one musician who said he "waited and waited and waited" for the "King" to come through the door, according to Hance, whose report continues:

"Presley, claiming he was sick with a cold, left here Saturday night promising to return Monday to fulfill his recording contract with RCA and to live up to his own slogan, 'Taking Care of Business.' When he failed to show in the studio RCA officials and his personal manager, Col. Tom Parker, reportedly 'got hot.'"

Parker, the tough businessman who has guided Presley's career for nearly 20 years was quoted as telling Presley, "Get off your tail, in that studio, fulfill your contract or there will be no more tours."

Hance said that Presley confidants contend that Ginger Alden, 20, Elvis' new girlfriend is "absolutely running him ragged. One time Ginger decided to leave Elvis. She walked out and the only way he could get her back inside the house was to fire a gun in the air."

Hance then talked with motel staff members and wrote: "'They're driving us all nuts. This guy (Elvis) has his days and nights backwards. He sleeps all day and is up all night. At 6 p.m. he wants breakfast. The first night he ordered cheese omelettes, four orders of bacon and six sweet rolls. The next thing you know he's demanding soup. No wonder his weight goes up and down like a balloon.'

"'And this security mumbo jumbo. They run in doors, out of doors, up and down hallways and elevators trying to hide from people. Who are they hiding from? No fans have come out here. Only you newsmen.'"

Checking this report out brought some insights. RCA Victor officials in New York, queried about the no-show at Nashville, referred all questions to Parker. Asked how Elvis' latest album, "Elvis Presley Blvd., Memphis, Tennessee," recorded at Graceland, was selling, the RCA spokesman referred that question, too, to Parker. Yet when Presley's records used to sell over a million, RCA, itself, released the information.

John Long, WHBQ Radio program director, said Elvis' latest single, "Moody Blues," was played on the station "three or four weeks, but it never broke out and in all justice we had to pull it off the air."

An Alden family spokesman said Ginger was out of town and there would be no comments.

A spokesman for the Nashville studio said six to eight musicians had been flown in from Los Angeles to back Elvis, that they sat around for days waiting, and, in disgust, went back home. The studio is now booked through March 28. Elvis, they said, will have to wait his turn.

Meanwhile, Elvis left Memphis for Las Vegas Monday night. He spent yesterday in Los Angeles celebrating the ninth birthday of his daughter, Lisa Marie. He was due back in Memphis today.

Memphis Press-Scimitar   July 22, 1977

Pity Poor Elvis —So Say Reds

MOSCOW (AP)—To hear the Soviets tell it, rock star Elvis Presley is now a broken and forgotten man demonstrating to the world the heartlessness of the American system of exploitation.

Aging and overweight, the former "king of rock" has been "mercilessly tossed onto the scrap heap of those who have gone out of fashion," the Literary Gazette, a Soviet journal, said yesterday.

The newspaper did not mention Presley's pink mansion, fleet of cars or the fact that he is a millionaire many times over.

"The Western show business industry is constantly manufacturing new trends and concocting new stars and idols, and it pitilessly dumps all those who have gone out of fashion," the newspaper said.

Once Presley could drive an audience wild simply by walking on stage "fitted out in his gold and pink rags, looking like a peacock, his hair combed over his forehead . . . his legs vibrating like mechanical drills," the newspapers said.

"Today this 42-year-old man has lost his taste for life, wrecked by his own success," it said.

In 1977, Elvis's health problems reduced the length of his show...

Elvis weaves that old wiggle magic

Elvis Presley inflicted two hours of Las Vegas and intermission pain on his Sunday night audience in the Stadium, then spent an hour licking the wounds.

The opening included some blaring horns, a gospel quartet plus one, a sexist comedian and a female singing trio. Two gospel basses demonstrated—literally—how low the show would go. With its yellow tuxes, black open-necked shirts, decorated denim jumpsuit and unmatched red pajamas, Act I definitely was tacky.

The audience, from grandmas and grandkids to lawyers and overaged greasers, remained remarkably polite. The announcement of a 25-minute break took many by surprise. They ended up sitting patiently through a 55-minute bummer, during which vendors hawked expensive Presley souvenirs. "Where is he?" asked one peroxided, bouffanted fan. "I can't stand the suspense."

FINALLY, TO THE overwhelming rumble of the "2001" theme, The Man stepped onstage. At 42, he has added a paunch and pounds but is still a phenomenon.

His outrageous white bell-bottoms were covered with baubles, bangles, beads, spangles and rhinestones. Diamond rings dripped from his fingers; medallions coated his chest.

He has changed from Elvis the Wet Look to Elvis the Dry Look. And from the looks of the flashing bulbs that greeted him every time he turned around, instant-camera stock must have zoomed.

As soon as he cranked up his opener, "C. C. Rider," the love affair with the fans ran wild. He carried his mike from one end of the stage to the other, passing out scarves from around his neck. Occasionally, he squeezed a hand that reached above the others among the front-row groupies. One woman passed him a 4-foot Panda, to which Elvis crooned a tune.

THE OLD ELVIS magic still works, even though his bulk has cut down on the famous bumps and grinds. But every now and then he still throws in a wiggle. Girls screamed and women swooned as he sang "It's Now or Never," "Don't Be Cruel" and "My Way." They cheered when he did "Jailhouse Rock," "Johnny B. Goode" and "What'd I Say."

He spent about a quarter of the hour introducing his musicians and singers. Maybe the trouble with Elvis is that after 20-odd years, there are too many favorites for one concert. Unfortunately, he attempted too few of them.

High-paying patrons deserve more than 15 songs and half a dozen hints of oldies.

The whole works goes 'round again at 8:30 p.m. Monday. Elvis probably is worth the wait, but be prepared.

...but his voice remained as clear and solid as ever.

Elvis Admitted to Baptist Hospital

Spring 1977 - Back in the hospital again

Entertainer Elvis Presley was admitted to Baptist Hospital early today after canceling a show at the last minute in Baton Rouge, La., and flying to Memphis with complaints of intestinal flu.

Dr. George C. Nichopoulos, Presley's personal physician, said the rock and roll star was admitted to Baptist about 2:30 a.m. and is undergoing treatment.

"He has intestinal flu with gastroenteritis (inflamed stomach and intestines), and that's all I can say right now," Nichopoulos said.

About 15,000 fans including Louisiana Gov. Edwin W. Edwards and many members of the Louisiana state Legislator were gathered in the Louisiana State University Assembly Center when the announcement was made last night that Elvis was canceling the show.

Howls of protest and shouts of "rip-off" filled the large hall as the announcer told the crowd ticket money would be refunded or ticket stubs could be kept to exchange for tickets to a later Elvis concert if it could be rescheduled.

All the warm-up groups had completed their acts, and the crowd had just reseated itself after intermission in preparation of Elvis' show when the announcement was made.

Elvis At Home; Hospital On Call

Elvis Presley was released from Baptist Hospital at 4 a.m. yesterday but continued to reserve his two-room suite at the hospital.

Vernon Presley, the singer's father, said, "Elvis has been resting at Graceland (his mansion in Whitehaven) since he left the hospital at 4 a.m.

"He decided to keep the rooms reserved and the security guards on duty at the hospital in case his physician wants to run additional tests. He is feeling fine and looking forward to returning to his personal appearance tours that begin April 21 at Greensboro, N.C."

Elvis was admitted to Baptist at 6 a.m. last Friday for what his physicians termed intestinal flu and fatigue after canceling a personal appearance at Baton Rouge, La.

The elder Presley said several members of Elvis' band also became ill during the tour.

King of Rock, Elvis, Dead at Age 42

British papers

Memphis's hometown hero is gone.

Memphis Commercial Appeal   August 18, 1977

Tributes Paid To Elvis Throughout World

From London to Moscow and Tokyo to Tel Aviv, millions mourned the King of rock and roll yesterday. One British pop star said, "If there had been no Elvis, there would have been no Beatles."

Throughout the world radios played Elvis Presley records almost continuously in tribute to the gyrating, pouting singer from Tupelo, Miss., who became the undisputed king of rock and roll and influenced a generation of popular music.

Banner headlines announced his death to stunned millions of fans. Radio and television as far away as Uruguay broke into regular programming to announce his death. In Northern Africa, where rock music is denounced as "indecent," government news agencies in Morocco, Tunisia and Algeria ran lengthy obits, usually reserved for heads of state.

"If there had been no Elvis there would have been no Cliff Richards, there would have been no Beatles, there would have been no . . . well, I believe all of us people who make our money from the pop side of show business," Richards, a top British pop star, said in London.

Fan clubs in London and Tokyo had been planning 21st and 20th birthday parties for later in the month. Now, both may turn into wakes.

"We've planned our 21st [anniversary] party for next Saturday," said Todd Slaughter of the official Elvis Presley fan club in Britain. "I don't know what we're going to do now."

Presley records appeared in the British top 50 up to the end of last year.

London RCA executive Rodney Burbeck, whose company issued Presley's records said, "He was the greatest. His death will have lasting effects throughout the entire record industry."

Les Perrin, British press agent for many top stars, said, "He was a great original. Many people tried to copy him, but he was unique."

Radio Luxembourg, one of the best known rock stations throughout Europe, canceled all commercials Tuesday night when the news was received and played Presley records as a tribute to the singer.

In Tokyo, Hideo Okamura, the Presley fan club's president, said a 20th anniversary party had been scheduled later this month. "But now it turned out to be a time of mourning," he said.

"I am in a state of shock," said Mrs. Kiyoko Yamachita, editor of the Tokyo fan club's newsletter. "I want to cry, but I can't."

In Tel Aviv, the government-controlled pop music station put on a three-hour special of Presley's songs and the Army radio station scheduled an all-night marathon for today.

In Paris, Presley's death was the top news event of the day for most of the newspapers. France-Soir, the largest afternoon daily, even took the trouble of interviewing a medical specialist on the cause of the singer's death.

A young waitress in a Montparnasse restaurant burst into tears Tuesday night when she heard the news on the radio.

"He was the king," she said. "I had all his records. No one will ever replace him."

The Paris newspaper L'Aurore called Presley "one of the most popular entertainers of the last 20 years."

"No, Elvis did not die either old, poor or forgotten," the French newspaper said. "Millions of Americans and Europeans who were in their twenties in the 1950s will never forget either his face or his songs, nor the rock and roll he made them discover at the age of love."

French singers, who modeled their careers after his, readily acknowledged their debts to Presley.

"It was Elvis whose songs were the lullabies of our first parties," said Sylvie Vartan, a popular actress and singer. "It may be because of him that many of us went on to become singers."

"It's my ego that is dying," said Johnny Hallyday, one of the top French singers, and now in his mid-30s. "He remained the symbol of a whole generation of youth as Sinatra had been for the preceding one and the Beatles for the following one."

In West Germany, where Presley spent two years in the U.S. Army, his following had been the largest on the continent. The RCA office in Hamburg, which was Presley's main distributor in the country, reported Wednesday that its telephone switchboard was jammed with calls from record dealers ordering thousands of his records.

Numerous German movie houses announced they will replay many of the Presley films during the coming weeks. And the leading German rock publication—Music Joker—will run a 184,000 copy supplement on Presley later this week.

In Italy, radio programs portrayed the singer as a "paradoxical idol."

According to one broadcast, Presley was "the kind of person hundreds of thousands of young people actually were—not just what they would like to be."

In Moscow, the Soviet literary journal Literaturnaya Gazeta wrote the Communist version of the singer's obituary three weeks before his death.

"Elvis Presley was in the style of the American legend of the bootblack who becomes a millionaire. This boy from the lower classes—dishwasher, truck-driver, and factory worker—in the 1950s became one of the most popular singers in the West who started the new wave of rock and roll.

"The industry of Western show business always produces new fashions, makes new kings and idols, and throws out those who are no longer in fashion," it said. "One of the victims of this cruel mechanism is the King of Rock and Roll."

But one of the most fitting tributes came from a Belgian grocer who was listening to the radio playing Presley's "Heartbreak Hotel."

"Listen, he's still singing even though he's dead."

Elvis Dies Quickly at Graceland After Suffering Heart Failure

by Ron Harris and Tim Schick

As friends, relatives and business associates slept quietly in his spacious home, Elvis Presley, international king of rock 'n' roll for more than two decades, died alone in the bathroom of his half-million dollar mansion.

But even if the others in his Graceland mansion had been awake, it would have been impossible for them to save the musical and motion picture star, the Shelby County medical examiner said.

According to Dr. Jerry Francisco, who along with other pathologists performed the autopsy on Presley yesterday shortly after his death, the entertainer died in a matter of four short minutes of coronary arrhythmia, an irregular beating of the heart.

Probably Presley's mild hypertension, which had plagued the idol of millions for the past few years, and a coronary disease which had gone undetected contributed to his death, Francisco said, but the precise cause has not been determined—and it may never be known.

"It may take several days (to determine the cause), it may take several weeks," Francisco said. "It may never be discovered."

Francisco said Baptist Hospital will continue lab examinations to determine the exact cause of Presley's death.

Presley died between 9 a.m. yesterday—when he was last seen by his fiance, Ginger Alden—and 2:30 p.m. —when his body was found face down and fully clothed on the floor in the bathroom of his home by Alan Strada, one of Presley's employees, Francisco said.

Presley, who doctors said had never complained or shown any signs of heart problems, apparently fainted in the bathroom as his heart began to beat irregularly—cutting off oxygen to his brain—and finally stopped, Francisco said. The entire process takes less than four minutes, he said.

Autopsy showed that Presley suffered from coronary atherosclerosis, hardening of the coronary arteries, Francisco said. The disease had caused scar tissue, but had not caused enough damage alone to cause the arrhythmia, he said.

Francisco said such coronary diseases are usually undetectable even in tests right up to death.

"Many times coronary artery disease can be at the point to cause heart attack and still be undetectable," he said. "I might have it right now and we would not know it."

Although Presley was taking drugs for hypertension and a chronic colon problem, there was no evidence of any drug use contributing to his death, Francisco said.

"He was using medication to control his blood pressure and for a colon problem," Francisco said, "but there is no evidence of any chronic abuse of drugs whatsoever."

Presley's personal physician, Dr. George C. Nichopoulos, said Presley had been taking "appetite depressants" earlier to curb a weight problem, but the medication was not amphetamines.

Nichopoulos, Presley's physician for the past 10 years, dismissed rumors that Presley had been taking hard drugs.

"If he was using cocaine I would have known about it," he said.

Nichopoulos said he had given Presley an extensive physical five days ago and found him in fit condition. The physician said, however, he had urged Presley continuously to curb his activities although many times the singer ignored his warnings.

"He thrived on entertaining people, and it is a very difficult position to slow him down," Nichopoulos said. "He was getting over an eye infection and a sore throat, but overall he was a healthy man."

Presley had spent part of the day prior to his death at the dentist and playing racquetball, Nichopoulos said. Presley left his home for a drive at about 11 p.m., returned home at about 2:30 a.m. and played racquetball until about 6 a.m. yesterday before retiring to his bedroom, Nichopoulos said.

Miss Alden was the last person to see Presley as she left the home at 9 a.m. yesterday, Nichopoulos said.

Presley apparently had fainted during the heart failure as he stood in the bathroom, his physician said. Strada found Presley on the floor and immediately summoned Joe Esposito, Presley's road manager, and they began applying mouth-to-mouth resuscitation and cardiac massage, Nichopoulos said.

Esposito called a Fire Department ambulance which transported Presley to Baptist Hospital as paramedics continued to apply cardiac massage, Nichopoulos said. Inside the hospital, the emergency resuscitation team worked on Presley for about 40 minutes before Nichopoulos said he discontinued efforts to revive him.

According to Maurice Elliot, vice president of Baptist Hospital, Strada and Esposito said Presley was without a heart beat and was not breathing when they found him in the bathroom.

Nichopoulos said he attempted resuscitation efforts because Presley's pupils were contracted when he was brought to the hospital, indicating that there was still some life. Usually the pupils become dilated after death, he said.

Outside the emergency room entrance of the hospital yesterday, dozens of onlookers waited in limbo for word of Presley's condition until at 4 p.m. hospital officials finally announced Presley's death.

Hospital officials busily answered constantly ringing telephones while trying to piece together details of the death for news reporters. On the second floor, where the body was held, a small group of police officers stood guard at the hospital's morgue and ushered all non-hospital personnel off the floor.

According to nurses, Presley's body was swollen and bloated as it was wheeled into the blood lab after being rushed to the hospital. A group of six pathologists, four from Baptist Hospital, began conducting an official autopsy on the body two and a half hours after Presley was pronounced dead.

The pathologists finished the autopsy shortly before 8 p.m.

Presley was admitted to Baptist Hospital April 1 with intestinal flu and gastroenteritis (inflamed stomach and intestines). He was also treated at the hospital twice, first from January 28 to February 14, 1975, and again August 21 to September 6 of the same year for a chronic colon condition. At the time he was diagnosed as having megacolon —an obstruction of the colon.

Elliot recalled the singer's previous visits to the hospital.

"I have been here since 1962 and have never seen a patient that creates as much interest," he said. "I was always impressed (with Presley). He was well mannered and a humble person. He was very gracious."

Asked about the gifts to hospital employees following stays at the facility, Elliot said: "The first I knew was when he gave the car to Mrs. (Marian) Cocke. It is contrary to hospital policy. We don't encourage it, but he was special."

Mrs. Cocke, a nurse at Baptist Hospital, was given a white Grand Prix because, "He knew how expensive it is to keep up a Cadillac," Elliot said.

Calls from around the globe— including calls from New Zealand, London, Anchorage, Alaska, Baltimore, New York, Los Angeles, and Canada—jammed the hospital's switchboard as word of Presley's death spread on the international news wire service, Elliot said.

Newsmen from across the nation began filing into the city last night and plane loads of reporters, fans and friends of the singer from across the world are expected into the city today.

A special edition of the Press-Scimitar was issued.

Memphis Press-Scimitar   August 17, 1977

Elvis Was to Wed On Christmas Day

Elvis Presley was to have officially announced his engagement to Ginger Alden, 20, on the first night of his Memphis appearance at Mid-South Coliseum, Mrs. Jo Alden, mother of Miss Alden, said today.

"Ginger and Elvis talked about it yesterday and he decided to announce their engagement at the concert August 27," Mrs. Alden said.

Mrs. Alden said her daughter was "still in a state of shock this morning" as she prepared to go to Graceland.

"We still can't believe it," Mrs. Alden said. "Ginger is under mild sedation," she said.

Elvis had given Miss Alden an engagement ring on January 26 and they were planning to get married in Memphis on Christmas Day, Mrs. Alden said. "She was having her dress designed in Los Angeles."

Mrs. Alden said Ginger had met Elvis in November when George Klein, former disc jockey and classmate and confidante of the singer, introduced them.

"Just last week Elvis and Charlie Hodge (a member of the singer's band) came to our house," Mrs. Alden said. "We gathered around the piano and he sang some of his old songs."

"He was such a good person and had a wonderful sense of humor." Mrs. Alden said. "He was really looking forward to starting his concert tour."

June 26, 1977—Elvis, Ginger, and Joe Esposito exit after the Last concert.

The Memphis Commercial Appeal   August 18, 1977

Carter Says Elvis is Symbol

WASHINGTON (UPI)—President Carter said Wednesday Elvis Presley "permanently changed the face of American popular culture" and became a worldwide symbol of his country's "vitality, rebelliousness and good humor."

The President, in a statement issued by the White House on Presley's death, said the popular singer was "unique" and is "irreplaceable."

"Elvis Presley's death deprives our country of a part of itself," Carter said. "His music and his personality, fusing the styles of white country and black rhythm and blues, permanently changed the face of American popular culture."

"His following was immense and he was a symbol to the people the world over of the vitality, rebelliousness and good humor of this country," Carter said.

Carter said Presley "burst upon the scene" more than 20 years ago "with an impact that was unprecedented and will probably never be equaled."

Thousands of mourners made the pilgrimage to Graceland.

Police, firemen, and the National Guard try to keep order.

The Memphis Commercial Appeal   August 18, 1977

Final Glimpse of Fallen Star Lures Faithful

by WILLIAM STEVERSON

Air National Guardsmen, police and firemen manned the gates of Graceland Mansion yesterday as thousands of persons, many openly weeping, gathered to mourn the death of Elvis Presley.

For most of the day, thousands flocked to the Whitehaven mansion, all hoping to get a chance to view the body of the king of rock and roll. Many saw those hopes vanish as a solid wall of policemen closed the iron gates to the house at 6:30 p.m.

The famous gates had been opened at 3 p.m. to allow fans of Presley to view his body in the foyer of his home. They were scheduled to close at 5, but because of the surging crowd, family members allowed the gates to remain open another hour and a half.

When 6:30 came, six officers manned each side of the gate and forced it closed while other policemen tried to restrain the last minute surge.

Tears rolled from the eyes of those closest to the front.

When an officer with a bullhorn asked the crowd to disperse, his request was met with chants of "No, no, no," and "One more hour."

After about 30 minutes, with the crowd still refusing to leave policemen

on motorcycles inched through the crowd with their sirens screaming and people began to leave. Shortly afterward policemen and sheriff's deputies picked up wooden barricades and walked into the crowd, pushing people away from the gate.

But even then hundreds still lingered, looking through the gate at the mansion.

Deputy Police Chief John Molnar said an estimated 50,000 to 100,000 persons visited Graceland during the day yesterday to pay their respects. He said as many as 20,000 persons were in the area at one time.

The crowd had dwindled to about 400 quiet mourners by late last night.

The mourners had come not only from Memphis, but from throughout the nation, many leaving their homes immediately after hearing of Presley's death Tuesday and driving all night to get here.

Private funeral services will be held at 2 this afternoon at Graceland. Presley's body will then be taken to Forest Hill Cemetery Midtown where he will be entombed in the cemetery's mausoleum.

Hotel and motel rooms in the city were booked solid through the week-

end, and spokesmen for passenger airlines said most planes arriving in the city also have been booked up. Delta Airlines added two flights from Atlanta to Memphis to help ease the demand.

Throughout the city there were scores of other tributes to Presley. Many radio stations devoted much of their air time to playing his records, and spokesmen for record stores said most of the stock of Presley albums has been depleted.

The Memphis Area Broadcasters Association said all stations in the organization would devote 60 seconds of silence to Presley's memory at 2 p.m. today.

In Nashville, Tennessee Gov. Ray Blanton ordered all state flags flown at half-staff today. The Constitutional Convention adopted a resolution calling Presley "an ambassador of the highest quality" for Tennessee. After passing the resolution, the delegates rose from their chairs for a minute of silent prayer.

Gov. Cliff Finch of Mississippi— the state of Presley's birth—declared today as an official day of mourning and ordered all state flags lowered to half-staff.

Spokesmen said hundreds of floral

wreaths and sacks of telegrams of sympathy were being sent to Graceland from all parts of the United States and from Elvis Presley fan clubs throughout the world.

The flamboyant entertainer, whose songs and pelvic movements created a cultural revolution in the United States in the 1950s, was found unconscious in his home Tuesday afternoon. He was rushed to Baptist Hospital where efforts to revive him were futile, and he was pronounced dead at 3:30 p.m. The Shelby County medical examiner's office said the death was caused by cardiac arrythmia, a form of heart attack.

After the autopsy at Baptist Hospital. Presley's body was taken to Memphis Funeral Home in Union. About 10:30 yesterday morning, as about 150 people looked on, the body was placed in a hearse with a police escort and taken down Elvis Presley Boulevard to Graceland.

Presley will be buried in a white suit, with dark blue tie and light blue shirt that his father gave him as a Christmas present.

Funeral Sermon Has Encouragement

By DEBORAH WHITE

C. W. Bradley, minister of Wooddale Church of Christ and longtime friend of the Elvis Presley family, presided at the entertainer's funeral services at Graceland mansion yesterday.

Bradley formerly was the minister at Whitehaven Church of Christ, where Presley's stepmother, Mrs. Dee Presley, is a member. It was through this association, he said, that he became close to the family. Following are excerpts from his funeral sermon:

"Words do not take away from a man's life in the sight of God. Though I will make several personal observations regarding Elvis, and from them seek to encourage us, it is not my purpose to try to eulogize him. This is being done by thousands throughout the world."

"We are here to honor the memory of a man loved by millions. Elvis can serve as an inspiring example of the great potential of one human being who has strong desire and unfailing determination. From total obscurity Elvis rose to world fame. His name is a household word, in every nook and corner of this Earth, though idolized by millions and forced to be protected from the crowds, Elvis never lost his desire to stay in close touch with humanity."

"Vernon told my wife and me one day while we ate and talked together that he had constantly stressed to Elvis that he must never forget his humble beginning. And I don't believe that he did. This could be seen in his regular contributions to so many who needed help. Truly I believe Elvis did not want to lose contact with humanity."

"In a society that has talked so much about the generation gap, the closeness of Elvis and his father and his constant dependence upon Vernon's counsel was heartwarming to observe. Elvis never forgot his family. In a thousand ways he showed his great love for them."

"In a world where so many pressures are brought upon us to lose our identity, to be lost in the masses, Elvis dared to be different. Elvis was different and no one else can ever be exactly like him. Wherever and whenever his voice was heard, everybody knew that was Elvis Presley."

"But Elvis was a frail human being. And he would be the first to admit his weaknesses. Perhaps because of his rapid rise to fame and fortune he was thrown into temptations that some

never experience. Elvis would not want anyone to think that he had no flaws or faults. But now that he's gone, I find it more helpful to remember his good qualities, and I hope you do, too."

"We are here to offer comfort and encouragement to Elvis' family. There is much encouragement in all the beautiful flowers sent by loving hands and hearts from around the world. There is much encouragement in the presence of so many who have crowded into our city in addition to those here. And also from knowing that literally millions throughout the Earth have their hearts turned in this direction at this hour. There is also much encouragement from the beautiful music. But the greatest comfort and strength come from knowing there is a God in Heaven who looks down upon us with love and compassion and who says, 'I will never leave you or forsake you.'"

Bradley then quoted the hymns by S.M.T. Henry displayed with this story and continued:

"We are here to be reminded that we too, must soon depart this life. The Bible vividly emphasizes the brevity and uncertainty of life. Once when King Saul was chasing David across the country, David said, 'There is but a step between me and death. And none of us knows when he shall take that step.'

"Elvis died at 42. Some of you may not live to be that old. But it's not how long we live that's really important, but how we live. If we reject the Bible then personally I find that life has no real meaning. The Bible teaches that God's plans and purposes for man culminated in the death and resurrection of His son on a cross, Jesus lives today. And because He lives, through Him we too can have hope of life beyond the grave.

"'O death, where is thy sting? O Grave, where is thy victory? The sting of death is sin; and the strength of sin is the law. But, thanks be to God; which giveth us the victory through our Lord Jesus Christ.' (I Corinthians, 15:55-57)

"Thus today I hold up Jesus Christ to all of us. And challenge each of you to commit your heart and life to Him. May these moments of quiet and thoughtful meditation and reflection on Elvis's life serve to help us also reflect upon our own lives and to re-examine our own lives. And may these moments help us to reset our compasses. All of us sometimes get going in the wrong direction."

Music magazines memorialize Elvis.

Swerving Car Kills Two Elvis Mourners

MEMPHIS (UPI)—An old-model car swerved toward a crowd of mourners outside the mansion where Elvis Presley lay in state early today, then "floor-boarded" into three women and a policeman in the street. Two teen-age girls were killed and another critically injured.

A patrolman, who gave chase and caught the car within a block, was injured slightly in a fight with the driver of the car, identified by police as Treatise Wheeler, 18, Memphis.

Wheeler was charged with two counts of second degree murder, drunk driving, leaving the scene, reckless driving and public drunkenness. He was held without bond.

Three juvenile girls in the car with Wheeler were charged with being accessories to second degree murder. Their names were not released.

Wheeler was driving a 1963 Ford Fairlane. When the officer who arrested him brought him back past the crowd to take him to jail, there were shouts of "Lynch 'em, hang him up."

"This really put a blemish on Elvis' memory. It seems like he just can't rest in peace," said Lynn Lassahn, 30, of Baltimore, among the hundreds outside the rock 'n roll superstar's mansion when the incident occurred.

The crowd had been holding an all-night vigil outside the 13-acre mansion, Graceland, where the body of Presley who died Tuesday of a heart ailment, lay

in state awaiting burial today in nearby Forest Hills Cemetery.

"The car came down the road," said Police Capt. G. L. Utley. "He swerved onto private property and then came back and hit the three ladies, who were in the middle of the road talking to a police officer. He appeared to floor-board it."

Patrolman W. Greenwood jumped out of the way, but the car struck the three girls and then sped on down the four-lane street named after Presley.

A policeman jumped into a parked patrol car and gave chase, catching the car within a block.

"He (the driver) came out fighting," said Utley, and the officer was hurt slightly in the altercation.

Utley said the grille and windshield of the car were smashed and police said a sixpack of beer, with two empties, was found on the front seat.

Two of the girls were pronounced dead on arrival at City of Memphis Hospital, according to Dr. Ralph Hamilton, and the other was hospitalized in critical condition.

The critically injured girl, taken to Methodist-South Hospital, was identified as Tammy Baiter, 17.

Police said the crowd was standing in the parking lot of a shopping center across the street from the iron gates to Graceland, where some 80,000 persons gathered Wednesday to pay their final respects to Presley.

Memphis Commercial Appeal
August 19, 1977

I know my heavenly
Father knows
The storms that would
my way oppose
For He can drive the
clouds away
And turn my darkness
into day.
I know my heavenly
Father knows
The balm I need to
soothe my woes
And with His touch of
love divine
He heals this wounded
soul of mine.
I know my heavenly
Father knows
How frail I am to meet
my foes
But He my cause will
e'er defend
Uphold and keep me to
the end.

The official funeral procession featured 16 white cars.

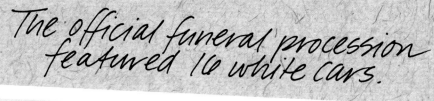

There were 5 official pallbearers: Joe Esposito, Dr. George Nichopoulos, Billy Smith, Charlie Hodge, and Lamar Fike.

Overcome with grief, Vernon Presley leaves the church.

287

Friday, August 19, 1977

From 'Floral Sea'
Wailing Elvis Fans to Receive Flowers

MEMPHIS, Tenn. (UPI)—Mourning Elvis Presley fans, barred from his private funeral, were promised a last souvenir today—a single flower each from the cemetery where the rock 'n roll superstar's body is sealed in a mausoleum.

Withered flowers plucked from a sea of 2,200 floral arrangements flanking the gray marble mausoleum were to be given to the mourners, who strained Thursday for a glimpse of the white hearse that carried Presley from Graceland, his 18-room mansion, to his final resting place at Forest Hill Cemetery.

Four miles from the midtown cemetery, only a handful of the 75,000 fans who had jammed the streets of Elvis Presley Boulevard during the three-day vigil, remained in front of the white-columned, hilltop mansion where Presley died Tuesday of heart failure at the age of 42.

An unusual floral arrangement

Memphis Commercial Appeal   August 20, 1977

TUPELO BUILDS FUND FOR ELVIS MEMORIAL

By Michael Arnold

TUPELO, MISS.—A special Elvis Presley birthplace memorial trust fund was established Friday at three Tupelo banks to finance a memorial to the famous singer at his boyhood home.

A commission will be appointed "as soon as possible" by Tupelo Mayor Clyde Whitaker to determine how the memorial funds will be spent. Whitaker has asked Tupelo residents to suggest names of persons to be appointed to the commission.

Mrs. Virginia Boyd, curator of the birthplace, said Friday that $900 was deposited to the trust by the East Heights Garden Club of Tupelo, which maintains the interior of the house and provides tours through it. She said additional contributions are being sought and donations may be sent to the Elvis Presley Birthplace Memorial Trust Fund, Tupelo, Miss.

On hand for the announcement were state Sen. Perrin Purvis, Reps. Tommy Brooks and Harold Montgomery, Vice Mayor James Williams, Lee County Board of Supervisors Chairman Charles Cain and Buster Davis, representing Gov. Cliff Finch.

Also at the announcement were the bank presidents who will administer the trust fund: Gene Berbette of the First Citizens Bank, Charles Causey of The Peoples Bank, and Jim Collins of the Bank of Mississippi.

The Presley birthplace, a white "shotgun" style frame house similar to many built here during the Depression, is managed by the Tupelo Park and Recreation Department.

Mrs. Dot Cooper, head of the department, said efforts have been made to keep the house "as authentic as possible." But those efforts have drawn complaints from a wide segment of the community that the department just doesn't want to spend money on the site.

Presley donated $10,000 to restore the house in 1956 and it is now surrounded by a 15-acre park with a swimming pool and recreation areas. Other two-room houses that lined the street next to the Presley place have been torn down.

Purvis said he hopes appointment of a bipartisan commission will get past conflict that has marked efforts to maintain the house.

Rep. Brooks said, "I think we're headed in the right direction by appointing a non-partisan advisory commission that can make decisions instead of selfish interest groups."

Memorials already suggested include expansion of the park around the birthplace, construction of a museum adjacent to the house or the building of a monument.

Brooks and Montgomery said they plan to offer a resolution during the special session of the Legislature scheduled in October memorializing Presley.

They said they may also offer a resolution to designate U.S. 78 between Tupelo and Memphis the Elvis Presley Memorial Highway, as suggested by Bobby Richardson, northern district highway commissioner for the state.

Meanwhile, Montgomery said Friday he has written NBC newscaster David Brinkley demanding a public apology for characterizing Elvis Presley as coming from a background of "poor white trash" during a special broadcast Tuesday night.

"Your reference to Elvis Presley and the community where he was raised as being 'poor white trash' was obviously not very well researched nor professionally presented," Montgomery wrote.

"Obviously you cannot distinguish between being poor and being 'white trash.' The latter phrase can apply to anyone, regardless of financial or material status."

Elvis's birthplace stands as a memorial.

288

Memphis Press-Scimitar   August 26, 1977

Presley Autopsy May Not Be Made Public

If an autopsy now under way shows that Elvis Presley died of unnatural causes, the report will be made public, Dr. Jerry Francisco, Shelby County Medical Examiner, said today.

"However, if it is found—and it now appears that it will be—that he died from natural causes, it will not be a Medical Examiner case, the private physician will sign the death certificate, and it will be up to the family whether to release the autopsy findings," Dr. Francisco said.

He said a portion of the autopsy is being done by the Medical Examiner's officer because Presley was found dead. An autopsy also is being performed at Baptist Hospital.

Dr. Francisco said the autopsy studies probably will continue for several weeks. Presley apparently died after a heart attack.

Memphis Press-Scimitar

The world press has been reporting inaccurately, that Elvis Presley died on Aug. 16, 1977, "two days after his mother, Gladys, died (Aug. 14) and at the same age, 42."

Those specializing in sensationalizing the news have gone on from that "fact" to say Elvis knew, or felt, he would die soon because his mother had died at age 42 in much the same way.

The fact is, Mrs. Gladys Presley was born April 25, 1912, died on Aug. 14, 1958—and unless they have changed rules in subtraction that makes her 46 at the time of her death.

Medical examiner Dr. Jerry Francisco announces the cause of death as heart failure.

Memphis Commercial Appeal   August 27, 1977

ELVIS' DEATH REPORT BLAMES HEART, LIVER

By BETH J. TAMKE

Elvis Presley's heart was enlarged, his liver contained fatty globules and he had an "abnormal amount" of hardening in the two main arteries leading to the heart, the Shelby County medical examiner said yesterday.

Dr. Jerry T. Francisco, who witnessed the autopsy and is conducting tests on the tissue samples, said yesterday his "provisional diagnosis" of the cause of death remains a heart attack.

"Hypertension, cardiovascular disease, atherosclerosis and coronary artery disease will probably play the major role" in Presley's death, the medical examiner said.

During an interview yesterday, Francisco said Presley's stomach contained "nothing identifiable" at the time of the autopsy. He also said his stomach had not been pumped during efforts to revive the singer.

Dr. George C. Nichopoulos, Elvis' personal physician, said earlier this week that the singer had been on a starvation diet and had eaten nothing for one and a half days prior to his death Aug. 16.

Francisco said if the singer had been on a crash diet prior to his death, it should not have contributed to the death.

He said Presley's heart was enlarged, weighing about 500 grams or [about] a pound, which is 50 to 75 per cent larger than normal. He said the enlargement could have been caused by the singer's labile (unstable) hypertension.

Francisco said he had been told that Presley's blood pressure was sometimes 160 systolic and 110 diastolic. Normally, blood pressure ranges from 100 to 150 systolic and 60 to 100 diastolic.

Nichopoulos said Presley's blood pressure sometimes was from 170 to 200 over 90 to 110 when he was under stress, and when resting it was 130 over 80.

The 42-year-old singer was constantly fighting a weight problem.

He weighed "more than 200 pounds," Francisco said. The medical examiner said he did not remember Presley's exact weight or the weight of his liver.

Elvis did not have an impacted colon at the time of his death, Francisco said. The singer had a history of colon problems since 1975, but the pathologist said it looked normal at the autopsy.

Francisco said there were no abnormalities found in the singer's throat, duodenum, bladder, pineal gland, spleen or arteries and veins in his limbs. There was no evidence of cancer, he said.

However, a source said Elvis had a slightly ulcerated larynx. The source also said Presley had cotton stuck in both ears at the time of death and puss indicating an ear infection was found in one ear.

The source also said examination of the singer's brain found absolutely nothing that could have led to his death. The source said all tests have not been completed, but thus far nothing has been found that could have caused the death.

Francisco said there were abnormal amounts of atherosclerosis, or hardening of the arteries leading to the heart.

The liver also contained an abnormal amount of fat globules in the hepatic cells.

"There is fat in the liver but to say it was covered with fat implies something that isn't true," Francisco said.

Francisco said he will stand by his original belief that Presley's death was caused by cardiac arrhythmia due to unknown cause, until the autopsy tests are completed, probably late next week.

He said the autopsy report will remain private unless the case becomes a medical examiner's matter or unless Presley's family decides to release it.

Memphis Commercial Appeal   August 27, 1977

Body Of Mother Of Elvis Moved To Mausoleum

By WILLIAM STEVERSON

The body of Gladys Love Presley, mother of Elvis Presley, was quietly unearthed and moved late yesterday into the mausoleum where her son was entombed last week.

In a 3-hour and 17-minute operation, 11 workers at Forest Hill Cemetery Midtown unearthed the massive steel and copper casket Mrs. Presley was buried in 19 years ago and sealed it into a crypt directly below the crypt containing the body of her son.

Vernon Presley, the entertainer's father, made the decision Thursday to move the body to the mausoleum.

Portions of the large tomb marking Mrs. Presley's grave were dismantled last night, but Ralph Davis, superintendent of the cemetery, said the five-foot tall cross and statuette of Christ will not be moved until Monday. He said his crews did not have the equipment necessary to handle the marble cross, which he estimated weighs more than 1,000 pounds.

No members of the Presley family witnessed the move, which began at 5:28 p.m. after the cemetery's gates had been locked. The only persons watching the 11 crew members exhume the body were four cemetery officials and two newsmen.

Davis said the move was not made public to ensure privacy for the Presley family. He said most employees at the cemetery were not told of the move, and the laborers were informed only minutes before they began work at the gravesite.

Mrs. Presley, who was 44 when she died in 1958, was buried a few hundred yards from the mausoleum.

The tombstone which marked Mrs. Presley's grave will be stored in a cemetery warehouse until the family decides where to place it, Davis said.

Before crews began digging at the gravesite, they removed a red carnation which had been placed at the grave earlier in the week by an unknown person, one of thousands who have come to Forest Hill to view the resting place of Presley and his mother.

Davis said the Presley family still has ownership of the plot in which Mrs. Presley was buried, but said he did not know what will be done with it.

Mrs. Presley's beige casket, identical to the one her son was entombed in least week, was buried in a copper-plated vault. After two hours and three minutes of digging with a backhoe and shovels, the vault was pulled from the ground and opened. The casket, without being opened, was then placed in the back of a pickup truck and carried to the mausoleum, where it was placed in the crypt beneath the unmarked crypt of Elvis.

A four-inch concrete slab was cemented over the crypt, and at 8:45 p.m. a solid block of white marble was locked into place in front of that.

Davis said when he met with Vernon Presley he obtained a signed statement giving the cemetery permission to move the body. Under Tennessee law, a permission statement must be signed by the surviving spouse or the remaining heirs before a body can be moved.

Davis said he and Vernon Presley discussed the possibility of placing the two bodies in a private mausoleum at the cemetery. However, he said no decision was made by Vernon Presley.

Gladys Presley was originally buried at this site.

Memphis Commercial Appeal   August 30, 1977

3 Charged in Body-Stealing Plot

By WILLIAM STEVERSON

Three Memphis men were charged yesterday with criminal trespassing in connection with what Police Director E. Winslow Chapman said was a plot to steal the entombed body of Elvis Presley.

The charges were made after police arrested the men who they saw fleeing from the mausoleum at Forest Hill Cemetery Midtown shortly after midnight.

Chapman claimed the three had conspired to break open the sealed crypt, take Presley's body from the casket and hold it for ransom.

Chapman said he did not know how much ransom the suspects planned to demand for return of the body.

The men were identified as Raymond M. Green, 25, of 981 Elizabeth Lane, Bruce Eugene Nelson, 30, of 5098 Quince and Ronnie Lee Adkins, 26, of 558 Storz. They were released on $50 bond each and face a preliminary hearing at 9 this morning in City Court Division 2.

A fourth suspect, arrested at Baptist Hospital shortly after the others were taken into custody near the cemetery, was released yesterday afternoon without being charged. Police did not give his name.

Chapman said the arrests came after police received a tip from a confidential source that there would be an attempt to steal the body of the entertainer who died Aug. 16.

Officers staked out the cemetery Friday and Saturday night and again Sunday night.

Chapman said police spotted the suspects near the cemetery Saturday, but that he thinks they were only in the area to check it out and did not intend to attempt to take Presley's body at that time.

Chapman said officers were hidden only a few dozen yards from the mausoleum early Monday when the suspects began [rattling] the large iron gate blocking the rear entrance of the mausoleum.

According to Chapman, the men entered the area shortly after midnight by climbing over a fence at the rear of the cemetery.

He said that at about 12:30 a.m. lights of a car traveling on Hernando behind the cemetery shined at the suspects who were at the mausoleum gate, and they apparently became frightened and began running.

The suspects were not armed and had no explosives, Chapman said. He said a shotgun was found in the trunk of the car.

Chief Roy Taylor of Special Officers, Inc., a private security force which patrols the cemetery, said three of the four suspects spotted at the mausoleum gates got into a car and sped away north on Hernando, then east on Person near the intersection with Elvis Presley Blvd.

The fourth suspect scaled the Interstate 240 fence and got away, Taylor said. Police said the man apparently injured a leg while fleeing, and was arrested when he went to Baptist Hospital for treatment. They gave no explanation why he was not charged.

Taylor said police took a number of weapons out of the car along with some type of explosive. However, Chapman said the shotgun in the trunk was the only weapon and there were no explosives.

Presley Is Target of Bodysnatchers

Fan Club button

Fans view the mausoleum where Elvis's body was later placed.

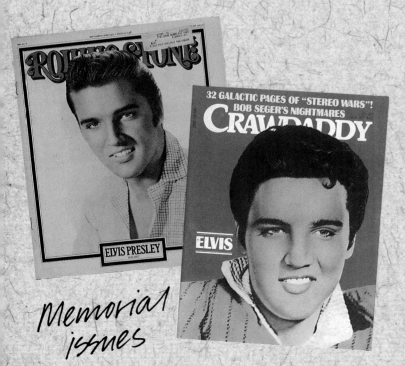

Memorial issues

Memphis Commercial Appeal   August 23, 1977

ELVIS' WILL NAMES 3 CLOSE RELATIVES

By Lawrence Busier

Elvis Presley named his father, Vernon Presley, executor of his fortune in a will probated here yesterday afternoon, but did not include his fiancee, Miss Ginger Alden, one of three witnesses who signed the will March 3, or his ex-wife Priscilla.

An inventory of the singer's wealth, believed to be millions of dollars is not expected to be filed for 60 days, but the will directs the elder Presley, 62, to distribute the net income for the welfare of himself, the singer's daughter, Lisa Marie Presley, and his grandmother, Mrs. Minnie Mae Presley.

The will was probated in a small room adjacent to the Probate Clerk's office during a 20-minute session before Probate Court Judge Joseph Evans.

The elder Presley, his attorney, Beecher Smith II, and guitarist Charlie Hodge and Smith's wife, Mrs. Ann Dewey Smith, both of whom also signed the will, were present.

Presley, who was hustled from the courthouse by two Shelby County Sheriff's deputies to a waiting white Lincoln Continental, declined to comment on the will.

"At this time we will have to let the will speak for itself," Smith said later.

According to the terms of the will, which was drawn up at Graceland, the elder Presley will receive his son's personal property, "including trophies and other items accumulated by me during my professional career."

He also will have "complete freedom and discretion as to disposal of any and all such property so long as he shall act in good faith and in the best interest of my estate."

Besides excluding the singer's former wife and his fiancee, Presley named no charitable organization as a beneficiary.

Priscilla Presley received more than $1.5 million in the couple's divorce settlement in 1973.

Miss Alden said the will was drawn up last March on the day Presley took her and her two sisters to Hawaii for a 10-day vacation.

"I was downstairs (at Graceland) until they called me up to sign it," she said yesterday. "There was no discussion. All I did was sign it."

She said she had not expected to be named in the will, even though she said she had accepted an engagement ring from Presley Jan. 26.

The will also authorizes the elder Presley to see to the health, education and welfare of "such other relatives of mine living at the time of my death who in the absolute discretion of (Vernon Presley) are in need of emergency assistance."

Upon the deaths of Elvis' father and grandmother, all remaining assets of the trust will go to Lisa Marie when she reaches age 25, according to the will.

The 13-page will was recorded and filed by Probate Court Clerk Bobby J. Dunavant after signatures were verified. Presley was shown to have been of sound mind and the will was recognized by the court to be authentic.

Presley authorized his father to appoint a successor to handle the trust and stated in the will that if the elder Presley is unable to continue as executor, the National Bank of Commerce in Memphis shall be appointed to oversee the trust.

The will does not call for the elder Presley or any appointees of the trust to furnish a bond or security for performance of specified duties of the will.

In addition to the inventory Vernon Presley makes of the assets, state and federal tax departments will make their own inventories to determine the amount of inheritance taxes to be paid.

Evans said yesterday the will likely will be "the biggest ever filed in the State of Tennessee."

Dunavant said the usual period in which an inventory is filed is about two months, but said yesterday the Presley will may be an exception.

"The size and complexity of it may cause them to run into difficulty in filing it in 60 days," he said.

Last Stop on the Mystery Train
An American legend: Elvis Presley 1935-77

Elvis's last LP before his death, plus a tribute LP by Elvis's backup group

ELVIS IN CONCERT

2 RECORD SET

APL 2-2587

ORIGINAL SOUNDTRACK RECORDING FROM THE CBS-TV SPECIAL PLUS ADDITIONAL SONGS RECORDED ON TOUR JUNE 1977.

ELVIS' Favorite Gospel Songs

QCA 362 STEREO

SUNG BY J.D. SUMNER & THE STAMPS QUARTET

FEATURING: "ELVIS HAS LEFT THE BUILDING"

Stereo Review

Elvis Has Left the Building

ELVIS PRESLEY was many different things to many different people—such was the nature of his special gifts and powers—but above all else, as three widely varying new albums suggest, he was a religious man. Indeed, this may be the only part of the Elvis myths that everyone agrees on. Both Merle Haggard's *My Farewell to Elvis* and J. D. Sumner and the Stamps' *Elvis' Favorite Gospel Songs* contain tributes to Elvis that stress his religiousness. Presley's own final album, *Elvis in Concert*, is highlighted by his reading of the gospel song "How Great Thou Art," which also appears on the Sumner album; according to Sumner, Elvis always called it "my song."

These three new releases are just the crest of the first wave of Elvis-related albums we can expect to see released in the coming year. It is pointless to ask whether they were done for money or for love, since they were obviously done for both. Fallen country stars have always inspired a rash of tribute albums—there were more than a dozen for Hank Williams—and country traditions die hard. Besides, Elvis was tastelessly and relentlessly commercialized (with his blessing) all his performing life, and there is no reason to expect anything different now. . . .

The New Yorker, August 29, 1977

. . . The only decent tribute I saw to Elvis was in the hallway of a building at the corner of Sullivan and Prince Streets. Somebody had put an old pair of blue shoes on a chest of drawers in the hallway with a handwritten sign. "Don't Step on My Blue Suede Shoes—In Memory of Elvis," the sign said.

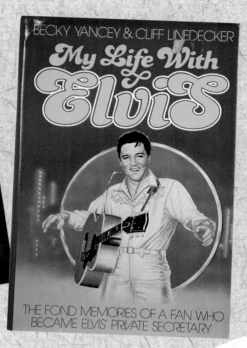

The Unique Appeal of Elvis Presley's Music Now Carries Over to Books About Him

Elvis Presley died, and a unique refrain in American music came to an abrupt end. Millions mourned him and reached out for anything to prolong memories. Record sales were staggering. Film retrospectives of Presley movies were immediately announced. Books made some of the most astonishing news of all. . . .

Elvis Was Getting Well

Elvis Presley adorers are still furious at the allegations by his ex-bodyguards that the late singer was on drugs during some of the unhappy phases of his incredible life and career.

However, I do ask Elvis lovers (of which I count myself one) to think rationally. If Elvis used uppers, downers and an occasional sniff of cocaine, does this really destroy fine memories of him or of his fantastic and unique talent: I think not. Anyone who abuses drugs is to be pitied, and I think it's important to try to know the truth about one whose life was fraught with all the vagaries of fame and success, the pressure of too much money, too many willing girls and too easy access to stimulants and depressants. . . .

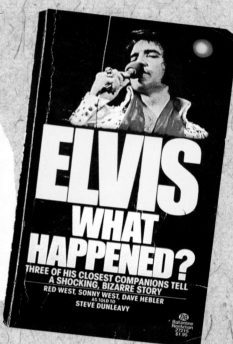

The infamous bodyguard bio released just 15 days before Elvis's death

Elvis fans hang onto $600,000 worth of tickets

Had Elvis Presley lived, more than 120,000 people would have paid about $1,300,000 to hear the overweight superstar belt out his famous songs during a 12-city tour that was to have ended Sunday night in Memphis.

But when the 42-year-old Presley died of a heart attack on Aug. 16, one day before the tour was to have begun, he left more than a legacy behind him.

Promoters, theater owners, and lawyers must now tackle a problem they rarely encounter—what to do with an estimated $600,000 in tickets adoring fans refuse to give up. . . .

Bodies of Elvis, Mother Are Moved

The bodies of Elvis Presley and his mother were moved to Graceland from Forest Hill Cemetery Midtown in a quick nighttime operation.

The move was unannounced. Two white hearses escorted by eight city police officers and five Shelby County deputies took the bodies of Elvis Presley and his mother, Mrs. Gladys Smith Presley, into the rear entrance of Graceland shortly after 7 last night. The move was completed by 8:30, police said.

The move had been set for 6 a.m. today, but last night was chosen because it was felt traffic would be lighter and the possibility of an incident would be less.

Police said there were no incidents.

Only a few watchers were outside the gates of Graceland when the cortege arrived, and at first some did not realize what they had seen.

The bodies were buried at the Graceland Prayer Garden Chapel. Vernon Presley, father of the singer, has said the graves will be under 24-hour guard and monitored by closed circuit television.

Elvis's body was entombed in the Forest Hill Mausoleum Aug. 18, two days after his unexpected death at age 42. His mother's body had been buried in Forest Hill Cemetery since her death at 46 on Aug. 14, 1958. Her body was moved to the Forest Hill Mausoleum after Elvis died.

The idea of moving the bodies from the cemetery to Graceland was first considered after an unsuccessful attempt on Aug. 28 to steal Elvis' body and hold it for ransom. Also, the crush of visitors to Forest Hill has inconvenienced many who wanted to visit graves of relatives. Souvenir hunters also have caused some problems.

The Board of Adjustment gave permission last Wednesday to rebury the bodies on the south side of Graceland estate. The 13-acre Graceland grounds are walled and patrolled by private guards.

This Inscription on Elvis' Tomb

*He was a precious gift from God
We cherished and loved dearly.*

*He had a God-given talent that he shared
With the world. And without a doubt,
He became most widely acclaimed;
Capturing the hearts of young and old alike.*

*He was admired not only as an entertainer,
But as the great humanitarian that he was;
For his generosity, and his kind feeling
For his fellow man.*

*He revolutionized the field of music and
Received its highest awards.*

*He became a living legend in his own time,
Earning the respect and love of millions.*

*God saw that he needed some rest and
Called him home to be with Him.*

*We miss you, Son and Daddy. I thank God
That He gave us you as our son.*

By Vernon Presley

Portrait of a grieving father :

Vernon pays tribute to his son.

No peace, even in death

Elvis and his mother were moved to Meditation Gardens soon after the bodysnatching scare.

Memphis Press-Scimitar   November 2, 1977

Doctor Group Shuns Elvis Issue

Memphis and Shelby County Medical Society has issued what one doctor termed "a non-committal statement" in the controversy surrounding the death of Elvis Presley.

Barring all but doctors and members from the auditorium at University of Tennessee Center for the Health Sciences, the organization last night voted to issue a statement that the society "had had no request from any authoritative body to evaluate the cause of death of Elvis Presley and we have no factual information regarding this matter."

Dr. Thomas Dorrity, president, said after the meeting the medical society will not seek any further information in the matter.

"Since we had no factual information this is the best we could do," he said. "We don't know what

the pathologist autopsy said. We don't know what the medical examiner's report said. It's like asking me to review a play I haven't seen."

A number of doctors voted against issuance of the statement, Dorrity said. The discussion of the autopsy was brought before the body because of controversy surrounding the cause of death of the 42-year-old singer who died Aug. 16, he said.

Dr. Jerry T. Francisco, Shelby County medical examiner, ruled that Presley died of hypertensive heart disease with coronary artery heart disease as a contributing factor.

Some autopsy results, however, indicate that Presley's body contained codeine, Placidyl and barbiturates, and that death may have been caused from a combination of drugs.

Memphis Commercial Appeal   October 19, 1977

Multiple Drugs May Be Ruled As Cause Of Elvis' Death

By BETH J. TAMKE

Multiple drugs may be ruled as the cause of death for Elvis Presley by Dr. Jerry T. Francisco, Shelby county medical examiner, sources told The Commercial Appeal yesterday.

Francisco and his staff met last night to review the information in the autopsy completed this week in an effort to decide what cause of death to place on the singer's death certificate.

The medical examiner, contacted at his office late yesterday, would neither confirm nor deny the reports, but said he would probably

hold a press conference on the autopsy Friday.

Francisco, along with Dr. Eric C. Muirhead, chief of pathology at Baptist Hospital, and several others met with Vernon Presley, the singer's father and the executor of the estate, yesterday afternoon to review the autopsy reports.

Sources said Presley was told his son had 10 drugs in his bloodstream at the time of death and they probably contributed to the death.

Among the drugs found in the bloodstream, sources said, were an antihistamine often used to control

hay fever or allergies; codeine, a derivative of opium that resembles morphine but is milder in action—less habit-forming—and is often used to relieve pain and found in some cough medicines; Demerol, a narcotic used as a sedative and analgesic, and several tranquilizers including Valium.

The sources said the drugs were all within prescribed levels but the interaction of all of them had an effect on the singer's diseased heart, which was at least 50 per cent larger than normal.

Pathologists and laboratory

specialists have been trying to determine the cause of the singer's death since Aug. 16 when he was rushed to Baptist Hospital after being found unconscious on the floor of an upstairs bathroom at Graceland.

One of the theories says the way he fell to the floor and the position he was in also contributed to the death. One source said Elvis apparently fainted or passed out while sitting in the bathroom and fell to the floor with his knees bent under his torso, cutting off circulation to his legs.

Long live the King

1977 – Present

" ... Elvis was and remained a working class hero, a man who rose from obscurity and transformed American popular art in answer to his own needs – and who may have possibly been destroyed by the isolation that being an American celebrity sometimes entails. He was as much a metaphor as a maker of music, and one, of telling power and poignancy."

John Rockwell
The New York Times

Many Are Cashing In On Memory of Elvis

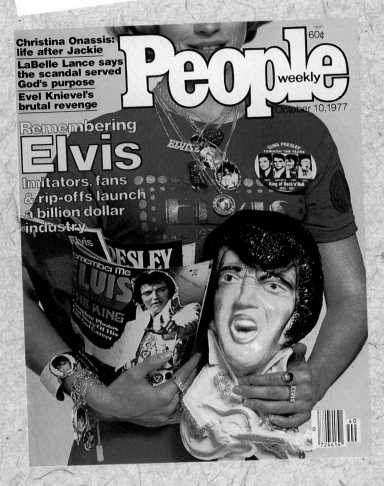

People weekly · October 10, 1977 · 60¢

Christina Onassis: life after Jackie

LaBelle Lance says the scandal served God's purpose

Evel Knievel's brutal revenge

Remembering **Elvis**

Imitators, fans & rip-offs launch a billion dollar industry

Souvenir buttons

Memphis Commercial Appeal   September 5, 1977

By AMANDA McGEE

The king is dead. But his memory is living not only in the hearts of fans but on T-shirts and bumper stickers and key rings; in magazine articles and special editions and paperback books; and in a blade of grass or broken tree branch from the lawn of Graceland Mansion.

Elvis Presley brought rock and roll into the forefront of American music. His initial appeal was only to the young, who were as fascinated with the beat of his music as with the swing of his hips. As his first fans grew up and had families, Presley's appeal remained and each year he gained more fans who were convinced he was the king.

But with the coming of the music of rock came other singers, some going out as fast as they came in, but on top of it all was Elvis, whose concerts continued to sell out year after year.

When the Beatles hit the music scene, so did Beatlemania with American youth buying Carnaby Street clothing and cutting their hair in the famous Beatle Bob. And although fans of Presley's music did not imitate his style, he was remembered.

In the aftermath of his death Aug. 16, anything and everything that was remotely connected with Elvis is being bought, borrowed, or stolen. . .

- A clump of grass from the lawn in front of the mausoleum where he is entombed. . .
- A twig or piece of a branch from a tree that overhangs the walls of Graceland Mansion. . .
- A broken guitar string. . . .
- A piece of styrofoam or a wilting flower from one of the many offerings left at the mausoleum in his memory. . .
- Anything that says "Elvis". . .
- T-shirts, patches on blue jeans and purses. . .
- Bumper stickers and posters. . .
- Key rings, jewelry, ball point pens, and buttons. . .
- Copies of his will. . .
- Reproductions of the concert tickets sold for his scheduled appearances in the city or the real thing. . .
- His records including copies of his first single for Sun. . .
- Copies of the films he made box office hits. . .
- Cassette tapes of Elvis himself, talking about himself. . .
- License plates. . .
- Editions of newspapers carrying Presley's story, special editions of both and books. . .

"I guess a lot of us, especially around here, took Elvis for granted. We all expected him to die an old man and all of a sudden he was gone," said Jim Godown, owner of T-shirts International. "I think the overall demand for Elvis souvenirs has naturally come because of [his death]."

Godown's firm has never printed any shirts dealing with Elvis before his death. He said the company had once drawn up some speculative art for a shirt but it was never printed.

"We had never really gotten into retail printing until recently but when we were doing cartoon printing, we rarely got requests for something to do with Elvis. But now everything we have that has Elvis on it is doing fine."

Another T-shirt firm, the Great American T-Shirt Co., had carried an Elvis shirt in stock for a little over a year. On his death, the firm ordered another type of shirt to add to the stack.

"Every other customer who comes in here wants one. When we heard about the death, we ordered as many shirts as we could get," said salesman Mike Chiles, "We'll order them as long as people want them. . . ."

ELVIS PRESLEY
INTERVIEWS AND MEMORIES OF:
The Sun Years

$4.99 REMOVABLE STICKER

The Sun Years bootleg LP

Belt buckle taken off the market for licensing infraction

Elvis dollar

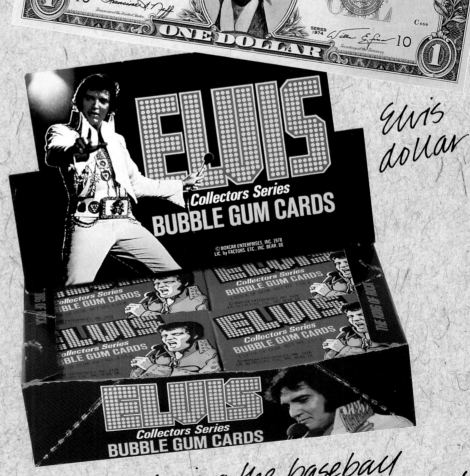

Newsweek   January 30, 1978

The Spoils Of Elvis

... **Exclusive Rights:** Shortly after Presley's death, his manager, Col. Tom Parker, made an agreement with Factors Etc., Inc., giving it exclusive rights to produce and market all Elvis memorabilia. "I didn't even like Elvis's music," says Factors president Harry Geissler, "but I was a fan of Colonel Parker. He's the king of promoters. I'm the king of merchandisers. It was only natural we got together." RCA Corp., which sold more than 500 million Presley records before his death, will not release sales figures since then but last week reported record corporation profits for the fourth quarter, spurred by "extraordinary posthumous demand" for Presley's records.

For Elvis zealots, no item is too trivial. Geissler has already brought his Elvis line to shows in Memphis and Chicago and now plans to tour nationwide. Fans are offered the chance to peruse items ranging from 15-cent bubble-gum packs to solid-gold $850 medallions—or to opt for such middle-range exotica as Elvis Christmas-tree ornaments, Elvis dollar bills ($3.50 a piece), Elvis wristwatches, gold-plated Elvis belt buckles and gold-plated replicas of the singer's army dog tag. Geissler says he turns down ideas he thinks are "duds or in bad taste." He gave the no-no, for example, to a company that wanted to market an Elvis air freshener. "You're going to see the Elvis market move away from the junk stuff entirely," he says, adding that negotiations are under way for a line of Elvis clothes and cosmetics. . . .

Before entering the baseball card market, Donruss produced Elvis bubblegum cards.

Bubblegum packs made to look like albums

Spanish-language fanzine

ELVIS WAS MURDERED!

The Motive: $500 Million
The Means: Poison Or Drugs

Rumors are sweeping the entertainment world that Elvis Presley was murdered.

The motive was money—not the several millions that Elvis had on hand at the time of his death, but the millions in anticipated revenues certain to be generated if Elvis died.

This money certainly has been forthcoming. Since mid-August 1977 the time of Presley's death, more than $500 million has poured into the entertainer's estate from the sale of records and thousands of souvenir items.

This is more money than Elvis had earned during the past 10 years he was alive. Some inside sources believe the sum actually surpasses Elvis' entire earnings during his 21 years as a superstar.

What's more, the money is expected to keep rolling in for years to come. One family intimate estimates the income to level off at no less than $100 million a year by 1981.

"There's no doubt that Elvis is worth far more dead than alive," he admits. "I'm sure that this is how these rumors about foul play got started."

Many, many persons have benefited financially from Elvis' death. Foremost among these are his father, his grandmother, his aunt and his long-time manager, Col. Tom Parker.

Elvis' 10-year-old daughter, Lisa, when she becomes 21, will receive funds now held in trust which probably will make her the world's richest woman, richer than Christina Onassis.

Presley's last girlfriend, Ginger Alden, is on her way to being a movie star thanks to her involvement with The King. His ex-bodyguards are counting a fortune from the sale of a book about their former boss—a book which strangely appeared the same week Elvis died.

Another book, by Elvis' ex-secretary Becky Yancey, couldn't find a publisher before the entertainer's death. Now it is a best-seller.

"Thanks to the fact that Elvis died mysteriously, when he supposedly was recovering his health after several scares and collapses, the rumors of murder are easy to believe," confides a Memphis police official.

"He could have been given a fatal overdose of a deadly drug, or an untraceable poison. It is very strange that his body lay undetected for hours although people were in the house.

"It can be construed that someone made sure he wasn't discovered to insure that he had time to die.

"However, the department is not launching a murder investigation because rumors are rumors and facts are facts, and you have to have facts to go on." Meanwhile, the money keeps rolling in. A good deal of it is going to people who never knew Elvis and who never were within 1,000 miles of him while he lived.

For instance, at New York's Statler-Hilton hotel, promoters recently put on display four lifesized dummies of Presley, dressed in clothes similar to those he wore onstage. Fans paid $5 to $10 a person for the privilege of viewing a lifelike Elvis dummy. A total of 35,000 people showed up.

An American businessman is busy in London, selling one-inch-square parcels of land from Presley's property in Mississippi. The promoter paid a stiff price for two acres of the land, but stands to profit by several millions by selling the tiny bits of real estate. Most of the "landowners" never will be able to visit their property.

In Las Vegas, the Hilton Hotel unveiled a bronze statue of Elvis and is charging tourists $8.25 a head just for looking at it. The sculptor, Carl Romanelli, shares in the bonanza and may soon be as rich as the late Pablo Picasso.

In 1954 and 1955, Elvis cut five records on the Tennessee-based Sun label. These were minor hits in the country-and-western market. Today, these records sell to collectors for $200 a piece and up, depending on condition. The jackets they originally came in bring even more since few exist.

"The whole money machine which has been in high gear since Elvis' death gives me the creeps and it's easy to believe that someone might have foreseen all of this and helped Elvis depart from this world," mutters a famed celebrity columnist.

"In most instances, a portion of the money goes directly to those who controlled Elvis. In his grave, Elvis is making millions for a lot of people."

The Men Who Would Be Elvis

Are They Helping or Hurting His Memory?

THE PRESLEY IMITATORS

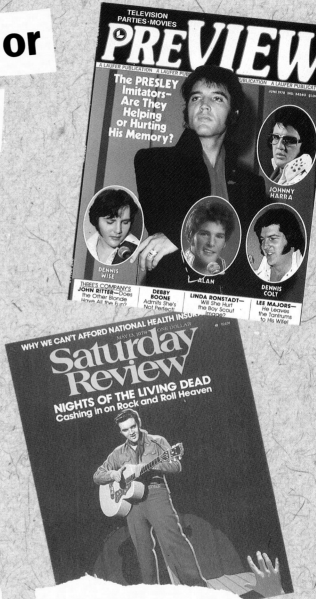

by FLANZY LEWIS

Elvis Presley is probably more popular today than he was five years ago . . .

As shocking as that statement may be to many of his fans, if you are one of the thousands—perhaps millions—who have bought records, photographs, memorabilia, or a xerox copy of Elvis' autopsy report, don't be offended. At first, the excessive promotion of Elvis items may seem crass while the excessive buying of these items appears ludicrous. But upon further examination, one must see that the merchandising of Elvis may ensure his immortality.

Undeniably, Elvis was more than a "likeness" stamped on a solid-gold medallion that sells for $850. He was more than the voice that's sold over 500 million records since his death. He was more than the lasting memorial that Graceland has become. Elvis was a phenomenon and, to truly appreciate him, one had to experience him in performance. But for far too many, that is not possible since the public was robbed of the opportunity by the 'King's' untimely death. For his fans now and for generations to come, the only hope of experiencing Elvis now is vicariously through an impersonator

There appears to be a definite need for Elvis "perform-alikes" . . .

or "illusionist." There appears to be a definite need for Elvis "perform-alikes." Yet, one wonders if the hundreds who are now doing that "King of Rock 'n' Roll's" act are also doing Elvis's image justice. Can so many people be that good at presenting the illusion of a performer who was considered unique? If the answer is no, then perhaps instead of helping to make Elvis immortal, they're making him into a dime-a-dozen-performer which younger generation will look at and ask: What was all the fuss about?

Many Elvis "perform-alikes" consider themselves "illusionists," not "imperson-ators." The reason most give is that they are not trying to imitate Presley, but rather create the "illusion" of him as a performer. Theoretically speaking, making the distinction is important. But from a practical point of view—well, as Gertrude Stein once said: "A rose is a rose is a rose. . . ."

> In the months since his untimely death, Elvis Presley's memory has been elevated to staggering legendary proportions. His films, records, and Presley memorabilia have become a tremendous and lucrative industry by themselves. But of all the tributes paid to the late "King of Rock 'n' Roll"—the most fascinating can only be the growing army of Presley imitators . . .

Rolling Stone   March 23, 1978

Elvis Presley: imitations in spirit and flesh

MORE THAN A HUNDRED impersonators are keeping the Elvis Presley legend alive throughout the United States (over thirty in Chicago alone), with shows ranging from small nightclub acts to sophisticated Las Vegas productions . . . .

ONE YEAR WITHOUT ELVIS

This album, which included a bonus greeting card, was released a year after Elvis's death.

His Loving Father's Memories

ALMOST A YEAR after Elvis Presley's death—which occurred on August 16, 1977—his records, movies and television specials are as popular as ever, if not more so. With these, his devoted fans can cheer and console themselves for years to come.

But there is one man for whom Elvis can never be replaced by vinyl, film or tape—his beloved father, Vernon Presley.

As Vernon bends all his efforts to please those devoted fans of Elvis with a mammoth convention in September at the Las Vegas Hilton, where Elvis played many times and never to an empty seat—a convention where a bronze statue of Elvis will be unveiled and the hotel's showroom will be renamed in his honor—Vernon has to turn inward for his own consolation.

For Vernon Presley has more memories of Elvis than does anyone else in the world going back to the very day when he was born on January 8, 1935. And it is those memories, most of them sunny but a few veiled in shadow that he must be calling up for companionship as the first anniversary of Elvis' death arrives. . . .

'ELVIS WAS THE LIGHT THAT SHINED ON EVERYBODY': A YEAR OF GRIEF, CONFUSION, RICHES

They flock to his Memphis mansion by the thousands every day—pilgrims shuffling down Elvis Presley Boulevard toward the charismatic relics of his life and his death a year ago. They pry the stones from the wall around Graceland, they steal bouquets from the grave, they rail against his death. Some angrily insist he is still alive and in hiding. Each morning hundreds of fresh flowers arrive. Without fail, two California girls send the same token of their grief every week—an arrangement in the shape of a broken heart.

His force and following seem undiminished. This week no less than 150,000 people are expected to converge on Memphis for the anniversary vigil and tribute. Presley enterprises continue to grow as bullishly as if he were still alive—perhaps even more so—forging a multi-million-dollar estate so complex it will take years to measure and untangle. Graceland remains as he left it. His upstairs living quarters have been locked, his clothes left hanging in the closets. His three cars stand idle.

Nothing is changed and everything is different. . . .

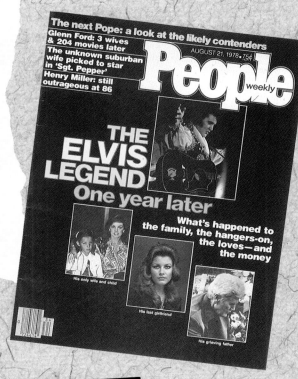

Souvenir button

A tribute album from Canada

TIME   August 28, 1978

Hound Dog Days in Memphis

A city survives labor turmoil and Presley mourners

It is a year since Elvis' death, and mourners are making the pilgrimage to Memphis and the grave of the rock king at his mansion known as Graceland. But the streets are eerily quiet as the evening advances. Only the buzzing of summer locusts in the crape myrtle trees breaks the silence. The police have been on strike for six days, and Mayor Wyeth Chandler, declaring a "state of civil emergency," has imposed a dusk to dawn curfew . . .

. . . The strikes and the curfew have persuaded some Elvis fans to stay home, but the hotels are still nearly 80% full (they had been booked solid for weeks in advance), and about 100,000 admirers have come to Memphis from the nearby dirt farms and even from as far away as Japan. . . .

A French import album

Drug testimony a bitter pill for Elvis fans to swallow

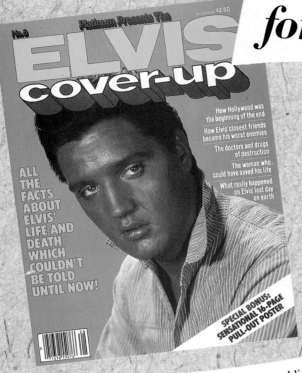

ELVIS cover-up

Platinum Presents The

No.8 $2.50

How Hollywood was the beginning of the end

How Elvis' closest friends became his worst enemies

The doctors and drugs of destruction

The woman who could have saved his life

What really happened on Elvis' last day on earth

ALL THE FACTS ABOUT ELVIS' LIFE AND DEATH WHICH COULDN'T BE TOLD UNTIL NOW!

SPECIAL BONUS: SENSATIONAL 16-PAGE PULL-OUT POSTER

Newsweek   January 25, 1980

DID ELVIS DIE FROM DRUG ABUSE?

. . . Late in the week, [Dr. George] Nichopoulos, 52, was found guilty of indiscriminately prescribing and dispensing controlled substances for ten patients, including Presley. He was found, for example, to have prescribed at least 10,000 pills for Presley in the twenty months before the singer died. The board voted to suspend Nichopoulos's license for three months and to place him on three years' probation. But the board also judged Dr. Nick not guilty of the more serious charges of gross incompetence, gross ignorance and malpractice. And it determined that he had "no involvement" in Elvis's death. . . .

. . . **ELVIS' TRUE** fans, [Beth Pease] believes, have a mystic relationship with him.

"You're going to think I'm right off the wall, but I'm not," [Beth] said. "I am a born-again Christian and I go to the Assembly of God Church. I have a friend who said she sees Elvis' image in the tiles in her shower with an angel floating above him. And she said the tree out in her yard—sometimes its branches look like Elvis singing into a microphone."

He means so much to her today that when she dies, she said, "I have left instructions for them to play Elvis singing 'Amazing Grace' at my funeral."

All the talk about the drugs that killed him . . . it doesn't matter to Elvis' true believers.

"I believe Elvis was called home to heaven to go up there and lead the biggest choir ever led," she said. "Who else in the world could sing like that? Who else in the world could lead heaven's choir?"

. . . **Medical examiner** Jerry Francisco, was not obligated to release results of Elvis Presley's autopsy to reporters because the post mortem had been requested by the star's father and not the state, the Tennessee Supreme Court ruled Monday. A suit against Francisco was filed by two reporters with the ABC program *20/20* after reports said the singer's body contained traces of drugs. Presley died in Memphis, Tenn., Aug. 16, 1977, with the official cause of death listed as a heart attack.

Vernon Presley 1916-1979

by Jerry Hopkins

. . . In 1975, just after Elvis' fortieth birthday, and his father's fifty-ninth, Vernon had his first heart attack and Elvis fell ill from exhaustion. The two shared adjacent hospital rooms.

After Elvis died, Vernon moved into Graceland with a nurse, whom some thought he would marry. There as his own health failed, he continued to supervise the business of the lucrative and thriving Elvis estate. He appeared in public frequently such as when the Las Vegas Hilton Hotel unveiled a life-sized statue of his son.

Vernon entered Baptist Hospital in late May complaining of an irregular heartbeat. He died a month later, a millionaire.

As fans commemorated Elvis's 50th birthday in 1985, they also viewed the graves of Vernon and Minnie Mae Presley alongside those of Elvis and his mother in Meditation Gardens.

'This Is Elvis': a film that loves him tender

Soundtrack album

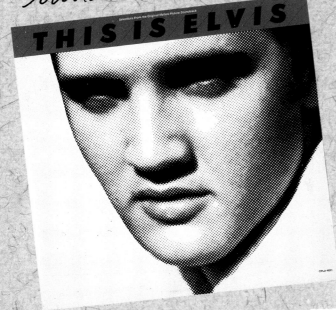

The docu-drama This Is Elvis re-enacted parts of Elvis's life. David Scott played Elvis at 18.

Film recalls life down at the end of Lonely Street

Memphis, Tenn.— Advisory to theater owners who book *This Is Elvis*, the Warner Bros. documentary: Stock plenty of Kleenex at the snack bar. For Presley fans, this is potent stuff.

The David L. Wolper production, which opened this week at 400 theaters in the South and will wind its way around the rest of the country, offers plenty of the celebrative moments during the rise and reign of rock's greatest star.

Through clips from home movies and outtakes from other films, *This Is Elvis* gives us a glimpse of the unguarded Presley: relaxing with his family at Christmas, horseback riding with his wife Priscilla, and clowning with his buddies. In one of the film's most amusing— and revealing—moments, Presley discovers that his boasts about sexual pursuits are being picked up by the microphone, and he quickly tries to cover up good-naturedly by singing an old gospel tune, "A Friend of Jesus."

We also get to see scenes from several early Presley TV appearances, including a marvelous 1960 segment with Frank Sinatra, where Sinatra sings Elvis' "Love Me Tender" while Presley sings Sinatra's "Witchcraft." And: There's the expected spectacular concert footage.

The final 20 minutes of *This Is Elvis*, however, centers on Presley's decline. The most powerful sequence is during the singer's final concert swing, when the bloated Presley looks so ill you wonder how he even made it to the arena. . .

. . . Malcolm Leo and Andrew Solt, who wrote, produced and directed *This Is Elvis*, began thinking about a Presley documentary while making their highly acclaimed 1979 *Heroes of Rock 'n' Roll* TV special. . .

. . . But there was no footage of Elvis before the age of 21, or of certain other key moments that Solt and Leo felt were essential to the story. So they decided on a risky (and sometimes intrusive) approach: about 20 minutes of "dramatic recreation," using four Elvis look-alikes, to cover different periods in his life. . . .

305

Elvis Presley's Graceland: An American Shrine

3764 Elvis Presley Boulevard

House & Garden

by **Martin Filler**

We are on U.S. Highway 51 South, yet another interchangeable part of the Great American Commercial Strip, which is virtually identical from Oxnard to East Orange. One by one, the familiar roadside litany of fuel and fast food: The Pancake Man, Texaco, Pancho's Taco, Shoney's Big Boy, Shell, Mobile, Exxon. Then, ahead on the left, is a sizable oasis of tall trees. As we approach this surprising curtain of green, traffic slows to a crawl, tour buses wheeze to a halt, and all eyes and Instamatics turn toward the peculiar white gate and the white-columned mansion on the hillside above it. The address is 3764 Elvis Presley Boulevard, Memphis, Tennessee. This is Graceland, the palace of the King of Rock-and-Roll.

Although it is one of America's newest shrines (it was opened to the public in June 1982), Graceland is nevertheless one of its most revered. Among recently hallowed places in this country it is comparable only to the Vietnam War Memorial in Washington in its ability to attract hundreds of thousands of people each year and to stir their deepest emotions. When Elvis Presley died suddenly on August 16, 1977, at the age of 42, an immense wave of public mourning was set off, on a scale that normally accompanies the passing of a national leader. But not all the grief was blind. When told of Presley's demise, John Lennon (who had once declared, "Before Elvis there was nothing") was said to have replied, "Elvis died the day he went into the army." He echoed the opinion of the many critics who felt that Presley's artistic greatness had long predeceased him.

Worse evaluations and revelations soon followed: scandalous reminiscences and debunking biographies told a lurid but lamentably believable tale of Elvis's dissipation: drug abuse, debauchery, divorce, depression, and the steady, sad decline of a young artist's gifts—this was the flip side of Presley's golden records. But to the legions of the faithful, none of this mattered, nor should it, for well before his death Elvis had ascended into America's Pop Pantheon. He had become a genuinely mythical figure, and the divergence of his public image and the private reality behind it is virtually irrelevant in terms of understanding Presley's lasting effect on the American psyche. . . .

Graceland was opened to the public in June 1982.

Thousands make annual August pilgrimage

EACH YEAR in mid-August, thousands of Elvis Presley fans pour into Memphis as a tribute to the King, who died Aug. 16, 1977. Last year the crowds were estimated at more than 25,000. Officials estimate that this year's Elvis International Tribute Week, through Saturday, may draw 35,000.

Fans—and entire fan clubs—will plunge into a round of remembrance. They will visit Graceland; see the new Relive the Magic museum; inspect the Lisa Marie, his personal jet; tour Sun Studio, where he recorded his first songs. Other events include Bad Bob's Elvis Impressionist Contest, the Elvis Sock Hop and the Elvis Presley Memorial Karate Tournament.

For many, the highlight of the week will be the Candlelight Ceremony at 11 p.m. Wednesday at Graceland. Again a torch will be lighted from the eternal flame at Presley's grave and taken to the gates of Graceland, where some 10,000 of the faithful are expected to be waiting. They will light their own candles from the torch and begin a long, silent procession to his grave. It is expected to take three to four hours for all to make their tribute to the King.

Meditation Gardens abounds with floral arrangements sent by ever-faithful fans.

Managing the Elvis empire

. . . "Elvis' business affairs were not of the best order," [Jack] Soden said in an interview from his offices at Graceland. "But it's worth noting that the style of managing not only entertainers but sports figures has changed dramatically since the '50s and '60s. The whole modern-day rules of management don't just put Col. Parker in a bad light; they put anybody of that era in a bad light.

"The condition of the estate that Priscilla came eyeball to eyeball with in the fall of 1979 is a whole 'nother story in itself. Priscilla could have panicked and run for cover. But the story that ensued is a neat one, and it's one I've been proud to participate in."

The key move was opening Graceland, which, on paper, was a crap shoot.

Priscilla and Soden decided to open Graceland to the public on a budget of merely $560,000, in June, 1982. The estate was prohibited from borrowing extra funds due to an imposing tax bill.

"I get a kick out of telling the story that we took the $500,000, plus $60,000 in pre-sold ticket revenues, and spent about every dime of it by the morning of June 7, 1982—and netted it back in 38 days," Soden said. "And that's a real fun statement to make. But the fact is that it wasn't a total shock that we netted it back in 38 days. I thought we'd net it back by the end of the summer."

Before opening Graceland, Priscilla and Soden, a former Kansas City investment banker, toured Hearst Castle in California and consulted with the Smithsonian Institution and the National Park Service, which manages famous American homes.

"Priscilla, most of all, had a very strong sense of how Graceland should be done," Soden said. "There was a great desire to open Graceland with a lot of dignity, and to a certain extent, that meant not catering to whatever current whims might exist. For example, we were under a lot of pressure in the spring of 1982 because the [Albert] Goldman book came out and he had done a hatchet job on Elvis. There was a great faction of Elvis fans who wanted the entire presentation of Graceland to be a rebuttal to the Goldman book.

"There were lots of whims blowing in every direction, and the course we set was a good steady one. It was to let this place and let these artifacts speak for themselves."

Fans express themselves on the stone wall at Graceland.

Elvis' Graceland: The rock king's Castle awaits his loyal fans

. . . The Presley legend received its biggest boost on June 7, 1982, when the gates of Graceland, his Southern-style mansion, were thrown open to the public. His fans could finally see some of his most beloved possessions—his guitars, cars, show costumes and much more.

Presley bought Graceland, a 23-room mansion on the southern out-skirts of Memphis, for $100,000 in 1957. For 20 years it was his private sanctuary, where he could relax among family and friends. It was, indeed, the King's castle, where he was shielded from public eyes by the walls of the 14-acre estate.

Then, on Aug. 16, 1977, the mournful news came from Graceland.

"SINCE ELVIS' death, requests to open the house to the public had been overwhelming," said Jack Soden, executive director of Graceland Enterprises. "The Presley family and executors of the estate felt there was no better location for a memorial museum than the mansion itself."

More than a half-million people a year visit Graceland, making it the city's No. 1 attraction and putting Memphis on the tourist map as definitely worth a detour. Presley is still playing to a full house. During the peak tourist season, some 3,000 visitors a day file through the home at 3717 Elvis Presley Blvd. . . .

Elvis mementos fill the Trophy Room behind the main house.

Presley's mansion is gaudy

April 24, 1982

MEMPHIS, Tenn. (UPI)—Elvis Presley's mansion, which will be opened to the public June 7, is crammed with gaudy furnishings that reflect the glitter of his stage life, a preview reveals.

A group of 300 bus tour operators was escorted through the white-columned mansion Friday so they could get an idea of what their customers could expect.

No picture-taking was permitted, and the upstairs bedroom and bath where the rock star was found dead Aug. 16, 1977, were placed off limits, with a security guard blocking the stairway.

The ground floor of the house presently has bright red carpet, but this will be changed before the tours start.

"The family has asked us to change the color scheme of the ground floor back to blue," a guide said. "They asked for that since it was blue for 18 out of the 20 years Elvis lived here."

In the front hallway hangs a photographic portrait of Presley's former wife, Priscilla Presley, and their daughter, Lisa Marie, as a child.

To the left of the front door is the dining room with an oval table with gold marbling on its mirrored surface. The floor is black marble and gold painted chairs with black upholstery surround the table.

Shelves and ornate cabinets along the dining room walls are filled with bric-a-brac ranging from a gold lion to two elaborate statues of Buddha.

At the right of the front door is the living room. Like the rest of the mansion, it is done in red tones and crowded with furniture, including Victorian style sofas covered with black and red sequined pillows.

Exotic stained glass peacocks extend to the ceiling between the living room and a small music room, where Presley sometimes entertained friends by playing the piano.

Down a flight of blue-carpeted stairs lies the mirror-lined TV room.

The basement room has lemon yellow carpeting and navy and yellow sofas. A matching yellow soda fountain stands in one corner of the entryway, equipped with pewter tankards and yellow plastic glasses.

To the side stands a bank of three 25-inch television sets.

"Elvis was a TV nut," the guide explained. "He had three so he could see himself on all three channels."

The living room and dining room at Graceland are ostentatious perhaps but not gaudy.

Graceland graces Virginia

Don and Kim Epperly spent much of last year creating this model of Graceland, the late Elvis Presley's Memphis, Tenn., estate, at their home in Roanoke, Va. She lights the mini-mansion nightly with Christmas lights and plays Presley's music through a speaker.

Kim Epperly shows off the miniature Graceland she and her husband have constructed in their yard.

Drugs may cancel Elvis stamp

The battle rages on over giving Elvis a stamp of approval.

Rep. **Edward R. Roybal** (D-Calif.), chairman of the House Appropriations subcommittee that approves postal subsidies, irked **Elvis Presley** fans by saying that a stamp honoring the late singer would send a "bad message to the youths of this nation" because of his drug use.

"I don't think he deserves a stamp because of his personal habits," Roybal said.

Rep. **Don Sundquist** (R-Tenn.), and **Pat Geiger** of North Springfield, Vt., who has led the fight for an Elvis Postage stamp, said Roybal was exaggerating Presley's drug problems and they plan to continue to push for the stamp.

"If you're going to wait for a perfect man, you will never issue a stamp," Geiger said. "Elvis had one failing and a million good qualities."

Fans want to see an Elvis stamp.

'Hire' Elvis, PO folk told

WASHINGTON—If the post office is really serious about making money, Pat Geiger has three little words of advice: Elvis, Elvis, Elvis.

By its reluctance to issue an Elvis Presley stamp, Geiger swears, the U.S. Postal Service is missing out on a great financial windfall.

"I hate to reduce Elvis' stamp to a mercenary thing, but with the postal service facing a $1.6 billion deficit, how can they turn their back on all this revenue?" asked Geiger, of North Springfield, Vt., who heads the Elvis Postage Stamp Campaign. . . .

No stamp now for 'the King'

Elvis Presley apparently won't be honored with a U.S. postage stamp any time soon.

Belmont Faries, chairman of the Citizens Stamps Advisory Committee, said no to the entertainer.

"The committee chooses people who have stood the test of time," Faries told Postal Life. The Postal Service last year got around to honoring opera star **Enrico Caruso** "so Elvis will have to wait." Elvis fans, citing his impact on popular music and his appearance on some foreign stamps, have flooded the Postal Service with letters, making Presley one of the most requested stamp subjects in recent years.

THE KING'S RANSOM

. . . Elvis Presley is worth more dead than alive—his memory earning 10 times as much as he made in his 42 years, and that was $100 million. Licensed Presley collectibles alone promise to gross $50 million in the next three years. The first 35 such items—like Royal Doulton mugs at $95 and pink toy Cadillacs for $15—have just come out, timed to capitalize on the media blitz leading up to Presley's 50th birthday on January 8. Plans to make Presley's Memphis home, Graceland, into a tourist wonderland are under way. Though it's 30 years this month since his first record—"That's All Right (Mama)"—was played on radio, Presley will be offered to a new generation of rock and roll fans on MTV. "A whole industry was built around an animated mouse named Mickey," says Joseph Rascoff, who became business manager of the Presley estate in 1982. "The next could be Elvis Presley. . . ."

Pre$ley $pell$ profit

Elvis mugs

Liquor decanters: (left) Unauthorized decanter made in Japan; (center) "Aloha Elvis" from McCormick Distilling Co.; (right) "Elvis' Teddy Bear" also from McCormick.

ELVIS' TEDDY BEAR

Commemorative Plates: (Top) "Elvis at the Gates of Graceland" by Delphi for the Bradford Exchange; (middle) "Jailhouse Rock" by Delphi for the Bradford Exchange; (bottom) "Loving You" by Susie Morton for Ernst.

Elvis still a gold hit commercially

There is now strong evidence that Elvis Presley has risen from the dead and returned to us as a cash register.

The August issue of *Life* informs that Elvis, who died in a hallowed, drug-ridden haze seven years ago this month, "is worth more dead than alive—his memory earning 10 times as much as he made in his 42 years, and that was $100 million." It's a tale of deeply felt fan reverence and equally passionate commercial exploitation.

"A whole industry was built around an animated mouse named Mickey," says Joseph Rascoff, new business manager of the rock legend's estate. "The next could be Elvis Presley."

Rascoff surely dreams of Chicagoans buying and selling Elvis futures on the Board of Trade. He already has firm plans for an onslaught of records, music videos and trinkets more varied than the dozens of Elvis impersonators (one of whom is said to earn $100,000 yearly in, where else, Las Vegas).

Officially licensed goodies soon to hit the market could gross $50 million within three years, suggests reporter Elizabeth Owen, and include Royal Doulton mugs for $95 and pink toy Cadillacs for a modest $15. A recently discovered 1956 recording will be released, as will a six-record set of golden oldies and an album tied to a video for airing on MTV. Remember, total Presley record sales already are an awesome $800 million.

Yearn for more? There'll be a cable TV tour of his beloved, 14-acre Graceland in Memphis, where 1 million visitors have paid $6.50 (adults) or $4.50 (kids) for tours since 1982. We'll also apparently get a Hanna-Barbera cartoon series for Saturday mornings, a line of Smurflike products and maybe even Elvis theme amusement parks in the United States and abroad. Imagine a glorious Jailhouse Rock Water Slide or All Shook Up Roller Coaster!

"Some weirdo keeps writing me to check a closet in the basement at Graceland because he's sure Elvis is living down there," Rascoff says. If that's the case, you can bet Rascoff will let you know and probably charge $7.50 for the news.

. . . It is at Graceland, however, that the largest number of musical pilgrims pay their respects.

"You get more reverence at the Presley home than you get at Mt. Vernon," observed one cynic.

A tour of Graceland takes visitors to the dining room, where Elvis habitually sat at the far end of the table so he could keep one eye on his guests and the other on a TV screen, and the music room with its gold-leafed Kimball piano, said to be worth half a million dollars.

In the carport, the singer's fleet of autos still awaits. Rising Sun, his favorite palomino, died last spring, but visitors can see his extraordinary costumes and stop at his grave in the Meditation Gardens close by the swimming pool.

Last of all, they can shop in the gift store for a bottle of "Love Me Tender" moisturizing bath, 16 fluid ounces for $4.99.

"They don't even have this in New York," admitted a visitor from New York.

There are a lot of things in Memphis that they don't have in New York.

Or anywhere else for that matter.

"Love Me Tender" bath products

The unlicensed "Kid from Tupelo" doll was not allowed on the market.

Elvis dolls: (left) "Elvis in Concert" from Starr Assoc. also plays micro-cassettes; (right) Elvis in a black phoenix jumpsuit from World Doll Inc.

ON THE MEMPHIS STREETS PRESLEY ONCE RULED, TV'S ELVIS REINCARNATES THE YOUNG KING

Elvis the tv series was launched in 1990. From left: Blake Gibbons played Bill Black, Michael St. Gerard starred as Elvis, and Jesse Dabson played Scotty Moore.

ABC Rocks with series on Elvis

ABC has announced that *Elvis: Good Rockin' Tonight,* a half-hour dramatic series about Elvis Presley, will be a mid-season replacement and ordered eight episodes from executive producer Rick Husky.

Husky is happy, of course, and more than a little relieved since he had spent about $1.5 million shooting the pilot in Memphis last May and that's a lot of money for a pilot.

"It was very expensive and we were the last pilot delivered to the network for consideration," Husky said in a phone interview from his Los Angeles office. "I think that hurt us in terms of coming on in the fall schedule."

In addition, Husky acknowledges that he was a little worried about selling the series, since it will not be "normal" television.

"It's not a sitcom or a lawyer story," he said. "It's a half-hour drama with music, which has never been attempted before. We're calling it a docu-series."

Michael St. Gerard will star as Elvis and the first eight episodes will focus on the early part of Presley's career, according to Husky.

"We'll begin early in 1954 when Elvis was starting his career, and went in to do a demo," he said. "If we're successful, we'll take it through the story of his life. . . ."

313

Elvis—A folk hero for our time

US   March 19, 1990

The Man Who Would Be King

Michael St. Gerard is a baby-faced hunk with bedroom eyes. A budding sex symbol, he has the manners of a choirboy: polite, attentive, ingratiating. And he is not at all pleased about it. "I sound like Donny Osmond," he laments, dejectedly stabbing a forkful of chicken as he looks down at New York City's Central Park from the lofty heights of Nirvana, a swank Indian eatery. "I don't mean to."

But Donny Osmond (even the new improved model) is about six galaxies removed from the part that might possibly launch St. Gerard into stardom's stratosphere. On February 6 the little-known actor made his television debut in the title role of the new ABC series *Elvis.*

Filmed on location in Memphis, Tennessee, and Tupelo, Mississippi, the half hour show—which is licensed by and has the full cooperation of the Presley estate—is a dramatization of Elvis' early years as a performer. The series opens in 1954, and Elvis is a 19-year-old truck driver. Before long he has his first Number One single, "Heartbreak Hotel," blowing Perry Como's "Hot Diggity" off the top slot on the Billboard charts. Elvis is deified, vilified, cheered, jeered, adored, outlawed, idolized and satirized. . . .

Michael St. Gerard also played Elvis in Heart of Dixie and Great Balls of Fire.

David Keith as Elvis in Heartbreak Hotel

Amusing 'Heartbreak Hotel' offers Elvis in a tall tale by Chris Columbus

Who's the mythic figure in the multicolored suit, the one who descends from on high to grant our wishes and make our troubles easier to bear?

Is it Santa Claus? Superman? Or, as opined by the slick and sometimes amusing new comedy "Heartbreak Hotel," is it Elvis Presley? . . .

. . . The film catches up with him in 1972, when he has taken to singing "Battle Hymn of the Republic" in a gaudy stage show geared to female fans old enough to be his mother.

(The particulars of Elvis's real stage act are nicely recapitulated, right down to the scarf handler who supplied the King with souvenirs he could toss to the fans.)

In all other ways, it shows the star to be the same sweet, gentlemanly, receptive and clean-living Elvis he always was. After all, this is a fairy tale. . . .

Musical salute to Elvis takes fast lively romp through his songbook

'Elvis: A Musical Celebration'

A multimedia, musical revue; written by Robert Rabinowitz, set by Douglas W. Schmidt, costumes by Jeanne Button, lighting by Jules Fisher and Peggy Eisenhauer, film sequences produced by Chrisann Verges; staged and choreographed by Patricia Birch.

Though tossing in just about every show business trick imaginable, minus only a fog machine and plunging "Phantom of the Opera" chandeliers, "Elvis: A Musical Celebration" is really just a harmless stage romp through the rock 'n' roll king's noteworthy songbook.

Creator/lighting designer Jules Fisher, who also thought up "Beatlemania," conceived this vehicle as a multimedia, Magic Kingdom salute to Elvis Presley, His Life and Times.

The whole thing is performed behind a giant, transparent movie screen that impressively covers the width of the Chicago Theatre stage. Near the back wall, a row of smaller screens projects alternate images, while in the middle, performers and dancers, including three Elvis impersonators, carry on, frequently surrounded by cinematic images. . . .

'Elvis': Broadway bound

It was probably inevitable: "Elvis, An American Musical" will open July 1, 1988—at the Las Vegas Hilton.

"Presley was the greatest star ever to appear in Las Vegas," reads an announcement from the Las Vegas Hilton, which is producing the Broadway-bound show. Presley appeared at the hotel "on 16 separate occasions from 1969 to 1977 totaling 47 weeks.

"He never played to an empty seat in the 1,600 seat Hilton Showroom."

Though there's no word yet on who will portray Elvis, the impersonator will be aided by two "immense screens, three 35-mm projectors, film clips and documentary footage."

ELVIS
AN AMERICAN MUSICAL

IN ASSOCIATION WITH THE PRESLEY ESTATE

Elvis: An American Musical was a stage musical that interpreted Elvis's life through his music.

315

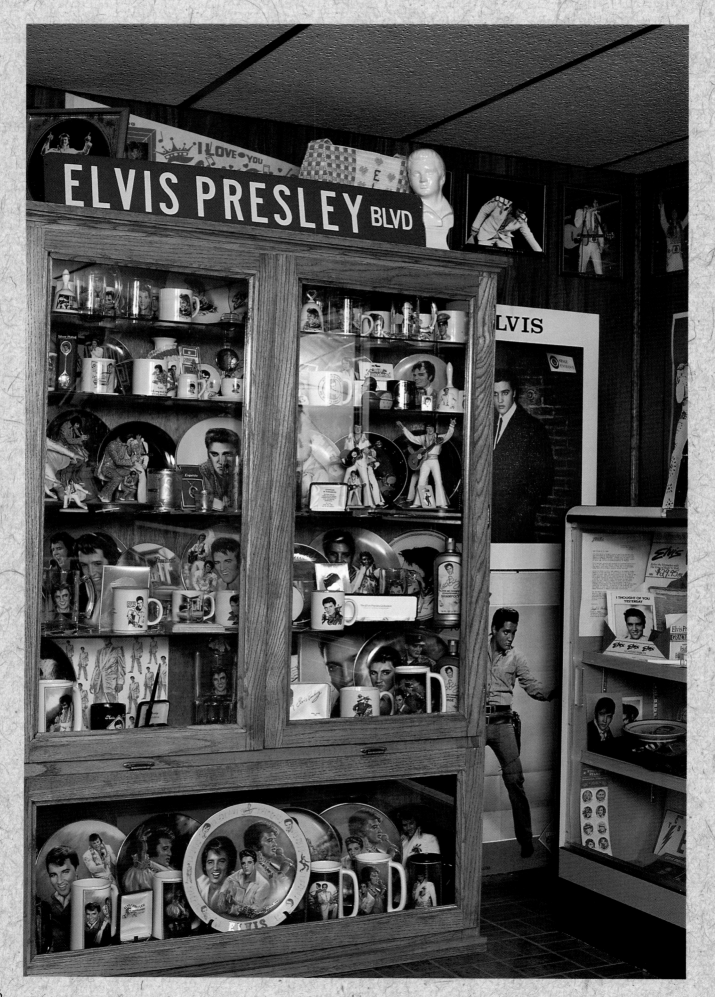

PHOTO CREDITS/COPYRIGHT

Bill DeNight operates The Elvis Presley Burning Love Fan Club of Streamwood, Illinois. A non-profit organization, the fan club works to keep Elvis's memory alive through charity work. Each year, the club matches in thousands of dollars the number of years Elvis has been gone. For example, on the tenth anniversary of his death, the club donated $10,000 to charity in Elvis's name. The club's motto is: "Just carrying on where Elvis left off." Because Mr. DeNight frequently donates parts of his collection to charity auctions, his assortment of Elvis memorabilia is ever-changing.

Sharon Fox, a lifelong fan of Elvis Presley, has been collecting magazines, fanzines, and newspaper articles about Elvis as well as other celebrities since the early 1960s. More an archive than a collection, her assortment of articles offers an important insight into the way Presley was perceived during his lifetime. Much of her Elvis collection consists of personal and rare items, including correspondence from the offices of Presley and his manager, Colonel Tom Parker. Ms. Fox has self-published a remembrance of Presley, *He Touched My Life,* as well as a compilation of clippings, *Elvis: His Real Life in the '60s.*

Ger Rijff became a fan of Elvis Presley at an early age. A native of Amsterdam, Holland, he owns and operates Tutti Frutti Productions—a clearinghouse for Elvis-related projects. Mr. Rijff has compiled a number of photo books, including *Elvis Close-Up* and *Memphis Lonesome,* which focus on brief periods of Presley's life. His Elvis Presley collection consists of many rare photographs, European magazines and fanzines that feature Elvis, sheet music, and posters and lobby cards for the European versions of Elvis's movies.

ADDITIONAL COPYRIGHT

INFORMATION

Fan Club, 1960 World Copyright by A. Hand, 202; Belt buckle, ©ADM Award Design Metals, 299; *Don't Be Cruel* sheet music, ©1956 Ahalirnar Music, 49; *Fans' Star Library*, The Amalgamated Press Ltd., The Fleetway House, 126; *Photoplay*, Argus Press Ltd., The Illustrated Publications Co., Ltd., 92, 126; *Weekend & Today*, ©1967, 1968, Associated Newspapers Ltd., 207, 215; *Musique*, 1959 by Belgium Notes Distribution, 131; *Elvis In The TV Film Stars*, ©1960 by Besscal Publications, Inc., 195; *Bolero*, 1964, 189; *Billboard*, © 1955 by BPI Communications, Inc., second subsidiary of Affiliated Publications, Inc., 32; Movie poster, ©1960 20th Century-Fox Film Corp., 149, 154; *Love Me Tender* poster, ©1956 20th Century-Fox Film Corp., 71; *Charro*, ©1968 by Clair Huffaker, Crest book, ©1969 by Harry Whittington, Fawcett Gold Medal Book, 224; *Cineavance*, 1967, 208; *Club Voor Fans*, 1959, 131; *Movie TV Secrets*, ©1960 Country Wide Publications, Inc., 156; *Crawdaddy*, ©1977 Crawdaddy Publishing Co., Inc., 293; *His First & Only Press Conference*, ©1972 Current Audio, Inc, 247; *Movie Teen Illustrator*, by Datsmith Publishing Co., 189; *Elvis Presley: Del Recuerdo*, ©1977 De Replica Publications, Inc., 300; *Screen Stories*, ©1968 by Dell Publishing, Inc., 217; *Dig*, ©1956, 1957, 64, 79; Bubble Gum packs, © Donruss, ©Boxcar Enterprises, 299; *A Tux for TV* Bubble Gum card, ©1936 Elvis Presley Enterprises, 48; Elvis Presley button, ©1956 Elvis Presley Enterprises, 60; *Double-Image* button, ©1956 Elvis Presley Enterprises, 60; *Hound Dog* Bubble Gum Card, ©1956 Elvis Presley Enterprises, 61; *Timeout Between Shows* Bubble Gum Card, ©1956 Elvis Presley Enterprises, 61; *The Fan's Friend* Bubble Gum Card, ©1956 Elvis Presley Enterprises, 61; *The Elvis Presley Eau de Perfum*, ©1957 Elvis Presley Enterprises, 62; *Elvis Presley Photo Folio*, ©1957 Elvis Presley Enterprises, 77; Elvis scarf, © Elvis Presley Enterprises, 61; *Love Me Tender* sheet music, © 1956 EP Music, 53, 70; *Hound Dog* sheet music, ©1956 EP Music, 49; EP Shampoo, ©1956 E.P. Music, 312; *Kentucky Rain* sheet music, ©1970 Elvis Presley Music, Inc., 234; EP Doll, ©1984, 1987, EP Enterprises, Inc., 312; Delphi Plate, ©1988 E.P. Enterprises, Inc., ©1988 Delphi, 311; Delphi Plate, © 1988 E.P. Enterprises, Inc., ©1988 Turner Enterprises Corp., 311; *Faces*, ©1975 Faces Magazine, 269; *Flaming Star*, 1982, 222; *Elvis Presley In Hollywood*, ©1956, Pub. by GIB Pub. Corp., 71; *Elvis and Jimmy*, The Girlfriend-The Boyfriend Corp., 65; *Now Or Never* sheet music, *Party* sheet music, ©1957 Gladys Music, 92, 143; *Hard Headed Woman* sheet music, ©1958 Gladys Music, 117; *Blue Suede Shoes* sheet music, ©1956 Hi Lo Music, 56; *Juke Box Favorites*, ©1956 Hill & Range Songs, 39; *TV Star Parade*, ©1956, 1958, 1976, by Ideal Publishing Corp., 130, 152, 277; *Rock 'n' Roll Battlers*, ©1956 Ideal Pub. Corp., 75; *Elvis In The Army*, Ideal Publishing Corp., © 1959, 125; *Movie Life*, ©1967 by Ideal Publishing Corp., 208, 214; *Movie Stars*, ©1975 Ideal Publishing Corp., 270, 277; *Melody Maker*, ©IPC Business Press, LTD., 288; *Country Music*, ©1975 KBO Publishers, Inc., 267; *Weekend & Today*, ©1965 K.M.R. Publications, Inc., 207; *Movieland*, ©1965 by K.M.R. Publications, Inc., 208; *Kristall*, 1957, 65; *Elvis Presley Hero Or Heel?*, ©1957 L. Miller & Sons Ltd. by agreement with Fawcett Publications, Inc., 78; *Jail House Rock* movie poster, ©1957 Loewis Inc., 104; *Elvis: One Year Later*, ©1978 Lorelei Publishing Co., Inc., 302; *TV Radio Mirror*, 1956 by MacFadden Publications, 57; *Photoplay*, ©1960, 1968 by MacFadden Publications, Inc., 135, 302; *Photoplay*, ©1968 by McFadden & Bartel Corp., 214; *Elvis Presley 1971 Album*, ©